1019
FH3

CATULLUS, CICERO, AND A
SOCIETY OF PATRONS

This is a study of the emergence, development, and florescence of a distinctly "late Republican" sociotextual culture as recorded in the writings of this period's two most influential authors, Catullus and Cicero. It reveals a multi-faceted textual – rather than more traditionally defined "literary" – world that both defines the intellectual life of the late Republic and lays the foundations for those authors of the Principate and Empire who identified this period as their literary source and inspiration. By first questioning, and then rejecting, the traditional polarization of Catullus and Cicero, and by broadening the scope of late Republican socioliterary studies to include intersections of language, social practice, and textual materiality, this book presents a fresh picture of both the sociotextual world of the late Republic and the primary authors through whom this world would gain renown.

SARAH CULPEPPER STROUP is Associate Professor of Classics at the University of Washington.

CATULLUS, CICERO, AND A SOCIETY OF PATRONS

The Generation of the Text

SARAH CULPEPPER STROUP

CAMBRIDGE
UNIVERSITY PRESS

CAMBRIDGE UNIVERSITY PRESS
Cambridge, New York, Melbourne, Madrid, Cape Town, Singapore,
São Paulo, Delhi, Dubai, Tokyo

Cambridge University Press
The Edinburgh Building, Cambridge CB2 8RU, UK

Published in the United States of America by Cambridge University Press, New York

http://www.cambridge.org
Information on this title: http://www.cambridge.org/9780521513906

First published 2010

Printed in the United Kingdom at the University Press, Cambridge

A catalogue record for this publication is available from the British Library

Library of Congress Cataloging in Publication data
Stroup, Sarah Culpepper, 1967–
Catullus, Cicero, and a society of patrons : the generation of the text / Sarah Culpepper Stroup.
p.   cm.
Includes bibliographical references and index.
ISBN 978-0-521-51390-6 (hardback)
1. Rome – Social life and customs.   2. Rome – Intellectual life.   3. Language and culture – Rome.
4. Catullus, Gaius Valerius.   5. Cicero, Marcus Tullius.   I. Title.
DG78.S88   2010
937′.05 – dc22   2010006648

ISBN 978-0-521-51390-6 Hardback

Tibi
Mira Naomi Lvovich
January 28 2005 – October 27 2006
London
. . . at certe semper amabo.

Contents

Quo uis cumque loco potes hunc finire
libellum:
uersibus explicitumst omne duobus opus.
lemmata si quaeris cur sint adscripta, docebo,
ut, si malueris, lemmata sola legas.

Mart. *Ep.* 14.2

Preface and acknowledgments

At many places in the writing of this book – a book about texts, and about textual culture, and about the peculiarly and painfully self-conscious sort of writing by which these texts are dedicated and this culture is defined – I have not been entirely sure what it is I need to do (or rather, to write) in order to make my point. This, I am happy to say, is not one of them (I attribute this fortuity to the fact that I have read several books myself). This is the part of the book where I am, first, to write of the deeply personal origins of this work. This is the part of the book where I am, second, to detail for you the ways in which these origins blossomed into the text you hold in your hands. This is the part of the book where I am, third, to thank solemnly the many people who saw this work to its fruition. This is the part of the book where I am, fourth, to express my deep affection for the many people in my life whose friendship, advice, and patience saw me through this work. In other words, this is the part of the book where I am to engage in a process of dedication. And so this is what I shall do.

Although I could not have said so at the start of this study, I know now that I wrote this book about texts and textual culture in part because I grew up in a household shaped (almost literally) by texts and (less literally, but only just) by textual culture. Every member of my family wrote and published; books were the most affectionate gifts we gave each other; we gave them on all occasions; we marked the act of prestation (what we used to call "giving") with an inscription in order to set that moment apart from all others. I wrote this book about texts – I'll just call them "books" for now – because growing up I had naturalized the world of the book qua object of affective social interaction, and I recognized the roots of this naturalization in the textual communities of the late Roman Republic.

This work began as a dissertation on a somewhat similar topic. As is the case with many dissertations, its most salient characteristic is that I completed it. I have to confess that I really enjoyed writing the dissertation – these were some of the best fifty years of my life – though I could not have done so, and certainly would not have enjoyed it as much, without the indescribable patience, sage advice, and indefatigable support of my committee at the University of California, Berkeley: my chair, Kathleen McCarthy, and my readers Erich Gruen and Andrew Stewart. I could not have hoped for better. I was also greatly aided by the guidance of Leslie Kurke, an inspirational scholar and exceptionally devoted teacher who led the dissertation group in which I participated in 1998–1999, and by Tony Long, my personal advisor throughout graduate school, a professor who always had the time to lead a reading group in whatever obscure philosophical text had struck my fancy, and, in a time of need, a friend. *Sine quibus non.*

Along the way, portions of this work have been read by a variety of individuals I am happy and humbled to have known. *In primis* are Alain Gowing and Brian Krostenko: the two individuals who taught me how to read – really *read* – Cicero and, not coincidentally, two of my most influential and inspiring professors. Thanks are due similarly to Tom Habinek and Nellie Oliensis, who graciously agreed to read portions of my drafts, picked up on things I'd not yet noticed, and guided me in better directions. Finally, I am grateful to my intellectually exhilarating cohort at the University of Washington's Simpson Center for the Humanities, where I was fortunate to be a fellow in 2002–2003.

I am thankful as well to the anonymous readers at Cambridge University Press, who did not read merely "portions" of this work, but indeed all of it. If this work is any good at all, it is in large part because of their advice, objections, support, and patient humor. (My favorite comment: "Page 268: You're having way too much fun." I did have fun. If writing is to be anything, it must be a bit fun.) Thanks are due as well to Michael Sharp of Cambridge University Press for his patience and encouragement. I am similarly grateful to Anne Marriott, my patient and diligent copy-editor, and one with whom it was a pleasure to work: any errors that remain are mine alone.

Parts of this project were delivered as talks at the 2001 APA meeting in San Diego (this talk later became an article in *MD*, and is rehashed and expanded here in Chapter 8), the 2004 APA meeting in San Francisco (delivered *in absentia* by Alain Gowing), a conference at Stanford University in 2005, the 2006 APA meeting in Montréal, and at the University of Calgary in 2006. Thanks are due to the University of Notre Dame Press for their permission to use, gratis, an excerpt of Michel Camille's chapter in *The Book and The Body* as the epigraph to Part Three.

In general, I must thank the following individuals for the many discussions, emails, arguments, irritated asides, and encouragement that helped things along: Elaine Fantham (a continuous inspiration and support), Brian Krostenko, Dylan Sailor, James Ker, Jed Parsons, Laurel Fulkerson, Amy Richlin, Larry Kim, Tom Habinek, John Dugan (an invaluable *sodalis*), Charles Murgia, Nellie Oliensis, Stephen Hinds, Cathy Connors, Ruby Blondell, Jim Clauss, John Morgan, Alessandro Barchiesi, Enrica Sciarrino, and the late Emanuele Narducci. To these usual suspects I must add the unexpected but delightful conversations I have had with rabbis Jonathan Singer and Will Berkovitz, both of whom have helped me think more meaningfully about dialogic and textual interaction in antiquity.

It is no surprise that I have learned a great deal from my students. *In primis* I count Marco Zangari, Alexander Dresser, Ryan Boehler, Christina Franzen, Erika Nesholm, Sam Beckelhymer, and Michael Seguin. I have amazing students, and this fact makes me happy beyond repair.

David Banta, the 1998–1999 fellow at the *TLL*, deserves special note. David helped me figure out *munus* (which had not yet been published). As much as this work is a *munus* to many, it is certainly a *munus* to David.

This work was first proofread, in a touching act of goodwill, by Paul Sherrard: I met Paul as a Stranger, and then I asked him to read my book, and then we became friends. Paul's humor, sincerity, intellect, and love of words and literature have been an inspiration both in the revisions of this text and, strangely, in how I think of future projects. Although we shall forever disagree on the proper use of the semicolon, em-dash, and a variety of other things (he is doubtless correct), I am glad to have met him. And so it goes.

To the bar staff at both Flowers and the Ravenna Alehouse: I am not sure I brought the wit, but you never failed to bring the wine. *Gratias ago.*

I am deeply grateful to the following individuals for the encouragement, friendship, support, humor, and love they have shown me throughout the years: Steph and Len Lvovich, David Summerlin, Lisa Kelman, Ryan Boehler, Trevor Layman, Chops and Jane Wong, Bryan Fujimoto, Scott Edwards, Miguel Pizarro, Jesse Anarde, Nancy Hartunian, Scott Barnett, Ilan Sharon, Ayelet Gilboa, and Mary LeBlanc. I ask merely that you all read Cicero, *Laelius* 88 (the Loeb translation will suffice). In short: little that is good in this world amounts to anything at all unless you have a person with whom to share the experience.

To my husband Richie: you are my best friend, greatest love, and trusted confidant: *plus oculis meis.* To my son Max: sweet one, you humble me: *sis in sinu semper et complexu meo.* To my brother, David Lewis Stroup: I'm not only glad you are my brother; I am glad you are my friend. I am glad you like books as much as do I.

To my parents, Edward Dixon Stroup and Marion Culpepper Stroup (*z"l*): you were my first teachers, and my best ones. If I love books (and I do), if I love teaching (and I do), if I do any of this (and I do): it is because of you. I miss you, and I regret that you are not here to remind me not to think too fondly of my own writing. In any other situation, this book would be given to you, who have given me so much. And yet –

During the revisions of this book, my niece, Mira Naomi Lvovich (*z"l*), died. Mira was the daughter of my best friends, Stephanie and Leonard Lvovich, and the sister of my beloved nieces Hannah Margaret and Ava Sarah. I remember vividly the day of Mira's birth and, even more vividly, the days of her passing. I have lived through loss: but the loss of a child in one's family is – as I am sure anyone who has experienced it knows – devastating.

Classical texts are sometimes unhelpful in the extreme. But sometimes they're a little bit of OK. Both Catullus and Cicero lost close family members during the course of their writing – Catullus, his brother; Cicero, his daughter – and both wrote deeply and painfully and honestly about their loss. Each man understood that the most pressing urge one feels when one has lost a loved one is that the world should never forget that this person existed. Each man sought to create in his writing a *monumentum* – a memorial – for the one he had lost: and, in the end, each man did. In some small way, then, I should like this book to be a *monumentum* for my Mira. It is not enough, but nothing would be.

SARAH CULPEPPER STROUP
University of Washington, Seattle

Abbreviations

For the most part, I have adhered throughout this text to the *OLD* standard citations for the abbreviation of classical works. In the citation of Cicero's works, however, I have chosen occasionally to diverge from the *OLD* standard in favor of what has seemed to me both a more logical and consistent system of citation and one that speaks more directly to the arguments presented herein. Thus, for example, I preface all letter collections with the abbreviation *Ep.* (for *Epistulae*: thus *Ep. Att., Ep. Brut., Ep. Fam.,* etc.) and have standardized my references to the *technica* as follows: *de Inv.* (*de Inventione*), *DND* (*de Natura Deorum*), *de Off.* (*de Officiis*), *de Div.* (*de Divinatione*), *de Orat.* (*de Oratore*), and *Lael.* (*Laelius uel de Amicitia*). The following works are referred to by abbreviation only.

ARV	Beazley, J. D. 1942. *Attic Red-Figure Vase-Painters.* Oxford University Press.
Bergk	Bergk, T. 1863. *Emendationes aliquot Catullianorum carminum.* Halae: Formis Hendeliis.
CIL	*Corpus Inscriptionum Latinarum.* 1863–.
CVA	*Corpus Vasorum Antiquorum.* 1925–.
E–M	Ernout, A., and Meillet, A. 1959–1960. *Dictionnaire étymologique de la langue latine*, 4th edn. Paris: Klincksieck.
FgrH	Jacoby, F. (ed.). 1923–1999. *Die Fragmente der griechischen Historiker.* 4 vols. Leiden: Brill.
GLK	Keil, H. (ed.). 1855–1880. *Grammatici Latini.* 7 vols. and suppl. Leipzig: Teubner.
*IE*²	West, M. L. 1992. *Iambi et Elegi Graeci ante Alexandrum Cantati*, vol. 2. Oxford University Press.
OCD	Hornblower, S., and Spawforth, A. (eds.). 1996. *The Oxford Classical Dictionary*, 3rd edn. Oxford University Press.
OLD	Glare, P. G. W. (ed.). 1982. *Oxford Latin Dictionary.* Oxford University Press.

PE   Gentili, B., and Prato, C. (eds.). 2002. *Poetae elegiaci testimonia et fragmenta. Pars altera.* Leipzig: Saur.

RE   Pauly, A. F. von 1980. *Paulys Realencyclopädie der classicshen Altertumswissenschaft,* 2nd edn. Eds. G. Wissowa, W. Kroll, and K. Mittelhaus. Munich: Alfred Druckenmüller.

TLL   *Thesaurus Linguae Latinae.* 1900–.

Introduction

The textual story of the late Roman Republic is a difficult one to tell. Where we would seek a breadth of representative sources, we have a handful of possibly anomalous ones; where we would hope for symmetry of aesthetics, activity, interests, and production, we have disparity in every category that would appear to matter; where we would value evidence for extensive communication between our most fully represented authors – or at least some indication that they recognized each other *as authors* – we have a handful of letters, one or two cryptic references, and frustratingly little else. We know there were textual "heavy hitters" in this period; we know there were men who wrote vast quantities of literature and men who seem to have captured the very essence of a genre in a few short lines. By the early Empire, the authors of the first half of the first century BCE (and with a few years added to the low end, this is the working definition of "late Republic" in this study) had come to be viewed with a sense of awe and nostalgia, as embodiments of a textual, social, and, in some ways, political world that had become impossibly out of reach. The story of this world seems an undeniably important and exciting one, but it does not give itself up easily.

My interest in the details of this story arose after several years of working "on" the late Republic produced the suspicion that there was a problem with my approach to these authors and texts. I realized that the literature of the late Republic is more pervasively influential on both our understanding of Republican literature as a whole[1] and the generic and lexical practices of later authors than any period that had come before it. I similarly recognized that Catullus and Cicero, while far from the only evidence from this period, constitute our most extensive sources for the textual

---

[1] As Goldberg 2005: 8 has noted, "the literary history of the Republic as we tell it is largely a first-century story."

world of the late Republic. And yet I had come to suspect that, when all was said and done, I – *we* – understood less of this world than we might.

This is not to say, of course, that the middle and late Republic have not been the subject of many excellent and highly influential studies – in terms of both broad social and political analyses and keenly focused author-centered works. Such studies have sparked and maintained my interest in the incredibly complex world of the late Republic and my own work builds upon, and is deeply indebted to, what has come before. But it is the "cultural work" of texts and the "generation" of texts that work culturally that lie at the heart of my interests in the Roman world. And when it comes to the textual life of the late Republic – not that of the earlier Republic, projecting forward, nor that of the Principate and Empire, projecting back – I suggest that we lack sufficient understanding of how the texts of this period functioned in the lexical, structural, and social contexts in which they were produced. Because I do not imagine that my own textual venture is any more or less self- and community-interested than those of the period with which I am concerned, I admit that what captures me about the textual world of the late Republic is that I find the cultural work of its texts simultaneously familiar and foreign to the practice of modern scholarly publication. The texts of the late Republic are at times tantalizing and at times frustrating, and in all cases I feel it is necessary to return to these texts and their generation (and the generations that produced them), and the work that they did, in order to understand why I think of them – and indeed what it means to write and publish a social and textual history – as I do.

If I were to be more transparent than is advisable, I would admit "*the* problem with the Republic" is really "*my* problem with the Republic." To put it in more optimistic terms, however, let us call this not a problem with the Republic so much as a puzzle over its textual praxis. If it is not a puzzle that can be solved *in toto*, it is one we can begin to unravel with a careful and focused return to the primary evidence of the period, however asymmetrical the evidence and however difficult it may be to read it in concert. It is this puzzle from which this study sets out, then, and the cautious unraveling of this puzzle is its goal. And if we are to address the puzzle of how texts worked culturally in the late Republic, we must start from the beginning of late Republican texts. And at the beginning – I am speaking not temporally, but in terms of our most fully preserved representative authors – we have Catullus and Cicero.

Catullus and Cicero. The former, an astonishing poetic genius and disingenuously apolitical socialite hoodlum, would have completed the whole of his corpus at about the age many graduate students in this field are completing their doctoral dissertations and beginning to search for a job. The latter, an ambitious political player and self-conscious bibliophile, turned to his markedly textual endeavors only at an age when most senior faculty might begin to reevaluate their retirement portfolios and notice that the undergraduates are now younger than their own children.[2] Catullus, a man who seems to hold himself aloof from the work of the forum – even as he is obviously well versed and deeply engaged with its activities, as befits his social status – offers the unique (and almost certainly anomalous; Lucilius is perhaps the only parallel) perspective of an upper-class individual who chose to play the outsider to, and observer of, late Republican politics. Cicero, a man who entered the forum eagerly and clung to it as long as he could (and even in death seemed to cling there still), offers the compelling (and, if not anomalous, at least anomalously productive) perspective of an individual who so identified with the Republican forum that his death came to mark, for later periods, the end of Republican oratory as a whole.[3] These two share ego (monstrous), talent (prodigious), and wit (witty). But other than that, it is at first difficult to imagine two more aesthetically opposed authors from whom to reconstruct the practice of a learned society: reconstructing the textual world of the late Republic can feel as though we are reconstructing an entire language based on but two of its native speakers.

The apparent asymmetry of Cicero and Catullus – both the documented distinctions of genre, age, and public and political activity, and the alleged (and as I shall argue, distorted) irreconcilability of aesthetic, social, and personal positioning – makes the pair a notoriously thorny one to combine in one study. Thus although recent years have seen a resurgence of studies on the late Republic, such studies – and there have been many excellent ones – have tended to address (with the outstanding exception of Krostenko 2001) the "Intellectual World" of Cicero and his group (so Butler 2002; Corbeill 1996; Dugan 2005; Fantham 2004; Rawson 1985; Steel 2001; Wood 1988) or the "Poetic World" of Catullus and his (so especially Janan 1994;

---

[2] Collins 1952: 11 has bought into these men's textual fictions rather eagerly. Catullus is the "uninhibited, ribald young poet... speaking and writing his mind with utter abandon and neglect of personal consequences" while Cicero is "vain, somewhat pompous" – and Catullus is *not?* – and a politician who "never used, not even in the mud-slinging *In Pisonem*, such lusty words as *confutuere...*"

[3] Thus Tacitus, *Dialogus*, has Maternus reckon the "recent period" of oratory *ab interitu Ciceronis* (*Dial.* 24.3).

Fitzgerald 1995; Nappa 2001; Skinner 2007; Wray 2001; Wiseman 1974a; 1982); but virtually never the two at once.[4] This thematic and generic schism does not detract from any of the individual works cited above (nor from the group as a whole); but our approach to the practices of this period has suffered from a methodological blind spot that it will be useful to address.

For all of their stylistic and situational asymmetry, Catullus and Cicero tend to strike modern readers as two of the most viscerally personal characters of Roman literary history.[5] There are few undergraduate classics majors who have not spent a wine-soaked hour or two contemplating the eternal truths of c. 85,[6] and few junior faculty who have not found themselves suddenly sympathetic to Cicero's anguished contortions over manuscript revision and dedicatory form as expressed in the letters to Atticus (cf. *Ep. Att.* 13.12, etc.). But the arguably deceptive intimacy with which these two are viewed is not restricted to those given over to study them – either for a year or a lifetime. In spite of the maddeningly opaque translations with which Catullus is often saddled (I have had more than one confused American undergraduate ask, "So, what does 'I'll bugger you and stuff your gobs' *mean*?"[7]), his youthful lust and social irreverence require no especial background in the classics to be savored. Cicero, conversely, is noteworthy for being the only classical author of whom I am aware who arouses such easy loathing even in those who seem to know little more than his name: "Cicero? I *hate* Cicero!"[8] Whether we adore or detest them, we feel strangely secure in our belief that we know them.

The striking emotional accessibility these authors elicit suggests that what might first appear to be a weakness in our pool of evidence is in fact a hidden strength. For as much as the operative conditions of Catullus' and Cicero's textual production – the "what and wherefore" of each man's

---

[4] Thus although Wiseman 1974a includes a chapter dealing with a few of Cicero's letters (pp. 146–157), his focus is on the content of the letters (most specifically as they relate to the Clodius affair) rather than their function as "literary" creations. Beard and Crawford 1985, Bloomer 1997, Fantham 1996, and Habinek 1998 bring both poetry and prose into their discussions, but only rarely in terms of interconnecting phenomena.

[5] In an article that takes the traditional position of setting Catullus and Cicero into aesthetic and social opposition, Collins 1952: 11 writes of the "dream" that Catullus and Cicero were familiar friends, "[this] does not reckon with the *actual personalities of the two men as we know them.*"

[6] A student recently told me he had read most of Catullus in the original; I asked him which class he had taken, and he said, "It wasn't in a class – it's just because I *like* him!"

[7] This quote is not apocryphal (translation is Lee 1990). The resultant facial expression, when I have rendered the Latin in terms understandable to an American undergraduate, is a sweet, sweet balm for the soul.

[8] This quote is also not apocryphal. It was spoken to me at a bar one evening, when someone had made the mistake of asking what I was working on (this book).

decision to write what he did – are undeniably asymmetrical, there are places in which the tonality of their texts speaks to a mutually recognizable textual and social aesthetic. These men knew each other; they ran in the same elite circles; they shared friends and enemies; it is not terribly difficult to imagine that they may have run into each other at the sorts of textually interested *convivia* mentioned by each author and examined in detail in Part II. And – if for different reasons and in different ways – they both wrote urgently and frequently about the social, textual, and political world they inhabited. Our story of the late Republican textual world will not be a complete one until we find a way to consider these men in the concert in which they lived rather than the opposition in which they have been placed. And for that, I suggest, we must locate points of intersection in the work they produced.

In *Cicero, Catullus, and the Language of Social Performance*, Brian Krostenko argues persuasively for several linguistic intersections in the descriptive language of performance and display used by each author and, in so doing, increases considerably our understanding of late Republican linguistic code. In this study, I argue for two further intersections in their texts: intersections distinct from those offered by Krostenko, but conceptually compatible with the late Republican worldview he sets forth. These intersections, as explained below, are those of terminological and social code, and rhetoric and sociopractical function; they are indicative of *textual* rather than linguistic praxis, and allow traditionally opposed authors and traditionally opposed spheres of discourse to be brought to bear on each other in ways that will broaden what we can say about "how people wrote" in a period in which there was indeed a great deal of writing going on.

In order to get at "how people wrote" in the late Republic, however, we must start by looking at what Catullus and Cicero wrote, and by plotting each man's writings against those of the other. We know these men are different; is there a way in which they are similar?

The result of such a plotting is difficult to overestimate in its implications. For in considering the literary endeavors of Catullus (polymetric love and invective; mythologically informed "learned" verse; witty social and political epigram) against those of Cicero (self-promoting *oratio*; a cycle of intellectually interested technical treatises – called in this study the *technica*; an ongoing run of epistles), what comes to light is not an incompatible tangle of warring aesthetics so much as a telling intersection in precisely those texts each author wrote *for* and dedicated *to* other members of his social group (by "dedicated" I mean "addressed to a named

individual" – by analogy with the artistic "response piece," I take the Catullan invectives as "dedicated" texts – and by "group" and "Society" I
mean not a card-carrying "club" of any sort, but "an informal network of
overlapping circles of textual production"). If Catullus and Cicero diverge
in terms of the sort of texts they wrote, they converge at the point of
what they did with many of these texts and, more significantly, how they
did it.

Catullus and Cicero meet, in other words, at the level of the dedicated
text. Whether it is a poem dedicated to Calvus or a dialogue dedicated to
Brutus,[9] a versified celebration of extra-forensic textual life or a dialogic
complaint of the situations that have made such a life necessary, the varied
dedications of Catullus and Cicero suggest not only a textual praxis that
could be adapted to vastly different sociopolitical situations, but one in
which a large number of men – their dedicatees, and those from whom
they received texts in return – engaged. As a sociocultural artifact, then,
the dedicated text provides not only an intersection of the textual practices
of Catullus and Cicero; it provides a valuable inroad into the textual world
of the late Republic, a world in which dedicated texts are a locus not only
for artistic and intellectual expression, but also for the "contestation and
negotiation of societal dynamics."[10]

In reading these texts against each other, and in spite of all their apparent
distinctions (issues of chronology and operative condition are discussed
in the last section of this Introduction), two commonalities arise – two
intersections not only of "what," but also of "how." The first, and one
that will be usefully informed by texts outside of the dedicatory corpus,
is that of terminological and social code: when these men discuss the
social and textual world in which they participate, they tend to use the
same terms of operation and figures of social interaction. This intersection
is the focus of Part I. The second intersection is that of rhetorical and
sociopractical expression, which, by drawing on the terminological work
of Part I, provides the focus for Parts II and III, each of which examines a
distinct expression of this intersection. Part II locates in the dedicated texts
a recurrent engagement with issues of elite performance and the judgment
thereof, and suggests that each man, in his own way (and the distinction in
these "ways" broadens our narrative), uses his dedicated texts to contain,

---

[9] Dugan 2005: 266 notes the similarities between Cicero's *Orator* and Cat. 50; in footnote 42 on the
    same page, Dugan suggests that *Ep. Att.* 9.10.1 similarly resembles the tone of c. 50.
[10] Tatum 1997: 483. Tatum specifies such texts as "literary," and his focus is on Catullus; although I
    find his generally "hierarchical" take on Catullus unconvincing, he offers a useful formation to the
    social function of dedicated texts.

critique, and in some cases improve upon "real world" opportunities for elite performance. As a likely outgrowth of the instinct to "house" elite performance in the pages of a dedicated poem or book, our authors – building on an earlier tradition but, in the case of Cicero at least, taking it to new heights – also tend to imbue their dedicated texts with a sense of materiality, and the compelling various textual materialisms of Catullus and Cicero form the focus of Part III. Fuller details of these intersections will be given in the last section of this introduction.

Because Catullus and Cicero meet at their dedicated texts, a return to such texts will not only help us reconstruct their personal approach to – and perhaps opinion of – the process and social function of textual dedication; it will also enable us to plot several points on the broader continuum of textual practice in the late Republic. Whatever else each may have written, it is in the dedicated text that each created the literary work and the literary *persona* that would prove the most broadly influential to the textual practice of later periods.[11] It is through these texts that we find our most fertile approach to the textual society in which Catullus and Cicero created themselves as distinctly textual beings, and I will argue that it is through these texts that the story of the textual world of the final decades of the Republic may begin to be told.

WHY A "SOCIETY OF PATRONS"? WHAT THIS BOOK
IS NOT – AND IS – ABOUT

Not about

It is awkward – if not dangerously precious – to include in the Introduction to a work any lengthy discussion of what that work is *not*. And yet in light of both the nature of the present study and the tenor of recent investigations into Latin literary and intellectual culture (and indeed the ways in which the former intersects with, and diverges from, the latter), it will be useful to say a few words on what might appear to be omissions in this study, and offer some explanation of why they are there (or rather, why they are not).

---

[11] *Pace* Conte 1994: 203, who claims that both Cicero and "his contemporaries" viewed him(self) as more of a politician than a "writer and thinker," writers of the Empire and later periods – from Seneca, Pliny *minor*, and Tacitus to Petrarch and de la Vergne – seem to have found rather greater inspiration in his dedicated dialogues and epistolographic habits than they did in his oratory. Tac. *Dial.* 32.6 includes a quotation from *Orator* in his summary of Cicero's impact: *et Cicero his ut opinor uerbis refert, quidquid in eloquentia effecerit, id se non rhetorum <officinis>, sed Academiae spatiis consecutum.* The quotation is from *Orator* 12.

Patronage

First, although this is a book about "patrons" – or more specifically, the textual habits of two patronal-class men and the degree to which they may speak of a more pervasive cultural praxis – it is not a book about patronage, either literary or social, either in the late Republic or any time before or after. The topic of Roman patronage, from the middle Republic through to the height of the Empire, is an interesting and complex one, and has been the subject of many thoroughgoing and excellent investigations, especially those dealing with the Principate and early Empire.[12] And if we are to understand such patronage in terms of a strongly socially hierarchical system through which textual "goods" (the currency of the nominally socially inferior member of the relationship: the so-called "client") are exchanged for material or social ones (the currency of the nominally socially superior one: the "patron"), then it is safe to say that some form of such a system – though one that would have differed greatly in form and function from the system as described by Tatum, White, and others – was in place from the mid third century BCE down through the early first. Indeed, most of our evidence from this period points to a fairly large number of precisely such hierarchical patronage relationships, in which the – usually poetic and performative – work of a social "inferior" (so Livius Andronicus, Cnaeius Naevius, Titus Maccius Plautus, Caecilius Statius, Quintus Ennius, Terence, Marcus Pacuvius, and Accius[13]) was written at the behest of, and dedicated to, a social "superior" (M. Fulvius Nobilior, D. Iunius Brutus, the Metelli, and so on) who then remunerates the poet for his product, by variously economic or social means.[14]

---

[12] Saller 1989 (cf. Saller 1982): 49 offers what seems to me, *pace* Badian and others, a good foundational definition of patronage: "First, [patronage] involves the *reciprocal* exchange of goods and services. Secondly, to distinguish it from a commercial transaction in the marketplace, the relationship must be a personal one of some duration. Thirdly, it must be asymmetrical, in the sense that the two parties are of unequal status and offer different kinds of goods and services in exchange – a quality which sets patronage off from friendship between equals." Contra Saller, see Badian 1982 and Brunt 1982. Among the numerous examples of excellent work on the topic, and in addition to those just noted, I would include among the most widely influential Brunt 1965, Deniaux 1993, Dixon 1993, Gold 1982 (note especially the contributions of White, Williams, Wiseman and Zetzel) and 1987, Tatum 1997, White 1978 and 1993, and the edited collection of Wallace-Hadrill 1989. Johnson and Dandeker's essay in Wallace-Hadrill (1989: 219–242), although it addresses social and political patronage rather than the literary sort, and although its focus lies in the post-Republican period, nevertheless makes the important point that we should never expect patronage to have been a monolithic or static system.

[13] Accius is placed in this group because of his known association with a patron, D. Iunius Brutus Callaecus. He is, however, something of an unusual case, as we know he also wrote *Didascalica* in mixed prose and verse, and was the dedicatee – late in life, unless this was a dedication made post-mortem – of Varro's early *de Antiquitate Litterarum*.

[14] On this see also Clarke 1978: 46–47, who notes that the client in literary patronage might hope to gain money (so Mart. *Ep.* 10.9; cf. Pliny *Ep.* 3.21), government post (so perhaps the case with

We have virtually no evidence for either how this remuneration worked or the forms it may have taken, but we might imagine return gifts of money, social favors, sought-after invitations to convivia, or private audiences, and more importantly – if the poem is a fine one, and the *patronus* does his job – a general increase in status and renown. The return gift received by the *cliens* will represent, at least ideally, an equitable token of exchange. But the complex reciprocal system of these non-commodities, in which the tangible tokens of text and dinner stand in for the (more highly valued) intangible increases in status and influence, requires that as much as these social "goods" should be theoretically equitable in value – it is to be a "fair trade" – they are never to be identical in substance. A literary *cliens* receives money (favors, invitations, etc.); a literary *patronus* – and we shall return to this point below – receives texts.

Yet a hierarchically based scenario of patronage is insufficient as a model for what we see in the late Republic, because it accounts for neither the turbulent political world of these years nor the large quantity of prose production of this and earlier periods. And indeed the middle Republic, as we shall see, offers evidence of an altogether different sort as well. It is that of a group of learned men who produced and circulated texts outside of a hierarchical patronage model; men who avoided the lexical tags – *patronus, cliens* – with which we commonly associate hierarchical textual exchange, and indeed the very men who serve as the conceptual ancestors of the late Republican practice with which we are concerned.

Two of the most renowned and influential literary producers of the middle Republic are Cato and Lucilius – with each of whom, it is worth noting, Cicero explicitly identifies, and with the latter of whom the fourth-century CE grammarian Diomedes would associate Catullus.[15] Although we have little detail of the dissemination and circulation of Cato's texts during his lifetime,[16] we know that he dedicated at least one of his treatises to his son – the *Praecepta ad Filium* – and so according to a structure that would have had nothing to do with the traditionally extra-familial hierarchical patronage of the period. Of Lucilius' practice we know even less. He had a close friendship with P. Cornelius Scipio, but there is no evidence of any form of patronage between the two;[17] the fact that he was

---

Horace?) or other benefits. The patron, in turn, might receive administrative assistance from the client in any number of ways, but the main token of repayment is of course fame.

[15] Diom. GLK I 485: *iambus est carmen maledictum . . . cuius carminis praecipui scriptores . . . apud Romanos Lucilius et Catullus et Horatius et Bibaculus.*

[16] For much of what we do know, see Sciarrino 2004.

[17] Cf. Gruen 1992: 280: "the evidence [for their friendship] betokens a relationship in which difference of status played little role. It possesses the flavor more of equality than of patronage and clientage." The whole of the seventh chapter of Gruen 1992 (pp. 272–317) does much to correctly reposition

the named dedicatee of others' works would suggest likely participation in what we might imagine to have been a textually productive group of learned social equals.[18] Even if Lucilius did not affix specific dedications to his books of satires or epigrams – the works are too fragmentary to tell us this; if Juvenal may be used as a valid comparison I suspect he did not – he stands as our first example of a member of the educated upper classes who chose the life of the poet over that of the politician and, standing coolly outside the world of the forum, criticized it actively.[19]

Although Cato and Lucilius differ in a great many ways, their paths intersect in their social status and production of literature.[20] Both men wrote and shared their texts with men of patronal class, and what we know of the middle Republic suggests they were not alone in this. As early as the late third and early second centuries, we have attested what was doubtless a Hellenistically influenced upper-class[21] engagement with the antiquarian, grammatical, and philological prose treatise outside of any identifiable (or even likely) system of patronage. The earliest of such authors included Fulvius Nobilior and Iunius Gracchanus (both authors of antiquarian texts); somewhat later came Lucius Aelius Stilo Praeconinus, Caius Octavius Lampadio, and Vettius Philocomus.[22] From the mid second century BCE onward, and at about the same time as the first *commentarii* began to appear (those of Aemilius Scaurus, Rutilius Rufus, Lutatius Catulus, and both Sulla – in Greek, and dedicated to Lucullus[23] –

Lucilius, and other writers of the period, vis-à-vis the so-called Scipionic circle – a "group" now recognized to have been an almost exclusively Cicero-influenced fiction.

[18] In the end it is unclear to what degree Lucilius (himself the dedicatee of Stilo, Antipater, and Clitomachus) dedicated his satires to others – either to make or deny the claim begs the very question of what a "dedication" meant at this time – but his (possibly epistolary) poems certainly engage in direct address and speak to a lively textual culture (on which cf. Habinek 1998: 117). Cicero praises Lucilius' *sal et uenustas* early in the *de Finibus*, and seems to identify himself with the poet (de *Fin.* 1.3.7), although he remarks that whereas Lucilius would have restricted his audience, he himself eagerly seeks the learned reader.

[19] Cf. e.g. vv. 1145–1151 of the fragments of Lucilius.

[20] The bibliographies on Cato and Lucilius are vast, and there is no need to duplicate them here. On the literary activity of Lucilius, perhaps the most helpful work is Gruen 1992: 272–317, as noted above; on Cato's literary interests in the *Origines*, see recently Sciarrino 2004.

[21] Suet. *Gramm.* 2 identifies Crates of Mallos as the first to introduce grammatical study (*studium grammaticae*) to Rome, but says later that the early proponents of "grammatical study" belonged to the equestrian class (*Gramm.* 3). The majority of later *grammatici* were freedmen or lower-born freemen, and functioned primarily as teachers (even if they gained great wealth and fame from such). Habinek 1998: 34–68 provides an excellent and wide-ranging analysis of the period that saw the "invention" of Latin literature.

[22] Praeconinus wrote commentaries on the hymns of the Salii and, possibly, the Twelve Tables; Lampadio divided Naevius' *Bellum Punicum* into seven books; Philocomus appears to have prepared an edition of Lucilius' satires.

[23] Plut. *Sulla* 6.

and Lucullus – dedicated, in turn, to Sulla), we see a rise in works of historical prose (so Sempronius Aselio, Coelius Antipater, Caius Fannius, Lucius
Cassius Hemina, and so on), both in the form of monographs (Antipater)
and annalistic accounts (Fannius, Hemina, Piso, Cnaeus Gellius); various
writers of verse (so the ethical and satirical verse epistles of Sp. Mummius
and the epigrams of Lutatius Catulus); and of course the regular composition and circulation of oratorical speeches and legal works (so those earlier
"writing orators"[24] who are the focus of much of Cicero's *Brutus*), which
probably would have accounted for most of the prose "publication" of this
period.

Save the memoirs of Lucullus and Sulla, we have no explicit evidence
of dedicatory practice in this period; it is impossible to say to what extent
these memoirs participated in any sort of formal system of dedication or
exchange,[25] but the reverberations of their practice are traceable into the
late Republic and beyond.[26] If we had more than we do from the period of
150–100 BCE, I think it is likely that we would witness a nascent system of
"publication-minded" literary dedication among a group of approximate
social equals. As it stands, however, what we have for these years amounts to
a slightly confused jumble of names, titles, and content descriptions pieced
together initially from the authors of the late Republic (Varro, Nepos and –
of course – Cicero), fleshed out somewhat by Suetonius, and giving us
virtually no information concerning the dedication or exchange of texts.
We know men of the educated upper classes were writing, and we must
imagine that these writings were shared or circulated – which is to say,
nominally published – among their peers by some means or other. Beyond

---

[24] The term "writing orator" will be expanded in Part III of this study, but for the most part it is used
here to indicate – as Cicero outlines in *Brutus* – that group of orators who wrote and circulated
their *orationes* after delivery. For a discussion of some of the second-century BCE authors and their
compositions (if mainly in the context of their written appraisals of Greek culture), cf. Saunders
1944; Frier 1999.

[25] In addition to the writers of the *commentarii*, who would likely have written their works with
the hopes that they provide the subject matter for another's expansion, I would include as prime
suspects for dedicatory practice – this based in part on a Hellenistic trend appearing first in the
late third century (am thinking here especially of the dedicatory prefaces of Archimedes, to which
I return in Part II) – the authors of the antiquarian and philological treatises.

[26] Of Cicero's "named" dialogues, four – *Cato*, *Catulus* (the name of the first book of *Acad. Prior.*),
Laelius, and *Lucullus* (the name of the second book of *Acad. Prior.*) – are named after figures
from this period (with Catulus and Lucullus as figures that transition into the late Republic),
all of whom were strongly associated with literary production and appreciation. Plasberg 1892
ad fr. 37 (cf. Purser 1892: 448–449) of the *Hortensius* suggests that this fragment (*bellum cum
mortuo gerunt*) may refer to a literary war raging around the memory of Cato. More than one
hundred years later it seems the war is still raging: the dialogic core of Tacitus' *Dialogus* begins with
the interlocutors' discovery of Maternus sitting in his chamber, holding a text of his *Cato* in his
hands.

that, in terms of second-century BCE evidence of textual praxis, we have precious little.

But of what we have from this period, two things are certain. First, a great deal of literature was created in a system of hierarchical, or "vertical," poet–patron exchange – what we have come to call "literary patronage" – and, if not coincidentally, revolved around various venues of public performance and display. Second, a goodly body of literature was created and circulated not according to the expectations of literary patronage and public display, but rather according to some horizontally aligned "other system" that claimed as its participants educated men of functionally approximate (non-patronage-dependent) social rank. As noted above, it is this horizontally productive other system, as it develops in the Republic, with which we are concerned, and the one I designate in this study as *isonomic* – meaning simply "of approximately equal social status" – in terms of both its members (men of roughly commensurate status) and the currency (texts) through which their exchanges were negotiated.

Book trade

Next, and precisely because this study concerns itself with the textual materiality of privately dedicated works of literature, I am of necessity not concerned with the "physical book" as a tool for the broader (post-dedicatee) dissemination of literature. The theoretical lens of textual materiality ("text as social stuff," one might say) through which I conceptualize these dedicated objects is one not especially current in the field at present;[27] but as I argue in Part III, it is a valuable one when dealing with the strange and powerful autonomy with which dedicated texts of all sorts are endowed. In theorizing the social and aesthetic properties of the dedicated text (a term I apply variously to the single poem, a collection of poems, or a dedicated treatise) as distinct from the economic and intellectual properties of the "book," I focus on those dedicatory or performative moments at which the text is made to express and generate its existence – as a repository for elite display, obligation, or affection – in a way that seems to defy its material substance. As these moments occur after the raw materials for the text have been acquired but – of necessity – long before the text will have entered the broader community as any kind of consumer good, this study is not concerned with the papyrus trade of the early first century BCE

---

[27] Dupont 1999 (see esp. pp. 111–127), Kuttner 2005 (on the *Lithika* of Posidippus), and Roman 2001 are notable and important exceptions.

(it is clear that there was a substantial one),[28] nor with the basic ins and outs of acquiring paper (while we know the Imperial *Horrea Chartaria* were located in the area of the Argiletum, we can only hypothesize on the location of their Republican counterpart), nor with the physical structure of the *liber* vs. the *libellus* (although I will suggest that the distinction is in fact one of function rather than size), and least of all with the public book trade (Catullus himself tells us of the *scrinia* – for Martial the term is *libelli* – but the context in which he does so makes it clear this is not *his* primary "publication" point).[29] The broader public consumption of the texts of Catullus and Cicero – whether this occurred by accident or design or both – remains an interesting issue. But our focus is on the "first order" nexus in which our authors' texts were written and dedicated, and the ways in which each man worked to distinguish those within the nexus from those outside of it.[30]

Everyone who wrote

Finally, this is neither a book "about" every individual who wrote and dedicated texts in the late Republic, nor one that will investigate in detail every member of the large and active isonomic class I have come to call a "Society of Patrons." This is in part because such broad (and useful) surveys of Republican literary culture have been done in the past and their content need not be repeated here. But it is in part because even in terms of the dedicatory focus of the present study the survey model presents various methodological difficulties, and it will be good to state these at the start.

In some cases, the difficulty arises because an author who we know participated in the isonomic textual reciprocity of the period has left us with no examples of the dedicated texts with which we are concerned. So Caesar, who received from Cicero – via Balbus and Oppius – a text copy of *pro Ligario* and dedicated to the orator his own *de Analogia*,[31] is certainly to be considered a member of this "group." But we are left with no primary evidence from which to map our intersection – we possess none

---

[28] On early Roman papyrus trade and production, cf. Plin. *HN* 13.68–90; on Pliny's account of the production of papyrus, see Dimarogonas 1995; on the role of papyrus in the book trade as a whole, see Turner 1968.

[29] Habinek 1998: 114–121 provides a helpful discussion of several of these issues. On some of the more technical details of production, see Cavallo 1975 and Kenney 1982.

[30] On the role of bookshops in disseminating aristocratically produced texts to a wider reading audience, see Starr 1987; on Cicero's publication of his own works, see Phillips 1986, Murphy 1998 and, more recently, Butler 2002.

[31] Cf. *Ep. Att.* 13.19.

of his dedicated writings – and so his involvement in the core of textual
production is made wholly dependent upon what others of the period
have said about it. Caesar surely had a "dedicatory voice," but it has been
silenced by the dearth of direct evidence.

Occasionally the source of the difficulty is that a member of the group has
left us with examples of dedicatory practice that are either too fragmentary
(so the case for many of the so-called "Neoterics," a term I do not use) or too
anomalous to bring into the discussion in a way that would not distract
from its overarching focus. Thus we know that Varro, an exceptionally
prolific and varied author (some seventy titles in 600 books are recorded
by some authors), dedicated his first grammatical work, *de Antiquitate
Litterarum*, to an aged Accius (we might propose a date in the mid 80s,
unless the dedication was made post-mortem), and his early *Ephemeris
Naualis* to Pompey (77 BCE).[32]

That we have reports of these dedications is important, as they point
to the dedication of prose texts prior to that of Cicero's *de Oratore*.[33] As
we possess nothing of these texts beyond title and dedicatee, however, it
is impossible to bring them into the consideration of this study in any
meaningful way. We do know, of course, that Varro later entered into a
relationship of textual reciprocity with Cicero: both the ninth book of the
Ep. Fam. and the thirteenth book of the *Ep. Att.* attest to Cicero's ongoing
anxiety over the matter. As early as 47, Varro had promised to dedicate
one of his works to Cicero (*Ep. Fam.* 9.8);[34] in 45, Cicero dedicated to
Varro his *Academica Posteriora* and complained to Atticus that two years
had passed since the intended dedication had been announced – and still
nothing from Varro! The promise of a *magna sane et grauis* προφώνησις
(*Ep. Att.* 13.12) was finally fulfilled between 45 and 43 with the appearance
of *de Lingua Latina*, twenty-one books of which were dedicated to Cicero.[35]

---

[32] That Accius was a freedman who wrote under the patronage of D. Iunius Brutus Callaecus adds
depth to the textual picture of the earlier part of the first century BCE and underlines the complexity
of textual dedication in this period. Accius seems *sui generis* in this apparent transition from being
a man who only gave literature, for most of his life, to one who received literature, in extreme old
age, from another individual. There is surely more to this story, but there is little more we can say
with confidence.

[33] The *Rhetorica ad Herrenium* would of course be another text to consider for inclusion in the earlier
period, but because we lack any definitive information concerning either author or chronology and
because, based on stylistic and structural grounds, I find it personally inconceivable that this text
dates before the late 40s BCE (I would likely put it closer to Varro's *DRR*; I discuss issues of dating
this text briefly below), it is not noted above as one of the possibly "pre-Ciceronian" dedications.

[34] On Cicero's correspondence with Varro and Paetus in 46 and 45, cf. Leach 1999. For a good summary
of Varro's work, with some helpful details of his relationship with Cicero, see Baier 1997.

[35] We have some of the dedication of *de Lingua Latina*, but it is sparse: *in his [libris de lingua latina]
ad te scribam* (*DLL* 5.1).

Save the early dedications mentioned above, Varro seems to have shifted into his more productive dedicatory period at close to the time Cicero did. In addition to the dedication to Cicero, he dedicated texts to Caesar (*Antiquitates*, in 47) and Atticus (*de Vita Populi Romani*, date unknown), and he is the only person apart from Cicero for whom we have sure evidence of the composition of a dialogue in the Republic – *de Re Rustica*, published in 37.[36] Because we possess the three books of this dialogue in their entirety (most of the dedicatory sections of the non-dialogic *de Lingua Latina* have been lost), it is a useful comparandum in our consideration of the more substantial evidence provided by Catullus and especially Cicero. And yet because we possess this dialogue in its entirety, we can say that the choice of dialogue form seems to be where the "dialogue" between Varro and Cicero is – surely intentionally – complicated: each book of *de Re Rustica* has a different setting (the first is set in the *Aedes Telluris*, the second in Epirus, and the third in the *Villa Publica*); the second book has a dramatic date of 67, while that of the first is likely (or at least ideologically) post-44, and that of the third is most likely 50;[37] Cicero is fairly absent, but Atticus is an interlocutor in the second book; and each book ends abruptly, jarringly, in a way that seems to speak to the sudden silencing of Cicero's own dialogic voice.[38] Somewhat more troublingly, each of the three books has a different dedicatee (the first book is dedicated to Varro's suspiciously "farmy" wife, Fundania;[39] the second to Turranius Niger; the third to "everyman" Pinnius)[40] and – this final detail is the most problematic for the purposes of this study – at least two of these three dedicatees (Fundania and Pinnius) may not have existed or are at any rate elsewhere unattested. Varro's strangely urban (or mainly urban) treatise on "country matters" surely plays an important part in the dedicatory praxis of the late Republic, but it shows few obvious meeting points with the texts of the two authors who speak most vehemently to the praxis as a whole.

[36] On this dialogue see Linderski 1985 (for the dramatic date); Green 1997.
[37] On this, see Linderski 1985.
[38] The relationship between Cicero's overarching dialogue project and subsequent dialogists – Varro, Seneca, and Tacitus – is the focus of a forthcoming study.
[39] The *DRR* is to my knowledge the only Republican text explicitly dedicated to a female recipient (if she is real). Dedications to family members were not uncommon (so Cicero's *de Officiis*) and may indeed carry their own connection to an earlier Republican form (Cato's *Praecepta*); nevertheless, the dedication to a non-writing wife – if Fundania is meant to be a real person and not a speaking name – falls outside the rubric of the isonomic ally-exchanging and homosocial society with which this study is concerned.
[40] Green 1997: 435, fn 22 discusses the "generalizing" tone of the name and notes that although Pinnius is an attested Roman name, it is likely that "the expectation that readers would have assumed that a specific, known . . . Pinnius was meant, would not preclude the author's selection of that name for metaphorical or allegorical reasons."

Finally, sometimes the difficulty lies in the author who surely fits into the
late Republican picture at some level but for whom questions of social status
make it impossible to determine in which sphere of literary production (the
hierarchical or the isonomic) he resided. Thus Lucretius is variously argued
to have been a learned aristocrat of the patron class (the members of which
we would expect to be the providers of patronage rather than in need of
it themselves) or a learned everyman of the client class (the members of
which we would expect to lack sufficient social or economic capital to
support either themselves or the publicity of their work).[41] Was Memmius
Lucretius' Atticus, that is to say, or his Maecenas? Wiseman would hold
the latter position. Although the jury is out, and though I suspect the
answer may not be so simple, the terminological intersections that provide
the focus for Part I of this study suggest at least that Lucretius was not
participating in the textual argot of the late Republic: of *otium, munus*,
and *libellus* – the three most heavily textual terms at which Catullus and
Cicero intersect – Lucretius uses only *otium*, and only once and in the
plural (5.1387; the plural is a form more common to poets of the Principate
and Empire). Further, while neither Catullus nor Cicero use the term
amicitia in any direct discussion of their dedicated texts and the term
never appears in the dedications of such texts, Lucretius states baldly that
his desire for the *amicitia* of his dedicatee has compelled his writing of
the poem (*sed tua me uirtus tamen et sperata uoluptas / suauis amicitiae
quemuis efferre laborem / suadet*, 1.140–142). As tempting as it is to include
his work in our sample, then, to do so would be to commit a distracting
and methodologically problematic *petitio principii*. We are looking for
intersections, and Lucretius is an off ramp.

About

Before we get to a more detailed description of the methodology and scope
of this study (see below), it will be useful to contextualize our authors
within the broader textual story of the late Republic. It is certain that
Cicero participated in relationships of hierarchical literary patronage, and
it seems likely that Catullus did as well. Everything we know of their relative
social standing, however, would have had them do so only in the role of
patrons – the providers rather than recipients of patronage – themselves.
For all of his dedicated *technica*, it is clear that Cicero never considered

---

[41] On this argument, see especially Wiseman 1974a: 11–43 and 1982, in the latter of which he convincingly locates Lucretius, with Archias and in contrast to Catullus, in the group of Memmius'
clientes.

himself to occupy anything other than the position of literary patron. But so too is it clear that Catullus – *pace* those who would posit him as the first and last villa-owning Republican aristocrat who willingly assumed the position of the *cliens*[42] – never dedicated a single poem, much less a *libellus*, to any man he either identified as, or considered to be, his patron.[43] Neither man, in other words, dedicated texts to any other man from whom he might expect to receive anything other than, perhaps, a text in return.

The hierarchical patronage we saw at work in the middle Republic continued as a vibrant system of literary production and publication in these later years.[44] Archias was both Cicero's literary *cliens* and friend (there is no reason to expect these categories to be mutually exclusive in the Republic or any other period), and when in c. 14 Catullus suggests that the *libellus* he received from Calvus had been given to Calvus by a *cliens*, it is clear that he identifies with the recipient of the literature (Calvus) and not its donor.

This last point in particular – one's relative role in the exchange of literary texts and how that role is conceived – is worth a closer look. As in later periods, the terms (*patronus*, *cliens*) by which we commonly identify the participants in textual exchange are used only sparingly by our Republican authors and never, in the literary sense, of themselves.[45] Yet because these terms do appear in contexts of textual reciprocity in the Republic and later (when they appear with slightly greater frequency and, more importantly, in cases of self-reference), and because the very nature of dedicatory texts encourages us to think almost exclusively of the gift's point of origin (the

[42] So Gold 1987: 55, who posits "several" patrons for the poet, but who notes that the matter becomes "confused," and that none of these patrons "seems to have influenced his work to any great extent."
[43] This point is made most compellingly by Wiseman 1982: 39: ". . . the picture we get of Catullus is of a man at the upper end of the Roman social scale, more likely to be the source of patronage in a small way than in any need of a patron for himself."
[44] On these years and some of the "client-level" participants in hierarchical literary production see especially Wiseman 1982, and 1974a.
[45] Catullus uses *cliens* (of an imagined author of a wretched poetic gift) only once, as cited above, at c. 14; *patronus* appears only at c. 49, addressed to Cicero. Here, the word is playfully opposed to *poeta*, but the sense of *patronus* must not be taken to mean "literary patron" but rather forensic "advocate." Catullus' use of the phrase *patrona uirgo* in c. 1 is discussed briefly in Part III; Sulpicia c. 11 refers to herself as a *cliens* of the Muse, and Aurelius Opillus (cf. Suet. *Gramm.* 6) writes that poets are bound to the Muses by *clientela*; cf. Gold 1987: 56. Although Cicero uses *cliens* with somewhat greater frequency, he too tends to avoid the term, and the contexts in which it appears make clear a forensic rather than textual tonality. The term is for the most part eschewed in the orations, the letters, and the majority of the *technica* (it appears once in *Brutus*, the most "textually interested" of the dialogues, once in *Cato*, and not at all in the *Laelius*, in which we might expect it to appear in the context of *amicitia*; it appears somewhat more frequently, but only in the forensic sense, in e.g. *de Orat.*). *Patronus* appears more often, but not in the sense of literary relationships.

writer), it can be tempting to define participants in a relationship of textual exchange based on the nature of what they give.

This "point of origin" focus has marked the majority of past investigations into the literary patronage of both the Republican period and, to a greater extent, those periods that follow. The evidence of the late Republic, however, suggests that it is more useful to define the identity of the participants based not on the substance of what each man gives, but on the substance of what he receives.[46] In other words – and to use those words our authors avoided – what makes a *cliens* a *cliens* is not so much the fact that he writes and dedicates literary texts to another, but that he receives in return a non-literary, non-textual good. What makes a *patronus* a *patronus*, then, is not so much that he gives a non-textual good to his exchange partner, but that he receives only texts from this partner to begin with (it is, then, tempting to wonder whether Varro's dedication to Accius might have served as an honorific textual gesture, elevating the man symbolically from the level of textual *cliens* to that of textual *patronus*). Although the upper-class production of literature is at times marked as a pursuit indicative of excessive leisure time (and this is a theme that will be explored in Chapter 1), the evidence from both the middle and late Republic shows that literary composition and dedication by the patron class was anything but anathema: it was an act of distinctly upper-class privilege. A book is the perfect gift for the man who has everything. To receive another's book was to assume one's place among the favored few, and we might suspect that, in some ways, the receipt of another man's text was enough to initiate a man into the Society of Patrons.

In the first century BCE, patronal-class Romans were *writing Romans*. If we do not see them using the terms of literary patronage to describe their textual exchanges, it is reasonable to suppose that this was not so much because they were especially worried about being mistaken for being another man's *cliens* as because there was no worry that this mistake could be made. Could it be argued that textual exchange between patronal-class men can nevertheless be considered a form of "patronage"? Perhaps. But to argue that the dedication and receipt of literary texts is a sufficient condition for patronage – an assumption of some for Catullus' dedicated *carmina*, though I have yet to see it voiced for Cicero's dedicated *technica* – is to expand our understanding of "patronage" so broadly as to deprive it of meaning. If we are to make any sense of the late Republic, we must

[46] Especially useful to this configuration of late Republican reciprocity are the works of Mauss 1990 (orig. 1950), Schrift 1997 (see esp. the essays by Benveniste and Sahlins, as well as the introduction, "Why gift?" by Schrift), Hyde 1983, Godbout and Caillé 1998, Gernet 1981, and Gregory 1982.

recognize in this period a powerful isonomic system of literary production as well.

In proposing a reevaluation of the dedicatory practices of Catullus and Cicero, then, I want to contextualize these practices in terms of the Society of Patrons mentioned above. This Society, a group of approximate social equals who participated, to varying degrees, in a form of indubitably "horizontal" – isonomic – sociotextual reciprocity is reconstructed most profitably based on the evidence provided by Catullus and Cicero, and it is to our late Republican sources that I give greatest credence. But when the late Republican evidence is supplemented by that of the Empire – Pliny, Plutarch, and Suetonius are especially useful – then this group may be expanded to include a fair number of the educated and politically active men of the patronal class: not only men such as Atticus, Brutus, Caesar, and Varro, but indeed Cinna, Hortensius, Memmius, Nepos, Q. Cornificius, Pollio, Q. Mucius Scaevola, M. Messalla (cos. 53, not his Augustan-period homonymous son), and M. Caelius Rufus – and even such shadowy figures as Furius, Aurelius, Egnatius, Fabullus, and Veranius. A brief prosopography of these individuals, divided into two groups of greater or lesser "probability of participation" and with details of literary production, textual exchange (in terms of either attested dedication or receipt), and "intra-Society alliances," is provided in the Appendix.

We know, then, that our Society comprised a fairly large group of fairly well-to-do and powerful men. And the men of this group, in addition to whatever other social and political activities with which they busied themselves, engaged in the pursuit of what they surely and explicitly considered as (modern debates over the term notwithstanding) "literary" endeavors.[47] But not only did these men write such "literary" texts (described variously as *uersiculi*, *sermones*, and *litterae* and ranging from bawdy epigram to complex philosophical dialogue) as the physical representatives of patron

---

[47] The problem of "what literature is" rages on, but is not of primary (or even secondary) interest to this study. Quinn 1979: 22–23 (esp.) suggests a kind of "pleasurable uselessness" as one of the main criteria for Roman *litterae*, and notes a Roman anxiety over such "Greekish" lack of utility; but even as he (pp. 2–3) notes that Cicero applied the term *litterae* to both poetry and prose (his own and that of others), he glosses over Cicero's own clearly literary efforts in the *technica*. I find attractive Quinn's suggestion that for the literary text (as opposed to one written primarily for legal or religious purposes) "usefulness is a secondary concern," but I would tweak it a bit by suggesting that even such apparently "useless" works of literature as Catullus' *carmina* or Cicero's *de Finibus* (this latter is Quinn's example) may have inherent in their original composition a first-order social utility. Suetonius provides an interesting classical view of the question, and suggests both a generous view of what constituted literature, and, as now, an ongoing debate over the terms (*Gramm.* 4). See also Dupont 1999 for an interesting and widely ranging survey of the "invention" of literature in antiquity.

class display; if we are to make sense of the evidence offered by Catullus
and Cicero, so too did they carefully dedicate them to, and circulate them
throughout, members of the social and intellectual peer-group for whom
that display would have been most recognizable and meaningful.

It is certain that the activity of this group grew out of the nascent isonomy
of the middle Republic, but whereas for that period we can identify little
more than a handful of 'probable' participants in such a system – those
listed above – the relative wealth of evidence for the late Republic gives us
our first substantive look at the how and why of learned literary exchange
outside of the structural hierarchy of earlier or later periods. The textual
production of the late Republic is marked, more than that of any period
prior to it, by patronal-class recognition not only that the dedicated text
could be constructed so as to move throughout this class in a system
independent of hierarchical patronage (a recognition we may trace to the
middle Republic), but that its ability to do so provided the members of
this class with a valuable intellectual, artistic, and social tool. For some
members of this class – and this may be Catullus' story – it was a tool of
choice; for others – the likely position of Cicero and men who had started
their intellectual life "outside the text" and turned to textual production
only as the Republic crumbled – it was a tool of survival. If the textual
story of the Republic starts with the dedicated text, then the consideration
of these texts is in part a consideration of their producers.

HOW A "SOCIETY OF PATRONS"? METHODOLOGY AND SCOPE

As I noted at the outset of this Introduction, the story I plan to tell is not a
simple one. It is inherently difficult (or at least puzzlingly untraditional) to
read Catullus and Cicero in the same work; as that is precisely what I shall
do in this study, I want to explain in rather more detail both why I think
this is not only a valuable approach, but perhaps even a necessary one and,
further, how I will situate these authors against each other. Although what
I intend to show is that they are far more similar than they are different
(although, again, that is not the point of this book), it is incontrovertibly the
case that analysis of these authors calls for different styles of interpretation
and approach. In what follows, I provide first a general discussion of how
issues of chronology and operative condition inform this investigation and
how they will be treated within it, and then a basic outline of the shape and
progression of each part of the study and the ways these parts fit together.

If we take 54 BCE as both the terminus for Catullan poetic activity
and the publication date of Cicero's first dedicated text, *de Oratore* (I have

nowhere encountered compelling arguments against either claim), then we have precisely no chronological overlap in the known or extant textual dedications of these two men. It is clear, however, that Cicero had been engaged in what he considered to be literary endeavors long before 54, and so it will be useful to consider these years and how they may have shaped his turn to the writing of dedicated literature. His *de Inventione* (84 BCE), if not the most stylistically sophisticated of treatises, speaks of a lifelong interest in literary composition, and when he claims, in the dedication of *de Oratore*, to be eager for a return to the studies of his youth (*ad eas artis, quibus a pueris dediti fuimus, de Orat.* 1.1.2), we suspect that although his eagerness is overstated, his interest in literature is not.

The thirty years between the publication of *de Inventione* and *de Oratore* were not textually inactive ones for Cicero. Aside from the regular publication of *orationes* throughout his career (Cicero does not include these in his notion of *litterae*, and so neither shall we – though at least some, such as the *Actio Secunda* of *in Verrem*, should probably be brought into the fold), we have notice of several poetic works that likely date from earlier periods (*Glaucus, Alcyones, Limon, Aratea*, the epic *Marius*). In 60 he tells Atticus that he has just sent him a *commentarius* on his consulship written in Greek (*Ep. Att.* 1.19), asks for his friend's opinions of it, and explains that he will next send off a Latin version and finally one in verse – doubtless this is *de Consulato Suo*, composed in three books and partially preserved in *de Divinatione* – just to make sure he has covered his bases (*ne quod genus a me ipso laudis meae praetermittatur,* 1.19.10; cf. 1.20.6 and 2.1.1).[48] In subsequent letters from this year and the next, we learn that he is expanding his library and is preparing – apparently at Atticus' suggestion – to write a *Chorographia* based on that of Theophrastus' geography (*Ep. Att.* 2.3; 2.4; 2.6; 2.7). We also have notice of an *Admiranda* (Plin. *HN* 31.12.51); the date of this work is unknown, but if I were a betting individual, I would place this similarly after 60 and before 54. In 56, Cicero approaches his friend Lucceius – himself a writer of histories – with the request that he compose a piece on Cicero's consulship and especially the details of his role in foiling the conspiracy of Catiline (*Ep. Fam.* 5.12). Cicero hopes his friend will grant him his request, but says that if he does not, he will be forced to do what many criticize – write about himself (*scribam ipse de me,*

---

[48] On Cicero's value as a writer of histories, cf. Plut. *Cic.* 41; on his value as an author, cf. Nepos fr. 2: *ille enim fuit unus qui potuerit et etiam debuerit historiam digna uoce pronuntiare, quippe qui oratoriam eloquentiam rudem a maioribus acceptam perpoliuerit, philosophiam ante eum incomptam Latinam sua confirmarit oratione. ex quo dubito, interitu eius utrum res publica an historia magis doleat.*

5.12.8). Lucceius does not write the history Cicero had so desired, and a year after the letter had been sent, Cicero began work on both *de Oratore* and *de Re Publica*, the former of which would be published in the year following, and the latter of which was circulated in parts between 54 and 51. In writing about the orator and about the Republic, I suggest, Cicero had begun to write about himself.

In other words, although Catullus and Cicero did not overlap in the years during which each wrote and dedicated texts, they overlapped quite significantly in the years during which each observed and engaged with the literary world of the late Republic. We saw above that not only did Cicero show lifelong interest in the production of literature, but his interest in writing more politically and intellectually engaged works of literature (and in discussing literary terminology, as we shall see in Part I) seems to have increased around 60: two years after his elaborately literary defense of the poet Archias, and just about when Catullus would have been in his mid 20s and actively engaged in textual production.

In our examination of the poems of Catullus – our focus will be both the dedicated poems and those that speak of the textual world in which such dedication occurred – we shall see that he participated in a world of isonomic textual exchange that must have been well established before his entry into it and that continued to evolve in complexity and form based on the activities of all of its members. And yet the form of the texts that were exchanged in this world is important to consider, as they appear to have been almost exclusively poetic in nature. Indeed, save Varro's dedication to Accius in the mid 80s (?) and to Pompey in 77 (each difficult to bring into the discussion both because they are lost and because there is no evidence that these texts were dedicated in a relationship of textual reciprocity), we have no evidence for the dedication of prose texts in the late Republic prior to 54. We know that at least two patronal-class individuals of the middle Republic had dedicated *commentarii* to each other, and so we might imagine that this practice had continued, in some form, in the years leading up to Cicero's decision to write and dedicate his *de Oratore*; but our map of the textual world into which Cicero was to enter suggests that poetry had provided the primary token of dedication and exchange.

Yet the world in which this exchange took place was one not populated by individuals devoted to poetry alone; indeed, all evidence is to the contrary. Many of those men to whom Catullus addresses or dedicates his poems, from at least some of whom it is likely he received or might have expected to receive poems in exchange, are men who were known to have written both poetry and prose, and indeed who not only participated actively in the political life of the Republic, but who had made their name and fame in doing just that. I noted at the start of this Introduction that one of the most frustrating things about the evidence from the late Republic is that in some ways it is fairly anomalous; thus in Catullus' apparent *a principio* rejection of political and forensic activity in favor of the world of the text, we have almost no one – indeed, no one about whom anything significant is known – with whom he may be compared in terms of operative condition. Because Catullus, something of a Lucilius of the late Republic, boasts that he never enters the forum save to dawdle (c. 10; contra this, of course, cf. at least cc. 39 and 53), he offers the rare perspective of a man whose engagement in the textual world was not merely all he had; it was all he wished to have. He tells us that the patronal-class choice of the text over the forum, even if this was not a common choice to make, was nevertheless a possible and defensible one, and because his discussions of his textual world seem in no way embittered by a negative relationship with the forensic and political one, he helps us reconstruct the "stakes of the textual game" as they would have differed for those who steered clear of the forum, those who kept a foothold there, and those who had been expelled from it by force. A "rare blend of engagement and detachment,"[49] we have in Catullus not a man who did not care about the Republic; we have a man who did not use his texts to try to change the Republic, because he chose to locate the cultural work of his texts in the textual world alone.

Cicero did not have that choice. If Catullus gives us a glimpse into the world of textual dedication before Cicero's declining political fortunes (and perhaps Atticus) encouraged him to enter it, then the terms by which Cicero constituted his entry can give us further evidence for the terms and interest of the Society as a whole. When we note that although the operative conditions faced by these men differed, their terminological, rhetorical, and sociopractical modes of expression often coincide, we can do several things. First, and as suggested above, we will be able to suggest an overarching shape for the textual community of the late Republic as it mediates between the practice of the earlier period (about which we know little) and that of the Principate and later (about which we know rather

---

[49] This quote is from Gruen 1992: 316, in a description of Lucilius that aligns nicely with my understanding of Catullus' situation: "Lucilius emerges as beholden to no person, faction, or political philosophy. He mocked friends and adversaries alike, lampooned public figures, and parodied public actions... [he was] a contentious critic who could laugh at his own quarrels and even taunt his own readership. He offered a rare blend of engagement and detachment. And he consistently guarded his fierce independence."

more). Second, by comparing the points of coincidence and disparity, we
will be able say something of the ways in which a man who felt he had been
"forced" from the forum engaged with the textual world in a way that was
functionally distinct from that of a man who had rejected political life from
the beginning. Third, we will be able to get a clearer idea of how Cicero
used his dedicated dialogues to respond to, and in some ways attempt to
change, the stakes of the textual game that he had entered. And fourth, in
fleshing out the shape of the late Republican community, in particular the
ways in which the dedicated text became more aggressively politically and
socially concerned, we may form a clearer image of a structural and stylistic
forerunner to the textual world into which authors of later periods would
retreat perforce. The textual community of the late Republic is of course
but one moment in the ongoing and ever-changing textual life of Rome.
A mapping of this community will add not only to our understanding of
the late Republic, but indeed to our understanding of how earlier periods
fed into it and why later periods responded to it as they did.

For all this, the period with which we are dealing is relatively brief, and
this study is confined almost exclusively to the evidence of Catullus and
Cicero. We have about twenty to twenty-five years of significant textual
activity at our disposal with, as noted above, no chronological overlap in
the dedicated texts of our two authors. We know virtually nothing of the
chronology and even less of the dissemination of Catullus' *carmina*, and
this makes problematic certain issues of their comparison and juxtaposition with Cicero's dedicated dialogues. If Sestius knew Catullus (c. 44),
then it is likely that Cicero did; and if he did, it seems inconceivable that
he would not have been at least moderately familiar with at least some
of the *carmina*,[50] especially after the poet's death, when they might have
entered broader distribution. In examining the terminological, rhetorical,
and sociopractical intersections of Catullus' dedicated *carmina* and Cicero's
dedicated dialogues, however, I will argue for no direct lines of influence
or response, as such are impossible to prove conclusively. Where the intersections are most compatible – those of terminology and the social code

---

[50] I base this not on Cicero's references to οἱ νεώτεροι, *poetae noui*, or *cantatores Euphorionis*, all of
which post-date the poet's death significantly, but on Cat. 49, which is our only evidence that the
two knew each other (Thomson 1997: 294 believes that c. 35 may refer to a letter Cicero wrote
to Catullus on the matter of Caecilius' poetry – an attractive idea, but one unsupported by the
evidence). The phrase οἱ νεώτεροι appears in a letter dated from 50 (*Ep. Att.* 7.2.1); *poetae noui*
appears in 46 (*Orator* 161), and *cantatores Euphorionis* in 45 (*TD* 3.45). Although such phrases may
refer to the poetry of Catullus (cf. Crowther 1970), they give us nothing in terms of reconstructing
an affective or aesthetic relationship between the two men. On Cicero's general encouragement of
poetic activity, cf. Pliny *Ep.* 3.15.1.

it entails, as discussed in Part I – the two authors will be considered in near synchrony (though with some allowance for diachronic progression in Cicero's use of such terminology, where such a progression seems both plausible and meaningful). Where there appear to be nuanced distinctions in the intersections – those of rhetorical and sociopractical expression, as discussed in Parts II and III – and where these intersections might tell us something significant about how each man's engagement in the textual community may have shaped his expression of it, then I will tend to adopt more of a diachronic approach, dealing first with the relevant Catullan passages, and then with those of Cicero, and suggesting general ways in which it appears Cicero might have responded to what had come before.

In the case of Catullus, I attempt a survey neither of his "overarching" poetic agenda (I believe he had several), nor of every poem that might be said to address any given individual (many of the addressees are listed in the Appendix, and in most cases little more can be said) or performative situation. By way of maintaining focus on the somewhat slippery questions at hand, I restrict myself to a consideration of poems of two basic sorts: those that are dedicated to another or appear to be written in response to a dedication, and those that speak more broadly of the textual world – the Society of Patrons – in which such dedication appears to have occurred.

As a result, many of the *carmina* that seem as if they could be brought into the discussion will not be addressed. I do not, for instance, consider the poet's offhand reference or uncolored address to individuals we might certainly include in our Society (as noted above, for this cf. the Appendix), if this reference does not at the same time speak to ongoing engagement with the practice of the Society as a whole. Thus although I include Cinna as an almost certain participant in the textual world of the late Republic, and although Catullus' poems to Cinna (cc. 10, 95, and 113) may well have functioned as tokens in the textual transactions of our Society, they do not in and of themselves reveal anything significant of its overarching practice. Similarly, while my analysis of textual materialism will bring into consideration several of the most "textually powerful" of the *carmina*, I pass over those many examples of Catullan invective – the Gallus, Gellius, and Mentula poems – that show no convincing trace of the expected textual reciprocity or terminological and functional quibbles with which we see the Society elsewhere engaged.

My approach to the *carmina* operates at a few levels. I try to take Catullus' claims at affective and functional face value: a poem written to a friend is indeed – at least, at first – a poem written to a friend, and a poem that claims to respond to a request for poetry has a real request in mind. But texts that are themselves dedicated to others (c. 1, etc.), and indeed those that engage in discussions of the world of textual production and exchange (cc. 12, 50, etc.), tend to be more "textually interested" than those that do not, and so I try to tease out what I see to be the metatextual function of these poems. It is not that I believe that Catullus only writes about writing; rather, that even when he does not immediately seem to be writing about writing, the language and imagery with which he presents apparently "non-poetic" social interactions – a chance meeting in the forum or a casual dinner with friends – often offer their most compelling meanings if read as metaphor for the textual world. Third, and because I wish to break the surface of these poems and reconstruct what I can of the textual world in which they were produced, I often interrogate the poet's claims of affection and disdain (most specifically, I tend to view invective as a poetically generative genre and not a true profession of anger), and look for those lexical, tonal, and rhetorical markers – shadowy innuendo and sly argot – through which a deeper textual practice might be revealed. C. 16 famously warns Catullus' readers, past and present, of the risk of engaging in biographical fallacy (I find it especially strange that a poem the entire message of which is "things are not as they seem" has been taken as evidence of Catullus' true affective state); with this poem in mind, then, I take this poet's verses with a grain of the salt with which they are so liberally seasoned. In so doing, my more textually oriented take on Catullus' dedications is supplemented, at the critical level, by work in the areas of fetish, collection, and gift theory; in the case of those *carmina* that suggest a cycle of reciprocal poetic invective, I have found it useful – it is admittedly slightly unorthodox – to consider relevant certain pop culture exempla of the "amicable feud" or "response piece" as a generative artistic tool in and of itself.

This study will seem, at times, like more of a study on Cicero than anything else, and it is indeed based more heavily on the Ciceronian evidence for several reasons. First, Cicero simply provides us with more evidence to consider; because of the breadth and extent of his corpus we are able to compare the textual concerns of the dedicated *technica*[51] (those primarily dialogic prose works of his later years) to similar such

[51] The dedicated *technica* as a whole include *de Orat.* (dedicated to his brother Quintus), *de Rep.* (Quintus), *de Leg.* (Quintus), *Brutus* (Brutus), *Orator* (Brutus), *Parad. Stoic.* (Brutus), *Part. Orat.* (Marcus *filius*), *Acad. Prior.* (Catulus [lost] and Lucullus), *Acad. Post.* (Varro), *de Fin.* (Brutus), *TD* (Brutus), *DND* (Brutus), *de Div.* (Quintus), *Top.* (Trebatius), *Cato* (Atticus), *Laelius* (Atticus), and *de Off.* (Marcus *filius*). It is likely that *Hortensius* was similarly a dedicated dialogue; there is an implied recipient of *de Opt. Gen.*, but no named dedicatee; whether or not there was a dedicatee for *de Fato* is unclear.

concerns as they are expressed in both the (mainly earlier) *orationes* and the (often contemporary) letters, and to trace a chronological progression and strong generic distinction that is impossible in the case of Catullus. Second, past investigations into the "literary culture" of the late Republic have focused almost exclusively on what little we know of the poetry produced at that time, and have used Cicero (and especially his *technica*, a fact that seems impossibly problematic to me) to provide corroborating "evidence" for a literary world in which he is imagined to have taken no part. In so doing, they have tended to naturalize what was by all accounts the highly anomalous situation of Catullus (the aristocratic poet who was politically interested, but not especially politically active), and to consider Cicero's *technica* – if they are considered at all – as non-literary products: unproblematic source material for the "real" (i.e., poetic) literary activity of the late Republic, or for the "intellectual life" of those who are simultaneously assumed not to have been powerful players in the textual world. I want to argue, by contrast, that both the *technica*, which were certainly *litterae* to the man who wrote and dedicated them, and Cicero – a man who held both political and literary interests, who wrote both poetry and prose, and who turned increasingly to the dedication of prose texts as the Republic faltered and failed – are more representative witnesses for the general character of the textual world of the late Republic from 60 on and may be profitably opened up by using what Catullus has to say about his textual world as a comparable source. Finally, although much has been written about the influence of Catullus – both in terms of language and in terms of poetic form – on the literature and textual life of the later periods, I will suggest that Cicero's use of the dedicated text to move outside of the textual community and "do things" in the world at large (never much of a concern to Catullus, as it seems) may be brought profitably into discussions of the socially engaged textual materialisms and dedications of the Principate and Empire.

My understanding of the *technica* – their overarching project of textualizing the orator's voice as much as their more specific task of transferring this textualization into the hands of others – has been informed by the many recent and excellent investigations into Cicero mentioned above and, at the theoretical level, by gaze, gender, and fetish theory as well as, in the case of *Brutus*, that of textual materialism. And yet because my understanding of the lexical, tonal, and stylistic work of the *technica* requires that we consider them as serious social and literary artifacts in their own right, I base my analysis of their project and form on internal evidence before all else: both the "face value" claims of those *technica* we will consider and, as with Catullus, the contests and negotiations that are suggested to lie just beneath the surface.

The immense and complex project of the *technica*, and in particular Cicero's "invention" of textual authority and prose *persona* in the latest of these works (a project investigated profitably by Dugan 2005), remains at the center of my understanding of the late Republican creation of the dedicated prose text as a tool for social and intellectual negotiation. As such, I have no doubt but that the *technica* were as innovative as they have proven influential. The internal evidence of the *technica*, however, suggests that the innovations they claim could only have resulted from, and were only allowed by, the isonomic textual world into which Cicero had entered. It is certain that the *technica* functioned as some of the primary "producing products" of this world, and that they continually shaped, reinforced, and added to its structure and intent. It is likely, if we cannot say certain, that when Cicero entered the textual world in 54, his dedication to Quintus of a highly artificial, highly literary dialogue would have been something relatively unheard of in the Roman textual world and, perhaps, something a bit unsettling. By 46, however, and with the publication of *Brutus*, it is clear that Cicero is not the only prose author playing the dedication game (and Varro's choice of a dialogic *DRR* makes us suspect that the game was a good one).

We must be careful, then, to approach the innovations Cicero claims for his texts with a critical eye. Just as Catullus 16 cautions against the bio-graphical fallacy, *Brutus* 11.42 (*concessum est rhetoribus ementiri in historiis ut aliquid dicere possint argutius*: it's OK for rhetoricians to lie in their histo-ries, if it's to make a point more sharply) cautions us that Cicero's claims of tradition and innovation are often cloaked in irony and innuendo. Cicero sends his *technica* into the textual community as a way of remaking the community in his own image. But the *technica* are produced producers: written *for* – and thus in a certain sense, *by* – this community, they shape the subsequent aesthetic and functional expectations *of* the community. There is no doubt but that they were innovative: but to consider them in absence of the sociotextual system upon which their composition, dedica-tion, and circulation were predicated risks a misleading overestimation of their "newness" and gives us only half the story of why Cicero's innovations mattered.

As noted above, this book is divided into three basic "Parts," each of which focuses on one of the major intersections between the texts of Catullus and Cicero; each part is then subdivided into chapters that address, in different sections, specific elements of these intersections. Owing to both the imbalance of the evidence and considerations of genre, some sections will address Catullus and Cicero in tandem while others will be weighted more heavily to the author (usually Cicero) who either had more at stake in his textual negotiations or has provided the more compelling evidence for a particular textual phenomenon. The goal of the chapters is not to provide a perfect balance between each author; such would be highly artificial, and would strain both points of contact and of disconnect. Rather, I wish to investigate each man's expressions of an intersection (terminology, rhetoric, practice), in whatever ways and to whatever extent he did, and to present these expressions against each other in a way that will tell us more about the structure, background, form, and interests of their world and, as is likely, the greater textual world of the late Republic as a whole.

Part I of this book, "How to write about writing," addresses intersections of terminology and social code and lays the interpretive foundation for much of the terminological and social coding that we shall see in subsequent parts of the study. I consider the two major conceptual markers – *otium* and *munus*, in Chapters 1 and 2 – and the one minor one – *libellus*, in Chapter 3 – at which our authors intersect most closely either in explicit use (*otium* and *munus*) or variously cautious circumlocution (*libellus*). I will suggest that these are the terms through which Catullus and Cicero conceived the social time, social space, and social objects of their textual exchanges; as they are terms that continue to be linked to the textual world of the Principate and early Empire, even as their connotations may shift, it will be worthwhile to start our study with a careful look at the language our authors used to "write about writing." As noted above, my approach to the evidence will show the greatest synchrony in Part I, as the high degree of congruity in our authors' use of these terms and social codes – Catullus writing wholly within the textual world, and Cicero writing first from its exterior and then moving to its core – is suggestive of a socially coded idiom of patronal dedication recognizable as such to all major participants of the period. The markers with which Part I is concerned respond more or less to three fundamental questions concerning how Catullus and Cicero write about the conceptual shape of a client-free textual Society: *when*, *what*, and *where*. *When* seeks the ways in which these authors conceptualize the patronal-class prerogative of "social time," during which their dedicated texts were produced and shared. *What* examines the ways in which these men conceived of their dedicated texts as material objects, and suggests that the term by which these men "materialized" their texts in terms connotative of reciprocal display and obligation will tell us much of the underlying expectations of the Society for which they were written. *Where*, finally, turns to a known and loved "little word" – *libellus* – and suggests that a recontextualized understanding of this term and its sociotextual function will open up a new way of thinking about what it means for a book to circulate.

Parts II and III build off the terminological foundation offered in Part I (and there will be some overlap in poems discussed), but investigate elements of the second major intersection, that of rhetorical and sociopractical expression. Part II, "The textualization of display," is the most substantial part of this study, and in its investigations into both possible causes and likely expression of the textualization of display – the transferal of cultural display and obligation into textual form – it functions as the core of the work as a whole. Chapter 4 begins with a consideration of the "problem" of liberal performance in the late Republic, and addresses the ways our authors engaged with late Republican concerns (and, in the case of Cicero especially, anxieties) surrounding upper-class public display and its censure. I suggest here that an increasingly unstable forum may have made the textualization of patronal display particularly attractive to Cicero in the years leading up to 54, but show that both he and Catullus participated in similarly "commodifying" censures of display or its estimation. In Chapter 5, I turn to Cicero's translation of the homosocial display of the forum into the homosocial display of *de Oratore* and *Brutus* and consider, via Catullus' Sestius and c. 44, the ways in which poet and orator would easily overlap in the textual interactions of the Society. In Chapter 6, the final chapter in Part II, I look to the role of patronal-class social and rhetorical obligation as it is co-opted and expanded by both Catullus and Cicero, and suggest that in adopting the form of "polite obligation" for their dedications, each man forged his textual dedication as the social tool best suited to create the offer, and the text, that could not be refused.

Part III, "The materialization of the text," constitutes the briefest part of this study but is in some ways the part that looks most to the future of textual production and dedication. Although it builds on the idea of the dedicated text as an embodiment of social practice and display, the specific focus of Part III is textual materialism as it emerged in the late Republic and, most specifically, our authors' fetishization of their dedicated texts as powerful objects – or peculiar little bodies – that move about and "do things" in the textual and, especially in the case of Cicero, social world. I begin with a brief consideration of how this textual materialism related to the process of the textualization of display and how it might relate to the post-Republican heirs to this textual fetishization (it is in the late Republican fetishization of the gift text that our authors found their greatest influence in the Principate and early Empire). In Chapter 7, I turn to Catullus' use of the fetish text as a tool of contract and payoff (cc. 1, 49, 68b), erotic stand-in and issue (c. 50), and – if more briefly – poetically generative invective (cc. 16, 42): the literary "response piece" that does not so much attack its dedicatee (and I will suggest that these are indeed dedicatory pieces) as it responds to, and subsequently incites, further artistic production and exchange. Chapter 8 focuses on Cicero's personification of the Republican voice, via the figure of *Eloquentia*, in *Brutus*. As a dialogue that marks a decisive moment in the orator's future course of textual activity (it is a dialogue that "breaks the silence" of Cicero's pen, *Brut.* 5.19), *Brutus* heralds the frantic textual explosion of Cicero's final years, in which dedicated dialogue moved closer and closer to theatrical piece, and the textual world was increasingly peopled with Cicero's dialogic personifications of a vanishing Republic.

PART I

How to write about writing

Intersections of terminology and social code: when, what, and where

> Cui dono lepidum nouum libellum
> arida modo pumice expolitum?
> Corneli, tibi . . .   Cat. 1.1–3
>
> To whom do I give this charming, new work–
> Just now polished up with dry pumice-stone?
> Cornelius! To *you* . . .

In his dedication of a small collection of poetry – a collection that would mark Catullus' brief career as much as it would 'make' the poet for generations of readers to come – Catullus asks a deceptively simple question: To whom do I give this charming new work?[1] Two lines later the poem provides its own answer – the *libellus* will be dedicated to the historian Cornelius Nepos[2] – but the question and its implications remain for the poet, the recipient, and the readers who have encountered it since. On closer inspection this simplest of inquiries becomes only more complex, more difficult to decipher, and more demonstrative of the anxieties of textual exchange and the author's desire to remain a subject even as he becomes, through his text, an object. Who will understand what the gift of a text means? Who will make sure that the right people read it? Who will be able to read it as it was intended to be read and who will, perhaps, make a gift in kind? What, at last, does it mean to entrust one's text – one's *persona* – to the care of another, and how does one write about this meaning?

Catullus and Cicero write about writing with some frequency and, when they do, with a great deal of care. They do so in different ways, of course; what it "meant" for each man to write, and so to write about writing, held a different meaning, and one necessarily implicated in his social, political, and personal situation. And yet, as I suggested in the Introduction, as much as Catullus and Cicero write about writing differently, those texts that seem

---

[1] The structure and order of the Catullan *libellus* is a topic dealt with extensively elsewhere and so will not be reviewed here; on this, see especially Hubbard 1983 and Minyard 1988. For an extensive bibliography of the corpus, cf. Scherf 1966.

[2] Auson. *Ecl.* 1.1 makes the identification of Nepos reasonably certain; cf. Thomson 1997: 197.

33

most concerned with the meaning of writing in the late Republic – the dedicated texts, and also those texts that show interest in textual production – tend to intersect in the authors' pointed and approbative use of a few, and as I shall argue socially charged, terms. It was when I began working with these authors' dedicated works that I first noticed, and not without some surprise, that certain terms – *otium, munus,* and *libellus* – not only appeared in the most "textual texts" of Catullus and Cicero but that, when they did – and in spite of the differences between the two authors' claims or apparent reasons for writing – they were used in ways that seemed both non-standard for the period (their most convincing reading is never merely "leisure," "duty," or "little book") but undeniably similar in tone and function.

A closer mapping of the texts in which these terms appeared convinced me that both Catullus and Cicero tended to place such terms at specific points in their texts in order to mark elements of textual production and function. *Otium* and its related terms, for example, tend to appear early in texts – or scenes within texts that talk about textual production – and, when they do, they are used to set the distinctly "textual time" within which intellectual discussion and textual production occur: *otium* in such usage never marks simple inactivity but rather a very specific sort of textual engagement. *Munus,* by contrast, is frequently used in these texts to designate the specific product of *otium,* the dedicated text, and as such it appears especially in discussions of how such texts could be used to engage relationships of textual reciprocity: the textual *munus* both "pays back" an earlier textual gift and seems to request one in return. *Libellus,* finally, is used to mark the text once it has left its author's control and has moved out into the world of circulation: never merely a "neat little book," *libellus* seems to provide the closest term for "a published text" that we have for this period.

The following chapters, then, consist of something of a word study, and word studies run the risk of tedium and circularity. I am aware that beginning an investigation into a lively textual world with a painstaking review of three single terms may not be the most exciting way to get things going. But precisely because the overlap in usage of these terms is so compelling, because the meaning of the textual discussions in which they appear is expanded by a more "textualizing" understanding of their function, and because these works are the most compelling textual markers of the period, an identification of this function will expand our general understanding of the ways in which patronal-class writers of the late Republic conceptualized their activity. In the process of this study, then, as the deeper significance of these terms unfolds, and as terminological intersections point to socio-textual ones, we shall find it useful to take occasional detours. Thus once we recognize that *otium*, qua "time to write," is often used to introduce scenes of secluded patronal-class conversation and conviviality, we will consider passages in which *otium* is not used as a descriptive marker of such conversations, but in which the descriptions themselves encode textually productive activity. Similarly, when we see that the first time Cicero uses *munus* of his dedicated texts he links it with a passage from Hesiod on the rules of reciprocity, it will be useful to consider subsequent citations of this passage that may have the social function of the textual *munus* in mind. When, finally, we note that the designation *libellus* underlines both the materiality and social function of "text set in motion" – this will be the primary focus of Part III – we will be able to understand more about how and why this textual materialism becomes as important as it does for later periods.

Although the function of these terms in later periods is not the focus of this section, the story of the textual world does not end with the late Republic any more than it begins with it. Indeed, each of the terms examined here continues to carry valences of textual production and textual society in the Principate and early Empire, and these continuations will be noted in brief at the conclusion of each terminological discussion. Just as we shall see a shift in designation from the middle Republic to the time of Catullus and Cicero, the connotations of these words shifts again in the later periods, but there remains an underlying late Republican "textuality" to these terms that informs our understanding of how later authors came into dialogue with the argot of the earlier. Finally, of course, I want to begin by taking a close look at the words these authors used to write about writing, both because neither man chose his words carelessly and because the somewhat more sociohistorical analyses of Parts II and III are predicated on an understanding of the ways in which these authors frame and engage with the very words examined in this section.

We start, then, with three markers of terminology and social code, *otium*, *munus*, and *libellus*, around which Chapters 1–3 are constructed. In the case of each marker we will see below that although there are often hints of the late Republican "social code" evident in the middle Republic, the New Comedy uses of these terms carry little of the social anxieties with which they are linked in the later period and none of the later and approbative connotations of literary, textual, or aesthetic concerns. In his study on the language of social performance, Krostenko noted a disjuncture between Plautus' use of, for example, *elegans* and *lepidus*, and that of later Latin authors,[3] and proposed that between the third and second centuries BCE there occurred a gradual "emergence of the language of social performance as a coherent set." Krostenko attributes this emergence to a shift in political and social aestheticism linked to the rise in convivial practices among the elite during this period.[4] As we shall see in the sections that follow, the language of textual dedication and exchange appears to have emerged along the same lines and during approximately the same time period (from that of Plautus, that is, to that of the late Republic), and may, I suspect, indicate a parallel emergence of terms of textual approbation arising from Krostenko's argued increase in second-century elite conviviality. Krostenko argued for a "display argot" that emerged from the aesthetic shift in terms that came to be associated approbatively with convivial display; what I think we have here is the emergence of a "textual argot" originating in a functional shift in terms that came to be associated approbatively with the dedicated texts these display-oriented communities had begun to produce.

In what follows, I move from the more generalizing and abstract of the terms (so the question *when*, to which the answer is *otium*) to the more exacting and concrete (*where*, to which the answer is *libellus*). Chapter 1 addresses *otium*, a term used at the end of the Republic (and periods that would follow, although the connotations change significantly) to describe broadly the "time" in which authors engaged in textual production and exchange. In Chapter 2, I suggest that *munus*, a term that carried connotations of reciprocity and implied obligation even in the middle Republic, emerges in the late Republic as designative of the sociomaterial object of textual reciprocity: the dedicated text itself. Chapter 3, the final chapter in Part I, argues that *libellus* emerges in the formative period of the textual community as the marker of that textual product expected, if anxiously, to experience public circulation beyond the affective confines of a closed textual world.

---

[3] Krostenko 2001: 21–22.
[4] Krostenko 2001: 1 notes the second-century BCE rise in the popularity of both *ludi* and convivia-embedded performance – both public and private – and linguistic display within the social and economic structures of the late Republic. On the increase of *ludi* and the effect of this increase on the Plautine stage, cf. Gruen 1996: 127.

CHAPTER I

When? Otium *as "time to write"*

THE SOCIOECONOMIC ORIGINS OF LITERARY LEISURE

The works of André and, more recently, Toner have been instrumental
to an overarching understanding of the definitions, form, and function of
otium in the Roman world.[1] While André's relation of *otium* to a Hellenistic
ideal[2] of leisure time is useful to the present study, he focuses on the uses
of the term (and its related concepts) in the political sphere, and gives little
consideration to the function of *otium* as a temporal and social marker
in the literature of the late Republic. Toner's discussions are more directly
relevant to the literary circumstances of the late Republic, and his remarks
on Cicero's interest in the construction of an "ideal" of leisure do much to
get at the problems at stake in this period in the intellectual realm.[3] The
textual connotations of *otium* as it is used in the late Republic, however,
remain largely unexplored by recent scholarship.

I start, then, with a brief consideration of why and when *otium* might
have shifted into the textual realm and a short survey of *otium* as it functioned in the New Comedy of the late third and early second centuries
BCE. I turn then to the use of *otium* in the late Republic, marking especially the semantic and spatial distinctions between *otium* in the city and
otium in the textual world. Both Catullus and Cicero used *otium*, and the
related *otiosus* and *otiose*, to mark the socially available "time" within which
each man's dedicated texts were read, produced, and exchanged. A review
of Cicero's use of the term in the orations leading up to the mid 60s (that
is, those that likely pre-date our Catullan evidence or are contemporary
with its earlier years) will show that in this period the public use of *otium*

---

[1] André 1966 and Toner 1995.   [2] André 1966: 41.
[3] Toner 1995: 26 cites also Wirszubski's remark that Cicero's use of the term "reflected both its popularity
and ambiguity" (cf. Wirszubski 1954); see also André 1966: 276, who summarizes Cicero's position,
"*Il a voulu définir . . . une orthodoxie de l'otium.*"

tended to mark a time free from political or military strife – a connotation "personalized" in Cicero's later textualizing use of the term – and one
that brought with it, as a result, the generally salubrious state of the body
politic.

Although we can say nothing of the determinative nuances of *otium* in
dedicated texts prior to those of Catullus, we shall see that in his purely
textual world *otium* stands wholly aloof from the public and display-
oriented "work" (*negotium*) of the forum and marks in every instance of its
usage neither political "peace and quiet" nor robust civic health, but the
distinctly private and almost inevitably "textual time" that patronal-class
individuals reserved for the production and enjoyment of their literature.
In Cicero's defense of the poet Archias in 62, however, surely due to the
content of the speech but also, I think, in recognition of an emerging
aesthetic, he makes use of a more textualizing sense of *otium* as a time
devoted to literary business. In *pro Plancio* (54 BCE) Cicero narrows the
sense of *otium* to indicate most specifically a time devoted to reading, and
in the dedicated *technica* and letters of the later years (especially those post-
dating the publication of *Brutus*), the term has become rooted in Cicero's
textual world as the argot for the "time to write."

Otium is a puzzle. We can say almost nothing of the etymological origins of the word,[4] nor need we, as my argument here is not one based on
etymology; it is in every case use, rather than etymology, that determines
meaning. By way of getting at the emergence of "textual *otium*," however,
it will be useful to take a brief detour into the relationship of *otium* to
a Greek word with which it seems conceptually linked – σχολή.[5] Quintilian, in his discussion of an excessively "busy" sort of oratory, describes
P. Popilius Laenas' "translation" of a Greek term thus: *nec inutili ex Grae-
cis ueteres transtulerunt, quod ab iis sumptum Laenas Popilius posuit, esse
hanc †inociosam† actionem* (*Inst. Orat.* 11.3.183). If we take for the nonsense †*inociosam*†, which appears only in the fifteenth-century MS P,[6] the

---

4 Suggested derivations from the Greek αὔσιος or αὔτως (the sense thus being that *otium* defines a
   time that is "empty" or done "in vain") have been rejected on the argument that there is no trace of
   an earlier *au-* form of the word and, at any rate, the adoption of *ō* for *au* is problematic. Cf. E–M s.v.
   otium; if *otium* entered Latin through the Greek, we would expect some indication of an earlier form
   such as **au-tiom*; E–M suggest rather that there may be some connection between this word and
   the formation of the somewhat rare and technical term *indutiae*. Walde-Hofmann 1965 s.v. *otium*
   provides a slightly fuller analysis of the term, but similarly concludes that the etymology of the term
   is uncertain.
5 I am grateful to Gregory Nagy for his clear articulation of the relationship during a discussion we
   had in the winter of 2000.
6 B, the eleventh-century codex, from which the majority of secure readings originate, has the meaningless *mocosam* (the reading retained in Winterbottom's 1970 Oxford Classical Text); Halm 1868
   suggests *negotiosam*, which is plausible but seems to miss the point of Quintilian's citation of Laenas.

(otherwise unattested) reading *inotiosam*, we can propose that at least by the early Empire (and possibly by the middle Republic, if Quintilian is actually quoting a source contemporary to Popilius), the adjectival *inotiosus* might have been considered a reasonable translation of the well-attested Greek ἄσχολος (*inotiosa actio* is thus the excessively busy sort of oratory described just before the phrase is used), suggesting perhaps even an earlier sense in which some aspect of *otium* was viewed to be akin to some aspect of σχολή.

If a kinship of *otium* and σχολή appeared in the late Republic, then this may explain something of why *otium* emerged as a term indicative of "intellectual activity within a social setting" at least by the mid to late 60s. As early as the fifth century BCE, σχολή was linked with the protracted talk that accompanied it (μακραί τε λέσχαι καὶ σχολή, Eur. *Hipp.* 384), and the sense that σχολή is a time not just for discussion, but for learned discussion – the natural "product" of the σχολή of an upper-class male – is attested by Plato (*Leg.* 820c) and Aristotle (*Pol.* 7.1.13). The term is linked to the textual sphere by Plato (e.g., *Phaed.* 227c and 228a)[7] and becomes even more closely linked to textual production later, when σχολή comes to indicate the physical text that is written during hours of σχολή: if σχολή produces learned discussion, then learned discussion produces the texts that record and remake it. This "talk to text" sense of σχολή – σχολή as a text the contents of which originated in discussion – is perhaps most fully developed in Plutarch,[8] but it appears to have emerged at least by the late Republic, when Philodemus – a Peripatetic philosopher who lived at Rome and was on friendly terms with Cicero – uses σχολή to refer to the physical text that is produced as the result of a social time.[9]

As we shall see below, at about the same time that we find *otium* linked with intellectual pursuits in the Republic, it is used first to determine the limits of "textual time" – in Catullus and Cicero's orations from the 60s – and then – especially in the *technica* dating after 46 – to serve as late Republican textual code for time that is most specifically "time to write."

---

[7] At *Phaed.* 227c, the word is actually ἀσχολία, which Socrates uses, in an appropriation of Pindar, *Isthm.* 1.1 (πρᾶγμα καὶ ἀσχολίας ὑπέρτερον θήσομαι), in his claim that listening to the contents of Phaedrus' conversation (σχολή) with Lysias would be, to him, "a greater thing than business" (καὶ ἀσχολίας ὑπέρτερον πρᾶγμα ποιήσασθαι). At *Phaed.* 228a, we learn that Lysias composed his speech κατὰ σχολήν.

[8] Plut. *Moral.* 790e, βίβλον ἢ σχολὴν περὶ πολιτείας ἐν Λυκείῳ γραψάμενος and 2.37c, σχολὴν γράψας; cf. further Plut. *Moral.* 326d.

[9] Philodemus *Acad. Ind.* P.74M, σχολὰς ἀναγράψαι. Cicero marks the textual aspect of σχολή qua temporal concept when he urges Atticus, in 59, ἐπὶ σχολῆς *scribe* ("write when you have time," *Ep. Att.* 2.6).

In Rome, *otium* is always firmly linked with the temporal aspect of writing rather than the physical (the physical and obligatory determinations of such texts adhere to *munus*), but Cicero seems to play with the "talk to text" sense of σχολή when, at the start of the first book of the *Tusculan Disputations*, he claims that he has contained the *scholae* of five days in as many books (*itaque dierum quinque scholas, ut Graeci appellant, in totidem libros contuli, TD* 1.4.8).[10] In a letter from 44 Cicero brings out the textual meaning of the term even more explicitly when he refers to a dedicated text – a text that would have been the product of *otium* – as a σχόλιον[11] (*Ep. Att.* 16.7).

Our focus here will be the ways in which this textualizing sense of *otium* is expressed in Catullus and Cicero. But because I am positing a late second-/early first-century emergence of the textual sense of *otium*, it will be helpful to consider first the use of the term in the middle Republic. In Roman New Comedy (*otium* does not appear in our sources prior to this) *otium* functions always as a temporal marker, but it lacks a stable semantic valence with regard to either what this time is for, where this time should be most properly spent, or whether one should "enjoy" *otium* in public or in private. The two dominant categories of signification (when such can be determined) are distinguished by whether the playwright defines *otium* as a time of activity, or as its absence – the difference between "I've a few minutes to get this done" and "Ah, I've a few minutes to myself." It is the former of these that is the more common signification in this period, and one I designate the *otium* of obligation. In both Plautus and Terence, characters of various social strata use *otium* in this way to mark, loosely speaking, a period of time during which to engage in a particular activity that has been requested of one and to which there is an understood element of expected obligation. This term appears frequently in the context of casually requested or promised conversation:[12]

LYCONIDES magna est res quam ego tecum otiose, si otium est, cupio loqui.
LYCONIDES I've an important matter I'd like to discuss with you in detail, if
        you've the time.   Plaut. *Aul.* 771

---

[10] On this, see also Douglas 1995.
[11] The use of σχόλιον in such a sense is rare, and seems almost entirely a Ciceronian invention.
[12] See also Plaut. *Cap.* 183: *em! uel iam otium est; Cas.* 214–215: CLEOSTRATA *mox magis quom otium mihi et tibi erit / igitur tecum loquar: nunc uale.* MYRRHINE *ualeas;* 544: CLEOSTRATA *sine eam: te nolo si occupatast.* ALCESIMUS *otiumst; Epid.* 655–656: EPIDICUS *abi intro ac iube huic aquam calefieri; / cetera haec posterius faxo scibis, ubi erit otium;* 423: PERIPHANES *at quaeso, ubi erit otium, / reuortere ad me extemplo; Poen* 857–858: SYNCERASTUS *fecero, / quamquam haud otiumst.* To these uses, cf. Ter. *Adel.* 419–420: *non hercle otiumst / nunc mi auscultandi!*

At Plautus *Mercator* 286–8 the social obligation implied by this usage of *otium* is made more explicit, and it is this sense of *otium* that will be an important aspect of the term as it is expressed in the texts of the late Republic:

DEMIPHO dicam, si uideam tibi esse operam aut otium.
LYSIMACHUS quamquam negotiumst, si quid uis, Demipho,
  non sum occupatus umquam amico operam dare.

DEMIPHO I'd tell you, if I saw that you had the interest or time.
LYSIMACHUS Though I'm busy, Demipho, if there's anything you want
  I'm never too preoccupied to serve the interests of a friend.

Far from a simple concept of "leisure time" or "holiday," then, the *otium* of obligation is a time set aside for a category of endeavor that, generally speaking, would fall out of the character's normal sphere of "work" but that, in the course of the play, carries with it some importance in the unfolding of the plot. *Otium* of this sort is not work per se, but the emphasis on the obligation implicit in granting the requested "favor" means that it is not a time utterly free from social obligation and expectation.

A second signification of *otium* in this period – one that appears less frequently but that further unfolds the meaning of the term as it develops in the late Republic – specifies it as the functional opposite of (and so freedom from) its privative, *negotium*. Deriving originally from phrases such as *mihi neg (nec) otium [est]* ("I've no *otium*"),[13] *negotium* designates not "work" writ large but a specific time or activity that has consumed, or obliterated, one's *otium*. It is thus a time of lack, a time that is not one's own: time that is obliged either to a master by way of social rank, or to an employer by virtue of economic need, or to a Republic by way of elite obligation. On the comic stage, *negotium* is used variously of business in general or a specified task or occupation.[14] But as all Roman New Comedy uses of *negotium* signify the lack of "one's own time," then we may conceptualize the *otium* that signifies a freedom from *negotium* – the "lack of a lack" – as the *otium* of personal autonomy, a concept that will be especially important for the textual world of the late Republic. In the middle Republic (most specifically the very late third and early to mid second centuries BCE), this

---

[13] Cf. E–M s.v. *negotium*.
[14] It is associated with the *urbs* as a whole (*negotio / mihi esse in urbe*, Plaut. *Merc.* 279–280), with the forum in particular (*apud forum negotium*, Plaut. *Most.* 884), with the "business of pleasure" (*lenonem . . . inter negotium*, Plaut. *Poen.* 1938) and, twice, in vague references to epistolary transactions – here the sense is "it's the business at hand" (*ita negotiumst: / mandatae quae sunt, uolo deferre epistulas*, Plaut. *Pers.* 693–694; *sed propera hanc pellegere quaeso epistulam – ita negotium est*, Plaut. *Pseud.* 993).

otium signals time set aside to do nothing save what one might choose to do – although the choice of what this is is rarely specified. It signals the absence of a required or expected activity or service even – and this where the *otium* of the earlier and later periods emerges – when that activity is explicitly literary. The prologue of Terence's *Hecyra* presents perhaps the closest collocation of *otium* and literature in the middle Republic, and here the prologue's whole point is that, for Terence, writing is work.[15]

Quod si scripturam spreuissem in praesentia
et in deterrendo uoluissem operam sumere,
ut in otio esset potius quam in negotio,
deterruissem facile ne alias scriberet.
Ter. *Hec.* 24–27

But had I then scorned the poet as he set out to write
And had I wanted to use my energies deterring him from the job,
So that he might spend his life in leisure rather than work,
I'd have easily discouraged him from writing further plays.

The signification of *otium* as "one's own time" is especially strong when the term is paired with a companion noun indicative of pleasurable inactivity.[16] As with the *otium* of obligation, the *otium* of autonomy marks an absence of *negotium* (even if this marked absence invokes an unmarked presence – *negotium* – as the norm). But whereas the former fills the void with the promise of, or request for, a "socially obliged favor," the latter offers no substitute for the work from which one has been freed. In the late Republic we shall see that there has emerged in the interim a distinctly "textual *otium*" that contains (though never entirely collapses) both valences of the term in its charge that time of one's own is best spent writing texts for others. Because the "textual *otium*" of the late Republic is configured as a time of both political autonomy and social obligation, it marks that time most suited to the enjoyment of belletristic pursuits.

LEISURE IN THE FORUM

If Plautus and Terence had little to say about the "what, where, and whether" of *otium*, Catullus and Cicero show a great deal of interest in the term. Their semantic positioning of *otium*, generally speaking, is determined by whether the *otium* under discussion belongs to a sphere of

---

[15] Cf. too *Phorm.* 1–3; on the *otium* / *negotium* distinction in Terence, see André 1966: 125–127.
[16] So *pax*, cf. Plaut. *Amph.* 208, and *silentium*, cf. Ter. *Hec.* 43.

public or private display, and whether (in the case of Cicero especially) this *otium* is *honestum* and significant of a more pervasive sense of civic well-being or *inhonestum* and indicative of mere refusal to participate in the *negotium* of the state. As a term that resided happily in two realms of signification even prior to the "textualizing" *otium* we see in Catullus and later Cicero, *otium* could be used with either approbative or derogative force, depending upon who is using the term (and in what context) and whether or not (and where, and by whom) the subject of *otium* – the *uir otiosus* – is observed enjoying the "act" of political autonomy.

On the whole, both Catullus and Cicero conceive of *otium* as traditionally incompatible with the necessarily public activity – *negotium* – of the political world. There is often emphasis on the performative aspect of *otium*, and each author relays the same message: however a man of the Republic should choose to spend his private hours, he should not be enjoying them *in public*. On this Catullus and Cicero meet precisely. We will soon get to the more political conception of *otium* as it appears in the orations of the mid 60s, but it will be useful to consider first an example of *otium in foro* in Catullus. In c. 10, an amusing and revealing commentary on the distinctions between appearance, reality, and the display of poetic *persona*, Catullus drives home the point that the "public display" of *otium* is to be avoided at all costs. Unless, of course, you are no man of the Republic:

> Varus me meus ad suos amores
> uisum duxerat e foro otiosum
> scortillum, ut mihi tum repente uisum est,
> non sane illepidum neque inuenustum . . .
>
> 10.1–4

> My Varus led me out of the forum and took me
> To meet his girlfriend, since I apppeared *otiosus*;
> A little tart, as I saw at once,
> But not altogether without her charms . . .

In the introductory lines of the poem, Varus[17] catches Catullus "hanging around" in the forum – the positioning of *otiosum* following *foro* is a

---

[17] The identity of Varus is not fixed; the man would have been either Alfenus Varus, an eminent jurist of about Catullus' age and cos. suff. in 39 (thus rather an attractive choice, considering that the poem sets out from the forum), or Quintilius Varus, friend of Vergil and Horace (cf. Hor. *Odes* 1.24). Frank 1920 argued for the latter; Thomson 1997: 232 notes that the evidence of c. 10 does not allow a solid identification, and remarks that whichever Varus was meant, he was an individual who "moved in the legal and literary society of the capital." One wonders whether this character is

dramatic one – and leads him immediately away.[18] The verb *duxerat* signals an important directionality: Catullus is taken *from* the forum (where he is, at least politically speaking, silent) *to* the private and erotically tinged company of Varus and the *scortillum* (where he speaks, if deceptively). He moves from a venue in which he lacks or has rejected verbal influence – one in which his display of leisure is inappropriate[19] – to one in which he is able to orchestrate the complex verbal and social displays of the "in crowd."

This poem engages in a dialogue of aesthetic estimations; it sets the judgments of the forum against those of the private home, and plays with themes of truth and deception as they operate in both the political and textual worlds. The first judgment is one of the political world: Varus spots Catullus in the forum, and – seeing that he is *otiosus*, and indeed because he is *otiosus* – leads him from it. Catullus, next, arrives with Varus

---

to be identified, via poetic name-swapping, with the Suffenus of cc. 14 and 23 (the latter addressed, perhaps humorously, to Varus): this would certainly add richness to our understanding of c. 22.

[18] There are some difficulties with the interpretation of *uisum* at the end of l. 2. Most commentators (cf. Fordyce 1961: 116; Ellis 1979: 23; Thomson 1997: 232) have taken *uisum* as the supine of *uisere* (rather than the perfect passive participle of *uidere*, as I have rendered it above), and have cited the use of *uisere* + *ad* with the sense of checking in on someone who is ill (Fordyce 1961: 116, followed by Ellis 1979 and Thomson 1997, cites Ter. *Hec.* 188–189 and several post-Catullan passages, but there are no parallels with having a supine of *uisere* introduce a prepositional phrase (*ad suos amores*) to argue for the meaning "Varus led me . . . to check up on his girlfriend" (who was ill, or at least pretending to be, as her request to visit Serapis in l. 26 has been taken to suggest). But this reading presents difficulties. The supine can certainly take an accusative direct object, but it is somewhat more unusual (and distinctly clumsier) to couple a supine with a prepositional phrase such as *ad suos amores* (*ad Caesarem gratulatum*, Caes. *Bell. Gall.* 1.30, does not provide a convincing grammatical parallel). Further, although *uisere* + *ad* can indicate the process of "looking in on" an invalid, the verb can do this just as well without a prepositional phrase (*Varus me suos amores uisum duxerat* would have the same meaning if not, assuredly, the same metrical value) that unnecessarily muddies the sense of the whole. If *uisum* is taken as a supine, and *ad suos amores* the idiomatic use of *ad* with *uisere*, the sense is: "Varus led me, *otiosus*, out of the forum, in order to check up on his girlfriend." This reading is not irreparably problematic, but it seems to me to miss out on an ironic twist of the lines. First, it passes by the *uisum . . . otiosum* bracketing of l. 2 (with both *uisum* and *otiosum* in agreement with the *me* of l. 1: "since he saw I was *otiosus*") as well as the nice resonance with the same participle at the end of l. 3: *uisum est*: Catullus was *uisum . . . otiosum* in l. 2; Varus' love-interest is *scortillum . . . uisum* in l. 3. Indeed, the playful chiasmus of "*uisum otiosum/scortillum uisum*" creates a lively conversation of silent "sizing up," as discussed above. If we take *uisum* as a perfect participle of *uidere* and in agreement with *otiosum* – and although *uisus* + adj. is without direct parallel in our sources (though cf. Cic. *Verr.* 2.4.7), I am not convinced that Catullus is not at least capitalizing on potential ambiguity – we see that the point here may be not just that Catullus was *otiosus* in the forum, but that he forefronts his display as such in order to get at deeper issues of appearance, reality, and deception.

[19] It is important to note that in the forum of the Principate the display of leisure seems less problematic (perhaps indeed because the "work" of the forum had changed so dramatically): thus Horace might stroll leisurely through the forum (cf. *Sat.* 1.6.133) without any sense of displacement or inappropriate display. He does not use the term *otium* to describe his wanderings, it is true; but his lines have no sense of the tension surrounding "public leisure" as it appears in the late Republic.

at the girlfriend's home – she is the erotically tinged excuse on which the transition from forum to home is predicated – sees her, and knows immediately (*ut mihi tum repente uisum est*, l. 3) that she is "a little tart," though there is nothing to suggest they had met before. Both Catullus' state of leisure in the state's place of business and the girl's status as "a little tart" are judgments based on appearance and not voiced expression; but we are nowhere led to suppose that Varus and Catullus are incorrect in their conclusions (he's at leisure; she's a tart) or that any deception has been attempted.

But as Catullus and Varus move from the realm of their silence – humorously, the very locus of Republican speech (although if this Varus is Alfenus the jurist, it is a realm in which he regularly resides) – to the one of their speech (*incidere nobis / sermones uarii*, ll. 5–6), as they move from the homosocial world of the forum to the gender-mixed world of the home and from the expectations of the Comitium to those of the convivium, the first deceptive act of display, and the penultimate act of judgment, occurs. For once he moves from forum to home – from the world he claims to reject to the world he claims to embrace – Catullus embarks upon a deceptive presentation of his poetic *persona*: in hoping to impress Varus' girl, he brags that he did well enough in Bithynia, and has brought back eight strong litter-bearers (ll. 18–20). The girl, of course, then asks Catullus if she can borrow the men, as she wishes to go and visit Serapis.[20] But there is something in Catullus' expression of the girl's over-exuberant request that suggests she was calling his bluff – and that he has "allowed" (made) her to do this in order to make a specific poetic point. The jig, as they say, is up. Catullus plays along, and once he has "confessed" that the litter-bearers belong to his friend Cinna – a reference that underlines the textual and political worlds this poem seems to straddle and set against each other[21] – he harshly upbraids the girl for denouncing his tall tale and unmasking his fictional *persona*. She is *insulsa* and *molesta*, and won't allow

---

[20] The reference to Serapis in l. 26 is often taken as indication that the *puella* is either ill or feigning illness, and is thus used in support of the reading of *uisum* discussed above.

[21] Cinna was in Bithynia with Catullus (for which cf. c. 4, the *Phaselus* poem, and c. 10), and a dizzyingly clever epigram written on his return intersects nicely with the terminological and sociopractical inquiries of this study: *Haec tibi Arateis multum inuigilata lucernis / carmina, quis ignis nouimus aerios / leuis in aridulo maluae descripta libello / Prusiaca uexi munera nauicula* (Cinna in Isid. *Orig.* 6.12.1; cf. Blänsdorf 1995: 222). A poem that echoes Callimachus (χαίρετε λεπταὶ / ῥήσεις Ἀρήτου σύμβολον ἀγρυπνίης, *Ep.* 27, which engages with the wordplay of Aratus' λεπτή acrostic at *Phain.* 783–787), even as it dedicates a translation of Aratus (itself of course a translation of Eudoxus; note that Cicero also produced such a translation), is dripping with the textual tonality of the late Republic, and deserves more space than I can give it here. On this epigram and echoes of Cat. 1, see Flores 1976 and Batstone 1998.

a man to let down his guard (*neglegentem*, l. 34; this echoes c. 12, which censures Asinius' ambush on convivial *neglegentiores* in similar terms) even in the company of friends. A poor poet engaged in a playful boast of his status, and she had the poor taste to call him out on it – how dare she!

Or is this what the poem is saying at all? A problem with Catullus' deceptions in these lines is that it is unclear in the end exactly whom he has in mind to deceive, or indeed whether the reference to the eight litter-bearers was meant as a deception, a revelation, or perhaps a more textually interested commentary on what it means for a poet to keep up his poetic *persona*. I noted above that the girl's judgment of Catullus' economic status was the penultimate judgment of the poem; the final judge of Catullus' poetic display is of course the reader. Ideally – from Catullus' perspective, that is – this reader would be a Varus or a Cinna: a man of the late Republic and one familiar with the terminological code of the late Republican textual world; a man who understood the tension and humor that underlay every literary expression of personal and poetic status. Things for us are not as straightforward. But the line-end emphasis of *otiosus* at the start of the poem – the use of *otiosus* as the hinge that both closes the door to the forum and opens the door to the home – seems a tip-off that whatever world Catullus is about to enter, and whatever he is going to do there, c. 10 is concerned with what happens in the space of *otium*, and what sort of display – and as a result, textual production – *otium* can allow.[22]

I will argue in the pages that follow that *otium* signals, in the late Republican textual code, "time to write" (and talk about writing) and that it would have functioned, especially in dedicated texts and texts that concern themselves with the textual community, as a terminological marker directing our "ideal reader" to a text's underlying point of focus. We will get to a fuller examination of the evidence below, but it is worth noting

---

[22] Segal 1970 rightly notes the "connection of poetry and *otium*" (he does not discuss the approbative uses of the term in Cicero), but suggests rather puzzlingly that this connection "can perhaps be traced back to Lucretius" (p. 28). Although issues of chronology make it difficult to determine, between Catullus and Lucretius, who wrote what when, there is little evidence that much of Lucretius' poem would have been even nominally published before his death in 55 (if we take that as a reasonable date: cf. Conte 1994: 155), making a proposed "Lucretian influence" on Catullus' linking of *otium* with poetry untenable. More to the point, however, is that Lucretius uses *otium* but once in his entire poem, at 5.1387 (*per loca pastorum deserta atque otia dia*); the context is indeed man's discovery of song, but what we have is not *otium* but the plural *otia* – a form popular in the Principate and Empire, but rare in the writings of Catullus and Cicero – which seems to indicate "places of leisure" (which may give rise to poetic production, which seems the thrust of the term in later Latin) rather than "leisure" itself (Segal's foonote 3, same page, seems to recognize the problem), for which the singular is always preferred in the Republic.

here that the only other time Catullus uses *otiosus* (cf. c. 50, discussed below
and in Chapter 7) he forefronts the word similarly: by placing it at line-end
(this time it is the first line), he uses it to introduce a poem that is not
merely moderately interested in literary production, but is perhaps one of
the most pervasively textually concerned poems of the corpus.[23] As we shall
see below, Cicero uses *otiosus* in several of his more "textually interested"
technica in order to establish the social time in which the interlocutors
engaged the conversations that would be turned into texts, as well as in
letters that discuss the private enjoyment of literature (cf. *Ep. Fam.* 9.18,
of 46 BCE).[24] In the texts of the late Republic – and indeed those of later
periods – the use of *otium* and the world it invokes serve to focus the savvy
reader's eye on the author's underlying message.

   If c. 10 is read as a poem that is in some ways "about" *otium*, the
textual world of the late Republic, and the relation of this world to the
political world that surrounded and helped form it, then it suggests that
the presumably intimate display of authorial *persona* may be more deceptive
than it might first appear. As noted above, prior to Catullus' entry into
the textual world of c. 10, everything was as it appeared: he was *otiosus*; the
girl was a *scortillum*. In the "world of *otium*" in which the *otiosus* Catullus
was properly resituated by Varus, however, it is more difficult to decode
the display of *persona*, and we sense a piling up of fictions in Catullus'
textual self-presentation. He claims first to be a man of leisure, and then
(in his conversation of his time in Bithynia) a man of business; first a
man of comfort, and then a man of want. We hardly know what to make
of him.

   As Wiseman has noted, Catullus came from a family of no small means.
His frequent protestations of poverty, therefore, are likely more a matter of
generic convention than anything indicative of fiscal reality.[25] Wiseman's
point that the group at the girl's house could have *believed* he had brought
back the litter-bearers is an excellent one and worth noting here, precisely
because it complicates our view of what seems to be the increasingly
fictitious world of texts that result from the conversations of *otium*. Indeed,
c. 10 is the only poem in the corpus in which Catullus engages in boasts of

[23] Segal 1970 notes the literary importance of the *otiosus* as it appears in cc. 10 and 50, but his claim that *otium* of this period had "disreputable associations" is, if not simply incorrect, an oversimplification of the situation, and his statement that Cicero was situated at the "opposite pole" of the aesthetic estimation of *otium* fails to take into consideration Cicero's use of the term in the *technica*.
[24] Similarly, *otium* is the first word of Varro's *DRR* (a dialogue that at least in some ways seems interested in testing the bounds of the literary genre). Continuations of this sense of *otium* in writers of the Principate and early Empire will be mentioned below.
[25] Wiseman 1982: 39.

his financial position, and we must suspect that the "lie" of the economically "rather comfortable" (*beatior*, l. 17) poet is in fact a momentary unveiling of his true status as a man of some means. The Catullus who went to Bithynia is a man who plausibly could have returned with a train of eight litter-bearers. The Catullus who moves about in the world of textual *otium*, however, has not a single one strong enough to lift the broken leg of an old couch (ll. 22–23). Of course the kicker here is that he does not say he has no litter-bearers – only that he hasn't any from *Bithynia*. This is not the talk of a poor man, but of a wealthy one who is underplaying his position in accordance with social and aesthetic rules: this is the rich man who plays the poor poet pretending to be a rich man.

   The *otium*-allowed display of textual *persona* is precisely that – a display – and those who know the rules of the game do not attempt to unmask its players. In c. 10, it is of course Catullus who engineers, as if by mistake, his own unmasking; and it is through the correction of the "little tart," who is wise to the rules of the game (she is neither *illepida* nor *inuenusta*, l. 4), that he seems to resituate himself in the *persona* of a man with a "wallet full of cobwebs." In a poem that marks itself off, via *otiosus*, as one interested in a consideration of the textual world, a "poor poet's" carefully wrought deception that he is a man of some means seems rather a sly wink to the textually savvy reader that Catullus knows how to keep up poetic appearances. As we saw above, σχολή evolves from indicating a time of discussion to indicating a time of literary production; in c. 10, *otiosus* marks a time of casual intellectual conversation – political conversation, as ll. 6–13 make clear – and social display that results in a textually interested textual fiction that "captures" this conversational world, critiques it, and displays it anew – as a poem, but of course also as a dialogue.[26] The reader, in the end, is the final judge of the poet's "deception," and it is the reader's understanding of the textual world in which the poem is set that will determine her judgment of the poet's textually wrought "mistake."

   Before we get to a fuller consideration of *otium* in the textual world, let us return to the *urbs*. In Cicero's orations, *otium* and its related forms (*otiosus, otiose*) appear a total of 108 times. For the most part, the terms are used infrequently in the pre-consular and consular orations (once in *Rosc. Amer.*, a few times in *Verr.* 1, once in *Caec.*, six times in the Catilinarians, and

---

[26] On the colloquialisms of c. 10, see Thomson 1997: 234 (with further bibliography). Sedgwick 1947, who sees c. 10 as a source for conversational Latin, notes of this poem "it is not poetry at all apart from the metre: it is a perfect specimen of... *elegans et urbanum iocandi genus.*" On this poem see further Coulon 1956 and Nielsen 1987.

seven times in *Mur.*). When they do appear, they are relatively unmarked, referring generally to a socially and politically "peaceful time" for the state (and thus explicitly opposed to *bellum*: *Caec.* 33 and *Cat.* 1.25), and are often grouped with companion nouns such as *pax, concordia, silentium,* and *tranquillitas* (cf. *Leg. Agr.* 23, 24; *Cat.* 3.17; *Mur.* 63). In the discursive sphere of public and forensic activity, *otium* was a tool of strong authorial approbation: any mention of the term invoked the specter of its privative, and offered this specter up for judgment. Thus a man whose *otium* is marked as *honestum* (vel sim.) is simultaneously marked for his many years of service to the state (the patriotic and skillful performance of his *negotium*); conversely, if a man's *otium* is marked as *inhonestum*, we know he has been marked for either a premature refusal of such service or, even worse, a rejection of it from the very beginning.[27]

A notable exception to Cicero's pre-consular use of *otium* is the *de Lege Agraria.* In these orations, which attack the agrarian law put forward by P. Servilius Rullus (but instigated by Caesar and further supported by Antonius), the terms appear a total of eighteen times. In the second oration, addressed to the *Quirites,* the newly installed consul promotes himself as a "man of the people" even as he promotes *otium* (along with *pax* and *libertas*) as that state of affairs which is not only specifically advantageous to the *populus Romanus,* but also well within their reach and destined to be shared communally (*quid enim est tam populare quam pax? . . . quid tam populare quam libertas? . . . quid tam populare quam otium?* 2.4.9). Although the primary sense of this *populare otium* functions much as it does in the remaining pre-consular and consular speeches – it is an idiomatic marker of a healthy body politic, and the salubrity of *otium* will indeed play an important role in the textual world as well – it also echoes the more "private" sense of *otium* at play on the earlier comic stage: that of autonomous time, time "of one's own," in direct opposition not only to *bellum,* but also to *negotium.*

But as much as *otium,* and the respite it entails, is presented as a public good, it is a good only meaningful – only productive – if it is balanced by its complementary force. When *negotium* and the healthy political contest and social emulation that this implies (one might think of Hesiod's

---

[27] On this argument, see further Balsdon 1960: 467. The collocation of *otium* with *honestum* appears only once in the speeches (at Sulla 26 [62 BCE]: *ego, tantis a me beneficiis in re publica positis, si nullum aliud mihi praemium ab senatu populoque Romano nisi honestum otium postularem, quis non concederet?*) but frequently in the letters and the dialogues, e.g., *Ep. Fam.* 4.4.4; 7.33.2; *Acad.* 1.11; *de Off.* 2.4; 3.3.

configuration of Strife as a socially ameliorative force at *Works and Days* 20–27; this passage will be discussed below) are removed, the unchecked surfeit of *otium* becomes as destructive as it has been beneficial:

Neque enim contionandi potestas erat cuiquam nec consili capiendi publici; non gloriae cupiditate efferebantur, propterea quod, ubi honos publice non est, ibi gloriae cupiditas esse non potest; non contentione, non ambitione discordes. nihil enim supererat de quo certarent, nihil quod contra peterent, nihil ubi dissiderent. itaque illam Campanam adrogantiam atque intolerandam ferociam ratione et consilio maiores nostri ad inertissimum ac desidiosissimum otium perduxerunt. (*Leg. Agr* 2.91)

No one (in Capua) had any means of summoning an assembly or gathering a public council. No one was carried away by the desire for renown, for where there is no public honor to be had, the desire for renown cannot exist. There were no quarrels out of rivalry or ambition – for there was nothing left to quarrel about. They had nothing to seek to gain in opposition to each other, nowhere even to disagree. And so it was by means of a wisely thought-out system that our ancestors transformed the arrogance and intolerable wildness of the Campanians into an utterly inactive and utterly useless *otium*.

Cicero returns to the theme of *otium* at the end of the oration. He reminds his audience of the civic good of *otium* even as he presents himself as a consul most deeply devoted to the civic cause:

Quirites, potest nihil esse tam populare quam id quod ego uobis in hunc annum consul popularis adfero, pacem, tranquillitatem, otium. (*Leg. Agr* 2.102)

Citizens, nothing can be so beneficent to the popular good as that which I – a consul of the people – bring to you this year: peace, tranquility, and *otium*.

Not only shall those who have always wished for *otium* enjoy it, the consul wryly explains: even those men for whom *otium* has been a hateful thing shall be transformed by the consul into men especially equipped to enjoy the tranquility of leisure (*quibus odio est otium quietissimos atque otiosissimos reddam*, 102). Although some individuals might have receded into *otium* on account of indolence (*propter desidiam*, 103), those who have seized their *otium* by virtue of hard work (*uirtus*) rather than laziness (*ignauia*) shall be able to hold fast to it. This speech, then, recognizes some of the negative valences of the term – the connection of *otium* with words such as *desidium* and *ignauia* – even as it promotes it, perhaps somewhat radically (as suggested by both the Campanian story and the sheer heavy-handedness of the argument), and, in a sense that will come into play in Cicero's later defense of *otium* as a well-earned textual time, as a distinctly public good when it is partnered with hard work, healthy competition, and civic responsibility. It is the just enjoyment of civic and political salubrity not so much earned as bestowed (as textual *otium* would be bestowed in the Principate and Empire), as public benefaction, by a "consul of the people."

Thus far we have considered *otium* in the city; but we are interested in tracing the emergence of a literary use of *otium* in Cicero. This appears first in a letter to Atticus in 68 BCE (*Ep. Att.* 1.5 [Shackleton Bailey 1965–1970, vol. 1] *oti ad scribendi*), though the term is unelaborated. The word appears again in this sense in 62, one year out of the consulship, and in his defense of the poet Archias. Early in the oration, Cicero explains to his audience that the peculiar subject of the contest (the political defense of a literary individual) will require a peculiar sort of speech:

... Patiamini de studiis humanitatis ac litterarum paulo loqui liberius, et in eius modi persona, quae propter otium ac studium minime in iudiciis periculisque tractata est, uti prope nouo quodam et inusitato genere dicendi. (*Arch.* 3)

... Allow me to speak a bit more extensively on the subject of literature and the arts, and – in the character of one who, on account of his own leisure-time studies, has but little experience in the trials and tribulations of the state – to make use of a somewhat unorthodox style of oratory.

Whereas one might expect the "leisure-time studies" (*otium ac studium*) to refer to Archias, they refer instead – and perhaps surprisingly, taken in the context of earlier orations and earlier uses of *otium* – to Cicero himself: in a move that presages a topos common to many of the dialogues, the categories of orator and poet are collapsed into each other. Rather than presenting himself as a forensic "insider" speaking on behalf of a literary "outsider," Cicero takes on a *persona* through which he was best able to defend not only Archias but also the production and enjoyment of literature as a whole. In assuming the fiction of a man who had more to do with the world of texts than the world of the forum, Cicero subtly forefronts both his own literary character (much of which would have been limited, in 62, to earlier composition of poetry) and that of his audience (a *concursus hominum litteratissimorum*) precisely in order to draw attention to the shared aesthetic interests of defendant and judges.[28] But one of the most interesting – and for this study, most important – characteristics of the *pro Archia* is that what begins as a defense of the poet's claim to citizenship comes to resemble, as the speech progresses, a defense of both literary

---

[28] Steel 2001: 91–98 makes an interesting argument for the orator's emphasis on both poetry and ethnicity in this oration. See also Dugan 2005, ch. 1.

studies as a whole and the orator's pursuit of these studies in particular. In a direct address to Gratius, Cicero turns again from a defense of Archias' activity to a defense of his own:

> Ego uero fateor me his studiis esse deditum: ceteros pudeat, si qui se ita lit-teris abdiderunt ut nihil possint ex eis neque ad communem adferre fructum, neque in aspectum lucemque proferre: me autem quid pudeat, qui tot annos ita uiuo, iudices, ut a nullius umquam me tempore aut commodo aut otium meum abstraxerit, aut uoluptas auocarit, aut denique somnus retardarit? (*Arch.* 12)

I freely confess that I am dedicated to these studies: let others be ashamed if they have so hidden themselves in books that they have been unable to produce anything out of them for the common benefit, anything to bring into the light of day. But why should I be ashamed, who for so many years have lived in such a way that my enjoyment of *otium* has never dragged me away from any man in his time of need; my love of pleasure has never called me away; not even sleep has held me back?

Although this *otium* is one yet suffused with tension vis-à-vis the work-ings of the state (and to some extent this tension runs through the lexical life of the term, though it is mitigated in both Cicero's *technica* and the literature of later periods), it is linked here first – in Cicero, at least – with explicitly literary occupations.

The non-literary valences of *otium* continue throughout the orations. In the years that follow, however, we see an increase in the distinctly literary force of the term. It is marked more and more frequently as a "time to read,"[29] but even in the *pro Plancio* of 54 it has not yet become – in Cicero's public presentation of the term – quite a "time to write":

> Ecquid ego dicam de occupatis meis temporibus, cui fuerit ne otium quidem umquam otiosum? nam quas tu commemoras, Cassi, legere te solere orationes, cum otiosus sis, has ego scripsi ludis et feriis, ne omnino umquam essem otiosus. etenim M. Catonis illud quod in principio scripsit Originum suarum semper magnificum et praeclarum putaui, 'clarorum uirorum atque magnorum non minus oti quam negoti rationem exstare oportere.' (*Planc.* 66)

Why talk about my hours at work, when not even my hours of *otium* were leisure-filled? For those orations, Cassius, that you mention you were in the habit of reading when you are at leisure – these are the ones I wrote during festivals and holidays, so I was never utterly at leisure. For I have always thought that what M. Cato wrote at the beginning of his *Origines* was especially notable, that "men of

---

[29] So *Ep. Att.* 2.6 (59 BCE) *sic enim sum complexus otium ut ab eo diuelli non queam . . . a scribendo prorsus abhorret animus*; to this cf. *Flacc.* 75 (59 BCE), *Harusp. Resp.* 19 (56 BCE), less favorably at *Sest.* 110 (56 BCE), and by implication at *Balb.* 15 (56 BCE).

fame and rank should provide an accounting of their hours of leisure just as much as of their hours of work."

Both *pro Archia* 12 and *pro Plancio* 66 provide important evidence for Cicero's emerging approbation of a "textual *otium*" in the years following his consulship and leading up to the composition of his first dialogic treatise. The first oration is notable because it introduces three topoi that appear again in the *technica* of 54 and following: that *otium* bears "literary fruit";[30] that it is an activity "for the shadows";[31] and that it is something that might "call one away" from formal duty. The second oration stands out in its ameliorative use of *otiosus*. Whereas his earlier use of the adjective – and it appears only rarely – was either strongly derogative or at any rate vaguely ironical (the sense, I think, at *Leg. Agr.* 102, cited above), the *pro Plancio* passage, which itself participates in a consideration of the fickleness of the Republic and the generally degraded character of the forensic audience (this passage is discussed in greater detail in Chapter 4), posits the state of being *otiosus* as indicative not of slothful inactivity but rather of active literary enjoyment. Although Cicero's claim that writing prevents him from being "completely at leisure" is slightly resituated by the reference to the proem of Cato's *Origines* – in which it seems Cato suggested that writing provides a defense of one's hours of *otium* – we can say that in *pro Plancio* Cicero engages with a "textual *otium*" that he links with the activity of reading, and moves the activity of writing into closer proximity with the textual world than he ever had before. The writing of *orationes* is not here figured as "work" so much as "work-related" activity; the claim that his forensic writing prevented him from ever being "completely at leisure" both defends the work of his private hours (Cato's *oti ratio*) and draws our attention to the ways in which politically interested compositions – and their author – can straddle the worlds of forum and of text.

LEISURE IN THE TEXT

Catullus' configuration of *otium* in c. 10 has been discussed above; as we turn to a consideration of his further uses of *otium* and *otiosus*, the sociotemporal outlines of the late Republican textual world – the social "shape" of the time in which literature was produced – begin to come into

---

[30] *Fructus*; cf. *de Orat.* 1.1.2; 2.5.22; *de Rep.* 1.7; *de Off.* 1.70; cf. *Ep. Fam.* 7.1.1. Approaching this word from a slightly different angle (and in the context of a radically different literary system), Bowditch 2001: 124 discusses an "economy of *otium*" in which the value of a material given a client by his patron is determined by the sort of return – poetry – it effects.
[31] Cf. *de Leg.* 3.14; *TD* 5.7; but cf. too *Mur.* 30 and *Balb.* 15.

focus. *Otiosus*, which we considered in our discussion of c. 10, appears again – and again is used to introduce the operative conditions of poetic activity – in c. 50. In c. 10, Catullus uses *otiosus* to point up the fact that the world of *otium* is precisely not that of the forum, and that it comes with its own rules of display and fictions of *persona*. In c. 50, the term again deals with issues of leisure-time display and the poetic products that issue from it; in this poem it is precisely because Catullus and Calvus have donned the character of *otiosi* – men who have found the time[32] to "take their time" in the textual world – that they are able to enjoy the intimate convivial (*per iocum atque uinum*) *otium* that will produce both this poem and, as I think is likely, c. 51. We will come back to c. 50 in Chapter 7, in our consideration of Catullus' textual materialism; in what follows I want to look more closely at his use of *otium* at cc. 44 and 68b and especially its triple appearance in c. 51.

We may deal with cc. 44 and 68b rather briefly: c. 44 because it will come into play again in Chapter 5, and c. 68b because *otium* here occurs in the plural – a form that poets of the Principate and early Empire commonly use to indicate their poetic pursuits[33] but one that is rare in the Republic – and although it may be one of the more erotically charged uses of the term it is the least obviously indicative of "textual time."[34] Poem 44, addressed to Catullus' Tiburtine (or Sabine, if you must) retreat – his *suburbana uilla* (ll. 6–7) – is written as a thanks-offering following Catullus' recovery there after he came down with a bad cold upon reading a particularly vituperative speech of the orator Sestius. Catullus' cough is cured by both the villa's *otium* and its nettles (*otioque et urtica*, l. 15); but whereas it is the nettles that must have soothed his textually provoked bronchial distress, it is the *otium* provided by the extra-urban retreat (the role of the *suburbana uilla* as a locus of textual production will be revisited in Chapter 5) that allowed him the time he needed to produce his poetic expression of gratitude. In c. 68b, the plural *otia* appears in a brief description, not of writing per se, but of the leisurely erotic hours or places – *libera otia* (ll. 103, 104) – of one of literature's most famous literary couples, Paris and his stolen bride.

---

[32] *Hesterno . . . die* (l. 1) underlines the point that Catullus and Calvus do not live in an uninterrupted state of *otium*, but retreat into *otium* – for the specific enjoyment of their texts – when time and situations allow.

[33] Although *otium* appears in the singular at Verg. *Georg.* 4.564, it appears more commonly in the plural, almost every case of which signifies the time given – often given *to* the poet by a patronal figure – to the writing of poetry, cf. Hor. *Ep.* 1.7.36; Ovid, *Trist.* 3.2.9; 4.8.7; 4.10.39–40; 4.10.105; Mart. *Ep.* 1.107.3–4 (in which it is clearly linked to poetic patronage: *otia da nobis sed qualia / fecerat olim / Maecenas Flacco Vergilioque suo*). To this, compare Tac. *Dial.* 10.3, which links poetic production and the time of *otium* in which this production occurs.

[34] For an extensive bibliography on c. 68b, cf. Thomson 1997: 488–491.

If the plural *otia* in c. 68b is both suggestively literary and suggestively Greek in tone, this might help us get at the most notable use of *otium* in the corpus, that of c. 51, in Catullus' appropriation and "transformation" of Sappho 31. Catullus adapts more or less faithfully the first three stanzas of the Greek model, but the final stanza breaks from it with jarring effect: turning from Sappho to himself, Catullus critiques his engagement with the textual world:[35]

> Otium, Catulle, tibi molestumst:
> otio exultas nimiumque gestis;
> otium et reges prius et beatas
> > perdidit urbes.   51.13–16
>
> *Otium*, Catullus, is bad for your health:
> In *otium* you revel and thrash about madly;
> *Otium* 'ere now has destroyed both kings
> > And bountiful cities.

Various arguments have been made as to why the fourth stanza takes the form that it does; whether it might have been a later addition to the poem or, perhaps, should be excluded from this poem altogether.[36] But if the textualizing force of *otium* is brought to bear on Catullus' departure from the Sapphic model – or rather, his sharp turn to self-address[37] and self-criticism – then a more subtle understanding of the poet's self-critique arises: he is pained not by the hours he spends thinking of his love, but by the hours he has just spent *writing* about her. If we take c. 50 as a partial dedication of c. 51 – a proposition that may be reasonably argued on the basis of internal similarities between these poems, as well as their parallels (if taken as a couplet) with cc. 65 and 66 – then the distinctly textual *otiosus* of c. 50 is neatly echoed in the "outpouring" of *otium* of c. 51. It is the enjoyment of *otium* that has allowed the poet "time to write," but

---

[35] For a summary of the arguments as to why the poet does not adapt the fourth stanza of the Sappho, cf. Thomson 1997: 329. For an excellent reading of this poem (if with a few points of misunderstanding of the term), see Segal 1970 and Wray 2001: 88–92; cf. too Finamore 1984; Woodman 1966.

[36] Thomson 1997: 327 discusses the problem briefly, and provides copious bibliography on the topic at 330–331. Jensen 1967 is representative of the arguments against including the fourth stanza in c. 51.

[37] Catullus engages in self-address in cc. 8, 46, 51, 52, 76, and 79. In at least cc. 8 and 51, this address seems to speak strongly to an extra-poetic *persona* who is posited as "viewing" the textual work of the poetic *persona*. In the other poems, self-address does not appear to indicate so forced an "intertextual / extratextual" divide, but rather to provide a momentarily metapoetic inroad to Catullus' thoughts on the poetic process. On self-address in c. 51, see Segal 1970: 30–31; on Catullan self-address and other characteristics of the Catullan "writing voice," see Greene 1995.

in taking this time – to toss and turn with desire for Calvus, to thrash about with desire for Lesbia, to carefully adapt a Sapphic original that only heightens his desire for each (and that might indeed mark the initial poetic coining of his beloved's name) – he has brought upon himself only greater distress.

It is writing that is bad for Catullus' health;[38] it is writing in which he revels and agonizes (as true for this poem as for c. 50); it is writing through which the poet, poetically speaking, destroyed himself in the first three stanzas; and it is *writing* (if the Sapphic reference is expanded to include not only the world of lyric but that of epic, to which lyric frequently responds) through which kings and cities are both created and "destroyed" – the destruction of Troy is a matter of poetry above all else – by the poets who create them. The *otium* that allows a poet to write can also threaten to obliterate the poetic *persona* in the obligations and expectations of that writing: in triangulating his erotic relationship with Lesbia, his "literary relationship" with Sappho, and his eroticized textual relationship with Calvus, Catullus seems in danger of losing himself.[39] In the harsh self-address of the final stanza, we seem to get a flash of the extra-poetic Catullan voice (we might think of a similar flash in the poet's swiftly retracted economic boast at c. 10); the near-destruction of his poetic *persona* has caused Catullus to view the hours he spends writing poetry with the gaze of a man raised to do other things.[40] In the final stanza of c. 51, we do not hear the voice of a poet telling himself that he spends too much time in idleness; we hear the voice of a man telling his poetic *persona* that he spends too much time *writing*. That this voice cannot help but write in Sapphic meter, of course, makes the censure an ironic one: Catullus may write too much, and he knows it, but he can afford not to care.[41] The ironic reclamation of poetic authority reestablishes the poet's *persona*: Sappho, Lesbia, and Calvus be damned – c. 51 is about Catullus, and the poetic ownership of the *otium* through which the poet is able to engage in the transactions of his world.

---

[38] Thomson 1997: 329 notes that the phrase *tibi molestum est* is often used for medical conditions, and that an amatory parallel can be found at Cic. *Cael.* 44. Similarly, the verbs *exultare* and *gestire* are linked at Cic. *TD* 4.13 and 5.16, each time in reference to uncontrolled desires.

[39] Svenbro 1993: 145–159 offers a complementary argument for the Sapphic original: "Sappho understands that, as a consequence of writing, she will be absent, even dead" (p. 152).

[40] The final stanza of c. 51 is so imbued with the tone of parental disapproval that it is tempting to imagine Catullus intends to give the impression of a father who has stumbled upon his son's fevered writings – a son passed out at his couch, stylus in hand and lamp burning low – and who leans down to add, in fitting meter, "Kid, stop wasting your time with poetry!"

[41] Segal 1970: 30 notes "his disavowal of at least the 'poetic' *otium* is by no means complete," and calls ll. 13 and 14 a "realistic personal appraisal."

Cicero's use of *otium* in the orations has been discussed above (cf. too *Ep. Att.* 1.5, noted above). In light of both the strongly private and literary program expressed in the *technica* and what we can construct of Catullus' use of the term, it is perhaps not surprising that *otium* and its related forms appear over twice as many times in the *technica* as they do in the orations. When the terms are used in the later *technica* (those of 54 and following; that is, all save the youthful *de Inventione*) and the letters (which will not be considered separately, as they follow most closely the uses of the *technica*), they not only echo the literary and erotic valences that we see formulated in Catullus, but also frequently expand upon them. Writing is thus the *fructus oti* (as cited above; cf. *opus oti, de Off.* 3.4[42]); *otium* is that time given over completely to reading,[43] to writing,[44] and to learning in general.[45]

In contrast to the usage of *otium* in the orations, *otium* in the *technica* never represents a dereliction of duties and is only rarely marked by the "political" valences of "peace and quiet" or "freedom from civic discord" (this last usage appears somewhat more frequently in the letters, especially those to Atticus: cf. *Ep. Att* 14.2.3; 14.21.2; 15.2.3). Whereas the orations represented *otium* as that which could threaten to call one away from duty to the state (so *pro Archia* 12, cited above), the *otium* of the *technica* is presented as an asylum to which one might escape in times of trouble; it is still a place of peace and salubrity, but now the source of war and sickness is the state itself.[46] No longer does *otium* detract from the duties of the Republic; it is now the Republic – in its deeply decayed condition – that detracts from the explicitly literary duties of *otium* (*de Orat.* 1.1.2–3). In a letter written to Volumnius Eutrapelus in 46 Cicero speaks in performative terms of his desire to put aside his earlier forensic *persona* and envelop himself instead in a world of honorable literary leisure:

---

[42] Cicero's sense of *opus oti* is echoed in the much later *Technopaegnia* of Ausonius, in which he writes, *misi ad te Technopaegnium, inertis otii mei inutile opusculum.*

[43] Cf. *de Rep.* 3.4: *in istorum otio ac litteris tractata*; *TD* 5.36.105: *quid enim is dulcius otio litterato*; see also *de Orat.* 2.14.59; 3.32.131; cf. *Ep. Fam.* 3.11.4, written to Appius Clodius Pulcher: *nam auguralis libros ad commune utriusque nostrum otium serua.*

[44] Cf. *de Orat.* 1.1.4: *quantum mihi uel fraus inimicorum uel causae amicorum uel res publica tribuet oti, ad scribendum potissimum conferam*; 2.13.57: *otium suum consumpsit in historia scribenda*; *Brut.* 24.93: *dein cum otiosus stilum prehenderat*; *de Off.* 2.4: *scribendi otium*; see also *TD* 1.6.

[45] Cf. *de Orat.* 1.21.95: *et otio et facultate discendi*. The author of *Rhet. Her.* uses the term similarly at 1.1, in the introduction to his work: *etsi [in] negotiis familiaribus i<n>pediti uix satis otium studio suppeditare possumus et id ipsum, quod datur oti, libentius in philosophia consumere consueuimus, tamen tuo nos, Cai Herenii, uoluntas commouit...*

[46] Cf. *Brut.* 2.8: *quo tempore aetas nostra perfuncta rebus amplissimis tamquam in portum confugere deberet non inertiae neque desidiae, sed oti moderati atque honesti*; *de Off.* 1.69: *ad otiumque perfugerint*; 3.1 *otium persequimur et ob eam causam urbe relicta.*

Mihi enim iudicatum est, si modo hoc Caesar aut patietur aut uolet, deponere illam iam personam in qua me saepe illi ipsi probaui ac me totum in litteras abdere tecumque et cum ceteris earum studiosis honestissimo otio perfrui. (*Ep. Fam.* 7.33.2)

I have decided, if only Caesar will either allow or will it, to strip myself of that *persona* in which I have so often proved myself to him, and to hide myself completely in the text and – in your company and in the company of the others who are eager for these pursuits – to make use of this respectable leisure.

Otium is still used, though rarely, in the New Comedy sense of "if only you have the time" (*si modo tibi est otium, et si uis, de Part. Orat.* 1.1),[47] but the request that follows is precisely one for the discussion contained within the dialogue itself – the request is for writing. *Otium* and the literary pursuits by which it is marked function as a psychic and spiritual curative;[48] it is sometimes presented as a marker of advanced age and by extension – drawing upon an earlier sense of the term – an active life in the Republic, though on occasion Cicero cannot resist noting that his own state of *otium*, literarily productive as he is making it, has been thrust upon him both prematurely and against his will.[49] It is never incorporated into the sphere of acceptable public or political display – as we know from Catullus, there is no "room" for textual *otium* in the world of the forum – but in the mid 40s we see Cicero begin to use *otium* to speak plainly of both the purely textual work that occurs within the private home and the division of *otium* between time spent reading and time spent writing (cf. *id autem omne consumebatur in legendo, scribendi otium not erat, de Off.* 2.4).[50] In what is likely the last of the dedicated *technica* (and one that is epistolary rather than dialogic in form), *otium* is represented as a completely defensible lifestyle and is favorably compared to that of political administration:

Illud autem sic est iudicandum, maximas geri res et maximi animi ab iis, qui res publicas regant . . . esse autem magni animi et fuisse multos etiam in uita otiosa, qui

[47] Cf. *Ep. Att.* 12.61, which includes a quotation of Ter. *Heaut.* 75 and specifies the reading of *Orator. Chremes, tantumne ab re tua est oti tibi, ut etiam Oratorem legas?*

[48] *Acad.* 1.3.11: *administratione rei publicae liberatus doloris medicinam a philosophia peto et otii oblectationem hanc honestissmam iudico.* To this, cf. *Brut.* 3.13 and *de Div.* 2.7.

[49] *Brut.* 2.8; *Cat.* 49: *nihil est otiosa senectute iucundius*; 82: *otiosam aetatem et quietam.* To this, cf. *de Off.* 3.2: *nostrum autem otium negotii inopia.* To this cf. esp. *Brut.* 2.8 and *de Off.* 3.1.2, as well as Varro *de Vita* fr. 71; Balsdon 1960: 47 likens *otium* to "retirement," but the term is never so unmarked for Cicero in the *technica*; the configuration of "forced" *otium* is picked up later by Seneca, and will be discussed briefly below.

[50] Cf. *de Rep.* 1.1: *certe licuit Tusculi se in otio delectare*, of Cato, and *Lael.* 104: *nam quid ego de studiis dicam cognoscendi semper aliquid atque discendi? in quibus remoti ab oculis populi omne otiosum tempus contriuimus*, of the *Laelius* itself and, I think, the *technica* as a whole.

aut inuestigarent aut conarentur magna quaedam seseque suarum rerum finibus continerent . . . (*de Off.* 1.92 (44 BCE))

We must then have the opinion that the most important activities – those indicative of a supreme mind – are those performed by men who direct the affairs of the state . . . but there are – and have long been – men of great intellect who, even in life marked by *otium*, have embarked upon inquiries of the greatest import, and who have taken upon themselves weighty tasks, and yet held to the limits of their own affairs . . .

Otiosa uita: a life marked – here it is clear that the marking is an approbative one – by the *otium* that was the source of both intellectual inquiry (*inuestigarent*) and the writing that this inquiry produces. The use of *otiosus* in the passage cited above nicely encapsulates the increasingly ameliorative lexical valence of these terms – and especially the adjectival form *otiosus* – in the *technica*. Although *otiosus* appears in the earlier of the *technica*, it does so but rarely (twice each in *de Oratore* and *de Re Publica*) and tends to be used in guarded or slightly ambivalent passages.[51]

Beginning with *Brutus* in 46, however, and continuing through to the last of the *technica* in 44, Cicero uses *otium* with increasing frequency and with an increasingly positive and textual valence. It is used in the introduction to the *technica*, much as it appears in Catullus cc. 50 and 14, as a way of both introducing the dialogue piece and providing a handy *mise en scène* for the project of literary and textual display at hand.[52] Elsewhere, it does similar work in the dialogue proper, as interlocutors simultaneously defend their activity and spur it along (*explicabo . . . quoniam otiosi sumus . . . totam Zenonis Stoicorumque sententiam*, *de Fin.* 3.14; *quoniam . . . sumus otiosi*, *Lael.* 16; cf. 17), occasionally even suggesting that the "work" of their hours of *otium* outweighs the more political "work" that it has replaced.[53] But the most striking characteristic of this term in the *technica* is the distinctly literary valence that pervades, if by extension, almost every example of its use. In the later of these treatises especially, *otium* becomes the primary word used to mark the literary pursuits of the orator and his friends, as well as the circumstances under which this literature may be produced (cf. *de Fin.* 3.10; *de Off.* 3.4). But once, and perhaps most unexpectedly

---

[51] *de Orat.* 1.20.102: *mihi nunc uos, inquit Crassus, tamquam alicui Graeculo otioso et loquaci . . . quaestiunculam . . . ponitis*; but cf. 1.51.219, where the term is used more amelioratively.

[52] Cf. *Brut.* 3.10: *cum inambularem in xysto et essem otiosus domi; de Fin.* 1.14: *quoniam nacti te, inquit [Torquatus], sumus aliquando otiosum; TD* 1.5: *philosophia iacuit usque ad hanc aetatem nec ullum habuit lumen litterarum Latinarum; quae inlustranda et excitanda nobis est, ut, si occupati profuimus aliquid ciuibus nostris, prosimus etiam, si possumus, otiosi.*

[53] Cf. *DND* 2.3: *minime uero, inquit Cotta, nam et otiosi sumus et his de rebus agimus quae sunt etiam negotiis anteponendae*, and *Lael.* 86.

(to us, perhaps, if not to the original readers), it is used to strangely mis-introduce a metrical adaptation of Homer made "while *otiosus*":

De cuius coniectura sic apud Homerum, ut nos otiosi conuertimus, loquitur Agamemnon . . . (*de Div.* 2.30.63 (44 BCE))

While at leisure I translated what Agamemnon says about this prophecy in Homer . . .

The lines that follow are indeed a fair adaptation of *Iliad* 2.299–330; the problem is that the lines are spoken not by Agamemnon at all, but by Odysseus. There is a chance, of course, that Cicero was mistaken in this attribution as he wrote this passage, but that the work was published – it is dedicated to his brother Quintus – before he had opportunity to emend it (for such post-publication emendation cf. *Ep. Att.* 12.6a.1). But Cicero knows his Greek sources (his familiarity with Hesiod is discussed below);[54] it is not only here that he translates Homer,[55] and it seems rather more likely (or at least somewhat probable, considering that he is referring to a version of the text he himself has translated) that the misattribution of speaker – a misattribution that would give somewhat more weight to Cicero's argument at hand – is not so much an honest mistake as an intentional "error" made precisely to underline the tonal redirection that is involved in any appropriative act of "translation." While we do not want to give too much weight to this passage, it is tempting to play Cicero's use of *otiosus* here against that of Catullus in c. 50. Cicero's use of *otiosus* at *de Div.* 2.63 introduces a philosophically and politically charged Latin revision of a Homeric original; Catullus' use of the term at c. 50 may well have introduced a poetically, literarily, and erotically charged revision of a Sapphic one. As Cicero qua textual *persona* takes pains to say in *Brutus*, a certain degree of poetic license – or outright revisionism – is due an orator who engages in writing "histories" so long as this license serves a broader literary purpose (*Brut.* 11.42, quoted in the Introduction). In Cicero's use of *otiosus* as a marker of the distinctly literary process of adapting and re-presenting an earlier intellectual product – and this is a process with which the majority of the *technica* claim to be engaged – he marks his state of "textual leisure" as a meaningful, creative, and active one even as it feigns a lighthearted or ostensibly casual textual project.

[54] As Steel 2001: 94 notes in the context of an apparent "mistake" in *pro Archia*, "Cicero hardly ever makes mistakes in his deployment of Greek myth." An innocent misattribution in this passage is possible, but highly unlikely.
[55] For translations of the *Iliad*, cf. e.g. *TD* 3.26.63; 3.9.18; 3.27.65, and *de Div.* 1.25.52; 2.39.82; for translations of the *Odyssey*, cf. e.g. *de Fin.* 5.18.49. On this see Sandulescu 1970.

By the late Republic, as we see, the relatively unmarked social implications of *otium* in New Comedy have all but disappeared; what has emerged in its stead is a kind of bivalent notion of *otium* that is both set in opposition to the political work of the forum (which is not to say that the term could not be used there approbatively) and, at least as early as the mid to late 60s (*pro Archia*, of 62, contemporaneous with the possible period of Catullus' earlier compositions), wholly in line with an aesthetic of upper-class literary activity. The *otium* of Catullus tends to be marked with erotic valence and, especially in cc. 50 and 51, a sense not just of literary enjoyment, but also of textual production and exchange. Cicero's use of *otium* in the orations is primarily oriented toward the interests of "public health," but the distinctly literary tonality of *otium* in *pro Archia* argues against a simple, or at least unchallengeable, semantic dichotomy by the end of the decade. Although it is perhaps always problematic – in this period, and if you are Cicero – to be seen displaying your *otium* in public, there is no evidence that the textually productive connotations of *otium* were in and of themselves anathema to public speech (even if they did not often come into play in forensic and political orations). In the later *technica* as well as in the letters (most of which fall into the post-consular years), however, we see an increase in *otium* both in terms of raw usage and the literary, homosocial, and "textually reciprocal" valences with which *otium* is imbued. The configuration is not "I write when I have time," but "when I have time, I write." *Otium* has come not merely to allow textual production, but to signal its expectation.

The middle Republican signification of *otium* as both a time of autonomy and a time of obligation seems to emerge in the late Republic – perhaps in response to a rise in second-century convivial culture and the texts that this culture would have produced – in a concept of *otium* that provides an approbative defense of how, why, and when a member of the patronal class might embark upon literary, rather than (or as was likely the case for most of the writers of the period, in addition to) political, activity. This *otium* is both dignified and textual,[56] and enters the argot of a group

---

[56] The collocation of *otium* with *dignitas* appears several times in Cicero: *Sest.* 98 (56 BCE) (twice): *cum dignitate otium* and later *neque ullum amplexari otium quod abhorreat a dignitate*; 100: *dum otium uolunt etiam sine dignitate retinere*; *de Orat.*, 1.1: *in otio cum dignitate*; *Ep. Fam.*, 1.9.21 (54 BCE): *cum dignitate otium*. Balsdon 1960: 47 suggests, "In public life 'otium' stood for peace and freedom from disturbance... [I]t was not a long step to using the word for acceptance of the *status quo*, acceptance of existing political and social conditions." This may well be, but the specific grouping of *otium* with *dignitas* in these years – and in these texts – carries with it both literary and political concerns. See also Boyancè 1941: 173; on the phrase *cum dignitate otium*, see further Wirszubski 1954.

of patronal-class writers who wish to signal the implications, justifications, and innuendos of their textual endeavors and to use those endeavors to expand, explain, negotiate their existence in a textual world. It is true that Catullus' textual *otium* seems to have resulted from the conscious decision to make him unavailable to the state, whereas Cicero's textual *otium* – once he has entered the period of his final and most productive years – appears to have emerged from the state's increasing unavailability to the orator. Each man found his textual *otium* in different ways and used it, as we shall see below, to different ends. But the ways in which each configured *otium* as a time of textual production are, if surprisingly, more alike than they are different, and speak of a pervasive recognition of *otium* as terminological code for "time to write."

A letter to Cicero from M. Caelius Rufus, written to the orator while he served as proconsul in Cilicia, encapsulates the dynamic of *otium* and textual exchange even as it demonstrates that the valences evidenced by Catullus and Cicero must have been current throughout a somewhat broader literary society:[57]

Estne? uici? et tibi saepe, quod negaras discedens curaturum tibi, litteras mitto? est, si quidem perferuntur quas do. atque hoc ego diligentius facio quod, cum otiosus sum, plane ubi delectem otium meum non habeo. tu cum Romae eras, hoc mihi certum ac iucundissimum uacanti negotium erat, tecum id oti tempus consumere. (*Ep. Fam.* 8.3.1 (51 BCE))

What then, have I won? And do I keep on sending you letters, which is precisely what you said I shouldn't do, when you were just leaving? It's true – at least if the letters I send reach you. And I do so all the more earnestly because, when I am at leisure, I simply have no place to enjoy this leisure. When *you* were at Rome, it was the sweetest certainty of my time away from business that I could while away my hours of *otium* in your company.

We see that if the literary force of *otium* was far-reaching, so too were the literary games implied by the term. Both the "give and take" of Catullus 51 and the use of *otiosus* to introduce and elicit reciprocal textual exchange in Cicero point to a pervasive understanding of *otium* as textual time. At the close of the letter, Caelius makes a request that both underlines the function of *otium*-words as indicators of affective sociotextual time (σύνταγμα: Cicero's use of Greek as a code for the cultivated intimacy of

---

[57] Cf. too *Ep. Fam.* 8.1, in which Caelius claims to have sent a *uolumen* to Cicero.

his *technica* is here echoed by his correspondent)[58] and connects this time to the affective sociotextual space in which it is enacted:

Illud nunc a te peto, si eris, ut spero, otiosus, aliquod ad nos, ut intellegamus nos tibi curae esse, σύνταγμα conscribas. 'qui tibi istuc' inquis 'in mentem uenit, homini non inepto?' cupio aliquod ex tam multis tuis monumentis exstare quod nostrae amicitiae memoriam posteris quoque prodat.

And now I ask of you that – if ever you are (as I hope will be the case) at your leisure – you dedicate to me a treatise of some sort, so that I might know that you have me in your thoughts. "Whomever do you have in mind?" you say, "clever man." What I want is that, from your great many writings, one should stand out that might also offer to future generations a testament to our *amicitia*.

Otium is not merely a time to write; it is (and this will become more important as we investigate the texts created in the "time" of *otium*) a time to create writing that binds men to their past and links them to their future.

THE IMPERIAL *NACHLEBEN* OF *OTIUM*

The political and literary valences of *otium* continue well into the Principate and Empire, when *otium* is to be linked with both the production of literature and the ways in which the hours needed for this production are achieved. *Otium* is used frequently to address the production of poetry (e.g., Verg. *Ecl.* 1.6; *Georg.* 4.564; Hor. *Ep.* 1.7.36; Ovid *Trist.* 3.2.9; 4.8.7; Mart. *Ep.* 1.107.3, and, in a reference to poetic production, Tac. *Dial.* 10.3),[59] but now tends generally to be a concept of "literary time," the availability of which depends upon another's agreement to grant it. No longer the deserved autonomy of a man of means, the textual *otium* of the later period (Mart. *Ep.* 1.107 demystifies the term most forcefully) is a gift given by another. The *otium* of the Principate and Empire continues to be a term linked with the literature it produces, but it emerges as a time uncomfortably dependent upon the wishes of another.

---

[58] The letters to Atticus in which literary matters are discussed are especially marked by the use of Greek, cf. *Ep. Att.* 13.12–13. 32. Greek is used for the titles of philosophical *technica* at *Ep. Att.* 13.12 (on his *de Finibus*, περὶ τελῶν, and his *Academica*, Ἀκαδημική), *Ep. Att.* 13.16 (on the *Academica*), and *Ep. Att.* 13.19 (on the *de Fin.*).

[59] See further Mart. *Ep.* 3.20.8: *an otiosus in schola poetarum / lepore tinctos Attico sales narrat?*; 5.20.3: *tempus otiosum*; 11.1.1: *liber otiose*; and Pliny *Ep.* 1.9.8; 3.13.2 (of reading); 7.2.1; 8.21.2; 9.6.4 (*otium meum in litteris colloco*); 9.32.1.

It is Seneca, perhaps, who felt the loss of *otium* as patronal-class birthright the most deeply of all later writers and who most resented its shift from inborn possession to imperial gift – or punishment. He does not merely link *otium* with the enjoyment of literature; he claims that literature is the only thing that makes *otium* – in his case it was an enforced *otium* under Nero – bearable (*otium sine litteris mors est et hominis uiuis sepultura*, *Ep. Mor.* 82.3). The now fragmentary *de Otio*, a dialogue (if in only loosely dialogic form) conventionally dated to 62 CE,[60] engages in a moving reconciliation of *otium* with the ideals of Stoic philosophy to which Seneca had been a lifelong devotee. Both the literary and political designations of *otium* are brought to bear in this dialogue: at 1.4 the unnamed interlocutor makes the wry observation that Stoics never truly enjoy *otium* in their efforts to fill all of their time with philosophical inquiry. At 3.2–3 two "types" of *otium* pursued by philosophers are presented. The Epicurean pursuit of *otium*, Seneca explains, is one of fixed purpose; politics are avoided save in case of state emergency. The Stoic pursuit of *otium*, by contrast, is one of special purpose; politics are to be practiced, unless for some reason one finds this an impossible endeavor. At 4.2 Seneca argues that the wise man is able to serve the Republic even in *otium* – and perhaps even better here than in *negotium* – by engaging in the liberal arts (that is, in writing; cf. *de Off.*, cited above). Although the dialogue as we have it does not engage in an extended discussion of the connection between *otium* and literary production, his defense of *contemplatio* (5.1–8) is suggestive of the very sort of written products of *otium* of which *de Otio* is itself an example, and at 6.4 we are given the *sapiens* – Seneca himself, we must imagine, though there are Ciceronian echoes here as well – who retires into *otium* with the conviction, or at any rate the *apologia*, that his "leisure" time will render an invaluable service to posterity and, perhaps, the only one of which he is capable.

Toward the end of the dialogue, and in a discussion of Chrysippus' views on political exemption, Seneca defends a lifelong "opting out" of a hopelessly corrupt political world: a complete and utter retreat into *otium*. His tone suggests both an understanding of the earlier circumstances in which a man might retreat into *otium* perforce (Cicero) or choose it from the beginning (Catullus), and bitter resentment over an early Imperial degradation of the intellectual world of *otium*:[61]

[60] See Williams 2003: 1–2 for a discussion of the dating of this dialogue.
[61] So Williams 2003: 7 suggests that the dialogue may subject "the traditional Stoic commitment to public life to renewed scrutiny in a time of authoritarian and, especially under Nero, increasingly wayward rule."

Quid autem interest quomodo sapiens ad otium ueniat, utrum quia res publica illi deest an quia ipse rei publicae, si omnibus defutura res publica est? (Sen. *de Otio* 8.2)

But what does it matter how a wise man comes to *otium*, whether because the state is unavailable to the man or the man is unavailable to the state – if the state is going to fail everyone, no matter what?[62]

The textual *otium* of later periods may have brought with it a veneer of autonomy but, as Seneca seems to suggest, the veneer was a thin one, and cracking at its borders.

---

[62] On my rendering of *defutura . . . est* as "is going to fail, no matter what," cf. Williams 2003: 113 on these words: "the periphrastic future signals pessimistic resignation to an unalterable state of affairs."

CHAPTER 2

What? Munus *as the "gift of duty"*

THE POETICS OF RECIPROCAL OBLIGATION

We saw above, in a discussion of the first terminological intersection in the textually interested works of Catullus and Cicero, that in the period between the middle and late Republic *otium* emerged as an approbative term indicative of the time during which – thus our question *when* – a person might engage in textual activity. In the following pages, as we move to the question *what*, we shall consider the second terminological intersection between these two authors and their texts: the word by which each man chose to designate the physical products of their hours of *otium*, products that serve as an *oti ratio*, if one is needed (and for Cicero, it often was), and, even if one is not (and for Catullus, it is not), products that speak to the sense of *otium* as a time during which one might engage, of one's own will, in relationships of social and sociotextual obligation.

In the following pages, I start with a quick survey of the archaic and classical Greek terms most commonly designative of gift-exchange objects, propose *munus* as the term used most habitually by Catullus and Cicero when designating the textual products of their exchanges, and consider briefly the use of *munus* by authors of New Comedy. I turn then to an analysis of the term in Catullus and Cicero, and suggest that these authors designate their dedicated texts as *munera* – and, as we saw with *otium*, they do so in surprisingly similar ways – in order to set off the textual gift as a distinctly singularized, "invaluable" object specific to the production of their patronal class. I close my consideration of *munus* with an investigation into the ways in which Catullus and Cicero (though perhaps rather more the latter, for reasons that should become clear) tapped into the inherent "reciprocality" of the term in order to imbue their dedicated texts – the product of their *otium* – with a sense of obliged gratitude and expected reciprocation.

In the exchange structures of archaic and classical Greece – the most useful comparandum for our inquiry – the words for such potentially exchanged equitables are many: δώς, δόσις, δῶρον, δωρέα, and δωτίνη[1] are all used of material goods (or the acts of giving that might be realized in this gift) and neither imply nor exclude – in and of themselves – a cycle of ongoing isonomic reciprocity. Other words, such as ἄγαλμα, χάρις, and ξένια, might well invoke cycles of such ongoing reciprocal exchange, but their lexemic sphere of application is relatively restricted in terms of whether the word designates an *object* (so, ἄγαλμα, frequently in the context of divine dedications), an *act* (or favor, or the sense of having received such, so χάρις), or a *category of object* that defines, and is defined by, the relationship in which it is given (so ξένια, as that set of objects correlative to the relationship of ξενία). Of all of these words, only δῶρον is used directly of the exchanged or dedicated text imagined to circulate "as a gift" of its author,[2] and there is almost no overlap in the discursive spheres to which these terms refer. Thus δῶρον may describe an exchanged object (even a book), but never a reciprocally performed "favor" or "delight"; ἄγαλμα is similarly a term restricted to the realm of material exchangeables, whereas χάρις, in its reciprocal sense, is restricted almost completely to ephemeral or at any rate intangible sources of pleasure.[3] Ξένια is similarly a word that signifies objects rather than acts, but its inherent correlation with the active and reciprocal relationship of ξενία makes it perhaps the most flexible and dynamic of these terms in relation to the systems of gift-exchange in which it is enacted.[4]

We see in the terminological intersections of Catullus and Cicero that the lexemic representation of reciprocity in the late Republic is structured, in many ways, along the lines of the Greek: *donum* (cf. δῶρον)

[1] Cf. Benveniste 1948: 9; he does not take into account the broader scope of terms – ἄγαλμα, χάρις, ξένια – that might similarly (or perhaps even more definitively) signify a system of gift-exchange. For general discussions of gift-exchange, cf. Finley 1973: 63–66; Mauss 1990; Kurke 1991: 85–107; and Wohl 1998: 61–62 (the latter two in the context of exchanges of the archaic Greek aristocracy); for a general survey of archaic Greek gift-exchange, see Morris 1976; for the intersection of cash and exchange economies, see Parry and Bloch 1989; for general theories of gift-exchange, see further Raheja 1988; Strathern 1988.
[2] Dionysios Chalcous is the first to use the term in this way, cf. IE²: 59 (PE, vol. 2: 1); this passage is discussed further in Chapter 6.
[3] An exception to this function of χάρις is the poetic play of χάρις and the personified Χάριτες, cf. Dionysios Chalcous (cited above); Mel. *AP* 5.148.1; and Call. *Ep.* 51, which may indeed be using the χάρις not only of a physical object (the fourth "newly-wrought Grace") but also, if the reference to Berenike is to extend coyly to the recently completed *Plokamos*, a physical text.
[4] The relationship of ξενία has received more scholarly attention than have the objects of that relationship, ξένια; on the latter, however, see Spitzer 1993. On the relationship itself, especially as represented in Greek tragedy, see Belfiore 1994; Padilla 2000; and Roth 1993.

signifies a physical object that is given or received, but without further
claims as to the relationship in which this prestation occurred, while *gratia*
(cf. χάρις) is restricted to the realm of intangible acts or "favors" that may
circulate within systems of reciprocity, but that do not themselves signify
the existence of such a system, and that are not applied, in this period,
to durable or material objects. But against the background of these more
discursively differentiated terms, we see in the middle and late Republic
one – *munus* – that is applied both to intangible and ephemeral acts and to
material and durative objects. *Munus*, a term that in the middle Republic
could designate variously act, office, favor, responsibility and love-token,
emerges in the lexical intersections of Catullus and Cicero (intersections
likely matched by Cinna)[5] as a designation applied to a poem, a book, or
any physical object of isonomic textual dedication.[6] What this means for
Catullus and Cicero (and indeed for authors of later periods, who pick up
on the "textualizing" power of *munus*) is that *munus* provides the lexical
repository within which textual gifts might be embodied, enacted, and
imbued with a sense of understood obligatory return.

I want to suggest that when an object or office is designated a *munus*
(and we shall see below how this happens), there are two immediate consequences. First, this *munus* must reject a condition of stasis, or non-
movement, which allows a market valuation. Once something has entered
a cycle of gift-exchange, once it is recognized as a singularized object,[7]
it cannot fall out of that cycle without losing its exchange-signification.
Much as we saw with *otium*, it is the identification, or naming, of a *munus*
that is the key to its sociotextual function. When an object or an office is
identified as a *munus*, it is transferred from the sphere of monetary transaction, and into a sphere of perpetual and non-monetary exchange and
obligation. In the first, monetary, sphere, a commodity may be reasonably reckoned or fixed against the value of another, and so given a price;
in the second, exchange, sphere (the sphere, that is, of patronal textual
dedication), a *munus* is singularized, made "priceless" and "invaluable," by
its refusal to be reckoned against the value of anything else. When the
munus is removed from (or rather, never enters into) the transactions of

[5] Cinna, fr. 11.4 (Blänsdorf 1995: 222), designates as *munera* those *carmina* that his *libellus* contains.
[6] Although Greek lacks a singular term by which to identify a given book as an "acting object," the
notion that the dedicated text is both a "possession" (κτῆμα) and a "useful thing" (χρῆμα) is noted
at Dion. Hal. *Comp.* 1.1.
[7] On this terminology see Kopytoff's excellent 1986 discussion of the "singular" (that which cannot be
saleable for money and which is not exchangeable for a wide variety of things) and singularization,
as opposed to the "common" (that which is saleable for money and can be exchanged in discrete
transaction for a counterpart) and commodification. Cf. esp. pp. 68–70, 73.

the monetary economy, when it enters into the reciprocal exchanges of patronal-class writers,[8] it is not frozen in place, as some have put it, but rather it is frozen in motion.[9] What I mean is that because the *munus* is able to reject economic stasis, it is able to reject the normative valuations of a monetary economy. It is priceless – and invaluable.[10]

In the context of the late Republic, the *munus* marks a path of circular reciprocity in accordance with the concerns of patronal-class favor and obligation. On the one hand, a *munus* is oriented toward the past as the physical memory of a gift given or service rendered or received – and we shall see in later sections especially that memory and recollection function as important "named" characteristics in the dedicated texts of Catullus and Cicero. On the other hand we see that a *munus* is also always oriented toward the future in its implied expectation that a gift or service will be exchanged in return – thus, indeed, the function of the dedication as a whole, which speaks to nothing so much as the hope that writing will beget further writing.[11]

A second important consequence of the designation of an object or an act as a *munus* is that this naming invests the object or act with social privilege: in the late Republic, as we shall see, this means that the designation of "*munus*" insulates the object or act within the non-monetary estimation of a patronal economy.[12] The value of such a *munus*, and this is especially important when that *munus* is textual in nature, resides in its rejection of commoditization (it is not something that can be purchased directly from its author) and its complete economic enclosure within the patronal

---

[8] Kopytoff 1986: 74 "... in effect, commodities are singularized by being pulled out of their usual commodity sphere."

[9] *Pace* Wohl's 1998 discussion of the Greek ἄγαλμα, which behaves in many ways (if not in its restriction to physical objects) like the Latin *munus*. Wohl describes a process of "agalmatization" (p. 68) in which that which is "agalmatized" (in this case, Iphigeneia of Aiskhylos' *Agamemnon*) is figured "too precious to be traded" (p. 71), an object "frozen" (p. 78) in its state of greatest value. Although I am inclined to agree generally with Wohl's analysis, I disagree with her insistence on the ἄγαλμα's stasis. It was, by the fifth century, a definitive characteristic of the ἄγαλμα that it be dedicated or traded; it is in this "necessity of motion" that both ἄγαλμα and the *reddendum* are most functionally related. This argument is made more fully in Sailor and Stroup 1999.

[10] In his discussion of singularization among the Aghem of western Cameroon, Kopytoff 1986: 75 notes "To be a non-commodity is to be 'priceless' in the full possible sense of the term, ranging from the uniquely valuable to the uniquely worthless."

[11] Cf. Kopytoff 1986: 69 on those particular exchanges that mark relations of reciprocity: "Here, gifts are given in order to evoke an obligation to give back a gift, which in turn will evoke a similar obligation – a never-ending chain of gifts and obligations. The gifts themselves may be things that are normally used as commodities ... but each transaction is not discrete and none, in principal, is terminal."

[12] That is, in an economy in which the worth of a *reddendum* resides in its "exchangeability" and the concomitant rejection of a market value. See further Habinek 1998: 106 on aristocratic rejection of economic interests.

sphere of exchange. The *munus* refuses that act of estimation (*aestimatio*) that reckons the value of one good against another.[13] We see this concept illustrated in the gift that claims greater value because it refuses all valuation: it is singular or original, one of a kind, a family heirloom. Consequently, if a *munus* is removed from the sphere in which it was first instantiated (by theft, misappropriation, the refusal to exchange; Catullus frequently frames such attempted intrusions, though one suspects they function more as humorous intra-societal censure), it returns to its original condition as a static and commodifiable object (or act) and ceases to carry value in the exchange sphere (a tension we shall see teased out in c. 12). Properly speaking, one cannot buy an heirloom. Or rather, one can – and indeed, the sale of such is good business – but the value of an heirloom that is purchased will be (to the *munus* economy, those who receive and exchange their items of value the old fashioned, non-monetary way) primarily a cash one: it will have been translated into the terms of a monetary economy and will have lost its value as an extra-monetary good.[14] Catullus and Cicero are not concerned with the buying of heirlooms, of course, but with the production and safekeeping of their dedicated texts. What this means for our broader Society is that texts produced and exchanged within its borders (whatever those might be at the time of production) claim their value precisely because access to these texts is yet limited by the terms of dedication and depends upon isonomic and homosocial understandings of obligation, favor, ability, and affection.[15]

The middle Republic shows some evidence of this later terminological development. In Roman New Comedy, *munus* is used of material objects that are exchanged, and social actions that are performed, with the expectation that the "giver" in each case will receive an equitable return. In this period, *munus* can designate either a gift or a service (if such expects a gift

[13] On *aestimare / aestimatio* and *existimare / existimatio*, see especially Habinek 1998: 45 and following. Habinek notes, "[T]he literal meaning of [*existimare*] is to evaluate or assess; according to Festus (23 Lindsay), the simplex *aestimare* refers to the establishing of a relationship between *aes* or money and other forms of property." On commoditization and singularization, see Kopytoff 1986.

[14] E. Oliensis remarks to me (and quite rightly) that individuals can certainly *feel* that they are buying something more than an object's cash value when they purchase an antique (an "instant ancestor" portrait, silver service, a collection of netsuke, etc.) and points specifically to Cicero's pained negotiations with Atticus on the purchase of Greek sculpture. Nevertheless, the lexical distinctions at issue are those between the *munus*-world, in which pedigree is not for sale, and the money-world, in which anything, at least theoretically, can be bought.

[15] In Republican texts, a *munus* is never "given" to an individual or corporate identity that is incapable (socially or economically) of participating in the exchange. So David J. Banta, 1998–1999 fellow of the *TLL*, remarks in private correspondence that in Roman New Comedy *munera* are not exchanged intramaritally. I am grateful to David for his own kind *munus* to me: the patient assistance and sound advice in the gathering and evaluation of the Republican *munus*-material.

or service in return; it is the expectation of return that distinguishes *munus* from *donum* and *officium*), but – and this will stand in contrast with the "textual *munus*" of the late Republic – never both at the same time. Indeed, perhaps the closest the middle Republican *munus* comes to bridging the gap between gift (*donum*) and service (*officium*) is in the frequently erotic and meretricious connotations of *munus*: it may thus designate variously "intimate favor" or "amatory (re)payment,"[16] (Plaut. *Cist.* 92–93 and *Pseud.* 177),[17] and in Plautus (though not in Terence) the plural *munera* is often related specifically to prostitution.[18]

Plautus also uses the term in combination with the verb *fungor*[19] in order to indicate an office, duty, or responsibility owed to or expected by someone.[20] The social context of the exchange is usually implicitly private, but it always invokes the specter of public display.[21] In other words, and perhaps in comparison to the *otium* of obliged favor, the phrase *munus fungi* can be understood to mean "to claim for oneself an obligation of exchange."[22] Depending on the social context of the individual drama, *munus* may be paired with, e.g., *donum*, or *officium*, but is in any case kept distinct from either the *donum* or the *officium* by – and this is an important aspect of the late Republican sense of the textual *munus*, to which we shall turn momentarily – the implication of return within an extended system of reasonably commensurate exchanges.[23] Similarly important to the late Republican application of *munus* to dedicated texts is the middle Republican sense that a *munus* is valuable in its ability to procure, sustain

---

16 See Adams 1982: 164: "*Munus* could also be used of the services of either partner." Adams cites Petron. 87.8; Cat. 61.222; *cf.* Hor. *Carm.* 2.5.2; Mart. *Ep.* 9.67.8; Claud. *Carm. Min.* 25.130; ps-Acron. ad Hor. *Epist.* 1.18.75.

17 *Cist.* 92–93: *Inde in amicitiam insinuauit cum matre et mecum simul / blanditiis, muneribus, donis*; Pseud. 177: *facite hodie ut mihi munera multa huc ab amatoribus conueniant.*

18 In addition to those passages cited above, see *Poen.* 1176; *Truc.* 310; at *Pseud.* 777, 781 the singular *munus* indicates specifically a *leno's* payment.

19 Zagagi 1982: 281 notes, "[T]he double meaning of *munus* might originally have been embodied in the [idiomatic] phrase *munus fungi* – 'to enjoy,' 'to consume,' 'to take upon oneself an obligatory exchange.'" See also Zagagi 1987: 129–132. For another middle Republican use of *munus fungor*, see Lucilius *Sat.* 1.8 and 5.202.

20 See Plaut. *Amph.* 827; *Cas.* 949; *Trin.* 1; *Truc.* 354; to these examples compare Ter. *Adel.* 764: *munus administrasti tuom.*

21 *Cf.* Plaut. *Amph.* 825–827: [Sos.] . . . *nisi si quispiam est / Amphitruo alius, qui forte ted hinc absenti tamen / tuam rem curet teque absente hic munus fungatur tuom.* Here *res* and *munus* are paired in a description of the doubled king's various duties: since at least one of the "duties" involved the impregnation of Alcumena, it is possible that here *res* refers to Amphitruo's political business and *munus* to his "spousal obligations," but the reference is ambiguous.

22 *Trin.* 1: *sequere hac me, gnata, ut munus fungaris tuom.*

23 Zagagi 1982: 280. On the root **mei-*, Zagagi cites E–M 422. See further Palmer 1956: 258–269 and Benveniste 1966.

or promote a desired, and often erotic, relationship or personal alliance.[24] In sum, and although at no point in the middle Republic is *munus* applied to a text, all examples from the comic stage indicate that *munus* in this period carried with it those designations of social obligation and equal return[25] that would seem to make it such a valuable "textual" word for the later periods.

THE GIFT THAT SINGULARIZES

By at least the first half of the first century BCE, *munus* is applied most commonly to the performance of a public office – a political post, for example, can be called a *munus Reipublicae* – that was both expected on the part of the individual who performed it and also endowed this individual with a degree of *gratia* at his ability to perform this duty. But it is also in this period, in the "textual texts" of Catullus and Cicero, that we see *munus* emerge as an evaluative term designative of the physical object of isonomic textual dedication. Whereas *munus* before had meant variously "love-gift" or "social obligation," it appears that the textual society of the late Republic applies the word to the physical, textual object that is traded between social equals. As we shall see below, whether that *munus*-designated text is one of intimate and erotic poetry or affective and politically included rhetorical dialogue, *munus* appears repeatedly (and especially in the *technica*, which appear – not surprisingly – to be more aggressive in their promotion of textual duty) as the term chosen to mark a text as a literary and social object that is imagined to participate in an ongoing cycle of reciprocation.[26]

---

[24]   The term is used similarly in e.g. Pomponius fr. 390 (*fungi munera*); Lucilius frr. 8, 202 (*fungi munus*); 149, 676 (of the public games); 166 (of a "gift" of *ingentes pisces*).

[25]   In a linguistic analysis of the term in this period, Zagagi 1982 notes, "*Munus* is a special type of *donum*, from which it is to be distinguished by its obligatory character, implied by its root **mei-*, which denotes 'exchange.' Once the recipient accepted the *munus* ('exchange-gift'), he was under a burden of obligation . . . to make a due return, whether in kind or by a service." In response to the suggestion that *munus* originally meant "gift" or something similar, and did not have a sense of reciprocity, Zagagi notes that the shift from "gift" to "duty" (the latter of which is a common late Republican meaning of the term) would have been unlikely. In the case of the *munera mortis* – the term commonly applied to the gladiatorial games that were originally part of an elaborate funeral display – it is entirely likely that even funerary *munera* were originally conceived to be in some sense reciprocal, in that the gladiatorial display amounts to a gift given the dead with the hope of some sort of return of *gratia* (compare to this Greek funeral libations offered up with the hopes of a return of χάρις).

[26]   In sharp contrast, the words *donum*, *beneficium* and *officium* ("gift," "service," and "duty," loosely speaking), although they might well serve an affective and reciprocal relationship, do not carry any linguistically fixed connotation of reciprocity in this period. Although any of these could be applied to objects or actions within the scope of reciprocal exchange, the terms do not imply reciprocity in and of themselves, nor do our Republican authors ever use these nouns to refer specifically to their

Both Catullus and Cicero include the "textual" sense of *munus* in their discussions of textual and social exchange in ways that will open up the meaning of the term. Examples of such appear more frequently, in terms of raw numbers, in Cicero than they do in Catullus: in light of the relative textual output of each, this is hardly surprising (and indeed a mathematical ratio of textual vs. non-textual uses of *munus* brings the two into even closer alliance), and, if we take into account the likelihood that Cicero[27] felt a far greater need to imbue his texts with a sense of politically authorized duty, it is all the less so. Later in this chapter, then, we shall look more closely at the ways in which Cicero in particular used the designation of *munus* to suggest that the dedication and exchange of textual gifts was in fact also the dedication and exchange of textual debts. But first, I want to look at Catullus' use of *munus* as a tool for the singularization of dedicated texts.

In general, Catullus' use of *munus* falls in line with the New Comedy value of the term, especially in its ability to imbue the *munus* object with erotic or homosocial connotations. Let us begin with c. 12, in which Catullus both uses *munus* to designate an object exchanged between *sodales* and suggests that the *munera* of reciprocal exchange might stand in for the individuals through whom the exchange is enacted:[28]

> Marrucine Asini, manu sinistra
> non belle uteris: in ioco atque uino
> tollis lintea neglegentiorum.
> hoc salsum esse putas? fugit te, inepte:
> quamuis sordida res et inuenusta est.   5
> non credis mihi? crede Pollioni
> fratri, qui tua furta uel talento
> mutari uelit: est enim leporum
> differtus puer ac facetiarum.
> quare aut hendecasyllabos trecentos   10
> exspecta, aut mihi linteum remitte;
> quod me non mouet aestimatione,
> uerumst mnemosynum mei sodalis.
> nam sudaria Saetaba ex Hiberis
> miserunt mihi muneri Fabullus   15
> et Veranius: haec amem necessest
> ut Veraniolum meum et Fabullum.

exchanged texts. It is important to note that the verbs *dare* and *donare* are not similarly limited (cf. Cat. 1.1): only the nominal constructions – only the actual objects of the exchange – are constructed in this way.
[27] In the *technica* and letters; the term is not used in this sense in the orations.
[28] On this poem and c. 14, see especially Forsyth 1985.

Asinius Marrucinus,[29] you make clumsy use
Of that clumsy left hand: in the middle of a *soirée*
You steal a fellow's napkin, if he's let down his guard?
You think this is funny? You don't get it, you ass:
What a base and blundering thing this is!   5
You don't believe me? Well, believe your brother
Pollio – he'd gladly pay a mint for your
Little theft: now, there's a kid just *loaded*
With elegant style and delightful wit.
Well then, either brace yourself for a gazillion   10
Of my versified barbs, or *give me back my napkin!*
It is not the cost of the thing that moves me, mind you:
It is a *mémoire*, in truth, of one of my pals.
You see, Fabullus and Veranius sent to me
Some Saetabian kerchiefs – to be a *munus* –   15
From Spain: I am bound to adore them
As I am to adore my dear little Veranius and Fabullus.

Alas, poor (and now eternally red-handed) Asinius. Whatever the man has done is unclear; almost the only thing of which we can be sure is that he probably *did not* attempt to pilfer a napkin.[30] He has committed an unforgivable blunder in an established cycle of textual reciprocity, and this blunder is remade in c. 14 in terms of a boorish and "real" attempted theft of an heirloom in the making.[31] The exchange value of the "almost heirloom" is made explicit in the twelfth line of the poem, when Catullus designates the *linteum* as a *munus*: it is not just a gift, but a gift made in a closed textual world. It is in this world that men let down their guard (*neglegentiorum*, l. 3; cf. to this *neglegentem* as the final word of c. 10) in order to engage in the display of those textual – and so in some ways, as with c. 10, fictional – *personae* through which their texts are produced and

---

[29] Whether or not Marrucinus should be taken as an official cognomen or an unofficial marker of provenance – either way it is a marker of formality and poetic distance – see Thomson 1997: 239–240.

[30] I must admit that I go back and forth on this question. As noted in the Introduction, I am inclined to read Catullus' more "textual" poems fairly metatextually, and so it is my instinct that Asinius' convivial *faux pas* consisted of an act linked to the convivial production of poetry. There remains a part of me, however, that gains pleasure from imagining Asinius (or at least, Catullus' Asinius, as that is all we have) as the geeky practical joker whose blundering party gags provided Catullus with fertile ground for a good-natured poetic barb on proper convivial behavior. As much as I doubt Asinius actually tried to steal Catullus' napkin, then, the poem is a bit funnier if he *had*.

[31] For a similar attack, see c. 25, in which Thallus is chided for having stolen a cloak (*pallium*, l. 6), a Saetabian "napkin" (*sudarium*, l. 7), and some Bithynian *catagraphi* (l. 7; with Thomson 1997: 267 I would take this otherwise unattested word to refer to some sort of writing tablet), which the thief is accustomed to display as heirlooms of his own: *quae palam soles habere tamquam auita* (l. 8).

exchanged, and it is from this world that Asinius, possibly by committing a blunder that challenged its fictions, has been at least momentarily
expelled.

Although we may assume that Asinius' gaffe was not economically motivated, Catullus' claim that it is not the monetary value (*aestimatio*) of the
gift with which he is concerned critiques the theft in distinctly economic –
and thus distinctly downmarket – terms. In charging that Asinius' "transaction" (the theft) was a cash-interested one, Catullus distinguishes both
the transaction, and indeed Asinius, from the non-monetary – that is,
textual – transactions in which he and his similarly refined *sodales* take
part.[32] In denying his own financial interest in the *munus*, Catullus shifts
onto Asinius the obviously insulting, if humorously disingenuous, charge
of base economic motivation. The *linteum* is valuable because it is a singularized *mnemosynum* – a *mémoire* (the Greek here adds a cachet of
refinement) – of both the giver and the act of giving. As such, it is an
incontrovertibly biographical object; a physical representation of social
identity and practice, which is imagined to be as singular and as irreplaceable as the human beings who gave it. In this capacity, the *linteum* is a
material expression of both the prior bonds of friendship between Catullus and his exchange partners and a promise of continued bonds, and
exchanges, for the future. Catullus is as bound (*necesse est*) to adore the gifts
as he is to adore his *sodales*. The *linteum* fixes the debt of this adoration –
and the obligation of future remuneration.

When Catullus specifies that the *linteum* he received from his *sodales* had
been given with the specific purpose of constituting a *munus*, he establishes
its value as a constructed non-commodity. Thus Catullus challenges the
social meaning of the theft when he asserts *munus* status for the *linteum*
given him by his *sodales*. As an object of aristocratic exchange and a gift
resistant to a cash valuation (*aestimatio*, l. 12),[33] the *munus* should by virtue
of this signification remain insulated from the economic motivations of
petty theft. According to the dynamics of patronal remuneration, a *munus*
can never be stolen.

---

[32] For a vitriolic remark on the connection between *munus* and *sodalis* in Cicero see *Verr.* 2.3.85 . . .
totam insulam cuidam tuorum sodalium sicut aliquod munusculum condonaras . . . ? In a lecture on
performance culture and literary culture, delivered at the 1998 Heller Conference at the University
of California at Berkeley, Thomas Habinek noted of the term *sodalis*: "Etymologically, the word
sodalis is linked to the Latin word *suus*, meaning one's own, and to Greek terms such as *hetairos* and
ethê, which refer to the 'selves' who form the context in which one's own self develops its individual
as well as collective identity."

[33] See Habinek 1998: 45–58 and following on *existimo, existimatio* in the context of literary evaluation
and authority; Fitzgerald 1995: 93–96 is especially good on this poem.

To put it another way, a *munus* that has been stolen (or exchanged "improperly" according to mutually recognized rules of play) must cease, semantically speaking, to be a *munus* at all. It falls from the cycle of exchange and so loses its signification as a singularized, non-comparable, object. What can only be a napkin (*linteum*, l. 11) to Asinius is an invaluable *munus* to Catullus (l. 15). Asinius has behaved inelegantly (*non belle*, l. 2; *inepte*, l. 4; *sordida res et inuenustast*, l. 5)[34] at a chic in-crowd party featuring "jokes and drinking" (*in ioco atque uino*, l. 2) and, we can be sure, the sort of verbal play that was a precursor to textual production (cf. c. 50.6: *reddens mutua per iocum atque uinum*). As such, the party would have been informed by the expectations of textual *otium*, and it doubtless involved both the display of textual *persona* (cf. c. 10) and the exchange of the erudite but well-lubricated and thus probably rude verbal "play" – *in ioco atque uino* – that this *otium* allowed. Catullus' *ioci*, I suspect, consisted of precisely the sort of humorous invective[35] that would later have been reworked into poetic form dedicated, as is c. 12, to the original "target" of the humorous abuse.

It is a bit odd for a poem that identifies its setting as one devoted to frivolity to then attack a participant in this setting for having behaved frivolously. It is impossible to retrieve the nature of Asinius' blunder or the degree to which it is anything other than another textual joke used to provide the basis for textual production. If we wish to imagine a "real" blunder lying beneath the surface of Catullus' charge of "napkin theft" (an attempted "theft" Catullus knows was intended as a joke), we might imagine that Asinius broke some rule of convivial or poetic (invective?) play. Both because Catullus' more "textually interested" texts offer their most attractive readings if read at a metatextual level and because the poet's offered repayment for the theft threatens (ll. 10–11) and is (c. 12) simply poetry itself, it is tempting to suppose that Asinius' "theft" may have been one of a purely poetic nature – the "stealing" of another's riff, or theme, or punch line, or draft – that only at the end of the poem materializes as a non-poetic object in the reference to Spain.

But if we cannot reconstruct with certainty what Catullus had in mind in describing Asinius' *faux pas*, we can take a look at how he goes about describing and responding to it. First, the nominal social equality of the

[34] On the poetic "display" connotations of *bellus* and *uenustus*, cf. Krostenko 2001; in the late Republic, all *inept-* words connote action that is awkward, "out of place," or "ill-suited" to a particular public, and usually display-oriented, setting (these words will be considered again in Chapter 5). The adjective *sordidus* is closely linked to *illiberalis* by Cicero at *de Off.* 1.150.

[35] On the idea of *ioci* as poetic invective through which individuals gain fame, see Mart. *Ep.* 5.15.

convivial guests, potential partners in textual exchange, is knocked out of balance by the charge that Asinius has taken what has not been given. Second, Asinius' "theft," when framed as such, represents the intrusion of cash values, *aestimatio*, into the exchange (*munus*-centered) economy instantiated by the time of textual *otium* in which the party is imagined to occur. The contrast between the formal address to Asinius (*Marrucine Asini*) in the first line, and the affectionate diminutive/possessive (*... Veraniolum meum et Fabullum*) of the last, distances the bumbling interloper from the friendship-bound *conuiuae*. Although it may well be the case that Asinius has "stolen the napkins" in an awkward attempt to join in on the game of (poetic?) exchange, Catullus' paratragic framing of Asinius' attempt humorously secures (and advertises) its failure. Where the interloper wanted an invitation to exchange, Catullus promises (*aut... exspecta... aut... remitte*, ll. 10–11), and simultaneously delivers, a fitting poetic remuneration: the abusive hendecasyllables of the poem itself, and perhaps a promise of future attacks (*trecentos*, l. 10, that numberless number which I have rendered with the nonsense numerical idiom, "gazillion")[36] if the *munus* – and now we really must not wonder whether this "napkin" does not refer to a poetic gift / theft[37] – is not returned to its rightful owner and if Asinius does not adhere more closely to the convivial rules of play.

Finally, we might consider Asinius Pollio, the younger brother of Asinius the dedicatee and, as Catullus makes explicit, the ultimate "in-crowd" charmer. Pollio, it is suggested, is also a *sodalis* of the poet (or at least a potential one; he would have been about seven years Catullus' junior), and one to whom Asinius is not just placed in social contrast but to whom he is related by blood. The appearance of Pollio (the first appearance of Asinius Pollio in literature, for what it is worth) complicates the problem in two ways. First, it says something about what makes a member of the "in-crowd." No one is born into the textual world: poetic chic is a matter

[36] The numberless hoards of avenging hendecasyllables (!) appear again at c. 42: *adeste, hendecasyllabi, quot estis / omnes undique, quotquot estis omnes* (ll. 1–2), this time to exact a "poetic" justice from a woman who has stolen the poet's writing tablets (*codicilli*), and to restore peace and safety to the world at large. In this poem, the verb *reddere* appears six times; five of these are in the second person singular imperative: "give them back!" It is possible that the poet intends his repetition to underline the woman's inappropriate and unwelcome intrusion into the poet's circle.

[37] I have long wondered whether the "foreign napkin" might not refer to a collection of poems (or perhaps a single poem?) Catullus' friends composed on their travels and brought back with them; Cinna fr. 11 attests to the practice of returning from foreign travels with a poetic gift. Bernstein 1985 argues that Catullus frequently uses *amores* to refer to his (and perhaps others') love verses; he tends to refer to longer poems by titles echoing the first words, lines, or theme (Cinna's *Zmyrna*, c. 95; Caecilius' *Magna Mater* or *Dindymi domina*, c. 35); could the *linteum* refer to a poem?

of nurture and not nature, and Asinius the younger is as full of charm as Asinius the elder is devoid of it. Second, however, the poem problematizes the idea of money in the *munus*-world, for Pollio's readiness to buy off his brother's *faux pas* for an enormous sum (a coarse commoditization of coarse social behavior) seems only to underline the impossibility of putting a price on the *munus*.[38] Catullus, of course, could accept no monetary compensation: the *munus* may have been only a napkin (if ever it was), but it is as priceless to the poet (and as irreplaceable) as the family crystal. In an excellent discussion of Greek gift-exchange, Richard Seaford has argued that violent vengeance may be expressed as the flip side of reciprocal gift-giving; Seaford notes that hostile and friendly exchange may be described by the same terms.[39] So here we see the potential violence of exchange made explicit in the poet's ready inversion of the normally affective characteristics of the poetic gift. Asinius had unexpectedly taken what had not been given; Catullus will forcefully give an unexpected return.[40]

Textual exchanges are again the subject of c. 14. But this time, the *munus* in question is explicitly textual in nature, and its designation as a *munus* underlines the importance of the poet's exchanges with his friend Calvus. The poem is written on the occasion of a literary gag gift; it both describes and rejects an attempted intrusion into the inner circles of isonomic reciprocal exchange:[41]

> Ni te plus oculis meis amarem,
> iucundissime Calue, munere isto
> odissem te odio Vatiniano:
> nam quid feci ego quidue sum locutus,

---

[38] At the same time, Pollio's readiness to "buy off" his brother's inappropriate behavior signals that only the truly chic understand that any amount of money is worth erasing this embarrassment. Thomson 1997: 240 takes *mutari* not in the monetary sense but as "*infectum reddere*," and *talento* as an ablative of instrument. Indeed, the idea that Pollio should "pay for" his brother's gaffe is a surprising one (it is of course also a joke), but the economic considerations elsewhere in the poem would suggest that the economic sense of these words must be meant to carry some weight.

[39] Seaford 1994: 25–29.

[40] An archaic example of this dynamic can be found in the myth of Prometheus (and especially the episodes surrounding the feast at Mekone) in Hes. *Theog.* 535–616 and *WD* 45–105. In each poem, Prometheus and Zeus engage in an exchange of deceptive gifts and non-gifts (withholdings, concealings), and it is Prometheus' specific act of taking what has not been given (fire) that initiates Zeus' aggressive prestation of an undesired (if ostensibly desirable) return (Pandora). The classic analysis of these episodes, and the way such rapid-fire exchange functions both structurally and conceptually, is Vernant 1990: 183–201.

[41] Of this poem Burgess 1986: 593 notes that Catullus responds to Calvus' literary *munus* of bad poetry with a reciprocal gift worse by far than that which he had received: "The first poetry determines the nature of the second." It is possible, however, that the *carmen* itself – with its threat of reciprocation – is meant to serve as the return gift, thus dodging Calvus' poetic provocation and deflecting an ever-escalating cycle of reciprocating trash.

cur me tot male perderes poetis?   5
isti di mala multa dent clienti,
qui tantum tibi misit impiorum.
quod si, ut suspicor, hoc nouum ac repertum
munus dat tibi Sulla litterator,
non est me male, sed bene ac beate,   10
quod non dispereunt tui labores.
di magni, horribilem et sacrum libellum!
quem tu scilicet ad tuum Catullum
misti, continuo ut die periret,
Saturnalibus, optimo dierum!   15
non non hoc tibi, salse, sic abibit.
nam, si luxerit, ad librariorum
curram scrinia, Caesios, Aquinos,
Suffenum, omnia colligam uenena,
ac te his suppliciis remunerabor.   20
uos hinc interea ualete abite
illuc unde malum pedem attulistis
saecli incommoda pessimi poetae.

If I didn't love you more than my very eyes,
Calvus my darling, I'd hate you with a *Vatinian*
Hatred for that *munus* of yours:
What have I done to you – what have I said –
That you should do me in with all these poets?   5
May the gods damn that *cliens* of yours,
Whoever sent you such a crowd of bastards.
But if – as I suspect – it is "poetaster Sulla"[42]
Who sends you this marvelously *innovative munus*,
Then I don't care – in fact I'm absolutely thrilled,   10
That your labors haven't been wasted.
Great gods – what a god-awful little rag!
And this you sent to your Catullus,
To do him in on the very next day of the
Saturnalia – the best day of all!   15

---

[42] On *litterator* as "poetaster," cf. Suet. *Gramm.* 4, on the difference between *litterati* and *litteratores*. Nepos, we learn, wrote a *libellus* in which he indicated that *litteratus* is a term often applied to men who can speak and write with authority, but that should be restricted, technically speaking, to interpreters of poets. Suetonius then notes, however, that some make a distinction between *litteratus* and *litterator* (cf. the Greek *grammaticus* and *grammatista*), using *litteratus* to indicate a "master" of a subject and *litterator* to indicate an individual who is merely "proficient." A letter from L. Orbilius Pupillus is adduced to explain the distinction as it would likely have held for the late Republic: *Quorum opinionem Orbilius etiam exemplis confirmat; namque apud maiores et, cum familia alicuius uenalis produceretur, non temere litteratum in titulo, sed litteratorem inscribi solitum esse, quasi non perfectum litteris, sed imbutum.*

But you won't get away with it, wise guy,[43] oh no.
At the crack of dawn I'm off to the stalls
Of the booksellers: I'll gather together Caesii, Aquini,
Suffenus – all of that loathsome crap,
And this is how I'll pay you back – with punishment!   20
Meanwhile, you poets: adios! off with you!
Go back to that place whence you bore your vile feet,
You eternal buffoons, you foulest of poets.

In this poem, the innate reciprocity of textual exchange is made specific in the poet's language of patronal and economic exclusivity.[44] The affective and isonomic nature of the exchange is emphasized at the outset by means of intimate and textualizing vocabulary (ll. 1–2). We know that something has been given, that it has been given in the context of an exchange – *isto munere* – and that the poet is not happy about it. Three lines later we discover the nature of the *munus*: it is not an ill-chosen love trinket or personal favor gone wrong, but rather a book of crappy poetry, sent by Calvus to Catullus, as a private textual joke. We do not know, of course, who gave this *libellus* to Calvus – a *cliens*, perhaps, or Sulla the cut-rate literary *poseur*; but the donor remains ultimately nameless – even as he is knocked down a social peg or two: *cliens*[45] – and even though the *libellus* is represented as consisting of a poetic collection (*poetis*, 1.5; *impiorum*, l. 7), one wonders if the gag is not that this is a book of horrible poetry Calvus had tried to pull off as his own. Someone, at any rate, has attempted to blunder his way into what Catullus imagines as an exclusive sphere of

---

[43] With Thomson 1997: 245, I read here *salse* (as in the G family) rather than the reading of manuscripts of the OR family, *false*.

[44] Burgess 1986: 583 notes that c. 50 presents a similar image of poetic *amicitia*; Laughton 1970: 1–7 suggests that c. 49 (*Disertissime Romuli nepotum*) represents Catullus' poetic reciprocation for a poem sent by Cicero (*gratias tibi maximas Catullus / agit*, ll. 4–5), and notes the strong antithesis between *poeta* and *patronus* in the final three lines. Laughton would have this poem function as a callous rejection of one sent by Cicero, but the humorously abusive tone of c. 49 is not far afield from that used to address Furius and Aurelius, *comites* of the poet (in c. 11) in, e.g., cc. 15, 16, 21, 23, 24, and 26. If anything, I would take c. 49 (together with c. 65, discussed below) as persuasive evidence of the overlapping of poetic and rhetorical social and literary circles. For earlier and influential interpretations of the poem, cf. Baehrens' 1885 edition, (pp. 225 ff.) (following Schwabe 1862: 127, who argues that the poem is earnest, and the reference is to the *pro Caelio*).

[45] The actual social positioning of the interloper is irretrievable and unimportant: the language of the poem fabricates a textual reality more compelling, powerful, and permanent – for poet, addressee and "accused" – than the mutable hierarchies of extra-textual status. Of the terms and vocabulary of poetic patronage, Gruen 1996: 79 remarks, "The patron/client relationship . . . serves as a model, in most interpretations, for the nurturing of poet by potentate . . . Reciprocal advantages follow: *otium* and support for the poet, enhanced fame for the patron. Of course, the terms *patronus* and *cliens* were generally avoided: it would be impolite to call attention to the dependency." The application of the label *cliens* provides an intentionally awkward and socially unattractive disembedding of the normal exchange of texts.

textual exchange (we are reminded of Asinius' gaffe in c. 12). This unlucky individual, textually reduced to the status of *cliens* or poetaster, is summarily disqualified from the poetic competition that must occur between equals – a poetic competition (if of a rather metapoetic sort) that is now between Catullus and Calvus alone. The wretched poets (made even more nameless than the donor of the *libellus*) who made this gag gift possible are conflated with the wretched *munus* of their poems; perhaps more accurately, they are personified in the *libellus* in which their poems are contained. The only sort of textual exchange enjoyed by these *pessimi poetae* is at the hands of others and, what is worse, as a *joke* (the singular *Suffenum* in l. 20 makes one wonder if there is not a side project going on here);[46] at the end of the poem they are dismissed without further comment, and with Catullus' valedictory *ualete, abite* we imagine nothing so much as a book of poetry tossed, with disgust, into the trash. So much for the retention of poetic subject status.

The humorous poetic vendetta appears early on (*nam quid feci ego quidue sum locutus / cur me tot male perderes poetis?* ll. 4–5). As with so many of Catullus' poems, the theme here is that of textual exchange; but textual exchange with a hilarious Saturnalian and metatextual twist.[47] Catullus recognizes that Calvus' *nouum munus*[48] was meant as an erudite – "innovative" – gag, and he has fun writing about what happens to such a gift when it enters into an ongoing relationship of poetic remuneration and literary one-upmanship. Thus a game that is normally a matter of "who can give a better textual gift?" has become, in the days of clever social inversions, its inverse: "who can give the *worst* textual gift of all?" Catullus asks, with wide-eyed innocence, "What have I done to deserve this?" (we can practically hear him gasp). But this innocence is surely feigned: c. 14 suggests that not only does Catullus know *exactly* what he did "to deserve this" – the textual world of the late Republic would have doubtless offered many opportunities for gag gifts, and Catullus lets us know he knows where to find them – but that he and Calvus must have spent a sidesplitting hour

---

[46] Cf. Thomson 1997: 246; Thomson agrees that there is something pointed in the use of the singular, and suggests that he is "uniquely bad." Aquinus may be the poet mentioned at *TD* 5.63.

[47] Gag gifts were of course expected during Saturnalia; the theme of Saturnalian joke texts is explored perhaps most thoroughly (and brilliantly) by Martial in his *Apophoreta*. A textual "collection" (indeed a *libellus*, 14.2.1) that both demands (14.1.5–6) and defies distribution, *Apophoreta* reduces the value of all its "gift texts" to a two-line lemma – a volume of Catullus (14.195) equal to a volume of Homer (14.184) – that has value only if it is retained within the collection as a whole. On the textual deceptions of Martial's Saturnalian joke texts, cf. Stroup 2006.

[48] Here, I suggest, the poet's use of the adjective is sarcastic and pejorative, and should be read "strange, odd, weird, unheard of." For this use, see Cic. *de Orat.* 1.137; *Lig.* 1.1; *Verr.* 2.2.8.24.

or two rolling through the verses of inferior poets before Catullus sat down to compose his poetic return.

Perhaps because the poems being exchanged are not his own, Catullus speaks more freely of the interlocking system of texts, promises, exchanges, and (joking) retributions here than anywhere else in the corpus. It will be good to look more closely at Catullus' careful designation of the *munus* as a *libellus* (ll. 2–12). The use of *munus* at l. 2 makes it clear that something was given to – or done for (we do not yet know that the *munus* is an object, much less that it is a book) – Catullus under the pretense of reciprocity. Between lines 5 and 9, we learn that the *munus* is a collection of poetry, given first (also as a *munus*, l. 9) to Calvus and only then, via Calvus' joke, to Catullus. If there is a point to this poem – to whatever extent poems ought to have points – it might be merely this: not all textual exchanges are created equal.

The affective value of any gift is inexorably embedded in the type of relationship in which it is given. Thus while the gift of one's own text, the "normal" sort of exchange in which Catullus and Calvus engage, may bring with it the highest of affective values and obligations (and, by way of the personal dedication, allow the author to maintain his subjecthood), the gift of another's text, the foundational theme of c. 14, may disempower the author of that text – in cleaving to his *libellus*, he has become objectified and commodified right along with it – and reduce this author's value in the textual world to that of *cliens* or "dabbler." In his snide charge that the *libellus* could have been given only in a system of hierarchical patronage, and in his dismissive suggestion that, therefore, it must have been given in earnest, Catullus shores up the borders of his relationship with Calvus. A gift given sincerely in a system of hierarchical exchange can enter the isonomic circles of reciprocity only as a bad joke. At the same time, however, Catullus' configuration of the *munus* as a *libellus* underlines the materiality of this and all textual exchange. For although he promises a poetic remuneration in the form of second-rate and purchased literature, which would be the "fair trade" in response to Calvus' gift, c. 14 enacts its own repayment (just as in c. 12, the promised "avenging hendecasyllables" are reified in the poem). This poem is itself a textual *munus* with which Catullus dodges Calvus' poetic provocation and delivers a fitting but socially elevated return of poetic barb. This poem acknowledges the receipt of a *munus* even as it becomes a *munus* in order to repay the initial prank.

Catullus uses *munus* on four other occasions to indicate erotic interest or practice (cf. too the diminutive *munusculum* at cc. 64.103 and 78b.145 for "love-gifts"; this term is used by Cicero in his letters to Atticus to indicate the gift of a library). At c. 69.3 *munus* is used of clothing and jewelry meant to influence a woman's affections (vestiges of one of the main designations of *munus* in the middle Republic); at c. 61.43 of the office of Hymenaeus (the activity of the nuptial couch); at c. 61.227 *munere assiduo* is used of the sexual encounters between a young married couple; and at 65.19 of the *furtiuo munere* ("secret exchange") of a quince. This last occurrence of *munus*, both because it occurs in a dedicated text and because it is used to frame the textual exchanges between two men, is worth examining more closely.

> Etsi me assiduo confectum cura dolore
>   seuocat a doctis, Hortale, uirginibus,
> nec potis est dulcis Musarum expromere fetus
>   mens animi, tantis fluctuat ipsa malis –
> namque mei nuper Lethaeo gurgite fratris   5
>   pallidulum manans alluit unda pedem,
> Troia Rhoeteo quem subter litore tellus
>   ereptum nostris obterit ex oculis.
>   . . . [*deest uersus I*] . . . .
>   numquam ego te, uita frater amabilior,   10
> aspiciam posthac? at certe semper amabo,
>   semper maesta tua carmina morte canam,
> qualia sub densis ramorum concinit umbris
>   Daulias, absumpti fata gemens Ityli. –
> sed tamen in tantis maeroribus, Ortale, mitto   15
>   haec expressa tibi carmina Battiadae,
> ne tua dicta uagis nequiquam credita uentis
>   effluxisse meo forte putes animo,
> ut missum sponsi furtiuo munere malum
>   procurrit casto uirginis e gremio,   20
> quod miserae oblitae molli sub ueste locatum,
>   dum aduentu matris prosilit, excutitur,
> atque illud prono praeceps agitus decursu,
>   huic manat tristi conscius ore rubor.
>
> Although I am worn out by ceaseless sorrow
>   And care calls me, Hortalus, away from the learned maids,
> Nor is my soul able to bring forth the sweet progeny of the
>   Muses – tossed as it is by such swells of misfortune –
> For recently the tides of death, rising from swirling Lethe,   5
>   Have lapped at the death-white foot of my brother,
> Whom the land of Troy has snatched from my sight
>   And has hidden beneath its Rhoetian shore.
>   . . . .

Oh my brother, more beloved to me than life,   10
Shall I never see you henceforth? But certainly I shall love you always,
    Always I shall sing verses saddened by your death,
Just as the Daulian sang beneath the thick woodland shade,
    As she mourned the death of her Itylus, torn from her. –
But though in the midst of these overwhelming sorrows, Hortalus,   15
    I nonetheless send you these verses lifted from our Battiades,
So that you not think your request has flown from my mind,
    Entrusted in vain to the wandering winds;
Just as once the quince, given by a lover as a secret *munus*
    Rolled from the lap of the chaste young maid,   20
Who had forgotten – oh wretch! – that she had hidden it in her tender skirt,
    And up she leapt at the approach of her mother – out came the quince,
Out it sped straight for her mother, on a headlong course,
    And a guilty blush bloomed on the face of the sad young thing.

Poem 65 is addressed to one Hortalus, often, but by no means securely, identified as Cicero's oratorical rival Q. Hortensius Hortalus (on this see my discussion in the Appendix), and serves as a dedication both of itself – c. 65 is certainly a gift of its own – and of the translation of Callimachus' *Plokamos Berkenikês* (*aition* 66) that follows.[49] At the beginning of the poem (ll. 1–8), Catullus claims that he has been worn out by grief ever since the death of his brother. After a one-line lacuna, he briefly apostrophizes his deceased brother, and claims that he will forever memorialize his death in poetry (ll. 10–14). At line 15, the poet turns again to Hortalus – and even if he is not to be identified with Hortensius, Catullus' highly rhetorical address suggests that he is a man familiar with the style of the forum – and announces that although he is surrounded by sorrow, he will nevertheless send a new translation of the *Plokamos* of Callimachus (he uses the intimate familial "Battiades"), lest his dedicatee suppose that his request for poetry has been forgotten. The final six lines of the poem emphasize the affective relationship between the partners in this textual exchange. Catullus likens himself (ironically?) to a chaste young woman who has received, but forgotten, a quince sent as a love-gift from her young beau – here refigured rather strangely as the more mature orator and poet (if, at least, this Hortalus is Hortensius; even if not, the configuration is a

---

[49] On Catullus and Callimachus, see especially Clausen 1970; Buchheit 1975; Hunter 1993; and King 1988. On the form and imagery of c. 65, see further Kaiser 1950 and Van Sickle 1968. Cinna fr. 11 (Blänsdorf 1995: 222), also a dedication of a translation – one of Aratus – similarly uses *munus* to describe his dedication. On the relation of dedication and mock dedication to the "poetry of objects," see Hutchinson 2003.

surprising one).[50] Catullus claims that, unlike the young woman, he will not forget the (social and literary) obligation imposed upon him by his acceptance of his dedicatee's request.

The "poetic quince" undoubtedly refers to the love-gift given by Acontius to Cydippe in Callimachus *Aetia* 3 frr. 67–75,[51] and the practice of dedicating a translation with a poetic echo of the translated author (or some spin on this) may have been a favored textual flourish in the late Republic.[52] In the original *aition* the quince bore an inscription – an oath in the name of Artemis in which the reader (and recipient) is made to promise herself in marriage to the donor. The *munus* in this poem, then, was itself a kind of exchanged text. I suggest that when Catullus refers to the inscribed gift of the original *aition*, he is arguing for an important aspect of poetic exchange. Textual dedication that emphasizes the request of the dedicatee doubles as an act of "putting words (and an obligation) in one's mouth": to accept the textual gift is to become bound to the giver.[53] Once received, it establishes an obligation on the part of the recipient and serves as a reminder of both the transaction and the promised return.[54]

In c. 14, Catullus uses *munus* to describe a book of horrible poetry given him by his friend Calvus. In c. 65 we see the term again applied to a specifically textual object, and the poet's use of *munus* in this poem is at the heart of the late Republican revisions of this term. For when *munus* is

---

[50] On Hortensius' participation in the poetic sphere, and perhaps in support of the argument that he is to be identified with the Hortalus of c. 65, cf. c. 95.3 – dedicated to a Hortensius (but is this Hortalus?). Hortensius was born in 114 BCE, and so would have been between 50 and 60 years old at the time of this composition, some 30 years older than the poet. The difference in ages between the two underlines the subtle eroticism of the whole and strikes me as reminiscent of the language with which Caelius wrote to Cicero about their own textual exchanges.

[51] The scene with the quince – or "Cydonian apple" – is missing from the papyrus, but is supplied by *Dieg.* Z (P. Med. (PRIMI) 18, col. Z); cf. Aristaenetus I.10: Κυδώνιον ἐκλεξάμενος μῆλον ἀπάτης αὐτῷ περιεγράφηκας λόγον καὶ λάθρᾳ διεκύλισας πρὸ τῶν τῆς θεραπαίνης ποδῶν . . . ἡ δὲ κόρη κομισαμένη καὶ τοῖς ὄμμασι περιθέουσα τὴν γραφὴν ἀνεγίνωσκεν ἔχουσαν ὧδε· 'μὰ τὴν Ἄρτεμιν, Ἀκοντίῳ γαμοῦμαι.' ἔτι <δὲ> διερχομένη τὸν ὅρκον εἰ καὶ ἀκούσιόν τε καὶ νόθον ἐρωτικὸν λόγον, ἀπέρριψεν αἰδουμένη. See further Pfeiffer 1949–1953, vol. I: 70. Although the quince-as-love-gift is a common enough figure in both Greek and Latin literature, the *Akontios* and the *Plokamos* share the theme of catasterism (the first implicit, the second expressed) and the imagery of astronomy and meteorology. Daly 1952 agrees that the final lines of the first poem are meant to refer to the *Akontios*, but does not note the thematic parallels between the two poems. On this, see further Laursen 1989.

[52] Thus Cinna fr. 11 (Blänsdorf 1995: 222) dedicates a translation of Aratus with an echo not of Aratus, but of Callimachus praising Aratus (*Ep.* 27, praise of Aratus' acrostic at *Phain.* 783–787). A possibility that the final lines of Cat. 50, which I believe functions as a dedication of (or at least introduction to) c. 51, may convey Sapphic tonality is discussed in Chapter 7.

[53] On this theme as a whole, cf. Derrida 1994, *passim.*

[54] See Fitzgerald 1995: 192 for a discussion of some of the elements of reciprocal obligation in this poem.

applied to an exchanged text – as we will see more fully in the Ciceronian examples that follow – it is almost exclusively on the pretense that the text has been requested by the recipient (a theme to which I return in Chapter 6). In this way, the textual *munus* is simultaneously an object and an act of exchange. Thus although the *munus* of c. 65 clearly recalls the obligations of a love-gift received, it also emphasizes the explicitly textual nature of a prior (and possibly versified) request for poetry from Hortalus himself: *tua dicta*, l. 17. The imagery of the inscribed quince points up the material nature of the present *munus* – that is, the text as physical object. It also implies an underlying eroticism of private exchange and, because the recipient of the poem is himself an established orator, suggests that the private connotations of *munus* would have been well recognized in a broader and trans-generic circle – a "Society" – of textual producers. The written word, the poet suggests, is not bound by the ephemerality of the spoken voice: it will stand as an enduring reminder of obligation and reciprocity.[55]

Charles Murgia has remarked that this poem, addressed (as he feels, and as I am inclined to agree) to one of the greatest orators of the late Republic and a chief proponent of the Asiatic style of oratory, constitutes the first use of what will become a popular rhetorical trope in Latin poetry: the profession of poetic incapacity.[56] The structure of c. 65, Murgia notes, approximates that of the initial sentence of the *Rhetorica ad Herennium*,[57] and follows closely Cicero's early rhetorical advice for achieving the three-fold goal of the *exordium*.[58] Although the professed "inability to write" as an introduction to requested literary production appears also in Cicero's letters, Murgia remarks, "When [this] structure is lengthened by tension-building devices, such as parenthesis and apostrophe, the effect is to render

---

[55] Habinek 1998: 109 and following discusses the ways in which some poetry (Cat. 1 and Hor. *Odes* 3.30.1–2 are given special attention) may ascribe to itself the "physicality" (and so, immortality) of inscriptional writing, by pointing up the materiality of the textual presence. To the texts mentioned by Habinek, I would add at least Cicero's *Brutus* and *de Officiis*, both of which take pains to establish the text as a physical object.

[56] C. E. Murgia, in a lecture on rhetorical similarities between Cat. 65 and Quintilian, notes, "[*Carmen* 65] is a marvelous tour-de-force of both poetic and rhetorical technique, which belies by its careful crafted artistry the incapacity which it protests." I am grateful to Professor Murgia for providing me with a written copy of his lecture; it has not, as far as I am aware, appeared in published form.

[57] A double *etsi* clause is resumed with a *tamen*, and followed by a *ne* clause. For a similar *recusatio*-as-introduction, cf. the *prooemium* of Quint. *Inst. Orat.* 6.

[58] Cf. *de Inv.* 1.20: *exordium est oratio animum auditoris idonee comparans ad reliquam dictionem; quod eueniet se eum beniuolum, attentum, docilem confecerit.* Of rousing the general pity of the audience, that it might receive more kindly one's oratorical performance, the author writes, *deinde primus locus est misericordiae per quem quibus in bonis fuerint et nunc quibus in malis sint ostenditur . . .* (1.107). So Catullus claims that he is unable to write because of his extreme grief over the recent death of his brother, *namque mei nuper Lethaeo gurgite fratris / pallidulum manans alluit unda pedem . . .* (65.5–6).

the sentence more highly charged, more periodic, and more rhetorical."
I agree fully with Murgia's recognition of the poet's stylistic commixture
of Asian oratory and Republican lyric, but whereas he suggests that the
path of influence is one from the sphere of rhetoric to that of poetry, I am
hesitant to accept the rhetorical priority of this textual maneuver. First, the
style of c. 65 is clearly rhetorical, but rhetorical style does not necessitate a
singular rhetorical prototype. Second, the chronology of the *ad Herennium*
is problematic in the extreme – on lexical, stylistic, and formal criteria, I
agree with Douglas' suggestion that the text dates from ca. 50 BCE, but
arguments on dating abound[59] – and it is thus an exceedingly risky text
with which to date another. Third, although the prooemium of the *ad
Herennium* does indeed resemble the first lines of Catullus 65, Murgia's
subsequent rhetorical examples are either Imperial in date, or, in the case
of evidence from Cicero's *de Inventione*, concern not a difficulty in fulfilling an obligation of promised literature (the case of the *ad Her.* and c.
65), but rather a difficulty in speaking publicly on some matter or other
(cf. *de Inv.* 1.1). Finally, we will see in Chapter 5 that the prooemium of *de
Oratore*, which post-dates the Catullan corpus (if perhaps only just), shares
with the poem important characteristics of language, style, and dedicatory
scheme.

Elsewhere in Catullus *munus* refers once to the catasterized lock (and
perhaps, by implication, to the poem itself, c. 66.38); twice to an offering
of perfume given to the lock (c. 66.82, 92); once to a favor requested
from a friend (c. 62.7); once to the repayment of an earlier vow (c. 66.38);
twice to indicate (implicitly literary and poetic) graveside lamentation
(*munus mortis*: c. 101.3, 8);[60] and five times to a text exchanged between
poetic comrades (cc. 14.2, 9; 68a.10, 32; 68b.149).[61] The last of these makes
explicit both the poetic obligatory transaction – *carmen* and *munus* are
collapsed into one – and the intended result of this transaction: the ongoing
nature of *munus*-exchanges, an unending cycle in which poetic reciprocity
is identified with the imagined poetic immortality of both the relationship
and the individuals who participate in it:

---

[59] Cf. Douglas 1960; on further problems of dating, cf. Winkel 1979.

[60] This term is used elsewhere to indicate the gladiatorial games that originally constituted an important aspect of Roman funerary ritual; this is the final use of *munus* common at the end of the
Republic: cf. *de Off.* 2.16.55. In this sense too, however, *munus* functions as a marker of reciprocity,
as it forges an ongoing link between the living and dead, replacing lost obligations (and the ability
to assume them) with new "gifts" to the people whereby the deceased will be remembered.

[61] A similar interest informs the dedicatory poem, in which the author's status is clearly identified
with the renown of the text: *quare habe tibi quidquid hoc libelli / qualecumque; quod, <o> patrona
uirgo, / plus uno maneat perenne saeclo* (1.8–10). See further Habinek 1998: 110 and following.

Hoc tibi, quod potui, confectum carmine munus
    pro multis, Alli, redditur officiis,
ne uestrum scabra tangat robigine nomen
    haec atque illa dies atque alia atque alia.

68b.149–152

To you, this *munus* – the best I could manage – is wrought in a song
    And given in return, Allius, for your many kind favors,
Lest this day, and the next, and the ones after that
    Sully your name with their creeping rust.

Even when *munus* is not used to describe a dedicated text, however, I want to suggest that the late Republican *munus*-quality of the dedicated text glimmers just beneath the surface. The language, terms, and expectations with which Catullus dedicates the *libellus* in c. 1 speak deeply to the textual aesthetic within which *munus* is constructed. One rarely gets far arguing about why a term or figure is *not* used where it may have been (all the more so in cases of poetry), but the fact that Catullus does not use a term of textual evaluation in his dedication to Nepos might suggest that it is for Nepos to decide upon the social value of the gift – that it is for him to decode the meaning of the transaction; for him to engage in (or perhaps, reject) the reciprocal alliance that it offers. But the sense is clear. For future readers, the *libellus* remains a delightful new text (*lepidum nouum libellum*, 1.1)[62] made available to many via its publication – and this is the sense, I think, of *libellus* (which we shall get to momentarily) – but properly given, at least originally, to a single reader. For Nepos alone the *libellus* remains a priceless "original" gift of the highest poetic and material order (*arida . . . pumice expolitum*, l. 2).[63]

Cicero's use of *munus* is more semantically diverse than that of Catullus, but it develops along the same lines. In the majority of the

---

[62] It is possible that Catullus uses the adjective *nouus* not merely to indicate that his *libellus* is "newly finished," but also that it is an innovation on earlier Roman poetic form, cf. *nouo quodam et inusitato genere dicendi*, "a somewhat unorthodox style of oratory," Cic. *Arch.* 3, discussed above. As I shall discuss in Chapter 6, however, in a consideration of a fifth-century parallel to c. 1, Catullus' whole point to these lines may be to situate his practice within a sound poetic tradition. On the connotations of *lepidus*, see Krostenko 2001: 64–72.

[63] On the "epigraphical" elements of this poem, see further Habinek 1998: 112. I disagree with Fitzgerald's 1995: 40 suggestion that *pumice expolitum* is suggestive of prostitution (a suggestion drawn by analogy to Hor. *Ep.* 1.20.1–2: *Vertumnum Ianumque, liber, spectare uideris, / scilicet ut prostes Sosiorum pumice mundus*), but as I shall argue below, the diminutive *libellus* does carry tones of broad and commodified textual circulation. Although the Horatian verses cited by Fitzgerald clearly indicate a literary "pandering," I suspect that this is a later innovation on Catullus' image of the smoothly polished *libellus* at the moment it leaves the author's possession and moves into the world – as a published text.

orator's work – the earlier *technica*, and all of the speeches – Cicero uses the term *munus* in the sense of the expected or obliged political activities of an elite citizen class. It is in this public orientation of the term that we see that Cicero's *munus* is not just an act of exchange – it is an act of display. The duty or office designated by *munus* is implicated in the visible effects made available for the larger group, or the public at large – in this, it is definitively extra-domestic – and is often something that is explicitly repaid (though not with money: *munus persoluitur, Phil.* 14.34) or reciprocated (*munus . . . fungitur, de Off.* 2.20.70). This "political" *munus* is never fully identifiable with the office or duty with which it is coupled: it speaks to the expectations, social characteristics, and overall performative quality of the office or activity with which it is linked, but is semantically distinguishable from the office or activity itself.[64]

Cicero's *munus oratoris*, then, designates not "oratory" in the abstract or "the act of speaking" as a whole, but rather the obligations and expectations incumbent upon an orator in his activity (*de iure respondere, Brut.* 30.113).[65] The phrase *munus magistratus* (*de Off.* 1.34.124; cf. *munus aedilitatis, Verr.* 1.1.36; 2.1.14) emphasizes the magistrate's responsibilities to his fellows within the *ciuitas* and his obligation to uphold the honor of the state with the expected return – from the state in general, or a person in particular – of status and position. In all cases of this predominately public use of *munus*, the term is reserved for the usual or expected activities of the freeborn, and almost exclusively aristocratic, citizen class.[66] This "political" *munus* of the late Republic is constructed as an office that is owed, but never, to use the language of a cash economy, paid. It is coded as a favor, duty, or gift (and is thus coupled with *officium, beneficium*, and especially *gratia*)[67] that may be variously expected or promised, but it never participates in a cash-exchange, and is never identified with a source of income. When an individual designates his activity a *munus*, he is claiming for himself the social privilege of aristocratic exchange.

---

[64] As in Roman New Comedy, *munus* used in this register is often paired, but never identified, with the related terms *negotium* and *officium*.

[65] At *Ep. Fam.* 10.24.1: *. . . neque ego libenter pro maximis tuis beneficiis tam uili munere defungor orationis . . .* The *munus orationis* does appear to refer to the speech, which is in this case both an "act" (or favor) and a "text." To this cf. *Ep. Fam.* 10.24, in which Plancius writes to Cicero: *neque ego libenter pro maximis tuis beneficiis tam uili munere defungor orationis.*

[66] Thus at *de Off.* 1.34.124 Cicero discusses the *munus* of the magistrate as opposed to the *officium* of the foreigner (*peregrinus*) or resident alien (*incola*); at *de Orat.* 1.9.38 the author uses the term to indicate the "expected activities" of all *artes* in general.

[67] Cf. *de Inv.* 2.66: *. . . [appellant] gratiam, quae in memoria et remuneratione officiorum et honoris et amicitiarum obseruantiam teneat* and 2.161: *gratia, in qua amicitiarum et officiorum alterius memoria et remunerandi uoluntas continetur.*

In the letters of 60 and the following year, Cicero begins to use *munus* to refer to books he receives from others.[68] In the *technica* of 46–44, *munus* comes to be used of textual production and, more significantly, of the physical text itself.[69] To use the imagery Cicero develops in *Brutus*, we might say that the exchanged text becomes the "offspring" of his textual production. The term is used first in this sense at *Brutus* 4.15–16 (quoted below), a passage in which the orator may refer to Atticus' *annales* as the inspiration for *Brutus*, and fashions his dialogue as a distinctly Hesiodic *munus*. Cicero also uses *munus* as a term for the exchanged, and dedicated, literary text in the prooemium to the second book of *de Divinatione*, written shortly after the assassination of Caesar. At *de Div.* 2.4, Cicero refers to the act of writing philosophy (he includes in this category the major *rhetorica*) as a *munus Reipublicae*, and so implicitly establishes the whole of the *Respublica* as his private exchange partner: the text is not merely an "offering" to the Republic, but is a return for services rendered (and given in the hope of future recognitions).[70] Three sections later, he makes clear his proposed transition from the public *munera* of political activity to the private *studia* of textual production:

Id enim ipsum a Platone philosophiaque didiceram, naturales esse quasdam conuersiones rerum publicarum, ut eae tum a principibus tenerentur tum a populis aliquando a singulis. quod cum accidisset nostrae rei p., tum pristinis orbati muneribus haec studia renouare coepimus ut et animus molestiis hac potissimum re leuaretur et prodessemus ciuibus nostris qua re cumque possemus. in libris enim sententiam dicebamus contionabamur . . . (*de Div.* 2.6–7)

But I learned from Plato and his crowd that there occur naturally certain political revolutions – so that states are at one time held by princes, at another time by the people, and once in a while by single men. Well, when this happened to our state,

---

[68] Cf. *Ep. Att.* 2.1 (from 60 BCE), which refers to Cicero's *commentarius* on his consulship, calls Paetus' gift of a library a *munus*, and says that if Atticus takes care of getting this library to Cicero, that will count as a *munusculum*. Cf. too *Ep. Att.* 2.4 of 59 BCE.

[69] As my argument engages with late Republican literary chronology, it is useful to note that the *Auctor* of *ad Her.* uses *munus* once to refer to his writings, and does so in clearly reciprocal terms: *ut pro tuo in nos officio, nostro in te studio munus hoc adcumulatissume tuae largiamur uoluntati* (1.17.27). It is unclear whether the author means to refer to the act of writing (as at *de Orat.* 2.2.11: *sed, quo citius hoc, quod suscepimus, non mediocre munus conficere possimus . . . .*) or to the specific product of that writing, the book (as at *de Off.* 3.33.121: *habes a patre munus*), but we should not be surprised to see authors capitalizing on the possible lexical slippage between competing semantic registers (*munus* as act vs. *munus* as the product of that act). If the *ad Her.* dates from the early first century BCE, and I do not think that it can (*pace* Douglas 1960 and Winkel 1979, as cited above), we might take this as an indication that the term is coming to be available in this sense (*munus* = book) early in the first century BCE, but is only fully developed by the authors of the middle decades.

[70] *de Div.* 2.4: *quod enim munus rei p. adferre maius meliusue possumus quam si docemus atque erudimus iuuentutem.*

and since I had been deprived of my former political responsibilities, I began anew
these literary pursuits, so that I might both greatly ease my mind of these former
troubles, and also be of a help to my fellow man to as great an extent as possible.
For I had taken to speaking – *arguing* my judgments in books . . .

It seems clear that *haec studia* refers to the *munus Reipublicae* mentioned but two sections before. In this passage, Cicero promotes the
process of writing a suitable, or at least conceivable, replacement for
the public political duties of the orator. The orator's "written voice" (*in
libris . . . contionabamur*) is presented as a means of negotiating a social
status that had before depended almost exclusively on the opportunities
afforded by public display. With these words, Cicero appropriates for the
field of dedicatory literature a measure of the social authority of political
activity: the Muse has learned not only to write – but also to declaim in
writing.[71]
About two years after the composition of *Brutus*, he uses *munus* twice
again. Early in the third book of *de Officiis*, the term appears in a brief
lament of Scipio Africanus' lack of textual production:

Nulla enim eius ingenii monumenta mandata litteris, nullum opus otii, nullum
solitudinis munus extat . . . (*de Off.* 3.1.4)

For he left no textual record of his skill; we lack the fruit of his *otium*, the *munus*
of his time at rest . . .

Here, *munus* is explicitly associated with both *otium* and *monumenta*:
those durative (the latter term evokes a coy materiality) products of literary
production through which Scipio might have established for himself a
similarly durative textual existence.[72]
This "textualizing" use of *munus* appears again at the end of the third
book. In what is for us an eerily self-referential valediction, the author
exhorts his son:

[71] Cf. *Ep. Fam.* 9.2, written to Varro in 46: . . . *si minus in curia atque in foro, at in litteris et libris, ut
doctissimi ueteres fecerunt, gubernare rem publicam et de moribus et legibus quaerere.*
[72] Cicero is our first late Republican source for *monumentum* used to refer to the literary text (cf. too *de
Orat.* 1.66.201; 2.12.53; *Brut.* 7.28; 13.52; *Acad. Post.* 1), but the term is used frequently in this manner
in the Augustan and Imperial periods, as at Hor. *Odes* 3.30.1–2; cf. Habinek 1998: 110. A fragment of
the *Origines* points up the natural duality of *monumenta*, and the kinship between physical object
and written word: *propter eius uirtutes omnis Graecia gloriam atque gratiam praecipuam claritudinis
inclitissimae decorauere monumentis: signis, statuis, elogiis, historiis aliisque rebus gratissimum id eius
factum habuere* (Cato, *Orig.* fr. 83 Peter). Of this use of *monumentum*, Feldherr 1998: 21, 22 remarks,
"As a means of preserving the memory of events – a *monumentum* – written history could be classed
together with the paintings, statues, and dedications that created a visible record of a military
victory or other great deed."

Habes a patre munus, Marce fili, mea quidem sententia magnum, sed perinde erit,
ut acceperis. quamquam hi tibi tres libri inter Cratippi commentarios tamquam
hospites erunt recipiendi; sed, ut, si ipse uenissem Athenas (quod quidem esset
factum, nisi me e medio cursu clara uoce patria reuocasset), aliquando me quoque
audires, sic, quoniam his uoluminibus ad te profecta uox est mea, tribues iis
temporis quantum poteris, poteris autem quantum uoles. cum uero intellexero te
hoc scientiae genere gaudere, tum et praesens tecum propediem, ut spero, et, dum
aberis, absens loquar. uale igitur, mi Cicero . . . (*de Off.* 3.33.121)

So here, my son Marcus, you have a *munus* from your father – and not a bad one,
at least in my opinion: but its true worth will depend upon your reception. *Though
of course, you should receive these three books among your notes on Cratippus just as if
they were three guest-friends come to visit.* But, just as you would listen to me now
and again if I had come to Athens (I was halfway there, and would be there now,
if my fatherland had not called me back with voice sounding clear), so commit as
much time as you are able to these volumes, in which my own voice is set out for
you: and you will be able to commit just as much time as you desire. And when
I see that you take pleasure in this branch of inquiry, then I will talk with you
further – soon, I hope, and in your presence; but as long as you are abroad, *I will
speak through my text* [*absens loquar*]. So, farewell, my Cicero . . .

In designating his dedicated text a *munus*, Cicero encodes it – in a
way he must have expected both his son and subsequent readers to have
recognized – as a textual gift that responds to a request and initiates, in
its giving, the expectation for future such exchanges (is Cicero initiating
his son into the textual world or at any rate grooming him for the sorts
of textual exchange in which he will be expected to participate?). As with
Catullus' use of *munus* as a marker of both exchangeability and materialization (and we shall get to more of these momentarily), here the emphasis on
the physical distance between donor and dedicatee underlines the treatise's
function as a social and affective object. *Munus* here refers not just to the
act of writing or the ideas contained within the treatise, but to the physical
texts themselves: they are something for the young Marcus to have (*habere*)
and receive (*accipere*; *recipere*). They are the material keepsakes of his absent
father, a written voice that can stand in for the spoken. But this is not all.
In these lines, Cicero expands on the idea of the textual *munus* and actually
personifies his textual product. As Catullus' textual gifts from Calvus (c. 14)
and his *sodales* (c. 12)[73] could themselves represent the affective relationships between the poet and his comrades, here Cicero exhorts his son to
receive the three books of *de Officiis* as if they were guest-friends – *tamquam
hospites* – sent from his father. As the value of Catullus' *linteum* (c. 12) or

---

[73] So in c. 14 Calvus' "*munus*" to Catullus – a *horribilis libellus* – is later personified, and apostrophized,
in the poet's valediction: *uos hinc interea ualete abite . . . pessimi poetae* (ll. 21–23).

Calvus' textual joke (c. 14) was fixed by the friend's "in group" understanding of the spirit in which they were sent, the value of *de Officiis* is grounded
in the spirit in which the young Marcus will receive it. By first emphasizing the physicality of the exchanged text, Cicero is then able to create a
munus that is a stand-in for its author, a textual representative of the social
obligations that exist between donor and recipient. At the immediate level,
the return due Cicero's *munus* will be the promised future conversation, a
revoicing of the "inscribed word" that is constituted by the text. However,
Cicero also presents the dedication – and the valediction – as one from one
generation to the next, and imagines that he will receive from his son and
all future readers a reciprocal, and perhaps textual, remuneration.[74]

In the textual Society of the late Republic, *munus* signals a text that
has been created for the specific purpose of simultaneously initiating and
repaying a return in kind. The textual *munus* of the late Republic was a gift
that *needed* to keep on giving. And in order to do this, it needed to move
beyond the category of gift and into the category of debt.

FROM GIFT-EXCHANGE TO DEBT-EXCHANGE

In his own formulation of the word, Cicero emphasizes his familiarity
with – and interpretation of – the rules of what we might designate a kind
of "Hesiodic reciprocity." The opening passages of *Brutus* designate the
dialogue a *munus* intended for Atticus (in repayment for an historical work
presumably dedicated to the orator, cf. *Brut.* 4.15; the "double dedication"
of this dialogue is discussed in Chapter 6) and outline the "debt-exchange"
in which this text participates in explicitly Hesiodic terms:

> . . . Ipsa mihi tractatio litterarum salutaris fuit admonuitque, Pomponi, ut a te
> ipso sumerem aliquid ad me reficiendum teque remunerandum si non pari, at
> grato tamen munere: quamquam illud Hesiodium laudatur a doctis, quod eadem
> mensura reddere iubet qua acceperis aut etiam cumulatiore, si possis. (*Brut.* 4.15)

> . . . That treatise [of yours] cured me of my ills, Pomponius, and advised that I
> follow your cue, and remake myself; and that I return your favor with one of my
> own – if it is not a *munus* of equal value, it will at any rate be a welcome one.
> Albeit, the learned think highly of that Hesiodic saw: that it is best for you to
> return by a measure equal to that which you receive – and even more abundantly,
> if you can.

[74] As noted above, Cicero uses the term in this sense in the dedicatory letter for the first book of
Academica (*Ep. Fam.* 9.8.1) and the early sections of *Brutus* (4.15); it is used similarly in the prologue
of *Cato* (1.2; [44 BCE]). In each case, the emphasis is on the reciprocal and obligatory exchange of
literary and, by extension, social value.

The reference is a clever one: for whereas the orator first hopes only to repay Atticus with a *munus* that is "welcome, if not of equal value," he then adduces the precepts of archaic Greek reciprocity in order to suggest that the reciprocal tradition he is adducing is one that entails an inevitable accumulation of affective – and for Cicero, textual – interest. It is unclear to what extent the naming of the "Hesiodic saw" (*illud Hesiodium*) would have been necessary for Cicero's imagined audience. But that he makes it is significant, as the final lines of the clause – *eadem mensura reddere . . . aut etiam cumulatiore, si possis* – are not merely a reference to *Works and Days* 349–350, but a near translation of the second of these lines:

> εὖ μὲν μετρεῖσθαι παρὰ γείτονος, εὖ δ᾽ ἀποδοῦναι,
> αὐτῶι τῶι μέτρωι, καὶ λώϊον, αἴ κε δύνηαι . . .
>
> Take well from your neighbor, and return well, too,
> by the very same measure, and even better, if you can . . .

But if it is l. 350 that is paraphrased in *Brutus*, we might imagine that it is the next line – a line either wryly or tactfully omitted from *illud Hesiodium* – that Cicero knew would have resonated with an audience either familiar with, or with access to, the original. For this is the line that explains the underlying value of a "return with interest," and it gets at the heart of both textual reciprocity, and of Cicero's own personal and political situation in the mid 40s:

> ὡς ἂν χρηίζων καὶ ἐς ὕστερον ἄρκιον εὕρηις.
> So you might find him reliable, should you be in future need.

The *Brutus* passage then expands metaphorically upon the theme of *Works and Days* in terms that meld the agricultural with the textual. Cicero has no "first fruits" (*nouis fructibus*) with which to make his repayment, for his fields – the forum? – have withered and died. Nor can he offer a gift from his storehouses (*conditis*), as they are now consigned to darkness and his entrance to them has been blocked (*aditus . . . obstructus est*). He must start entirely anew:

Seremus igitur aliquid tamquam in inculto et derelicto solo; quid ita diligenter colemus, ut impendiis etiam augere possimus largitatem tui muneris. (*Brut.* 4.16)

I am, then, sowing something new, as if in an uncultivated and neglected field; and I shall care for it so diligently that I will be able to repay the generosity of your *munus* – with interest.

The references to parched fields and locked storehouses point to what Cicero perceives (to a large extent, quite rightly) as the death of his political and forensic career. He had not delivered a public oration since *pro Milone* of 52, and had become increasingly estranged from the forum that had offered him his most fertile material for publication. What Cicero is able to offer instead – his "new crop" sown in an "uncultivated field" – is the textually innovative *Brutus*: a dialogue set not in the shadowy past and shady venue of a *suburbana uilla* (as was *de Oratore*, published in 54), but in the vibrant present and the middle of the *urbs* from which the orator had become recently alienated. In his receipt of a text through which he might "remake" himself (*ad me reficiendum*), he is able to script for his future not only a new sort of literary venture[75] but one that carries with it, in the agricultural and economic language with which it is expressed, the unspoken expectation of an ongoing cycle of escalating reciprocity and alliance. Return in better measure, so that your neighbor is useful to you in the future.

We are not to imagine that Hesiod's somewhat cynical demystification of gift- (or rather, debt-) exchange lies at the root of Cicero's overarching plan for his personal, political, and social redemption through an aggressive scheme of textual reciprocity. In drawing attention to the possibilities for socioeconomic (remade here as sociotextual) increase implicit in such exchange Cicero asserts a cultural and literary pedigree for the historically "poetic" venture on which he is about to set out. In evoking the specter of a foundationally archaic cycle of favor and debt, and in fortifying this image with the language of ongoing agricultural increase, fertility, and prestation, Cicero situates his textual exchanges *in medias res*. *Brutus*, then, a dialogue designated a textual *munus* on more than one occasion,[76] is not merely a gift or repayment of favor: it carries with it an authoritative and socially sanctioned obligation of return. It is simultaneously the payment and receipt of debt.

If *Brutus* 4.15–16 seems to constitute Cicero's first attempt to endow his textual experiment with an element of archaic literary authority, it is far from the only one. It will be useful here, then, to take a quick detour into Cicero's subsequent expansion of the theme of productive textual *munera*. In his discussion of the economics of generosity in the first book of *de*

---

[75] One might think here of the terms by which he described his new oratorical venture at *pro Archia* 3, discussed above.

[76] Cf. *Parad. Stoic.* 5, also dedicated to Brutus: *Accipies igitur hoc paruum opusculum lucubratum his contractioribus noctibus* [of the *Parad. Stoic.*], *quoniam illud maiorum uigiliarum munus* [of *Brutus*] *in tuo nomine apparuit...*

Officiis, Cicero expands on the Hesiodic passage and produces a metrical echo of the original:

Quodsi ea, quae utenda acceperis, maiore mensura, si modo possis, iubet reddere Hesiodus, quidnam beneficio prouocati facere debemus? (*de Off.* 1.48)

But if, as Hesiod says, you should return in greater measure, if only you can, what you borrow in need, what are we to do when provoked with a favor?[77]

The phrase *si modo possis* both reasonably translates, and stands as the metrical equivalent of, the original αἴ κε δύνηαι: the *modo* alone ("if only you can") breaks from the original. But this is likely not so much a mark of uncertainty – an implication that perhaps you can't – so much as it is an addition *metri causa*, made precisely to turn the reader's mind (and perhaps eyes) to a further consideration of the original from which it comes. A letter to Atticus, dating from 45, engages in a more linguistically explicit theorizing of "Hesiodic reciprocity" and the ways in which this reciprocity might add a degree of authority to Cicero's present endeavors. He has anguished at length, we learn, over his hopes of entering into a relationship of textual exchange with his Varro:

... Ego autem me parabam ad id quod ille mihi misisset, ut αὐτῶι τῶι μέτρωι, καὶ λώϊον, si modo potuissem. nam hoc etiam Hesiodus ascribit, 'αἴ κε δύνηαι ...' (*Ep. Att.* 13.12.3 (45 BCE))

So, I was readying myself for what he would have sent me, that I might make a return in the very same measure, and even better, if only I could. For Hesiod *does* add, "if you can ... "

Here the line is quoted in full,[78] and there can be no doubt as to Cicero's conceived partnership of Hesiod's precepts and his ideas about the workings of the textual world he has entered. In the end, Cicero decides that he will dedicate to Varro his newly composed *Academica Posteriora*, for it contains *Antiochia* – the teachings of Antiochus of Ascalon, with whom Cicero had studied and with whose philosophy both Varro and Brutus had identified themselves – of which the dedicatee is expected to approve. In a letter that later serves as the dedication of this treatise, Cicero first refers to the dedication he himself awaits from Varro

---

[77] Cicero frequently couples the verbs *reddere* and *accipere* in his discussions of aristocratic exchange; in addition to these passages, see especially *Cato* 51 (again in an agricultural metaphor: *redit quod accepit*), and *Lael.* 26: *id acciperet ab alio uicissimque redderet* and 58: *ne plus reddat quam acceperit*.

[78] It is likely, I think, that the *si modo potuissem* of this letter – here clearly indicating an uncertainty as to the worth of his planned textual exchange – influenced the later metrical version of *de Officiis* 1.48.

as a *munus* (*etsi munus flagitare . . . ne populus quidem solet, Ep. Fam.* 9.8.1) and then, engaging in a provocative personification of the *Academica*, reviews, "Hesiodically," the rules of textual exchange – including the reasonable and excessive dilation of return – by which the two are bound:

> Misi autem ad te quattuor admonitores non nimis uerecundos . . . ex ea igitur media [Academiae] excitatos misi, qui metuo ne te forte flagitent; ego autem mandaui ut rogarent. expectabam omnino iamdiu, meque sustinebam, ne ad te prius ipse quid scriberem, quam aliquid accepissem, ut possem te remunerari quam simillimo munere . . . (*Ep. Fam.* 9.8.1 (45 BCE))

> But I've sent you four "reminders" [of your debt], ones not overly bashful . . . I shook them out from the midst of the Academy, and sent them off, and I fear they may make a demand of you – though I ordered them merely to ask. At any rate, I've been waiting for a long time now, and have held myself in check lest I write something to you before I have received a text, so that I might repay you with a *munus* as like yours as possible . . .

In the middle years of the Republic, then, the term *munus* was not only notionally linked with a poetic archetype of reciprocity; it worked together with this archetype to provide the lexical and socioeconomic framework upon which the textual exchange of gift – reworked, now, as a textual exchange of patronal debt – might be built.[79]

THE IMPERIAL *NACHLEBEN* OF *MUNUS*

Munus is an important poetic word for writers of the Principate and Empire, but it is only sparingly used to designate dedicated texts and – this may speak to the shift in the nature of textual dedication in the Republic – only rarely in the actual dedication. It appears most frequently to mean simply "gift," and often one that may be bestowed by a superior, or a god, or nature, or in a situation in which there is no clear sense of expected return (Hor. *Odes* 1.18.7; 4.10.1; at Ovid *Trist.* 1.1.20, the fact that he lives is a *munus dei*; cf. *Trist.* 2.11.49, however, where

---

[79] Although the dedicated dialogue would never reach the height of popularity that Cicero had perhaps envisioned in his final years, the late Republican formulation of *munus*-exchange extends well into the Imperial period. In a detailed discussion of social *beneficia*, Seneca echoes the language of the *technica* and letters, but by this time the sentiment of reciprocity seems to have been fully filtered through the language and imagery of the Republic. *Illud Hesiodium* has been utterly contained within philosophical doctrine, and what we have now is the exchange not of a text but of a person (*de Ben.* 1.8.1): *cui Socrates: 'quidni tu' inquit 'magnum munus mihi dederis, nisi forte te paruo aestimas? habebo itaque curae, ut te meliorum tibi reddam quam accepi.'* A Senecan theorizing of the temporal aspects of *munus* is addressed below.

the remunerative aspect of the term is made clear); and when it appears in the plural – as it frequently does – it is often in the erotic sense of "love-gifts" that we can trace back to the middle Republic (e.g., Verg. *Ecl.* 2.56–57; Prop. 1.3.25–26; 2.16.15; Tib. 1.8.29; 1.9.11–12). *Munus* is occasionally linked to the production of poetry; but the link is often not made explicit (Hor. *Odes* 4.3.21; Verg. *Ecl.* 5.53), and even when it is, the *munera* seem to be taken as precisely non-textual gifts that will be received in exchange for a poet's works (Hor. *Odes* 4.8.11–12;[80] Mart. *Ep.* 1.111; at 13.3, the point is that the distiches may be given *instead of* an edible *munus*).

Martial, who I feel is in many ways one of the most "textually interested" authors of the early Empire and who is certainly the most clued in to late Republican textual argot, stands out in this later period for designating his dedicated texts *munera*. Because I plan to address Martial's use of Republican argot and textual form – especially as it appears in the context of textual dedications and collections – in a subsequent study, I will give here just a brief summary of what we see. At *Ep.* 3.2, Martial dedicates a *libellus* to Faustinus[81] (or rather asks the *libellus* whose *munus* it would like to be, and compliments the choice) in playfully Catullan language. But whereas the first line (*cuius uis fieri, libelli, munus?*) would seem, according to late Republican argot, to set up an expectation of textual reciprocity, the second line (*festina tibi uindicem parare*) seems to quickly – and with the heavy-handed use of *uindex*, which is repeated at the end of the poem, somewhat pointedly – undercut the possibility of any such exchange. At *Ep.* 4.10, Martial again designates his *libellus* (l. 1) a *munus* (ll. 3 and 6) to Faustinus, and he again avoids direct address to his dedicatee, this time instructing a slave (*puer*, l. 3) to convey the light volume to his dear friend (*caro perfer leue munus amico*, l. 3), and at *Ep.* 5.15, addressed to the Emperor, he notes that no man has complained of being harmed by his invectives (*ioci*), but rather that the reader delights to see his name thus honored, and gains "deathless fame" (*uictura . . . fama*, l. 4) by his textual *munus*. Martial is savvy as to what it means to apply *munus* to textual dedications and addresses, but he is also aware that textual *munera* written for a patron and under an emperor fulfill a different social function than they had in the years when this designation had first been made.

---

[80] *Gaudes carminibus; carmina possumus / donare et pretium dicere munus.* Horace's use of *donare*, a verb that never expects a return gift, and the economically loaded *pretium* seems to speak to the hierarchically conceived exchanges that mark the textual production in the later periods.

[81] On Martial's relationship with Faustinus, see e.g. Sullivan 1991: 18.

Writing somewhat earlier, and in the dangerous literary and political world that emerged under Nero, Seneca – an heir to the late Republican (and especially Ciceronian) practice of textual dedication and exchange and an active producer of his own brand of dialogue – theorizes the dynamics of *munera*-exchange in terms that will be good to keep in mind as we move on from this section:

Quidam, cum aliquod illis missum est munusculum, subinde aliud intempestiue remittent et nihil se debere testantur; reiciendi genus est protinus aliud in uicem mittere et munus munere expungere. (Sen. *de Ben.* 4.40.4)

Some people, when they are sent an insignificant *munus* of some kind or other, send one back straight away and with no sense of timing, and claim that they don't owe anything; it constitutes a kind of rejection to make an immediate return, to obliterate *munus* with *munus*.

The problem with this premature reciprocation, Seneca goes on to explain, is that an exchange relationship of this sort (durative, affectionate, isonomic, useful) requires the participants to place themselves in a position of relative obligation and, by extent, emotional vulnerability. The state of being indebted to another – of owing a *munus* to one from whom a *munus* has been received – places one in a kind of social jeopardy, an erotically tinged vacillation between servitude and power. But it is through this state of vulnerability, this state of being in another's "debt," that the affective relationship, within which *munera* are exchanged, is able to accrue interest. A debt paid off immediately settles all accounts. One that is carefully drawn out is able to increase both the underlying value – credit – of the relationship it serves and the imagined "worth" of the eventual return-gift. The timing of the transaction, as Seneca notes, is key. A too-speedy return of gift or favor (an intimate present met immediately with a return; a casual loan paid back within hours) can come off as either disaffective in its zeal to discharge all obligation – "OK, are we even now?" – or, worse yet, an intentional commoditization of the relationship as a whole.[82] A debt carried overlong (a dinner invitation never reciprocated; a friendly email left unanswered; the promise of a dedication put off too long, cf. *Ep. Fam.* 9.8.1), however, can similarly degrade the underlying relationship precisely by ignoring the reciprocal rules by which it is structured. I do not want to suggest that we can apply Seneca's remarkably perceptive theorizing to the textual community of the late Republic whole-cloth. But Seneca was a

---

[82] cf. Sen. *de Ben.* 4.40.4: *et, ut breuiter, qui nimis cupit soluere, inuitus debet; qui inuitus debet, ingratus est.*

man deeply interested in how the social formulations of the late Republic had shifted – or maintained – in the period in which he wrote, and as we move on to consider what happens to a text that is conceived of as a *munus*, and especially the ways in which Catullus and Cicero play with the notion of request, hesitation, and the passage of time, Seneca's formulation is suggestive of the Imperial interpretation of Republican textual reciprocity.

CHAPTER 3

Where? Libellus: *polished and published*

For modern scholars, Catullus has done for *libellus* what Jawaharlal Nehru has done for the jacket, what Coco Chanel has done for the Little Black Dress, and what Flava Flav[1] has done for wearing a full-sized wall clock around one's neck. He has transformed fashion into a social signifier and, in so doing, has made it eternally his own. But as much as the poet has come to be identified with the term – and seems credited, though wrongly, with its earliest usage[2] – he uses it only four times in the whole of his corpus: twice in the dedication to Nepos (c. 1.1; 1.8), once in the context of an unwanted gift of a book (c. 14.12), and once – probably – to indicate an area of bookshops or booksellers' stalls (c. 55.4).[3] Even in the dedication to Nepos, it is unclear exactly what the *libellus* included.[4] Contemporary evidence (cf. too Cinna's *libellus*, noted below) suggests that *libellus* could have designated a single long poem (introduced by a dedicatory poem), or a collection of many poems, or anything in between. A passage of Tacitus'

---

[1] Flava Flav, born William Drayton (1959) and a classically trained pianist, is best known as the comically flamboyant, and highly talented, rap artist of the politically progressive group Public Enemy. His trademark accoutrement of the large clock worn around his neck – so those who see him will know "what time it is" (that is, the current social and political situation of which they should be aware) – is in hip-hop circles so fully associated with this performer that the wearing of a neck-clock alone marks one as definitively (and I apologize for the adjective) "Flavian." Although this last example might seem somewhat the furthest from the Catullan appropriation of *libellus*, Flav's use of the clock as a social and political signifier – a claim as to his own relative position vis-à-vis the political status quo – allies itself rather nicely with Catullus' lexical claim on the marked tonality of *libellus*.

[2] This seems the point of Strodach 1933: 29.

[3] The line is problematic: *te in Circo, te in omnibus libellis [quaesiuimus]*. Various emendations have been suggested (among which are the unsatisfactory *ligellis, tabernis,* and *tabellis*), but if the term is taken here to indicate "bookshops" (at the risk of Imperial retrojection, Mart. *Ep.* 5.2.8 may be useful) then we have with the plural *libelli* a clever geographical extension of the singular *libellus*. On this see further Thomson 1997: 336 and Wiseman 1980.

[4] On *libellus* and c. 1, cf. Singleton 1972. The bibliography on c. 1 is extensive; cf. e.g. Cairns 1969; Clausen 1976; Elder 1966; Thomson 1997: 200–201 provides a fuller bibliography.

Dialogus[5] links the distribution of *libelli* with private recitations of poetry; as such, it may have been something of an "audience handout" that served also as first-run copies of an author's latest works (*Sest.* 51.110, cited below, see note 12, may support this reading). Although we want to be careful about applying later formulations of the word to the earlier period, *libellus* is the most fixed of the textual terms we are considering; from the middle Republic[6] to the early Empire, it connotes the publication or sharing of texts. It seems not inconceivable that the dedication to Nepos[7] might have prefaced a private recitation of a selection of "new poems" or that, alternatively, it was later appended to a written version of such a selection as a matter of affection and gratitude. In the end, of course, we simply do not know enough about the circumstances surrounding the dedication of c. 1, or the broader publication of Catullus' poems, under whatever title they may have circulated, to do more than speculate. I do not, then, propose we abandon the catchphrase "Catullan *libellus*," but if we wish to get at the nuances of this word in the late Republic, we need to shelve our Catullan *libellus*, as it were, and examine some contemporary but non-Catullan uses of the term.

Varro and Cinna each use *libellus*. Varro uses the term twice: once to describe some published books of Lucius Abucius (*DRR* 3.2), and once of his own *Antiquitates*;[8] Cinna (fr. 11) designates his translation of Aratus as an *aridulus libellus* ("nicely polished publication"). Cicero, the only other Republican author to use *libellus*, uses the term with greater frequency. It appears first in his earliest surviving oration, *pro Quinctio* (81 BCE), in reference to public placards and bills of sale.[9] In the *Verrines*

---

[5] *Dial.* 9.3, *hi [uersus] enim Basso domi nascuntur, pulchri quidem et iucundi, quorum tamen hc exitus est, ut cum toto anno, per omnes dies, magna noctium parte unum librum excudit et elucubrauit, rogare ultro et ambire cogatur ut sint qui dignentur audire, et ne id quidem gratis: nam et domum mutuatur et auditorium exstruit et subsellia conducit et libellos dispergit.* Mayer 2001: 115 suggests that *libelli* here might indicate "invitations," but he seems unconvinced. The term could also mean something like "programs" (which for some reason Mayer feels would amount to the same thing as an invitation), and I believe this is on the right track. The passage entails a narrowing of spatial focus and a span of time leading straight up to the recitation: borrow a house; outfit an auditorium; drag in the couches; distribute the *libelli*. The suggestion that the *libelli* in this passage *could* refer to brief written invitations to a recitation (Mayer cites Pliny *Ep.* 3.18.4) is not compelling. The thrust of the passage seems to be that the *libelli* are placed (on the couches?) within the auditorium just prior to the recitation.

[6] *Libellus* appears in New Comedy only once, at Plaut. *Pseud.* 706, of a writing that is shared with another: *in libello hoc obsignato ad te attuli pauxillulo.*

[7] Nepos published a text later called a *libellus* (Suet. *Gramm.* 4); he does not use the term of his own writings, but the sense adheres.

[8] Cf. Varro, *Ant.* Cardauns fr. 204: *cum in hoc libello dubias de diis opiniones posuero, reprehendi non debeo . . .*

[9] Cf. *Quinct.* 6.27; 15.50; 19.61; 20.63; 22.73. For this use, cf. Petron. 28.

(70 BCE)[10] a request to bring forth a set of two *libelli* as material witnesses for unlawful export activity is strangely predictive (in language, if not in meaning) of Catullus' dedicatory poem:[11]

Sed tamen quicquid erit in his libellis, quantulumcumque uidebitur esse, hoc quidem certe manifestum erit: (*Verr.* 2.2.183 (70 BCE))

But whatever is contained in these *libelli*, and however unimportant it might seem to be, this at least will be clear:

The sense here is not so much dismissive as it is technical: these are documents that are to be brought forth as evidence in court; to be put in the hands of the public (and in the case of the *Actio Secunda*, this is of course a reading public alone) in order to be evaluated for their contents. The emphasis in all of these earliest uses of the term is one of publication, differentiation, and evaluation: these *libelli* are not "little books." They are written documents of various lengths that are designated *libelli* because of their social function as texts potentially accessible to a broader circle of readers.[12]

In the *technica*, the term appears frequently, and is used to refer in general to rhetorical or philosophical "handbooks" written specifically for publication and circulation.[13] It seems that Cicero is occasionally uncomfortable with the idea of patronal-class individuals participating in the production and broader circulation of *libelli* (though he uses the term of his *Philippics* at *Ep. Brut.* 2.4, so by later in life any discomfort has vanished), and this is certainly the sense he gives in Antonius' admission that he had published a *libellus* of his own (*de Orat.* 1.21.94, discussed below). The point is not, I think, that *libelli* might not constitute "serious intellectual endeavors," but patronal composition and publication (to whatever degree it occurred) had

---

[10] In addition to the passage cited in the text, cf e g. 1.6.17 (of a list of names); the term appears again immediately following 2.2.183 and with the same meaning.

[11] C. 1.8–9: *quidquid hoc libelli / qualecumque.*

[12] Cf. *Arch.* 26: *ipsi illi philosophi, etiam in eis libellis quos de contemnenda gloria scribunt, nomen suum inscribunt: in eo ipso, in quo praedicationem nobilitatemque despiciunt, praedicari de se ac nominari uolunt.* The emphasis on the philosopher's desire for named authorship and the renown that that might engender seems, to me, clear indication that these *libelli* are intended to be published – circulated outside of a self-selecting group of literati – rather than merely exchanged among peers. As early as 62 BCE, the term is used to indicate philosophical texts written specifically for public circulation of some sort, and some years later, in *pro Sestio* (56 BCE), Cicero uses the term to indicate the textual "commerce" implicit in convivial activity (*libelli pro uino etiam saepe oppignerabantur,* *Sest.* 51.110).

[13] Cf. e.g. *de Orat.* 1.19.85 and 3.30.122 (both uses are vaguely dismissive, and the second is Cicero's only collocation of *libellus* with *munus,* though the latter term is used with the sense of "task," or "duty" and not "text"); *de Fin.* 4.22; *TD* 3.43. To these, cf. the term at *Arch.* 26 (cited above) and *Ep. Fam.* 5.12.7; *libellus* is used for "account book," *Ep. Att.* 6.1.5.

a sound Republican history of which Cicero was surely aware. The anxious and vaguely dismissive tone that comes out in Cicero's use of *libellus* may, I think, point to his awareness that patronal-class publication was on the rise in the late Republic and, perhaps, to his own desire to enter into this practice on a broader scale.

It might be suggested that the derogatory force of *libellus* as it appears occasionally in the *technica* is to be expected from the diminutive, and this is worth consideration. But the potentially derogatory valence of the diminutive is neither strictly nor simplistically critical: it always casts its criticism in terms of opposed – or at least, contested – spheres of evaluation, and stakes a claim, by way of that criticism, to ownership or expulsion in an explicit or implied group. In the case of *libellus*, the directionality of derogation is invariably aimed at the uncomfortable fact that these texts have entered into more or less broad publication; the recognition of this directionality gives us a better sense of the late Republican *libellus* as a whole. When a text moves out of strict authorial control and enters the public world – when it is "published" – it makes itself, and its author, vulnerable to the suspicious gaze of consumers and critics. Its identity as the valued product of a textually savvy "in crowd" become contestable, and when our late Republican authors choose to mark a text as participating in such context, they do so with the diminutive.

In a strange passage of *de Oratore*, occurring toward the end of the first round of verbal banter between Antonius and Crassus, the former is made to note that he once (unwillingly!) published a "certain *libellus*" on the matter of eloquence and the men who possess it:

Tumque ego, hac eadem opinione adductus, scripsi etiam illud quodam in libello, qui me imprudente et inuito excidit, et peruenit in manus hominum, disertos me cognosse nonnullos . . . (*de Orat.* 1.21.94 (54 BCE))

And so, since I had been led to this very view, I went so far as to write down in a certain *libellus* – which slipped away from me without my knowledge or permission, and fell into the hands of the people – that I had known a certain number of eloquent men . . .

That Antonius should have published at all is meant to come as a surprise. It is true that Cicero plays up, only to knock down, Antonius' reputation as an uneducated man of action throughout the dialogue;[14] but Antonius' claim to have engaged in this endeavor targets the social and

---

[14] This is just the first of many such references; at the beginning of the second book Cicero refers to the youthful *opinio* that Antonius was *omnino omnis eruditionis expertem atque ignarum.*

textual sensibilities of the imagined audience. Although we can be sure that at least some patronal-class men were writing and publishing their texts in 91 BCE (the dramatic date of the dialogue), Cicero – perhaps in an effort to make his own publication of a dialogue seem all the more innovative to readers in 54 BCE – is careful to represent Antonius' publication as an accident, and something of an embarrassment; not, in other words, the sort of thing men like Antonius went around bragging about. Indeed, this dialogue promotes (and subsequently undermines) what may have been a "gentlemen's agreement" that idle discussion and written theorizing on the topic of rhetoric (we might include philosophy and politics) constituted a foreign and effeminate perversion of active involvement in oratorical life.[15] As Cicero presents it, the received view of *otium*-inspired conversation and composition was associated, as late as 91, with the kind of luxurious and non-political Greek learning that found no favor with a patronal class defined by its active involvement in the political life of the Republic. Indeed throughout *de Oratore*, Cicero makes clear his interlocutors' acquaintance with, and polite disdain for, both Greek learning and the literature produced by it. But we should not be so quick to take Cicero's word for it; for just as he has Antonius and Crassus – the very *maiores* of his *mos maiorum* – express disdain for leisurely conversation and composition, he writes a dialogue that acts out precisely such activity and, in the *persona* of Antonius, reveals that although patronal-class individuals may long have denied interest in composition and publication it was certainly an activity in which they had long engaged.

Indeed, as *de Oratore* (and the many *technica* that include defenses of Latin literature in their early sections[16]) is largely about the importance of writing – oratorical, philosophical, or political – as a powerful social mechanism, it is essential that Cicero establish early in the dialogue a solid Roman pedigree for upper-class discussion, composition, and publication of rhetorical theory. Thus Antonius' self-interrupting admission of having

---

[15] Cf. Crassus' reluctance to speak at 1.22.102: *quid? mihi nunc uos . . . tamquam alicui Graeculo otioso et loquaci, et fortasse docto atque erudito quaestiunculam . . . ponitis?* To this compare 1.47.221: *ineptum et Graeculum . . .* and Juvenal 3.78: *Graeculus esuriens.* Of Roman involvement in Greek studies, Zanker 1995: 212 suggests that, "In the Roman imagination, the cultivation of Greek literature was desirable, but only as a means for perfecting one's skills in public speaking or one's style in the writing of history." This is certainly what Cicero would have his readers believe, but it does not jibe with the picture of the late Republican textual world.

[16] This is one of the main threads that run throughout the *technica*, and the diologic remaking of Greek prototype is indeed one of Cicero's most powerful influences on the dialogues and epistolary practice of the Prinicipate and Empire. For defenses of Latin literature in the dialogues of Cicero, see esp. *de Leg., Brutus, Opt. Gen., Parad. Stoic., Part. Orat., Acad. Post., de Fin., TD, DND*, and *Top.*

written for publication (*scripsi etiam illud*), his anxious decentering of the composition as a "certain *libellus*" (*quidam libellus*), and his well-bred (if slightly overplayed) horror at its publication (*imprudente et inuito excidit*) adhere to the rhetorically established topos of a genteel reluctance to speak, much less write, professionally – even as they turn this topos soundly on its head. For once he has admitted to the writing and publication of this text (to which Cicero refers twice again: 1.67.206, 3.49.189[17]), he proceeds happily with a short description of its contents (1.2.94–95). To a certain extent, of course, it is Cicero who truly "publishes," and who indeed possibly "wrote," the *libellus* he attributes to Antonius in these lines (we do not know that such a *libellus* did not in fact exist, but we do not know that it did); it may well be through *de Oratore* alone that "Antonius'" oratorical opinions have fallen into the hands of men. But in positing a tradition of such rhetorical *libelli* at least three decades old at the time of the publication of *de Oratore*, Cicero fabricates a textual heirloom – politically active patronal-class men casually engaging in textual production and publication – that fits perfectly with the needs of his program of 54. He is tying his "modern" manufacture (in 54) of the artistic rhetorical treatise – the fictitious dialogue – to the ancient authority of literary composition and circulation.

As Hanssen and others have noted, the Latin diminutive carries almost endless valences and (like the English) is only rarely indicative of absolute (or even relative) physical "size."[18] Both Cicero and Catullus use diminutives enthusiastically,[19] but neither author's use of *libellus* means "a small book" any more than Cicero's use of *lectulum* at *Cat.* 1.4.9 (*qui . . . in meo*

---

[17] *de Orat.* 1.67.206: *quid si, inquit Crassus . . . petimus ab Antonio, ut ea, quae contineat, neque adhuc protulit, ex quibus unum libellum sibi excidisse iamdudum questus est, explicet nobis, et illa dicendi mysteria enuntiet?* At 3.49.189 Antonius is made again to emphasize that the *libellus* is one he himself wrote, and here there is no reference to anxiety at its publication: *ego uero, inquit Antonius, inueni iam, quem negaram in eo, quem scripsi, libello me inuenisse eloquentem.*

[18] Cf. Hanssen 1952: 45–47; on the diminutive, see further the studies of Hakamies 1951, who makes the unconvincing claim that a *libellus* is at its core an "*acte judiciare, titre*" (p. 121), and Strodach 1933, who is dead-on in his observation that *libellus* is a diminutive that indicates a specific relationship with its primitive (p. 32), but whose suggestion that *libellus* meant originally "a book written in pages" (p. 33, argued from Suet. *Iul.* 56, *epistulae quoque eius ad senatum extant, quas primum uidetur ad paginas et formam memorialis libelli conuertisse . . .*) is not compelling. It may be that some *libelli* of the Republic constituted notebooks in "page form" and were used for drafts and accounts (this is possibly the sense at *Ep. Att.* 6.1.5), but Martial (*Ep.* 1.2) is the first Roman author to refer to literary works written thusly; page-form publication is indicated by the phrase *breuibus membrana tabellis* (l. 3), which emphasizes the material quality of the book, rather than *meos libellos* (l. 1), which specifies its social and literary function (as circulating literature).

[19] As Hakamies 1951: 36 notes, Laurand 1927–1928 has counted 244 diminutives in Cicero's orations; to this, Hakamies adds 288 in the letters, and 367 in the *technica* (by contrast, as Hakamies points out, Seneca uses 163 in his letters, 58 in his *QN*, *de Ira* and *de Ben.*, and 9 in the tragedies; Tacitus uses only 55 total). In the Catullan corpus there appear 44 substantive diminutives and another 26 in adjectival or adverbial form (cf. p. 40).

lectulo interfecturos esse pollicerentur) means "small bed," nor Catullus' use of *ocelli* at c. 3.18 means "little eyes." Indeed, such a size-specific valence would be the exception in the Republic, not the rule, as what is often at stake is desired diminution not of size but of easy availability: the diminutive is not, then, a quantitatively "small" version of its primitive, but a qualitatively "scarce," "precious," or "vulnerable" one.[20] Diminutives are often used to evoke an intimate or conversational tone[21] (they are a favorite form of New Comedy) and are thus similarly able to draw out and defend the valence of a term and thus to personalize its evaluation, a function especially important for the late Republic and later periods. Various diminutive forms are used relationally or oppositionally, in order to stake a claim as to the relationship in meaning to the primitive form ("this is a *libellus* [and not a *liber*]")[22] and to draw attention to an object as being "other than what is expected" in a way that both demands and leads to a careful evaluation of use value (so Cicero refers to his *Paradoxa Stoicorum*, dedicated to Brutus, as an *opusculum*).[23] In the application of the diminutive to possessions, the form may be used to mystify value; to conceal (if seductively) the core value of what one either possesses or desires to possess.[24]

All of these aspects of the diminutive are at play in the late Republican formation of *libellus*. But it is the appropriative function of the diminutive – the ability for the diminutive to indicate anxious special interest: to apply that special interest in a way that transforms the diminutive into something other than the primitive – that is of greatest interest to this investigation. As Hanssen and others make clear, the diminutive partakes of lexical encoding. It claims ownership of a term and hopes to control the evaluation of its quality and use (its semantic "reception") and, when it takes the form of a substantive, it places the coded object in stark relation to the primitive, both vivifying and personifying it.[25] In the case of *libellus*, I suggest, the anxiety around which this coding is constructed is over potentially large-scale literary publication: the circulation and reception of one's written text outside a sphere of competent textual fellows – out of the sphere of one's control – and into the world at large.

---

[20] Hanssen 1952: 45 notes that this sense of qualitative smallness is also at work – but in reverse – in the configuration of the so-called "derogatory" diminutive.

[21] On this cf. Strodach 1933: 32: "[Diminutives are used] in order to express a nuance not conveyed by the primitives."

[22] So Strodach 1933: 32, but cf. my note above.

[23] *Parad. Stoic.* 5: *Accipies igitur hoc paruum opusculum lucubratum his contractioribus noctibus, quoniam illud maiorum uigiliarum munus in tuo nomine apparuit . . .*

[24] Cf. Hanssen 1952: 37.   [25] Cf. Hanssen 1952: 45.

This "*libellus* designative of authorial anxiety" is at work, I think, in the vaguely dismissive tone Cicero uses in the *technica* passages discussed above: the semi-personified *libelli* of rhetoricians and philosophers are texts that have escaped from their owners' control and that now circulate, virtually autonomously, with only nominal connection to their creators (so *Arch.* 26). But we see it worked out even more strongly elsewhere in the *technica*, where the term is used to evoke a sense of intimacy and idiom (*Top.* 1, of a shared poring over library contents; cf. *Ep. Att.* 12.3.1) or benign disinterest and jovial modesty.[26] It is in the later letters, however, that the evidence gains momentum. For in those post-dating 50 BCE, and although the term continues to be used almost exclusively of books produced with the intended or collateral result of moving into publication, *libellus* seems to have lost, for Cicero at least, any glimmer of its formerly negative valence. In these writings, *libellus* is associated with textual reciprocity in general and – only after 45 BCE – the exchange of written oratorical sentiments (*causae*) in particular.[27] The term continues to connote anxiety over authorship and "out of group" publication, but by the late 40s at least it seems to function as an ameliorative idiom for a sort of literary practice that had become increasingly common.

What we see at work with *libellus* in the late Republic, then, is that in addition to the multiple valences of the diminutive of which it partakes, the term marks a text destined, at least potentially, for "publication" outside of the textual society in which it was created. It is, in short, a book made available for public consumption (and so figures frequently in introductory poems, lines, and passages), and the potential dangers implicit in this consumption – most notably, the danger of losing authorial subject status, as happened to the *poetae* of c. 12 – forces anxious significations over value and ownership. Although the term may be used dismissively when applied to works produced exterior to one's own intimate sphere, when Catullus and Cicero use it of their own texts they encode it with an intimate directive as to how the text should be received, cared for, and circulated further.

Libellus is a term of slippery hesitation. Unlike the more affectively "certain" *munus*, the socially, economically, and textually "ambiguous" *libellus* signifies, both in the late Republic and in later periods, a "book in motion"; and indeed this is the valence especially evident in Ovid (*Trist.* 1.1.9; 1.7.19 and 33; 1.11.1) and Martial (e.g., *Ep.* 1.1.1; 1.2.1; 1.4.1; 2.1.3; 2.6.1; 6.1.1; 7.3.1). A book that is in motion, however, is a book that may be in

---

[26] Cf. *de Orat.* 1.57.242; 2.55.223; *Brut.* 44.163 (of Antonius' *libellus*); *Top.* 62.

[27] Literary exchange: *Ep. Fam.* 16.183; *Ep. Att.* 6.1.3; 9.13.7; 11.1.1; 15.24.1; 16.16a.2. Exchange of the written voice: *Ep. Att.* 15.24.1; 16.16a.2; *Ep. Brut.* 3.4.4.

danger. In a book's flight from its author's direct control and ownership, and in its cautious voyage into the world beyond direct dedicatees and intimate exchange-partners – a shift from unmarked *liber* to marked *libellus* and a destabilization of authorial subject status – it is thrust into a world in which it must defend its reception even as it must recognize that that reception is open to endless and ongoing reevaluation: *quidquid hoc libelli, qualecumque.*

PART II

The textualization of display

Intersections of rhetoric and social practice (1): from display to text

> Ligarianam praeclare uendidisti. posthac quicquid scripsero tibi praeconium deferam. quod ad me de Varrone scribis, scis me antea orationes aut aliquid id genus solitum scribere ut Varronem nusquam possem intexere. postea autem quam haec coepi φιλολογώτερα, iam Varro mihi denuntiauerat magnam sane et grauem προσφώνησιν.
>
> *Ep. Att.* 13. 12. 2–3 (45 BCE)

You have done a tremendous job marketing my *pro Ligario!*[1] From here on out, whatever I write – I will leave the publicity to you. As for what you write to me of Varro, you know that in the past I have written my *orationes* – for lack of a better word – in such a way that I could never weave Varro into the tapestry. But just as I have begun these more literary pursuits, now Varro has announced that he will dedicate to me a work of some substance!

In 45 BCE, at the end of a long and successful career as an orator and shortly before his own untimely death, Cicero wrote to Atticus for advice in the matters of textual publication, composition, and exchange. These lines, in which Cicero first tips his hat to the orality of his origins (*orationes*)[2]

---

[1] On Atticus' role in the promotion of his *pro Ligario*, cf. *Ep. Att.* 13.19.2: *Ligarianam ut uideo praeclare auctoritas tua commendauit. scripsit ad me Balbus et Oppius mirifice se probare ob eamque causam ad Caesarem eam se oratiunculam misisse.* The verb *commendare*, which can of course mean merely "to bring something or someone to the favorable attention [of someone else]," is also the word used for the transfer of orphans to new custody (cf. *Verr.* 1.151) and of what seems to have been a semi-formal act of "recommending" that one individual be accepted into the *amicitia* of another (cf. *Ep. Att.* 2.22; *Ep. Fam.* 9.13; 13.6; 13.10; 13.13; 13.17, etc.; *Ep. Frat.* 1.2). That this is also one of Cicero's favored words for the act of commiting something to writing (*Phil.* 9.10; *Ep. Fam.* 5.12) should not surprise us. Catullus uses *commendare* at c. 15.1, where he transfers himself and his *amores* (ostensibly his boyfriend, but perhaps his poetry; cf. Bernstein 1985) to Aurelius.

[2] The importance of Cicero's choice of *oratio* to describe his *technica* will be discussed below, but it is worth noting at the outset that when Cicero designates his *technica* as *orationes* that are written (*scribere*), he seems to do so not merely because they profess to "contain" prior acts of discourse, but because they replace that primary act completely, and endeavor to "do" social and political work through the text alone. To this, cf. Tac. *Dial.* 9.1, where the *Dialogus* is itself designated an *oratio*, and 9.2, where we learn that the problem with Maternus' "politically interested" historical dramas is that they are not effective at establishing or strengthening social relationships. At *Lael.* 25.96 a published speech is designated an *in manibus oratio*.

and then praises the potential of his recent and more literary compositions (*haec* . . . φιλολογώτερα), embody the competing concerns that faced the textual communities of the late Republic. Even as the dedicated texts of this period claim variously to mimic (Catullus) or to replace completely (Cicero) established arenas of patronal-class display, these texts challenge, ignore, or uproot the traditional primacy of display by means of translating it into textual form.

The following chapters, then, investigate the second major intersection of Catullus and Cicero that arose in my mapping of their dedicated texts, and a second "act" in our textual story. Whereas the intersection investigated in Part I of this study was one of terminological and social code – the way each man "wrote about writing" – the intersection investigated here is one of rhetorical and sociopractical expression – most specifically, the way each man, in his own way, both engaged with the anxieties that surrounded patronal-class display and sought to contain and remake that display in his texts. The display-interested concerns addressed in this part of the study, strictly speaking, stand apart from the terminological intersections discussed above. But just as, early in my investigations, I began to notice intersections in Catullus' and Cicero's use of "textual terms," so too did I notice that each man, often via his use of terminological markers and the situational nuance that accompanies them, wrote his dedicated texts as "textualizations" of various aspects of patronal display. In so doing, each man displayed in turn his awareness that the dedicated text might provide an attractive repository for upper-class discourse, fiction, and social expectation.

An investigation into the modes and means of these textualized displays will enable us to do two things. First, we will learn more about how members of a textual community that seems to have emerged during a period of heightened convivial activity may have negotiated between modes of convivial and forensic display as they carved out a place for themselves in the increasingly active textual world of the late Republic. It would be reasonable to expect that Catullus, when he includes in his poems display representative or suggestive of the convivium, would adhere to the modes of convivial display. It would be reasonable also to expect that Cicero, when he writes his *technica* in the form of lengthy arguments on matters of political and philosophical import, would adhere to the modes of forensic display. Either of these things would be reasonable to expect, but neither of them would be completely correct. Although early convivia surely included patronal-class composition and performance of poetry, what we know of this poetry, *pace* White,[3] is that it was likely semi-historical in subject matter, probably patriotic in nature, and composed by the *conuiuae* (who were distinctly *not* "poets").[4] The textualization of leisure-time display is not without precedent in the poetic world (and we shall get to this below), but we have almost no evidence for it in the Roman world prior to Catullus; his tendency both to engage in such textualization and to set the tone of the public world against that of the private one (so cc. 10, 65, etc.) may speak to a late Republican recognition of the social power of display and a desire to tap into this power by textualizing it. Cicero, by contrast, as politically and rhetorically informed as his *technica* are, does very little to ape the form of forensic oratory (if anything, the style of the *technica* runs closest to epideictic, which is the only form of oratory not discussed in *de Oratore*) and indeed, by setting every one of his dialogues in a private home – save *Brutus*, the setting is always a private home outside of the *urbs* – and often involving or suggesting the props of the convivium, he seems to blur the public and private worlds even more greatly than does Catullus. Second, because authors of the Principate and early Empire often imply (or indeed, complain) that the text offered the only meaningful venue for their acts of display – indeed, because the Principate is often considered a time marked by the large-scale literary retreat from the display context of the forum and into the private concerns of textual exchange – an understanding of what seem to be the roots of this retreat into the text will add depth to our understanding of the sociotextual background against which later authors constructed their exodus.

---

[3] White 1974: 42: "insofar as Romans applied any literary activity to their carouses, it was probably expressed in epigrammatic form." Although White's formulation fits nicely with the literary world of the Principate and early Empire, it elides the vibrant textual world of the late Republic, in which patronal convivia were productive of far more than epigrams.

[4] Cf. *TD* 1.3: *quamquam est in Originibus solitos esse in epulis canere conuiuas ad tibicinem de clarorum hominum uirtutibus; honorem tamen huic generi non fuisse declarat oratio Catonis in qua obiecit ut probrum M. Nobiliori, quod is in prouinciam poetas duxisset...* (cf. *TD* 4.3, at which we learn that post-convivial poetic composition was indeed a *mos maiorum*; at 4.4, we learn that Appius Claudius Caecus apparently wrote a *carmen* that Cicero deemed "Pythagorean" in nature). Cato (we are told) felt that patronal-class poetic composition and performance was unproblematic; what lacked *honor* was the practice of dragging *poetae* with one into the provinces so that they could compose on one's behalf. In his analysis of Cat. 44, Sandy 1978 takes the *TD* passage somewhat differently, reading *conuiuae* as "clients" (p. 70); but this does not jibe with the thrust of the passage, which is in defense of poetry, and it ignores the evidence of *TD* 4.3 and *Brut.* 19.75, in which it seems clear that the *conuiuae* are of patronal class. Cicero does not especially avoid the use of *poeta*, but he seems to reserve it for what may have been conceived of as "professional" poets. Catullus' use of *poeta* may point to similar connotations of professionalism; he uses the term on only seven occasions (cc. 14 *bis*, 16, 35, 36, 49 *bis*), four of which are combined with the adjective *pessimus* (the sense of this at c. 49 is discussed below), and at least three (five, if we count c. 49) are aggressively negative in tone. We shall return to Catullus' use and avoidance of *poeta* and *poema* in Chapter 7.

Catullus' and Cicero's uses of textual terminology align nicely. Owing to the operative conditions under which each man produced his texts, however, the distinctions in their attitudes toward patronal display and their relative desire – or need – to contain that display in their texts are more significant. The textualization of display is a characteristic of each man's dedicated texts (although more overwhelmingly so for Cicero); but this textualization functions in different ways and is employed, we must imagine, for different reasons only some of which we shall be able to reconstruct. Catullus' interest in the textualization of his display is manifest, and two such textualizations (cc. 10, 12) have been discussed above. But the textualization of display will mean one thing to a man who seems never to have participated in public display other than to observe or comment upon it (cc. 52, 93, and 103, though cf. c. 53, which does indeed engage in a textualization of forensic display), and another thing to a man who has made such display his life and who likened its absence to a kind of death. And indeed, Cicero both gives us more evidence for this process of textualization and the anxieties that accompanied it, and likely provides our best representation of the concerns and practices of the broader Society – most members of which, as noted in the Introduction and expanded in the Appendix, participated in both forensic display and the textual sort. Because Cicero had more at stake in the game, he gives us more to go on. In the pages that follow, then, I shall focus more heavily on the evidence provided by Cicero – his expressions of "performance anxiety" in the orations and *Brutus*, and then his textualization of display and social obligation in this dialogue and *de Oratore* – and I shall use examples of Catullan textual display to point up both how these men differed in their expression of such, and how and where (and, perhaps, why) they seemed to meet.

I would like to suggest three display-interested characteristics in Catullus' and Cicero's production of dedicated texts that will be good to keep in mind as we move ahead; these are three similarities in how these men textualize their display and, as such, they provide a useful starting point as we begin to tease apart the differences. The first characteristic is that each man tends to construct his texts as venues of private display with – ideally – all of the social and aesthetic authority of their "real-life" parallels. The second is that each man uses the display represented in his dedicated texts to forge and define the terms and obligations of their textual world, both with respect to the dedicatee and, as I think is likely, with respect to other members of that world who figure in the display. The third is that each man seems to recognize – and promote – the dedicated text as a tool of social negotiation and interaction; to view it as a means of initiating, challenging, and reestablishing the bonds of the textual community. Catullus' participation and influence in the display-oriented textual world of the late Republic was highly developed and has long been recognized (even if occasionally misrepresented, to my mind, as indicative of hierarchical poetic activity). What we shall see in this section is that a close look at Cicero's *technica* (and *de Oratore* in particular) will show not only a cross-generic engagement in the textualization of patronal display, but also that Cicero took an active role in the translation of public display into a private, literary, and exchangeable form.

In what follows, Chapter 4 investigates the connection between display and exchange in the late Republic; I offer an analysis of why the translation of display into text is so fraught a topic for Cicero – but also why it would have been such an attractive one – and look for those characteristics of public display that Cicero tried to translate into written form. I am especially interested in the orator's criticisms of performance and of the audience in *de Oratore* and *Brutus*, as these dialogues – marking, as noted above, the beginning of his dialogic efforts (*de Oratore*) and the resumption of these efforts in his final years (*Brutus*) – are especially illustrative both of Cicero's role in the promotion of textual dedication and of his efforts to historicize its social function. In Chapter 5, I identify specific instances of the display of social identity as they are reproduced in Cicero's *technica*, and analyze these performances against a background of what we know about the language and form of public performance. Here we will look especially to the echoes of the *tirocinium fori* and the convivium in *de Oratore*, a dialogue which served not only as a textualization of established patronal ritual but also as a textual model for Cicero's program of initiating his readers (and prospective, if not yet actualized, partners in production) to the newly wrought "paper forum" (or "book-roll convivium") of which he was an active producer.[5] Each of these acts of "textual display," as we shall see, functions as a replication, in written form, of the social power of a public, non-textual original. I turn then to *Brutus*, and suggest that it was conceived as a privatization of the orator's traditionally public audience; as Cicero had come to feel that he could no longer compete for status in a forum under the control of Caesar, he turned his attentions away from the forum and instead to the textual realm of production and display. In recreating his audience as one not of the forum but rather of the

---

[5] Echoes of the *laudatio funebris* and concomitant presentation of the *imagines maiorum*, both of which function as important structural devices in *Brutus*, will be discussed in Chapter 8.

convivium – by replacing, that is, the judgment of the many with the judgment of the few – Cicero transforms oral performance into elite literary display. Finally, in Chapter 6, I turn to the challenge our authors faced in fabricating a sense of written obligation for these "display texts"; in writing and dedicating texts that could convey enough social authority to ensure not only favorable reception and dissemination but, more importantly, a textual gift dedicated ("to" an individual, but "for" the Society at large) in return. In *Brutus*, as we shall see, Cicero argues that oratorical authority depends upon textual production. But how exactly is a "man of the forum" to replicate the authority of the forum in the pages of a non-forensic text, and in what ways might the textual obligations of "no man of the forum" speak as loudly as the public voice he had chosen to reject?

CHAPTER 4

The problem with liberal performance

"THE GAZE CRAMPS MY FREEDOM"

By the final years of an increasingly display-driven Roman Republic, foren-sic oratory was the only profession of ritualized and secular public display that was both suitable for the privileged classes and fixed within the sys-tem of liberal-political and civic hierarchy.[1] As both Edwards and Barton have argued, active participation in theatrical and gladiatorial display – the "pleasure industries" of both the Republic and subsequent years – was in this period confined almost exclusively to foreigners and the lower social strata.[2] These types of display were illiberal by definition and operated at a social, geographical and ideological remove from the discourse of the privileged classes.[3] Members of the cultural elite were allowed to patronize

---

[1] The private convivia of this period also provided fertile fields for the cultivation of status. Strictly speaking, of course, the sponsoring of – and performance at – private convivia cannot be considered a "profession." Nevertheless, I will consider the importance of the convivia as theatrical inspiration for Cicero's dialogues later in this section. Edwards 1997: 86 notes that actors, gladiators, and prostitutes, although certainly performers of a sort, were habitually excluded from the social and political hierarchy that demanded the possession of a publicly recognizable voice.

[2] Edwards 1997: 86: "The appearance of members of the senatorial and equestrian elite onstage and in the arena is first *attested* [my italics] under the dictator Julius Caesar." Suetonius reports that in 46 (the year of the composition of *Brutus*), two *equites* fought in gladiatorial contests in the forum, and another appeared in a theatrical performance (*Iul.* 39.1). Barton 1993: 13–14 notes that "by the end of the Republic, somewhere around half of all gladiators were volunteers." On this, see also Ville 1981: 255, 299–301. Cicero vilifies the "business of pleasure" as he includes it in his list of *sordidi quaestus* (*de Off.* 1.150, cited below). On this, Edwards 1993: 83 notes "*uoluptas* is regularly used of the experience of watching the games, as well as of the more commonly recognized pleasures of the flesh." *Quaestus* appears elsewhere in usages consistent with the Ciceronian evidence. Although Cato uses the term only once (*Ag.* 1. 4), and to indicate the laudable profession of agriculture, the term almost always carries negative economic connotations in Roman New Comedy; cf. Plaut. *Asin.* 511; *Pseud.* 1197; *Rud.* 291. For the term elsewhere in Cicero, see especially *Rosc. Com.* 24; *Verr.* 2.3.21; 2.3.38; 2.3.111; *Cluent.* 101; *Cat.* 4.17; *Ep. Fam.* 16.9.4. The author of the *Rhet. Her.* is careful to specify the reasons for his writing thus: *non enim spe quaestus aut gloria commoti uenimus ad scribendum.*

[3] The exclusion of the freeborn classes from onstage participation in theatrical performance is perhaps one of the most remarkable distinctions between Greek and Roman drama. Edwards 1993: 66 remarks, "Actors, gladiators, and prostitutes in ancient Rome were symbols of the shameful. Their signal lack of reputation was reflected and reinforced in the law, which, in the late Republic and

or produce these performances; but they were discouraged from becoming part of a performance itself. They could attend the theater, but only as viewers and not, strictly speaking, as the viewed. There was a problem with liberal performance in the late Republic – this problem is the focus of the following section – whereby the patronal classes were driven to engage in the forms of public display around which the Republic was built, but they did so at the risk of making the status that allowed this display vulnerable to critique or derogation. Cicero was as aware of this problem as any, and in his discussion of the ways in which a man of the liberal classes might acceptably earn his living, he included an analysis of those vocations fit only for the illiberal classes:

Iam de artificiis et quaestibus, qui liberales habendi, qui sordidi sint, haec fere accepimus . . .
. . . minimeque artes eae probandae, quae ministrae sunt uoluptatum:
                cetarii, lanii, coqui, fartores, piscatores,
ut ait Terentius; adde huc, si placet, unguentarios, saltatores, totumque ludum talarium. (*de Off.* 1.150 (44 BCE))

Now as to the trades and vocations – that is, which ones are thought noble, and which vulgar – the received opinion is, generally speaking, as follows . . .
. . . And least respectable of all are those trades that serve pleasure:
                "Fishmongers, butchers, cooks, poulterers, fishermen . . ."
As Terence puts it; add to this, if you will, perfumers, dancers, and the whole vaudeville crew.

In contrast to the many opportunities for illiberal public display, the forum offered the solitary locus for the "high" public performance of the Republican elite. But because the activity of the forum was clearly analogous to that of the "low" performative arts, and because it was itself a kind of inversion of the social and spatial dynamic of the theater, the orator's participation in the forum was inevitably fraught in terms of class and gender. The parallels between the work of the orator and that of the actor were manifest and many, and were highlighted for comedic effect in Plautus just as they were for didactic effect in Cicero.[4] The fame of the

early Principate, classified them as *infames*." Edwards 1997: 118 notes that practitioners of these "unspeakable professions" ("the etymology of [*infamis*] also suggests 'without a voice'") were not afforded the same physical and legal protection as Roman citizens (p. 124) nor were they allowed to vote. Connolly 1997: 3 inverts the observation: "as a class, [the disenfranchised of antiquity] were excluded from rhetorical discourse."

4 Cf. *Lael.* 26.97: *quod si in scene, id est in contione* . . . To this cf. Quint. *Inst. Orat.* 11.181: *non enim comoedum esse, sed oratorem uolo.* The points of contact between orator and actor have found their way into almost every recent work on Roman rhetoric and performance; see especially Corbeill 1996; Connolly 1997; and Gleason 1995, ch. 4. The privileged classes of the late Republic took pains to

actor, the dancer, and the gladiator threatened the orator from all sides, then, but these trades themselves were considered illiberal or – by a natural extension of the insult – effeminate.[5] The orator finds his power in the maintenance of this social distinction, this tension between the liberal and illiberal: the successful orator must have the alluring *uenustas* of an actor and the austere *grauitas* of a *pater conscriptus*. He can increase his status as a performer only by first endangering that status by performing, by becoming at least potentially the source of another's pleasure – another man's *uoluptas*.[6]

We can accept the following two things as certain. Public – and specifically forensic – performance in the early first century BCE was the source of strong social and political anxieties even before Cicero encountered his own personal difficulty in the forum. Corbeill, Edwards, Gleason, and others have demonstrated that these anxieties were expressed, most frequently, along the lines of social hierarchy and sexual subservience. A standard means of attacking a performer in the Republic, in other words, was to bring into question (or challenge outright) that performer's social status or gender. This displacement was especially vivid and necessary when the combination of performer and performance threatened to destabilize the social norm. Thus although a low-born actor of only moderate popularity might only occasionally raise the hackles of the social elite, a well-born

underline the distinctions between the actor and the orator and to fix each of them in terms of space, time, and social standing: it is no coincidence that the Roman courts admitted no business on *dies festae*. The two professions played distinct but complementary roles in the life of the city, and each played off the audience's knowledge of the other. The prooemium to Cicero's *pro Caelio* is a particularly rich source for the theatrical satire (on which see further Geffcken 1973 and 1995); the prologues of Plaut. *Amph.* 34 and Ter. *Heaut.* 11, *Hec.* 9, 10 use the language of the forum to humorous ends (on which see further Hughes 1997: 183–186). Cicero and his friend Roscius are reported to have discussed regularly the distinctions between orator and actor, and the latter is said to have written a book in which he compared the two professions (Macr. *Sat.* 3.14.11–14). See also Graf 1992 on the similarities of gestures used by actors and orators.

[5] Foucault 1990: 215: "[there exists] a principle of isomorphism between sexual relations and social relations. What this means is that sexual relations – always conceived in terms of the model act of penetration, assuming a polarity that opposed activity and passivity – were seen as being of the same type as the relationship between a superior and a subordinate, an individual who dominates and one who is dominated, one who commands and one who complies, one who vanquishes and one who is vanquished." For all of this in a classical context, see especially Connolly 1997: 1–15 (for an excellent discussion on the "effeminacy" of rhetoric as a whole); 62–110 (on the "proximity of perversion" in *de Oratore*) For the problematized gender of the Roman orator, see Corbeill 1996; Gleason 1995 (on the sexualization of speech in general): "Judgments about speech were sexualized because speech was an essential variable in the social construction of masculinity"; Gunderson 1996; and Richlin 1992, 1997: 90: "The orator's gender was a crux of Roman culture."

[6] *Brut.* 50.188: *delectatur audiens multitudo et ducitur oratione et quasi uoluptate quadam perfunditur.* Cicero's double qualification of *uoluptas* (*quasi . . . quadam*) underlines the highly performative nature of oratory and the problematic "pleasure" provided by the successful orator.

fellow suspected of engaging in low performance might easily be criticized by his peers in terms – *cinaedus, pathicus* – that marked him as socially and sexually less than a Roman man ought to be.[7]

As has been argued in studies across cultural and chronological divides, however, criticisms of status and gender often point to a deeper political or economic anxiety; in the Roman charges of paid performance as a sign of sexual immorality we may decode, without too much imagination, criticisms of pervasive social degeneracy. The very existence of these criticisms – the fact, that is, that they were expressed in the first place – suggests that the illiberality or, by extension, effeminacy of public display was not so much a native characteristic of the act as a projected and appropriative evaluation of it: a mark of the linguistic and semantic conventions that inform the language of public approbation. To call a (Roman) performer a *cinaedus* – in modern terms, an "illiberal pansy" – may have less to do with what you think of his sexual subject status than it does with what you think about the social implications of his performance qua Roman.

But if calling someone an illiberal pansy does not necessarily mean you think he is an illiberal pansy, what does it mean? The recognition of sexual and social criticisms as allusive and symptomatic, rather than demonstrative and explanatory, is not enough for the present project. For whereas allegations of illiberality or effeminacy – or both at once, as in Torquatus' accusation that Hortensius' display was that of an actor or dancing girl[8] – may speak to a generally recognized problem of display, they do not indicate the actual source of the underlying anxiety: to accuse an orator of conventionalized effeminacy is not the same as explaining why oratorical performance might be conventionally criticized as such in the first place. Similarly, derogations of status and gender, taken as such, demand consideration of the manifest parallels between political and literary patronage in the Republic. Although orator and poet might at first seem polar opposites in terms of social power and indebtedness, and

---

[7] On this, see further Edwards 1993, as cited above.

[8] Gellius *NA* 1.5.3, where we learn that Hortensius both dressed with such excessive care and spoke with such dramatic fervor that he was criticized of "acting like an actor" in his court cases (*multaque in eum, quasi in histrionem, in ipsis causis atque iudiciis dicta sunt*). In the trial of Sulla, one of the Torquati – both father and son participated, and so we cannot be certain who Gellius has in mind – lets fly with a storm of such insults that doubtless aimed for, and received, appreciative laughter: *sed cum L. Torquatus . . . non iam histrionem eum esse diceret, sed gesticulariam Dionysiamque eum notissimae saltatriculae nomina appellaret, tum uoce molli atque demissa Hortensius, 'Dionysia,' inquit, 'Dionysia malo equidem esse quam quod tu, Torquate,* ἄμουσος, ἀναφρόδιτος, ἀπροσδιόνυσος.' I contend that is impossible to read this passage and not conclude that Hortensius was a pretty smooth operator. A pretty smooth operator, indeed.

although the recipients of their labors may differ in terms of social rank or political engagement (then again, they may not), suspicions of status and gender are leveled at the forum-bound performer (who offers his speech to an audience of various social statuses) in much the same way as they are at the patronage-bound poet (who offers his text to a patron of implicitly – and certainly functionally – elevated rank).

If we look beyond the conventionalized accusations of degraded status or inverted gender, however, two aspects of public display come to light that are both especially problematic to Cicero in the final years of his life and especially important in his revision of patronal-class display into textual form. First, the interdependence between an orator and his audience: Cicero had always depended upon his audience for his success but he finds the audience of the late Republic increasingly beyond his sphere of control.[9] Second, the association between public display and the illiberal acquisition of gain: Cicero recognized that the orator was a source of public entertainment, but in the elite crisis of the late Republic all manner of public display became increasingly associated with base economic activity.

Any investigation into the Roman culture of display brings with it the inescapability of subjectivity. It is a small point, perhaps, but one worth mentioning in this context, that the Roman fascination with public display of all types – in the Republic and beyond – has been largely naturalized by the modern (and most notably, American) cultures that have studied it. American culture, of the last century and this, has both fetishized the social fictions of display[10] and tended toward enthusiastic self-deception with respect to the equation of artistic or athletic talent to social, ethical, or political sophistication and expertise. This is not to say that these particular tendencies show up to any extent in recent scholarship on ancient display and performance (they do not), nor to suggest that we are hopelessly crippled in our investigation by our collective impressions of display and fame (we are not). Rather, it will be good to denaturalize both ancient and modern attitudes toward display, and to underline the fact that these

[9] The "uselessness" of the imperial audience – an audience that has effectively abandoned the sphere of oratorical control – is a theme that runs throughout Tacitus' *Dialogus*.
[10] The specific fictions to which I refer are twofold: (1) the identification of a performer with her performance and (2) the identification of the ideological fabrication of performance with the cultural substratum in which that performance was created. I forego the expected references to the iconofaction of both the cinematic cowboy and the cinematic action hero, as well as the subsequent election of such to some of the most powerful (and increasingly display-centered) political offices in the country. The phenomenon of Arnold "The Governator" Schwarzenegger is happily spoofed in an utterly creepy wall calendar published by Andrews McMeel (2005).

attitudes are both particular and historicizable. Societies of greater political complexity than the Roman, and of greater artistic sophistication than our own, have flourished without nurturing a *Schaulust* so irresistible as to transform outlandish social theatrics – the forum and convivium and gladiatorial *ludi*,[11] the Academy Awards and *American Idol* and Super Bowl Sunday – into the cornerstones of cultural identity. Certainly, all cultures locate self-recognition in various acts of public and private display; these acts provide ways to gaze at others in order that we might discover our own identity. However, it is essential that we recognize in these Roman performances our own peculiar naturalizations, and that we take a more critical approach to the ways in which a surprisingly familiar display fetish manifested itself in the literature and social practices of the late Republic.

It will be useful to consider briefly recent theoretical work on visuality and the gaze. The work of Jay, Mulvey, and Kaplan,[12] each of whom discusses the gaze in terms of "ocularcentrism," or the privileging of the gaze in terms of gender and objectification, has informed my approach. Because Republican display, and especially the display of the forum, was in all cases a predominately male and homosocial phenomenon, the application of a general sense of gendered ocularcentrism (for which Kaplan 1983 provides a useful summary) to an overarching analysis of the "Roman gaze" – the complex social dynamic between a performer and his audience – will be particularly good to think with. But as much as the underlying structure of gendered ocularcentrism will provide a starting point, and as much as the contributions of Jay, Mulvey, and Kaplan will prove valuable to the analysis, the theoretically (and in particular, art-historically) fraught term "gaze" is developed by these authors in different ways and to somewhat different ends. For the sake of consistency, then, and by way of sidestepping completely a quagmire of aesthetic issues that have little or nothing to add to the discussion, I will use the term here in a somewhat simplified sense and one that adheres most closely to the ocular terminology of Sartre (his is the terminology adopted by subsequent theorists), who speaks of the gaze as that act of visuality and evaluation which originates in the Other ("the one who is not me") and upon which our self-recognition, and recognition of self-worth, as free individuals, depends.[13]

---

[11] On the "theater" of the convivium, and for a compelling argument for the presence of a convivial "audience" (ἀκολούθοι) in the Imperial period, see D'Arms 1999.
[12] See Jay 1993; Mulvey 1989; and Kaplan 1983, ch. 1: "Is the gaze male?"
[13] See Sartre 1956; this work and Lacan 1977 remain points of departure for any thoroughgoing discussion of gaze and the Other; Irigaray 1985 has been the most influential French feminist to attack the "phallologocentrism" of twentieth-century vision theory. In the context of a discussion

FROM THEIR EYES TO THEIR HANDS: SHIFTING THE AUTHORITY OF DISCOURSE

As much as the relationship between the Roman performer and his audience was one of potential, if vacillating, hierarchy, so too was it one of naked co-evaluation and interdependent pleasure, status, and validation. As problematic and occasionally combative as the relationship may have been, it is clear that both performer and audience looked to each other for entertainment, authority, and approval. The audience sought its enjoyment in the spectacle both from the performer's act and from its own role in providing this act with social meaning (without an audience, it is not a spectacle); the performer, in turn, sought approval for his act and validation of his theatrical or rhetorical skill (without a performer, an audience is just a crowd). Each partner in the equation was at any given time hierarchically indebted to the other; this hierarchical indebtedness vacillated continuously between the viewer and the viewed, but the partnership as a whole served only to validate the social order in which public display took first honors. "I see *myself*," noted Sartre, "because *somebody* sees me."[14]

The orator was potentially threatened by this interdependence because the practice of oratory was constructed, if never (in the Republic) actively defined, as a categorically liberal pursuit. Oratory is excluded, rather notably, from Cicero's list of liberal occupations at *de Officiis* 1.151; [15] and the sense of Cicero's list is that because the orator is not paid in cash for his public display, but presents it rather as a kind of voluntary offering to his client and the well-being of the Republic as a whole, he resides completely outside of any sphere of cash economy through which his display may be evaluated and thereby socially cheapened. The delivery of his voice might function as the *munus* or *ars* – a reciprocal gift denotative of status, or a learned skill – of a reputable and skilled freeborn male, but never as his *quaestus*: never as a means of monetary income through which his performance becomes a paid one.

of the body in Greek art, Stewart 1997: 13–15 provides a helpful survey of recent work on "visuality, gaze, and glance." Stewart, following Sartre and Lacan, distinguishes between the gaze and the glance, and remarks of the former, "as soon as I register the Other's gaze, become conscious of being looked at, I not only tend to freeze and look away but also to adapt my behavior to it. By thus turning me into Another's object, the gaze cramps my freedom." On this cf. too Jay 1993: 279 and following.

[14] Cf. Jay 1993: 289. On the recognized importance of the gaze in Pliny (*Ep.* 2.3.8, of Livy) and Tacitus (*Dial.* 10.2, of a poet), see further Habinek 1998: 105.

[15] Cicero's list of liberal occupations (*artes*) at *de Off.* 1.151 (the preceding section of which was cited in part at the head of this section), includes medicine, architecture, teaching, large-scale trade, and – as the apex of liberal activity – agriculture: *omnium autem rerum, ex quibus aliquid acquiritur, nihil est agri cultura melius, nihil uberius, nihil dulcius, nihil homine libero dignius . . .*

In the ideal (or at least, idealized) scheme of things the audience serves as an appreciative observer of the orator's skill and beneficence, and the orator is ostensibly the socially superior *subject* of any given forensic display. But in practice the role of the audience is much greater. The very act of oratorical performance demands that the orator enter into a reciprocal hierarchy with the audience. It is a hierarchy that of necessity muddles the lines between subject and object, and it is in this muddling that we may locate the underlying anxiety of performance expressed in criticisms of effeminacy and illiberality. For when the orator – a socially elevated speaking subject – presents himself for observation and approval, the orator becomes, or at least threatens to become, the socially inferior and disempowered object of the audience's discerning gaze.[16] It is not that an orator's act resembles the behavior of a pathic or lower-class male (or actor, or dancing girl), but that in transforming himself, via his display, into the object of the male ocularcentric gaze he threatens to become socially analogous to a pathic or slave. As the object, rather than the subject, of the evaluative gaze, the orator who pushes the envelope in terms of personal *habitus* and rhetorical style makes himself "too viewable" and, as such, a target for culturally coded derision.

In the case of a learned and reliable audience, whether that audience consists of the Senate or the Roman people, the orator occupies a relatively safe position in the hierarchy. Although he is dependent upon his audience's approval, he can trust an aesthetically refined audience to judge his display fairly and – whatever the outcome of the actual case at hand – to give merit where it is due. When an orator cannot trust the tastes and judgment of his audience, however, the hierarchical dependence between orator and audience becomes riskier. Cicero emphasizes the potential problems of this hierarchy when he speaks of a public gaze that is both forever out of the control of the orator and, as a consequence, always potentially aggressive toward him. He expresses his relationship to his audience in distinctly local terms: when observed by his public, the orator is located, quite literally, "in their eyes."[17] Thus in the same year he wrote *de Oratore*, and in one of

---

[16] At one level, the performer becomes the "visual slave." Edwards 1997: 76 notes of the "infamous" professions (actors, gladiators, prostitutes), "One striking feature of the legal position of the infamous is their assimilation to slaves . . . [W]hat made the infamous like slaves was that they too served the pleasures of others, they too had no dignity, they too were bought and sold." The penetrative qualities of the gaze are perhaps best – if most disturbingly – summarized by Sartre 1956: 79, on the sexual objectification of the gaze and the writer Jean Genet: "Sexually, Genet is first of all a raped child. This rape was the gaze of the other, who took him by surprise, penetrated him, transformed him forever into object." Cited also in Jay 1993: 295.

[17] The formula used for this ocular positioning is normally *in oculis* + a genitive of possession (*populi, senatus, omnium*) + an appropriate verb of action. Cf. *Q. Caec.* 27: *in oculis conspectuque omnium*;

the final orations delivered before he perforce turned his rhetorical energies away from the forum, Cicero reflected on the orator's need to be in the public line of sight:

Nam postea quam sensi populi Romani auris hebetiores, oculos autem acris atque acutos, destiti quid de me audituri essent homines cogitare; feci ut postea cotidie praesentem me uiderent, habitaui in oculis, pressi forum; neminem a congressu meo neque ianitor meus neque somnus absterruit. (*Planc.* 66)

Well, as soon as I realized that the people are a bit hard of hearing, but have 20 / 20 vision, I stopped giving a whit as to what they might *hear* of me: instead, I thenceforth made sure that they *saw* me right in the middle of things every day: I lived in their eyes, I held fast to the forum; neither my doorman nor sleep barred anyone from my company.

Cicero not only recognizes the Republican obsession with visual display; he is aware of his inability, qua orator, to dismiss his dependence on the gaze of his audience. In the passage above, Cicero seems to imply that an audience that once had a highly refined aesthetic taste for oratory now hungers only for a surfeit of visual stimulation. Although the emphasis here is on what the people might hear about Cicero and not what they hear from him, the implication is nevertheless that his voice is no longer as powerful as the physical presence of his body alone: *the reputation of his oratorical ability*, he quips, is not as important as *the fact that he is seen*. The defense of Plancius comes relatively early in Cicero's career, but as we have seen above it is a speech that shows a great deal of awareness of social form and expectation, and one that has begun to recognize *otium* as a time linked with the enjoyment of literature, away from the activity of the forum. What we may have above, I suspect, is a Cicero who has begun to ponder aloud the end result of an unbridled – and uneducated – ocularcentrism. In criticizing what he perceives as an obsession that can undermine the long-recognized power of the orator's voice, Cicero describes an excessive and destructive ocularcentrism. A gaze that had before served to validate social order now threatens to invert it. Cicero has himself perceived the need to "live in public" and to receive visitors in the dead of night. This final observation, "neither my doorman nor sleep barred anyone . . . " (a surely intentional – and likely intentionally textual – allusion to the

---

Leg. Agr. 2.90: *in oculis senatus populique Romani*; de Dom. 101: *in oculis ciuitatis*; Planc. 66 cited above; Phil. 13.5: *in oculis haerebant*; de Orat. 2.41: *in foro atque in oculis ciuium*; TD. 2.63: *si in oculis . . . multitudinis*; de Off. 3.3: *in oculis ciuium quondam uixerimus*. At Lael. 104 Cicero remarks of the relationship between public life and private work: *in quibus [studiis] remoti ab oculis populi omne otiosum tempus contriuimus.*

[non-] *exclusus amator*), points to the conventionalized allegations of performance and effeminacy even as it hints at a nascent linking of his past,
oratorical endeavors with his future, more literary ones. By presenting himself here as an *amatus* who must be ever receptive to the overtures of his
amatores, Cicero bears witness to the problematic social position of the
successful oratorical "subject" who must also be the "object" of his clients'
advances.[18]

But even if the orator could risk "capture" by the gaze of his audience
in order to achieve an increase in status and fame – a kind of counter-
capture, to be sure[19] – it is important to note that status and fame were
never guaranteed. For although an audience has the ability to recognize
the orator's performance with its gaze, it can also avert its glance, withhold
its recognition and approval of the orator's display. The withholding of
recognition is more than just an inconvenience, however. As Bennett has
noted, in the context of traditional theatrical display, but equally applicable
to that of the forum: an act without an audience is no act at all.[20] In the
language of social interaction, public performance can occur only if both
performer (actor or orator) and audience (theatrical or forensic) agree to
participate.[21]

Some eight years after the delivery of *pro Plancio*, and in a work that
is intent on making a case for the textual voice, Cicero again considers

---

[18] Of course, to a certain extent *clientela* of any sort – political or forensic as well as literary – is always
at least implicitly homoerotic; it is occasionally manifestly so. The *cliens'* approach to the *patronus*
resembles that of an *amator* (as in the above passage); to his *amat(us)* he is a suitor who would
establish himself in an asymmetrical relationship of favor and influence with the object of his social
and political desire. Oliensis 1997: 152 calls *clientela* an "asymmetrical friendship," and remarks that
(p. 151) "[a] man who happened to be out and about near daybreak in the first-century B.C.E.
Rome might witness . . . a kind of 'changing of the guard': disheveled young men staggering home
after a night spent on the doorstep of the beloved, while toga-clad clients scurry toward a patron's
door in anticipation of the morning reception." Oliensis notes further that *cliens* and *amator* are
represented as displaying similar virtues (constancy, eloquence) and encountering similar obstacles
(rivals, fickleness). Aelius Aristides describes the effect of the orator on his audience as one of erotic
magic (*Or.* 33.26); on this see also Gleason 1995: 123.
[19] Cicero makes this enslavement gloriously specific in his description of the successful orator's
aggressive and dynamic effect on the audience at *Brut.* 50.188 *[multitudo] gaudet dolet, ridet plorat,
fauet odit, contemnit inuidet, ad misericordiam inducitur ad pudendum ad pigendum; irascitur miratur
sperat timet.* See also *de Orat.* 2.72; 2.178; 2.185.
[20] In her work on the relationships between theater and audience, Bennett 1997: 86 calls theater
an "obviously social phenomenon," and remarks further, "[theater] is an event which relies on the
physical presence of an audience to confirm its cultural status." Bennett is correct, but in the context
of the classical world I would extend her formulation beyond the theater "qua theater" and into all
areas of ritualized public display.
[21] *Cf.* Jay 1993: 288: "The nonreciprocity between look and eye, between being the subject and object
of the gaze, is in fact related to a fundamental struggle for power. For the one who casts the look is
always the subject and the one who is its target is always turned into an object." Georges 1976: 321
inverts the Cartesian *cogito*: "*l'Autre me voit, donc je suis.*"

the orator's dependence on his audience. Whereas the defense of Plancius presented an orator who had merely recognized an inconvenient but necessary symbiosis with his audience, *Brutus* hints at a more sinister world, and one in which an orator depends upon his audience not only for his success, but also for his very voice. After the *persona* of Cicero delivers an amusing anecdote about Plato[22] (whose appearance in the dialogues often introduces a defense of Cicero's textual endeavors), the point of which is that a poet need please but a small crowd, while an orator must move *popularis adsensum uolgi*, Brutus is made to respond:

> Ego uero [inquit Brutus]...ut me tibi indicem, in eis etiam causis, in quibus omnis res nobis cum iudicibus est, non cum populo, tamen si a corona relictus sim, non queam dicere. (*Brut.* 51.192)

> Well, to be totally honest [said Brutus]...even in those cases in which we are concerned with the decisions of the judges, and not the approval of the people, all the same, if I am deserted by my *corona* of listeners, I find myself altogether unable to speak.

The implications first hinted at in *pro Plancio* are here developed in the passage from *Brutus*. Whereas in the earlier text Cicero suggests that he could continue his relationship with the public audience as long as he could adjust himself to its demands, *Brutus* makes the tricky case that the orator's dependence upon his audience's interest and goodwill may have become too great a liability. Although the late Republican relationship between an orator and his audience had always been a symbiotic one, Cicero nevertheless understood well that an orator's success depended upon the presence of a willing and predictable audience. By 46 BCE, when the Republican forum had come too fully under the power of his political opponents, Cicero felt, for all intents and purposes, as though his *corona*[23] of listeners had deserted him. He could no longer find a public that would engage in the reciprocal conversation through which his oratorical fame

---

[22] The anecdote is that Antimachus, while once reciting a lengthy poem before a large crowd, was deserted by everyone but Plato. Surprisingly unflustered by the exodus, Antimachus declared cheerily that he would keep on reading, as Plato was as good as a hundred thousand (*legam, inquit, nihilominus; Plato enim mihi unus instar est centum milium*). Cicero then claims that if Demosthenes had been deserted by all but Plato, he would not have been able to speak a single word (*Demosthenes...uerbum facere non posset*). This anecdote not only underlines the shakiness of the forensic audience and the problems with oratorical dependence upon that audience; it also suggests Cicero conceived of Plato as the idealized and ultimate "reader" of his *technica*.

[23] For another mention of this forensic *corona*, and clear evidence of Catullus' at least occasional attendance at forensic trials, cf. c. 53.1. Thomson 1997: 332–333 identifies this trial as that of 58 BCE; Gruen 1966 argues rather for a date of 54; on the relation of this poem to Cicero, see also Knobloch 1969.

was constituted. He had lost a forum in which he could speak, and so he had lost – for the moment – his means to speak at all.

It is clear that Cicero recognized his dependence upon the will and wishes of the audience. It is clear too that in the changing political climate of the mid first century BCE he saw this dependence as an increasingly negative element of oratorical practice. One of the most pressing dangers of the audience, and one Cicero hopes to lessen or avert with his entry into the textual community, is that the taste and education of the forensic audience are not in the control of the orator. There are two main reasons for this. The first is that the forensic audience – and its gaze – was a corporate phenomenon. It was both impossible and impractical for the orator to relate to the members of his audience on an individual basis; he could be concerned only with the response of the audience as a whole. To a large extent, this is a result of the social dynamics of display as much as it is the physical practicalities of the forum: the architectural and topographical structure of performative venues precludes individual reciprocation of visual contact. It is true that a performer might occasionally "catch the eye" of one or two members of the audience – Cicero's use of apostrophe in the orations provides us with after-the-fact stage directions for his glance – but he could not, as an individual, return this gaze *en masse*. Turning to the imagery of reciprocal gift-giving (Mauss and Levi-Strauss are of use here), just as an intentionally non-returnable gift may serve to "flatten" or "crush" an opponent, a functionally non-returnable gaze serves in part to "deaden" the performer in his inability to respond in kind.[24] And indeed we see that although both Cicero and Quintilian discuss the orator's eyes,[25] the eyes are treated only as an observed phenomenon – as a physical element of his rhetorical arsenal – and never as an active or perceiving sense: the orator is seen, but cannot seem to gaze in return.[26]

[24] See Mauss 1990: 37 (on "flattening" one's rival) and 123 (on the Kwakiutl p!Es, meaning "to flatten" or "to crush") and Lévi-Strauss 1969: 53. In *Slowness*, Kundera (1997) captures the specter of the non-returnable gaze when he refers to the audience of social performance as a "great throng of invisible people ... an infinity with no faces."

[25] Cf. esp. *de Orat.* 3.59.221 and *Inst. Orat.* 11.3.75–6.

[26] In his general discussion of ancient ocularcentrism and a Greek ambivalence toward both seeing and being seen, Jay 1993: 28 discusses a somewhat related phenomenon, the "look that kills": Narcissus, Orpheus, Medusa, and Argos Panoptes. Of course, even the technically "silent" player (the gladiator, the *triumphator*) compels the audience by virtue of his physical appearance, a "corporeal voice." Jay 1993, ch. 1 notes that in the case of Greek (and I would add, Roman) ocularcentrism, all other faculties were relegated to "second-place" standing behind the Look. On the silent "voice of the body," see especially Cicero's theatrical characterizations of Fannius and Piso in *in Pisonem*. On the effect of this "voice" on the viewer, cf. *de Leg.* 1.27: ... *oculi nimis arguti, quem ad modum animo affecti simus, loquuntur et is qui appellatur uultus ... indicat mores.* Here the weight of *indicare* is doubled, "to betray" and "to put a price on"; the worth of the individual is fixed by the external observation of his *uultus*; the face is "active," but only to the extent that it is *seen* by others.

As aware as the orator might have been of the necessity to impress individual members of the audience (and he may be more concerned with the opinions of some than of others), it is a by-product of the venue that the public voice is reified only through the favorable recognition of the viewing body.

A second and more important obstacle to the orator's control over his audience is the matter of aesthetic and political diversity. The forum was a definitively public space, and oratory must always seek to draw a crowd. In the Republic, most public orations were delivered in either the area of the Comitium in the event of political addresses, or that of the second-century Basilica Aemilia in the event of civil trials. In either case, we must imagine the orator surrounded by throngs of people of all classes, political sympathies, and levels of education. He would have had to make himself heard and noticed over a great deal of noise – cries of assent and disgust, no doubt – and a healthy dose of impatience, boredom, gossip, ridicule ("Hortensius is a dancing girl!" "Good gods! that *salaputium* can actually talk!"[27]), and, occasionally, outright threats.[28] It would have been a disruptive, dirty, chaotic mess, but it was throughout the Republic the primary pitch on which an orator tested himself again and again.

In many instances a crowd in the forum would have resembled an audience in the theater – Cicero refers to the forum *quasi theatrum* in *Brutus*[29] – and we should expect that at times the orator had as little control over the temper of his audience as did the actor or playwright. Cicero was entirely subject to the audience as it came to him: although he might plant the audience with his supporters, he was in no position to select listeners whose education, tastes, and political allegiance were in line with his own. Rather, he needed to anticipate, and play to, those aesthetic predilections over which he had no power. Both Cicero's exasperation with the situation, and his scheme to transform both his display and that of his audience into textual form (a "scheme" of which the dialogic display of *Brutus* is, of course, an embodiment), are evident when he "transforms" Brutus' "no audience at all" into the audience that is present – but perfectly useless:

[27] Cf. Cat. 53. Although the jeered *di magni salaputium disertum* is clearly meant to be vulgar (even if not especially aggressive; one wonders whether Catullus did not even know the identity of the "someone" from the *corona* who yelled out the insult), the meaning of *salaputium* – the MSS have *salapantium* – is yet unclear. On this question, cf. Bickel 1953; MacKay 1933; and Weiss 1966, who argues that *salaputium* represents an Oscanism.

[28] During Cicero's unsuccessful, and later revised, defense of Milo in 52, he cites the presence of armed Clodian thugs as the source of his anxiety and hesitancy of speech (*Mil.* 1.1).

[29] Cf. *Brut.* 2.6, in reference to Hortensius' career and untimely death.

Ut si tibiae inflatae non referant sonum, abiciendas eas sibi tibicen putet, sic oratori populi aures tamquam tibiae sunt; eae si inflatum non recipiunt aut si auditor omnino tamquam equus non facit, agitandi finis faciendus est. (*Brut.* 51.192)

For as, if a piper blows into his flutes and they make no noise, he figures that the best thing is to be rid of them, so for the orator the ears of his audience are rather like flutes; that is, if they don't respond to his breath [then they should be discarded]; to put it another way, if your listener is altogether like a horse who utterly fails to "giddy-up," you must stop trying to spur him on.

In this passage, Cicero likens the orator's audience to the silent flute or a dumb animal: it is valuable to the orator only insofar as it responds to his oratorical stimulus. A flute responds to the learned breath of the *tibicen*, but is itself an undifferentiated, senseless object; a flute is valuable to the *tibicen* only insofar as it fulfills his purpose of making music. Cicero knows that his audience is fickle, and that circumstances can be such that it is no longer of any use to him. But we saw in our discussion of *illud Hesiodium* that Cicero situates meaning in elision, and the reader is invited to follow Cicero's logic through to the end. For even if a piping-man's *tibiae* refuse to sound, the man himself does not leave the profession of piping. Rather, he finds himself a new set of pipes. Similarly, the frustrated equestrian may rid himself of an unresponsive horse, but only so that he might find a better one, not that he might cease to ride altogether. If we read this against the social and literary background of *Brutus*, we see that it is neither making vague references to a fickle audience nor – as *Brutus* would appear to claim – giving up the ghost. He is challenging his dependence on the forensic audience and promoting – both in his words and through the display of his dialogue – the possibility of breaking free from this dependence. Like the *tibicen* with a broken flute or the equestrian with an unruly horse, Cicero knows that he must find a new mechanism for the display of his craft. He must create for himself an audience that will be responsive, predictable, and sympathetic to his literary and social needs. Whereas he used to live in the eyes of the audience, he will now reside in their hands.[30]

Cicero fashions such a transition in *Brutus* by systematically devaluing the traditionally forensic listening audience and offering in its place the educated reading audience through which dedicated texts are circulated. Cicero was acutely aware of the problems inherent in an orator's relationship to his audience, but he could not do away with his audience without

[30] Although the image of "living in the hands of the audience" is my own, Cicero uses the imagery of "falling into one's hands" to refer to literary publication (so *de Orat.* 1.21.94) and circulation (*Brut.* 35.133); cf. too *Lael.* 25.96, cited above, Part II, note 2.

undermining the basis of his intellectual and forensic authority. What he does instead is recreate *within* his dialogues an ideal listening audience of carefully selected patronal-class individuals – Brutus, Atticus, Varro and his brother Quintus; but also Crassus, Antonius, Laelius, and Cato – who then serve as (even as they replicate) the ideal reading audience for the texts themselves. Where he used to offer his forensic display for the approval of a wide-reaching and indiscriminate public, he now offers his textual display for the approval of a select and discriminating few. By turning from a relationship of increasingly unpredictable political hierarchy to one of familiar and manageable textual isonomy, Cicero created for himself a new kind of audience – and with it, a new kind of display.

NON TAM UENDIBILIS: A LEXICAL CRITIQUE OF POPULARITY

By the middle of the first century BCE, public display in Rome was more pervasive and more widely accepted than ever before. By the time Cicero turned his thoughts to writing *de Oratore*, at least fifty-seven days each year were devoted to the display and enjoyment of the public games,[31] and at just about the same time that this treatise would have first circulated among his friends Pompey the Great dedicated – amidst lavish display – the first permanent public theater ever to be built in Rome.[32] But even as public display had become more widely accepted, it had become increasingly associated with suspicions of base economic activity. These suspicions invaded even the elite display of the forum and the convivium where we see the idea of widespread "popularity" expressed with the terms and imagery that had been previously reserved for lowbrow mercenary activity and petty trade. There was a problem with being deemed excessively popular in the late Republic, especially if this popularity hinged on the public valuation of one's public display. The problem with popularity was felt more

---

[31] By the first century CE the number of days would increase to seventy-seven; by the end of the fourth century that number would reach almost 150. *De Oratore* itself claims to be a discussion that took place on the days of the *ludi Romani* (to this cf. the introductory sections of the first book of Varro, *DRR*).

[32] The traditional date for the dedication of the building is 55 BCE, the year of Pompey's second consulship. The dedicatory festivities included a *ludi* and a *uenatio* featuring 500 lions, an elephant fight, and other amusements (Cic. *Pis.* 65; also Plut. *Pomp.* 52.4). Five shrines were located throughout the theater, the most important being that dedicated to Venus Victrix. Tertullian (*de Spect.* 10) relays the delightful story of Pompey's dedication of the theater complex: he invited people not to the theater itself but to the temple of Venus, explaining that the theater was no theater at all, but simply a long stairway leading up to the temple proper. Tertullian suggests that Pompey did this in order to avoid censure from the old guard – it had previously been the custom for Romans to stand when they attended the *ludi* – but as Richardson 1992: 384 points out, Pompey's invitation must have been made with tongue firmly in cheek.

keenly by Cicero, the orator dependent upon his *corona* of listeners, than it was for Catullus, the poet whose *corona* consisted of a small circle of friends and readers, most of whom – it is likely – were the same men. Catullus considered the problem with display-driven popularity from the margins of the forensic *corona*, as it were, and Cicero from its core; but as we shall see in the following pages, both men were keenly aware of the problems inherent in public judgment of patronal-class display, and both use the textualization of display in order to comment wryly on public opinion or escape entirely from its fickleness.

Throughout the middle and late Republic – and likely as the result of ever-increasing immigration, professionalized display, and economic productivity – patronal-class Romans devalued purely economic pursuits and idealized those pursuits that professed little concern with monetary gain. As Thomas Habinek has noted, the members of the elite in this period tried to distance themselves from any social activity that could be directly linked to the acquisition of cash and economic indebtedness. The patronal class, generally speaking, did not like to talk about their role in the acquisition of money (we may think of Catullus' swift self-correction of his economic boast in c. 10) and took pains to distance themselves from these suspicions in discussions of oratorical display and literary publication.[33] Whatever other benefits Catullus or Cicero might receive in exchange for their display or political (or merely politically interested) engagement,[34] neither received monetary compensation for their services. And yet neither Catullus nor Cicero was exempt from allegations of economic motives (Catullus himself spoofs these motives in cc. 10 and 28; Cicero skirts the accusation in his list of liberal occupations at *de Officiis* 1.151), which functioned in this period as a standard way of criticizing public – and perhaps especially forensic – display.

Of particular interest in this regard are *uendibilis*, a term that normally means something like "attractive for sale," but which Cicero uses on three occasions to indicate an orator's failure to achieve widespread popularity

---

[33] Habinek 1998: 106 on the topic of elite literary circulation: "aristocrats do not talk about money, except with one another . . . [A]ncient authors did not think it appropriate to talk about profiting from their books. They want their readers to believe that, unlike modern workers, they can eat prestige." Cf. also Habinek's discussion of *existimatio* as a marker of aristocratic self-evaluation (pp. 45–59).

[34] I am inclined to include Catullus' travels to Bithynia in the *cohors* of Memmius in the category of "political interested engagement." Catullus makes it clear that the reason he has not returned with "eight strong litter-bearers" (assuming he has not) is because Bithynia turned out to be a poor province, with little to give up. As Wiseman 1982: 42 notes (the context is c. 28), "the *beneficium* [Catullus and Veranius and Fabullus] are looking for is a share in the exploitation of Rome's empire, a much greater prize than any aimed at by a client in the ordinary sense of the term."

with his audience, and *uendere / uenditare*, which Catullus uses to censure base acts of display. *Vendibilis* is a rare word in extant Latin literature, but it will be worthwhile to consider the occasions on which Catullus and Cicero (the latter of whom does not just use the word, but theorizes its use) apply *uendibilis* and related terms to the context of public display. The Republican use of *uend-* words can be summarized quickly. The positive adjective *uendibilis* does not appear before Cicero, but the related verb *uendere* (from *uenumdare*) is a favorite of New Comedy and its frequently mercenary concerns.[35] Varro, the only other Republican author to use *uendibilis*, applies the adjective to a particularly "sellable" plot of land in a somewhat peculiar discussion of agricultural economics (*DRR* 1.4.2). Cicero similarly uses *uendibilis* to describe an attractive plot of land (at *Leg. Agr.* 2.36), a fact that makes his subsequent uses of the term all the more interesting; for twice in *Brutus*, and once in *Laelius*, he uses *uendibilis* to designate not a tract of land or traditionally recognized commodity, but rather an orator and his acquisition of public approval.

But what does it mean for Cicero to use *uendibilis* – a word that should mean, and in every other case does mean, "sellable" – as an indication of an orator's popularity? Are the connotations of the word necessarily negative, or has the orator simply coined a new term to indicate increasingly sought-after popularity with the Roman people? Let us consider briefly *uendibilis* as it is used in *Brutus*, where Cicero uses the "unsellability" of his textual display to theorize on the desired "sellability" of forensic display, and the problems that arise from a situation in which popularity is assumed to be coterminous with ability: we are told of L. Gellius, [*ille*] *non tam uendibilis orator quam ut nescires quid ei deesit* ("not so much a 'sellable' orator as one who seemed to lack nothing," *Brut.* 20.264), and of C. Visellius Varro, *in quo fateor uolgi iudicium a iudicio meo dissensisse; nam populo non erat [ille] satis uendibilis* ("in the case of this fellow, I admit I disagreed with the judgment of the crowd; for he wasn't sufficiently 'sellable' to the masses," *Brut.* 20.264).[36] Whatever else we make of Cicero's criticisms in these passages, his use of *uendibilis* on the whole is telling, as the term is never

---

[35] The use of the privative *inuendibilis*, at Plaut. *Poen.* 341 and in the context of *mercatus meretricius*, suggests that the positive degree of the adjective would have been in common usage. Although the verb does not carry with it any particularly negative connotations in Plautus, neither is it used as anything but a concrete description of traditional monetary transaction.

[36] The term appears again in *Laelius* in the context of C. Licinius Crassus; the word is this time applied not to the man himself, but rather to his oratorical skill: *tamen illius uendibilem orationem religio deorum . . . uincebat* (96). Finally, Cicero uses the word at *de Fin.* 1.12, of literary production; at *Verr.* 2.1.105, in a cynical observation of public approval; and at *Leg. Agr.* 2.36, in an economic and agricultural sense.

used to indicate popular judgment with which he is in agreement. In the
Brutus passages just noted, Cicero uses the term for men[37] who possessed
a great deal of innate skill and refined learning, but who fell short in
recognition because they were not attractive enough to a public who had
come to view oratory as just another kind of entertainment offered up for
their consumption. But this leaves us with two important questions. First,
what is wrong with popularity? If an orator must rely on the approval of his
audience for his status, why does Cicero mark the lack of approval in such
strongly cynical terms? Second, what is it about *uendibilis* in particular
that makes it Cicero's term of choice when he wants to criticize faulty
public opinion? Why would the relatively unmarked economic designation
"sellable" enter the marked sphere of forensic evaluation when an orator
has failed to impress an increasingly untrained audience?

Let us take a moment to compare the semantic weight of *uendibilis* to
that of the English "popular" and related terms of approval and distinction.
"Popular," like the Latin *uendibilis*, is used as a subjective and often economic indicator of public judgment and approval, and thus marks an individual or her talents as particularly attractive to the aesthetic predilections
of the majority. But even if "attractiveness to the aesthetic predilections of
the majority" is an acceptable working definition of this sense of "popular,"
the semantic force of the term (whether is it approbative or derogative)
depends upon the speaker's aesthetic identification at the moment of assessment. We might, for example, overhear a speaker claim that the blockbuster
Gladiator was an exceedingly popular movie. But knowing nothing of the
speaker's self-identification, we do not know whether the assessment is an
approbative or derogative one. If she wishes to ally herself with the people,
her use of "popular" is approbative and inclusive: for this speaker, a movie's
popularity is a sign of its cultural worth. If, on the other hand, she wishes
to distance herself from the judgments of the people, her use of "popular" is pejorative and a source of distinction: the designation of popularity
functions as a derogation of aesthetic value. There is of course always some
difficulty involved in trying to decipher the tone of a work of literature;
but in the context of *Brutus*, Cicero's use of *uendibilis* as an assessment of
oratorical popularity can have been nothing but a damning and cynical
criticism of public taste. When Cicero tells us of two fine orators who did
not gain the public approval they deserved, he is underlining one of the

[37] Lucius Gellius Poplicola, close in age to Crassus and Antonius (*horum aetati prope coniunctus*),
would have been born ca. 137/136 BCE; Caius Visellius Varro was a cousin of Cicero's and held
various political offices, but we have no other record of his oratorical career; cf. Sumner 1973:
102–103, 138–139.

most important problems with using popularity as a measure of skill or ability. Popularity is a mark of the public aesthetic – and sometimes the public can be wrong.[38]

The second problem with *uendibilis* as a mark of public approval lies in the first-order meaning of the word as "sellable." From a modern perspective, there is nothing particularly problematic in equating an orator's public reception with his economic potential. We often hear that a popular actor is "big at the box office," and so are accustomed to the widespread equation of fame with economic returns. But in the literature of this period, words of the *uend-* root normally indicated base – or at least, clearly illiberal – economic activity: in other words, the very sort of activity from which elite performers of the Republic sought to distance themselves as objects. When Cicero uses *uendibilis* in his dialogues to describe the "popularity" of an orator and his forensic display, then he is doing more than offering an uncritical observation of the judgments of the people. Rather, he is commenting on the degraded taste of the forensic audience as a whole. To revisit the passage quoted above:

> In quo fateor uolgi iudicium a iudicio meo dissensisse. nam populo non erat [Varro] satis uendibilis . . . (*Brut.* 20.264)

> In the case of this fellow, I admit I disagreed with the judgment of the crowd; for [Varro] wasn't sufficiently "sellable" to the masses.

Here the implication seems to be that the display of the forum had become for the audience nothing more than one more variety of cheap entertainment: Varro was not "popular" enough for the crowd because he did not play sufficiently to their base aesthetic judgments. When Cicero describes Varro's oratorical ability in these terms (he had skill, but it was not attractive enough to the *populus*), he both questions the audience's faculty of judgment and underlines the problems with lowering oratory to the status of the theater or other paid entertainment. The orator's performance, so Cicero has it, is defined in part by the fact that it is not for sale: in his refusal of direct economic remuneration, the orator is able to fashion his voice into the very symbol of elite Republican liberality. In contrast to this, the display of the theater was wholly commoditized. The actor accepts a cash payment in exchange for his physical skill and becomes a caricature of illiberality; both the performance and the man seem wholly up for sale.[39]

---

[38] For Cicero's views on the "problem" of popular fame, see also *TD* 3.2.3–4.

[39] Successful actors and gladiators could earn large sums of money; cf. Edwards 1997: 78. The gladiatorial contests, originally given as funeral games or *munus mortis* ("gift" of death – that

The orator's craft was ideally dislocated from the cash economy, and so from the "act" of acting. And yet the anxieties surrounding performance, and the remuneration for it, ran deep, and the charge that an orator was either "improperly (excessively, illiberally) entertaining" or suspiciously wealthy set the tone for many forensic jibes over an orator's status as a *uir bonus*.[40] As much as the orator might try to disassociate himself from suspicions of lowbrow display, the world of late Roman spectacle had become so fully developed that any act of public display threatened to be taken as an act of theatrical pandering.

The fraught interrelation of display and economy is made explicit several times in the invective poetry of Catullus, which tells us that even though a man might eschew the world of public display in favor of that of the text, he nonetheless (or perhaps all the more) would have been aware of both the dangers of display and the protection of the page. Although Catullus usually avoids terms explicitly indicative of economic activity,[41] he uses the verbs *uendere* and *uenditare* on a few occasions to criticize – in terms smacking of prostitution and pandering – public behavior that is incompatible with the aristocratic aesthetic.[42] We may confine ourselves to

is, for the deceased, cf. Cat. 101.3), involve a somewhat complicated transaction of performance and identity; cf. esp. Barton 1993 and Edwards 1997: 77–78; Barton 1993: 12 describes the gladiator as "crude, loathsome, doomed, lost (*importunus, obscaenus, damnatus, perditus*) ... throughout the Roman tradition, a man utterly debased by fortune, a slave, a man altogether without worth and dignity (*dignitas*), almost without humanity." See Barton 1993: 12 and following for the problematic "volunteerism" of the gladiators.

40 Edwards 1997: 76: "What made the infamous like slaves was that they too served the pleasures of others, they too had no dignity, their bodies were bought and sold"; on the "paid performance" and the sexual suspect, cf. p. 83: "Actors, gladiators,and prostitutes, and those who hired out their services, were regarded with profound ambivalence by their fellow citizens... [and] were all associated with forms of transgressive sexual behavior." Torquatus' accusation that Hortensius' appearance and delivery were "improperly entertaining" has been discussed above. On the suspicions that may accrue to an orator who becomes quickly and excessively wealthy, see Tac. *Dial.* 8.3 and 8.4, in which "Aper" describes Marcellus and Crispus, men of no particular ability or character (*sine substantia facultatum, neuter moribus egregius, alter habitu quoque corporis contemptus*, 8.3) who become fantastically wealthy – even as they lose their public voice – under the patronage of Vespasian.

41 Catullus uses neither *pecunia* nor *quaestus*, for instance, and *pretium* only of a woman whom he had charged with a greed "greater than a hooker's" (*plus quam meretricis auara est*, 110.7) and of a friend who has destroyed the bonds of *amicitia* (67).

42 Elsewhere Catullus uses *uendere* at 79.3 and 106.2. The first is an attack on Lesbius: *Lesbius est pulcher. quid ni? quem Lesbia malit / quam te cum tota gente, Catulle, tua. / sed tamen hic pulcher uendat cum gente Catullum, / si tria notorum sauia reppererit*. The second, a cynical commentary on public display or literary publication: *cum puero bello praeconem qui uidet esse / quid credat nisi se uendere discupere?* The nuances of this poem are difficult to translate. Thomson 1997, following others, takes *praeco* as "auctioneer"; but Cicero's use of *praeconium* (*Ep. Att.* 13.12) would indicate that these terms had likely entered wry literary idiom ("publicist" / "publicity") by at least the early middle decades of the first century BCE. So too, the *puer bellus* of 106 may refer – if we hold

the most representative use of *uenditare*, that of c. 33, a vicious attack on the unspecified antics of a father-and-son team that are here written up in terms of base sexual and economic display:

> O furum optime balneariorum
> Vibenni pater et cinaede fili
> (nam dextra pater inquinatiore,
> culo filius est uoraciore),
> cur non exilium malas que in oras   5
> itis, quandoquidem patris rapinae
> notae sunt populo, et nates pilosas
> fili, non potes asse uenditare.

> Oh you master of bathhouse thieves,
> Father Vibennius and that faggot son of yours
> (For the father has the filthier hand,
> The son the greedier ass),
> Why don't you go straight to hell,   5
> Since everyone is on to
> The father's snatchings – and that hairy ass of yours?
> Son, you couldn't pimp it for a dime!

Although father and son are censured in terms of illiberality and effeminacy, the poet's insult underlines the "spectacular" nature of the offense in terms of thefts "known to all" (*notae sunt populo*, l. 7)[43] and the base pandering of a streetcorner whore. The father is turned into a petty criminal; his son becomes both a pathic and a pansy and, as his undepilated derriere would suggest, he fails in a most base act of display.

The accusation of petty thievery occurs frequently in the corpus and especially in discussions of poetry and convivial culture.[44] Whatever the father has done (his name is elsewhere unattested, and Wray suggests he was "a person of relatively little consequence"),[45] his performance has reduced him, in poetic idiom, to the lowest social order imaginable – he

to Catullan idiom and tonality – to a young poet whose faulty (and perhaps too eager?) poetic "performance" has fallen victim to Catullus' cutting criticisms. Krostenko 2000: 286 argues for the sexual sense of *bellus* in this poem, and renders *puer bellus* "pretty boy." Surely this is one of the senses of the poem as a whole, but to my ear Catullus is double-playing the slang of sexual license with that of poetic appetition: publicist is denounced as a "salesman," eager poet as "gigolo." For the argument that *praeconem* is the subject of *discupere*, rather than *<puerum>* (as Krostenko notes, a semantically easier reading; the *se* is ambiguous), see Bushala 1981.

43 Wray 2001: 120, in an excellent analysis of this poem in the context of political and personal invective at Rome and its potentially legal ramifications, suggests that these words may imply that Vibennius and his son had already received the general condemnation of the community.

44 Thomson 1997: 289 notes similar thefts at Plaut. *Rud.* 382–384 and Petron. 30.8.

45 Wray 2001: 120; cf. Thomson 1997: 289.

is Asinius times two, expelled from the clique of poetic approval and cast into the realm of the definitively déclassé. The son's behavior is similarly obscure and similarly culpable. Catullus begins with the charge of pathic behavior (*cinaedus*, l. 2),[46] progresses quickly to one of active whoring (l. 4), and ends with an accusation of blatant – if doomed – self-sale (*nates pilosas... uenditare*, ll. 7–8). The accusation that a man is a *cinaedus* is a commonplace in Catullan invective. The final position of *uenditare*, however – an iterative I have rendered "to pimp" – underlines the poet's criticisms: inappropriate display, whether public or poetic, is recast in terms of base economic activity.

We will never know the details of the social infractions that may have so angered (or amused) Catullus, and indeed the elision of the original offense, in this poem and others, may open up further the argot by which members of this textual community used their texts as both loci of display (in that the text captures and remakes private display and then "publishes" it to the text's readers) and receptacles of social negotiation (in that affective and sometimes political alliances are worked out in, and transferred through, dedicated texts themselves). This poem addresses, and so may be functionally "dedicated to," Vibennius – if the man existed at all. But it is also, and perhaps even more so, addressed to Catullus' broader reading audience. However the crimes are to be read – if we can be confident that Asinius did not steal a napkin, then we can be confident that neither *pater* nor *filius* stole garments from a public bath or engaged in small-scale hookery[47] – Catullus speaks of a world in which display and text have collapsed into a single object of social affection (or, as here, disaffection). We might imagine that Vibennius knew what he had done, as did – more to the point – the earliest circles of Catullus' readers: either because these latter had witnessed the "crimes"; or because they heard about them later; or because the argot of the poem would make it clear what Catullus had in mind. Because the criticism is cast in terms of display (Vibennius acts like a thief; his son acts like a prostitute), and because of the nuances of exposure that emerge from the notion of both taking another man's clothes and removing one's clothes for another man, it is tempting to suspect that at least one of the men may have "exposed" or otherwise intruded upon

---

[46] *Cinaedus* was a term regularly linked to public behavior perceived as inappropriate or base according to generally accepted social standards. As a term often applied to actors and other performers, *cinaedus* resonated with anxieties over public display and its evaluation.

[47] So Thomson 1997: 289, "C.'s charges against Vibennius... and his son are the small coin of public pasquil-verse, and are not intended to be taken literally." Thomson rightly identifies clothes-stealing as a variant of convivial napkin-theft (cf cc. 12 and 25) and notes that approximately one-third of the poet's lampoons offer a sexual insult similar to *cinaedus*.

some aspect of Catullus' poetic *persona* (so cf. cc. 10 and 12). As difficult as it may be to reconstruct the act behind the argot, however, the heavily coded language of c. 33 suggests that Catullus' "ideal" readers not only would have chuckled at Catullus' carefully wrought poetic rant; they also would have appreciated, or at least understood the significance of, his ability to censure another man's display by means of crudely sexualizing and commercializing poetic invective.

Catullus' configuration of *uenditare* can help us decode the anxieties that accompanied forensic activity. By definition, the *homo liber* cannot be a passive object of sale:[48] a man who is sold in the Roman world is either (1) no longer a man or (2) no longer free.[49] When Cicero uses the term *uendibilis* of the popular orator, then, we can be sure that he is aware of the potentially negative economic implications of the term and that he uses the term to underline the problems with an oratory that had moved too far away from its original place as an unquestionably elite pursuit. By transforming the political constraints on the exercise of oratory in the mid 40s BCE into a claim that the whole of Republican oratory had become irreparably degraded (this is a theme Tacitus takes up in *Dialogus*, his own "dialogue with a dialogue"), Cicero has charged that an orator could gain popularity only with the potential loss of his autonomy. He could buy status only at the cost of selling himself.

But what does it mean for Cicero to degrade oratorical popularity in a text that is concerned at least ostensibly with outlining the past successes and failures of Rome's orators? We saw above that Cicero sought to escape the traditional problems of orator–audience interdependence by turning his interest to the production of private texts and a newly fashioned "reading" audience. In the case of Cicero's negative references to oratorical popularity in his use of *uendibilis*, we see a second indication of a problem the orator felt he could solve by turning his interest to the written text. The *Brutus* passages that discuss popularity do two things. First, by

---

[48] Habinek 1998: 105 suggests, "Aristocrats are supposed to act, not be acted upon, which is why they must take preemptive action against the possible confusion of their texts with themselves." I believe that in the late Republic, however, we see writers who strive after a careful identification of text with author.

[49] Servitude implies effeminacy. The slave is not a fully functional sociopolitical male; he occupies a political space closer to the female or the immature male (on which see further Arist. *Pol.* 1 *incip.*). On the decentering of servile sexuality and the concomitant problems for the free man, Foucault 1990: 215–216 remarks, "Slaves were at the master's disposition, of course: their condition made them sexual objects and this was taken for granted . . . on the other hand, everything in the way of sexual behavior that might cause a free man . . . to bear the marks of inferiority, submission to domination, and acceptance of servitude, could only be considered shameful: a shame that was even greater if he offered himself as the obliging object of another's pleasure."

underlining the distinction between Cicero's judgment and the judgment of the crowd (even if the two are usually in accord), these passages bring into question (here, as throughout the text) the audience's faculty of judgment, its ability to decide for itself which qualities were most indicative of oratorical excellence. Second, by representing oratorical popularity in economic – and by this time definitively negative – terms, these passages suggest that it is time for the orator to remove himself from a forum that had gained the ability to harm an orator more than help him. But just as Cicero underlines the social dangers met by the orators of his day, he also offers in *Brutus* a possible escape from these dangers. For if the audience of the forum has become too great a liability in its tastes and judgments, the orator can still turn to the private and definitively non-monetary exchange of literature as a means of securing his intellectual and social status. The exchange of literature mimics the dynamics of oratorical performance in terms of audience (the texts' recipients) and transaction (the texts' circulation). By turning to the text as a venue of private display – by following, in short, the path of the poet – the orator might gain the approval of a learned audience without running the risk of becoming "popular" with the indiscriminate crowd.

CHAPTER 5

From public display to textual display

TIROCINIUM FORI AND THE MAKING OF MEN

At least as early as the final decades of the Republic, oratory was constructed as an androgenic phenomenon. Just as oratory originates from men, so too does it make them,[1] and an essential part of this process was the so-called *tirocinium fori*: that ritual of forensic recruitment and training – we might think of an apprenticeship – that included the donning of the *toga uirilis* (the "toga of manhood") and the transfer of upper-class young boys from the tutelage of one adult male guardian (usually the father) to another (usually a family friend or colleague), as Cicero describes in this passage of the *pro Caelio*:

[pater] ut huic uirilem togam dedit – nihil dicam hoc loco de me . . . hoc dicam, hunc a patre continuo ad me esse deductum; nemo hunc M. Caelium in illo aetatis flore uidit nisi aut cum patre aut mecum aut in M. Crassi castissima domo . . . (*Cael.* 9 (56 BCE))

As [his father] gave the young Marcus the *toga uirilis* – I'll not mention my own involvement . . . but I will say this: his father transferred the young boy to me, straightaway, and from that moment on no one ever saw Marcus Caelius, in those rosy years of his youth, but with his father, or with me, or in the most irreproachable company of Marcus Crassus . . .

The *tirocinium* served the elite social order in two important ways. First, the *tirocinium* sought to introduce the young apprentice to the ins and outs of political life and by extension a forensic career: under the protection and guidance of a learned and beneficent elder, the young boy was able to achieve proper training and a safe entry into the dangerous world of Republican politics. Second, the *tirocinium* served to establish and solidify

---

[1] I am of course indebted to Gleason 1995 for the most thorough and influential modern discussion of Roman self-presentation and the androgenic phenomenon; see esp. pp. 103–130, on the Roman rhetorical writers. See also Connolly 1997: 111–152, who discusses the "pedagogy of manliness" in Quintilian's *Inst. Orat.*, and Richlin 1997 on rhetoric's "production of manhood."

the homosocial bonds between adult males – almost always members of the patronal classes – among whom the young boys were circulated. As Richlin has noted, this transfer of young boys is often constructed in erotic terms in rhetorical and pedagogical texts, and indeed Cicero's description of Caelius' childhood (*Cael.* 9–10; cited in part above) both underlines the nuances of the transfer and, in the orator's defense against charges of an "excessively close" relationship between Caelius and Catiline, points to the danger of unsavory speculation should the transfer go awry.[2]

But if we consider the process of the *tirocinium* in light of the kinship of Roman display and the projection of sexual suspicions, we can read this transfer of young men also as an act of carefully crafted social display. The ritualized transfer of young men (and the training that follows it) is at the same time the first public display – their social debut, as it were – of these men. It is precisely the act of being given and received that initiates their transition from the sphere of the potentially given object (a sphere shared by women and slaves) into the sphere of the potentially giving subject. At the same time, the exchange of young men constitutes an act of display on the part of the exchangers: the ability to participate in this "traffic in men" in so public a way is itself a social performance of significant power. The *tirocinium fori* both reestablishes the adult exchanger as an important player in the elite political drama and introduces the exchanged youth as the hottest new star in the theater of political operations.

It is the display and observation of the youths that provides the essential element of the exchange. In his defense of Caelius, Cicero describes the process in visual terms: the youth is transferred to him (*hunc... ad me esse deductum*) in the very flower of his youth (*in illo aetatis flore*). After his introduction into forensic life, no one ever saw the tender thing (*nemo hunc uidit*) but in the company of his father or Cicero, or in the unimpeachable presence of Marcus Crassus. Both in this passage and at the beginning of *Laelius*,[3] where Cicero mentions his own *tirocinium*, he emphasizes the *toga uirilis* as the signature costume of the mature Republican political *persona*. The *toga uirilis*, precisely because it is a costume, underlines the tensions

---

[2] *ad [Catilinam] si accessit aut si a me discessit umquam... tum existimetur Caelius Catilinae nimium familiaris fuisse* (*Cael.* 10). Cicero mentions his own childhood mentors at *Brut.* 89.304–90.312 and *Lael.* 1–2; Tacitus at *Dial.* 2: *quos [oratores] ego in iudiciis non utrosque modo studiose audiebam, sed domi quoque et in publico adsectabar mira studiorum cupiditate et quodam ardore iuuenili... At de Orat.* 1.29.133–1.30.134 (a mature) Crassus and (a much younger) Cotta "discuss" the training of the orator in similar, vaguely erotic terms: *[inquit Cotta,] quid praeterea esse adsumendum putes? tum Crassus arridens: quid censes, inquit, Cotta, nisi studium, et ardorem quemdam amoris?*

[3] *Lael.* 1–2: *ego autem a patre ita eram deductus ad Scaeuolam sumpta uirili toga ut, quoad possem et liceret, a senis latere numquam discederem; itaque multa ab eo prudenter disputata, multa etiam breuiter et commode dicta memoriae mandabam fierique studebam eius prudentia doctior.*

between intimacy and publicity: it emphasizes both the private man who wears it and the public realm in which this man lives.

These tensions are encapsulated in the ritual exchange itself. Because the initial transfer of the *tirocinium* implies an actual change of vestment – because the youth actually as well as symbolically is unclothed as a boy and clothed again as a man – the *tirocinium*, as much as it is a public performance, must also hint at things private, domestic, and at least potentially erotic. As in any initiation that centers around an actual or symbolic change of vestment (and, cross-culturally speaking, this includes a good many of them), it is at the moment between costumes – here, that moment between boyhood and manhood, between exclusion from and inclusion within the political life of the city – that the importance of the ritual as a producer of social identity is most exemplified. In Rome, the hint of a youth's vulnerability, his "objectivity," at the moment of this change only underlines the danger of the public life into which he will enter. For just as tender Caelius must be protected from the salacious overtures of corrupt Catiline, so the mature orator must be on guard against the clumsy leer of an untrained audience.

Cicero is fairly reticent on the topic of his own adolescent striptease (for some omissions in the corpus we are to be grateful), yet he is acutely aware of the affective, erotic, and potentially pathic implications of the ritual transfer of boys. Indeed, he capitalizes devilishly on the similarities between the *tirocinium*-transfer of young men and the marriage-transfer of young women in one of his final works. The piece is the never-delivered – and highly literary – second *Philippic*, and the context is a wittily acerbic (one might almost say "Catullan") description of Antony's youth:[4]

Sumpsisti uirilem, quam statim muliebrem togam reddidisti . . . Curio interuenit, qui te a meretricio quaestu abduxit et, tamquam stolam dedisset, in matrimonio stabili et certo collocauit. (*Phil.* 2.44–5 (44 BCE))

As soon as you put on a man's toga, you turned it into a hooker's . . . Curio came on the scene, dragged you away from your business of whoring, and – as if he had given you a housecoat – set you up in sure and stable wedlock!

Cicero's acerbic reference to the *toga muliebris* – the "woman's toga" prescribed for registered prostitutes – hints at the pathic connotations that might have accompanied any ritual training of the young by the old, just

---

[4] So Tac. *Dial.* 35.1 complains of the indiscriminate entry into the scholae of the Empire: *nam in loco nihil reuerentiae est, in quem nemo nisi aeque imperitus intret; in condiscipulis nihil profectus, cum pueri inter pueros et adulescentuli inter adulescentulos pari securitate et dicant et audiantur.*

as the frisson created by *meretricius quaestus* invokes what had become an established construction of political and sexual behavior as two sides of a fragile social coin. The goal of this passage, and indeed the whole of the *Philippics*, is to destroy Antony's character by any means necessary. But this is no empty vituperation: the harsh innuendo of the *tirocinium* joke would fall flat did it not capitalize on an already deeply embedded social understanding of the act as one that, if bungled, could effectively "unmake" the men it sought to produce.

Ten years prior to the publication of this "textual oration," the characters of Cicero's *de Oratore* engage in a somewhat more ameliorative rehearsal of the initiation of the young by the old. But whereas we might expect the potentially dangerous eroticism of this ritual transfer to be so underplayed as to be absent in such a text, what we see is that far from denying the eroticism of the institution, the characters are made to emphasize it to such a degree that the whole of the dialogue might be read as a seductive textual *tirocinium*.

"I NEVER LEFT HIS SIDE": *DE ORATORE* AND THE EROTICS OF HOMOSOCIAL EXCHANGE

Ego enim [inquit Sulpicius], qui ab ineunte aetate incensus essem studio utriusque uestrum, Crassi uero etiam amore, cum ab eo nusquam discederem ... (*de Orat.* 1.21.97 (54 BCE))

And indeed [said Sulpicius], as soon as I reached manhood I burned with enthusiasm for each of you – in fact, I was absolutely wild for Crassus, and nowhere left his side ...

One of the most remarkable and innovative claims of Cicero's dedicated dialogues is that dedicated texts of this sort provide for their author, and his readers, a venue of private and secondary display distinct from the questionable hierarchy of formal public display. Starting with *de Oratore* in 54 (our earliest example of a dialogue in Latin and quite possibly one of the first composed)[5] but continuing on with the publication of his subsequent *technica*, Cicero sought to textualize his oral performance as a way of avoiding the problems that arose from an increasingly unreliable

---

[5] As noted above, it is impossible to claim that no one had written a dialogue in Latin prior to Cicero's *de Oratore*, but Cicero certainly never points to a predecessor in the practice, which is what we would expect to see if there had been a significant tradition of such prior to 54. On the survival of this dialogue and, more specifically, its relationship to the form of the Platonic model, see Fantham 2004: 49–77.

Republican audience. As Cicero makes explicit in many of these treatises, but as is clear even in many of the orations of the earlier periods, it is his hope, and certainly a matter of his professional posturing, that his voice be construed as synonymous with the ideal of Republican liberality. But when, following Cicero's post-consular political setbacks and the continued rise of his political enemies, the hierarchical display of the forum became socially and politically unsafe for him and his allies, the orator and his friends turned to private literature as a new venue for rhetorical display. As is now generally recognized, the dialogues were not written as actual records of real discourse:[6] what they constituted, as I argue, were complex textual encapsulations – dramatic transformations bordering on a form of historical drama[7] – of elite public performance.[8]

We shall see in this section and the one that follows that Cicero weaves into his dialogues numerous, and specific, mimeses of elite performance. These textual rehearsals of established types of social display – the youthful and erotic initiation of the *tirocinium fori* and the erudite interchange of elite convivia (*de Oratore*, in particular, but a convivial tone runs through many of the *technica*), the display and judgment of the forensic sphere (so *Brutus*), the extra-urban and *otiosi sermones* of social equals who have fled the *urbs* in order to retreat into both villa and text – surely add to the dramatic force of the dialogues. But beyond that, they challenge and even remake the traditional boundaries between elite literary and social performance. *De Oratore*, the dialogue that sets the whole of Cicero's textual

---

[6] Indeed, Cicero comments twice on the fictions of his dialogues, first at *Ep. Att.* 4.16.1 (54 BCE): *Varro, de quo ad me scribis, includetur in aliquem locum, si modo erit locus. Sed nosti genus dialogorum meorum. Ut in oratoriis, quos tu in caelum fers, non potuit mentio fieri cuiusquam ab iis qui disputant nisi eius qui illis notus aut auditus esset*, and again in a letter to Varro at *Ep. Fam.* 9.8.2 (45 BCE): *puto fore ut, cum legeris, mirere nos id locutos esse inter nos quod numquam locuti sumus, sed nosti morem dialogorum.* It is interesting to note that in the years between 54 and 45 the *genus* of his dialogues had become a *mos*.

[7] That Tacitus may have felt similarly about the work and form of the dialogue comes out in the early sections of *Dialogus*, when the interlocutors come upon Maternus holding his *Cato* – an historical drama delivered the day before and one that had roused the anger of those in power (2.1) – in his hands (3.1). *Dialogus* is steeped in a world that has become so deeply textual, and so distantly removed from the orality of the forum, that only texts are imagined to have voices that are able to "do something." Maternus seems dead set on engaging in political criticism in his tragedies (historical or otherwise, cf. 3.3), but Tacitus (through "Aper") warns that not only does poetry fail to "do things" in the world at large (9.1–2), but any form of oral criticism of the state is inescapably dangerous even in the somewhat relaxed literary world under Trajan. *Dialogus*, by moving into dialogue with Cicero's own version of the historical drama, seems to suggest that the only place for "voiced" criticism of the political world (and I read *Dialogus* as darkly critical) is within the "silent" pages of a dialogue.

[8] On the interconnection of oratory and literature in this dialogue, see most recently Fantham 2004, esp. pp. 131–160.

program in motion, contains in its early sections a careful interweaving of the *tirocinium fori* and the elite convivium that serves in sum to transfer these performances from public to private; from world to text. Through a process of hints and shadows, of echoes and suggestions, the dialogue redesigns the initiation-display of the *tirocinium* and the reciprocation-display of the convivium for both the young (intra-textual) interlocutors and for all subsequent (extra-textual) readers of dialogue. And in the interweaving of the shadows of the convivium with those of the *tirocinium*, the text subtly shifts the scene from forum to dining hall, from unpleasant business to the business of intellectual pleasure. In capitalizing on the innate interconnection between elite convivium and the sharing and circulation of poetic and rhetorical texts, *de Oratore* completes (for itself and its author) this important first step in the transformation of public world to private text.

These elusive (and allusive) shadows of the *tirocinium* are simply sketched: Crassus and Antonius (the knowledgeable and experienced elders) introduce Cotta and Sulpicius (the naive and zealous youths) into a new world of social intercourse by means of epideictic display and some lively give-and-take concerning precisely the sphere into which the traditional *tirocinium* would introduce young men: forensic performance and (as an ever-present subtext to the dialogue) political maneuvering. But in *de Oratore*, a dialogue which questions the future of the Republican forum even as it considers its past (and this is a theme that will be taken up again in *Brutus*), the world into which the youths are introduced is one not of public, formal, and forensic oration, but rather of private, casual, and textual discourse.

A first *tirocinium*-like initiation appears early in the dialogue, at the end of Cicero's dedicatory narrative and just before the start of the discussion proper. The dramatic date of the dialogue is September 91 BCE, on the eve of the Social War. More specifically, the dialogue occurs during the days of the *ludi Romani*, and Lucius Crassus has retired to his Tusculan villa in order to escape the troubles of a weakened Senate. He is joined soon thereafter by Quintus Mucius Scaevola – who would himself sponsor Cicero's *tirocinium* – and Marcus Antonius, the former of whom was Crassus' erstwhile father-in-law, the latter of whom a partner in his political cause (*consiliorum in republica socius*, 1.7.24). Immediately after the elder men have been introduced to us, however, we learn they are not alone: the young Caius Cotta and Publius Sulpicius have journeyed with Crassus to his estate. Of the individual young men we are told almost nothing: only that each is on the verge of entering into public life, and that they represent the elders' final hope for a revitalized Republic.[9] In reality, of course, both Cotta and Sulpicius have passed the tender age at which boys were normally first handed over to their social and political mentors. But by locating in these "young men" all of Rome's (past) desires for a brighter future, and by contrasting the age of the youths (*adulescentes*) with the hopes of their elders (*maiores*), Cicero remakes Cotta and Sulpicius into Republican debutantes flush with enthusiasm: talented and socially promising young men who embody the potential of a resuscitated Rome.

The group of five spends the whole of their first day (although this amounts to fewer than seven lines of Oxford text) discussing the crisis of the Republic and the deplorable state of politics in general. The political discussion to which these lines allude serves as a foil for the rest of the dialogue; it is the somber backdrop against which Cicero's invention of the new "textual patron" is formed. The group talks not only of present affairs in the Republic, but about the future as well: by the end of the discussion, Cicero writes, the three elders (Crassus, Antonius, and Scaevola) had foretold all of the future woes that would befall the state.[10] Their thoughts, then, must be on crafting a new future for the Republic.

The discussion draws to a close together with the day, and as the men bathe and recline for the meal, the mood shifts abruptly from the political to the private; from the memory of Rome's past to the education of its future. The youths, we soon see, are to be initiated not into the political anxieties of the public forum but rather into the intimate pleasantries of the aristocratic villa. In other words, it is kind of a reverse initiation – a transfer of the young men not from the house to the forum, but from the forum to the house. The first stages of the initiation are marked by a striking description of the transformation:

Eo autem omni sermone confecto, tantam in Crasso humanitatem fuisse, ut, cum lauti accubissent, tolleretur omnis illa superioris tristitia sermonis; eaque esset in homine iucunditas, et tantus in iocando lepos, ut dies inter eos Curiae fuisse uideretur, conuiuium Tusculani. (*de Orat.* 1.7.27)

But when the conversation was finished, Crassus displayed such refinement that, as soon as they had bathed and reclined for dinner, all the sadness of the previous discussion had vanished; the fellow was so delightful, and with such a charming wit, that it seemed as though they had spent the day in the Senate house, and dinner in Tusculum.

---

[9] 1.7.25: . . . *in quibus magnam tum spem maiores natu dignitatis suae collocarent, C. Cotta, qui tum tribunatam plebis petebat, et P. Sulpicius, qui deinceps eum magistratum petiturus putabatur.*

[10] 1.7.16: *quo quidem sermone multa diuinitus a tribus illis consularibus Cotta deplorata et commemorata narrabat, ut nihil incidisset postea ciuitati mali, quod non impendere illi tanto ante uidissent.*

In this passage, Crassus' discourse is described not in the austere political language of the forum (there is no mention here of his *grauitas, seueritas*, or *eloquentia*), but in the intimate and affective language of private literary display and evaluation (*humanitas, iucunditas, lepos*).[11] The imaginary transfer from the Curia to the convivium marks the beginning of the initiation, and the sorrow of the forum is replaced by the wit of the dinner table. The effect of this description is twofold. First, we understand immediately that Cicero is up to something new. This dialogue is no mere record of a previously delivered oration; nor is it a colorless mimesis of an epideictic or deliberative display. Cicero is promoting both a new language with which the orator can be described, and a new style of literature in which he can be represented. Second, we encounter – in the swift shift from the sorrow of the political world to the delightful camaraderie of the villa – what will become a recurrent theme in the dialogues and the letters: literature heals the soul.[12] The convivial and literary wit (*tantus in iocando lepos*) with which Crassus is credited can do more than merely cure sadness. It can transform the world of the orator by allowing him to rewrite his own future.

But if the stage is set on the first evening, it is on the next day that Cicero presents the first "act" of his new, and distinctly textual, *tirocinium*. For following immediately upon the phrase *convivium Tusculani*, we learn that:[13]

Postero autem die, cum illi maiores natu satis quiessent, et in ambulationem uentum esset: dicebat [Cotta] tum Scaeuolam, duobus spatiis tribusue factis, dixisse: cur non imitamur, Crasse, Socratem illum, qui est in Phaedro Platonis? (*de Orat.* 1.7.28)

---

[11] *Iucunditas*, which is here used in an approbative sense, can have only deleterious connotations when used in a political or forensic setting, where it means something like "inappropriate effeminacy." Krostenko 2001: 1–19 includes *lepos* (and *lepidus*) in his lexicon of "the language of social performance." In Chapter 1, Krostenko notes of *lep(idus)*, "as a broad ameliorative, *lep(idus)* described mainly the response of an observer to a stimulus, whether or not the stimulus was intended to elicit the observer's favorable response." Krostenko argues that by the end of the Republic, *lep(idus)* had become "performatized, that is, it came to require of its referents that they be performed actions." Krostenko is certainly correct, but I would add to his formulations the observation that a *lep(idus)* performance belongs in the convivium, not the Curia: when Cicero uses *lepos* in reference to Crassus, he does so to define the social space in which that performance occurs. On the use of display terms in *de Oratore*, cf. Krostenko 2001: 202–232.

[12] A version of this sentiment appears in the orator's defense of the poet Archias: *nam ceterae neque temporum sunt neque aetatum omnium neque locorum; at haec studia adulescentiam acuunt, senectutem oblectant, secundas res ornant, aduersis perfugium ac solacium praebent, delectant domi, non impediunt foris, pernoctant nobiscum, peregrinantur, rusticantur* (*Arch.* 16). See also *Brut.* 3.13–4.15.

[13] I presented the argument on the invocation of Phaedrus in *de Oratore* first in Stroup 2007, of which the paragraphs below offer a paraphrase.

On the next day (as Cotta relays), when the older men had rested up and everyone had gone out to the garden-walk, Scaevola said, "Crassus, why don't we imitate Socrates in Plato's *Phaedrus*?"

The reference to *Phaedrus* is telling, as the group decides to recline beneath a plane tree to embark upon their discussion. At the most obvious level, it introduces the genre of the literary dialogue, with a nod to its most famous practitioner,[14] and thus gives us a clue as to what it is that Cicero has in mind for his own return to literature. But for this, any other of Plato's dialogues would have served equally well; the reference to the plane tree seems unnecessary if all Cicero means to do is inform his readers that he is about to write a dialogue. Cicero invokes *Phaedrus*, I want to suggest, for two more textually interested reasons. First, *Phaedrus* shares with *de Oratore* both a deep concern with the tensions between spoken and written rhetoric, and, to a lesser extent, the conviction that rhetoric and poetry are linked in their goal to "guide the human soul" by means of *eloquentia* (as I have noted, the comparison of poetry and oratory is a favorite theme in later *technica*). Second, as much as *Phaedrus* would seem to devalue the "sullen absence" of the written word in relation to the "lively presence" of the spoken – it is a text commonly accepted as Plato's "critique of writing" – it can just as profitably be viewed, as Berger has noted, as a literary dialogue written *in defense* of the composition of literary dialogues when these dialogues are restricted to a highly learned and carefully circumscribed reading audience.[15] In his reference to *Phaedrus* – a reference at once painstakingly casual and almost comically unexpected: "Here's an idea: let's pretend we are Socrates!" – Cicero transports the Tusculan villa into the center of a deeply historical, deeply textual, and altogether fictional mental landscape. In shifting from the sorrowful work of the public forum to the delightful leisure of the private *convivium*, in offering an image of men young and old reclining comfortably on cushioned benches,[16] Cicero invites his readers into the familiar world of intellectual display and textual reciprocity.

[14] We know that Cicero had a portrait of Plato at Tusculum: cf. *Ep. Brut.* 6.24.

[15] Cf. Burger 1980. Plato's Socrates does much to criticize the "silence" of writing (275d) because it, "like painting," will not respond to questions asked of it; as Berger suggests, however, much of Plato's critique lies with the problem of bad readers, a theme surely picked up by Cicero.

[16] 1.7.29; Zetzel 2003 (with further bibliography) argues that the addition of cushions (and benches) to the otherwise Platonic setting of this passage is suggestive of Cicero's desire to "insulate" his readers from the naked irrelevance of Greek doctrine. The use of *puluinus* is a bit odd: a somewhat rare word with frequently lofty connotations, its etymological link to the *puluinar* (and by extension, *lectisternium*) may be playing off the preceding reference of Socrates' speech as *diuinitus*. I discuss these scenes in somewhat greater detail in Stroup 2007: 33–36, and the phenomenon of the "text as villa" is the focus of an ongoing project.

The opening sections of *de Oratore*, then, set the tone for reading this text as a *tirocinium*, and the themes of initiation and education run throughout the remainder of the dialogue. In the sections that follow, the elder interlocutors will consistently provide the structure for the information that is presented, but the young Cotta and Sulpicius will invariably provide the motivation for the dialogue itself. *De Oratore* is not just a conversation between men of experience; it is a textual exercise in the private education of the inexperienced young.

The shadow of the *tirocinium* appears again in the first book, again immediately preceding a renewed conversation that is motivated by the young men's desire for training. Crassus and Antonius have favored the youths with a brief discussion of oratory, but seem – at least to Sulpicius' thinking – reluctant to proceed. The conversation momentarily stalls, and it seems uncertain whether the elders will continue with their discussion of rhetoric, though the readers know they must. The youths' desire (*cupire, amor, ardor*) is answered by the older men's restrained acquiescence (*obsequi*),[17] and the young Sulpicius eventually conquers his elders' reticence with a reference to the bond they share. At 1.21.96, Sulpicius confides to Crassus that he had ardently hoped (*insperanti mihi . . . sed ualde optanti*) for just such a discussion (*sermo*) on the topic of oratory in language reminiscent of Cicero's earlier description of his brother's request for *de Oratore* (1.1.4, *tibi vero . . . hortanti . . . roganti*), and also tells us something important about the relative roles of recipient and benefactor. For just as in c. 65 Catullus rewrites the relationship between himself and Hortensius as one between a shy beloved and her aggressive *amator*, here Cotta and Sulpicius are fashioned as eager young lovers who have repeatedly pursued private *sermones* with their senior mentors.[18] In the passage with which the request is made, the homoerotic tensions of the situation are played to the full:

---

[17] See 1.23.106: *ad quam [disputationem] te duo excellentis ingenii adolescentes cupiunt accedere*; of Cotta's desire to learn of rhetoric, see 1.20.34–35 [*ardor amoris*]; for *obsequi* see 1.22.99 and 1.47.206. Adams 1982: 164 notes that *obsequium* "sometimes indicates wifely obedience in a non-sexual sense," and cites *TLL* IX.2.181.688 ff., and Ovid *Ars* 2.179 ff. (of male subservience); Adams adds, "[*obsequium*] was transferred euphemistically to the female and passive role in intercourse, as at Livy 39.49.9 *eum puerum . . . exprobare consuli . . . solitum, quod sub ipsum spectaculum gladiatorium abductus ab Roma esset, ut obsequium amatori venditaret* and Col. 6.37.9 *asellus admovetur, qui sollicitet obsequia feminae.*" Such homosocial erotics are also especially evident in Catullus' Calvus poems.

[18] Sulpicius implies that he had been "handed over" to Crassus upon his initiation into manhood: *cum ab eo nusquam discederem*; cf. Cicero of the young Caelius' *tirocinium: numquam ad [Catilinam] accessit; a me numquam recessit (Cael.* 4.10).

Ego enim [inquit Sulpicius], qui ab ineunte aetate incensus essem studio utriusque uestrum, Crassi uero etiam amore, cum ab eo nusquam discederem, uerbum ex eo nunquam elicere potui de ui ac ratione dicendi . . . quod quidem si erit a uobis impetratum, magnam habebo, Crasse, huic palaestrae et Tusculano tuo gratiam, et longe Academiae illi ac Lycio tuum hoc suburbanum gymnasium anteponam. (*de Orat.* 1.21.97–98)

And indeed [said Sulpicius], as soon as I reached manhood I burned with enthusiasm for each of you – indeed for Crassus I felt the fires of love, and never left his side; yet I could never squeeze a single word from him on the force or theory of eloquence . . . But if indeed you give us what we want, Crassus, I shall be forever in debt to your "Tusculan *palaestra*" here, and I shall count this almost-urban training ground of yours far superior to the famed Academy and Lyceum.[19]

In these lines Sulpicius adduces the language of the *tirocinium fori* (*ab ineunte aetate incensus*; *cum ab eo nusquam discederem*) as a way of reminding Crassus that their present project is an initiation as well.[20] For although in the past the old man had contributed to a certain degree of the youths' training, he is reminded here that work remains to be done. Whereas Sulpicius had earlier been introduced into the forum, he must now be given an education in the elite discussion of *ratio dicendi*. As the remainder of the dialogue makes clear, Cicero's new vision of the youth's initiation is based heavily on the composition and circulation of rhetorical treatises. For as the elders discuss various theories of rhetoric and oratorical style, the evidence they adduce comes from prior and private discussions not only on matters of rhetoric but also on the detailed rhetorical handbooks with which they would all have been familiar. In a sense, of course, Cicero is giving us just one more rhetorical handbook. But by placing the information of Greek *praecepta* within the form of the self-aware exchanged dialogue, he is asserting for his "speaking" text a new kind of power over the circulation of information. Lest Quintus (or any of Cicero's anticipated readers) miss

---

[19] It is difficult to convey the full meaning of *suburbanum gymnasium* in a neat translation. In using *suburbanus* to describe Crassus' *gymnasium*, it seems Cicero does three things. First, he emphasizes not only that the discussion is extra-urban (an important detail, as I discuss further in Chapter 8), but also that it is almost-urban: not quite city, it is true, but in a space of intellectual and social dialogue *with* the *urbs*. Second, he emphasizes the future of elite discourse: the orator's voice had previously found its place in the forum; it will now be located in the safety of the private home (which is to say, the text; for this sentiment, see also *Ep. Fam.* 9.2 and Leach 1999: 167–168). Third, Cicero of course points to his own *suburbanum gymnasium*: that located in his own Tusculan villa, which he had purchased from Vettius in ca. 70 BCE (cf. *Ep. Att.* 4.5) and which had originally belonged to Q. Lutatius Catulus, the son of the Catulus of this dialogue. On Cicero's use of *suburbanus* to refer to the *praedia* of the wealthy, cf. *Verr.* 1.54. The (Loeb) translation, "semi-rural," of Sutton and Rackham 1942, inverts the directionality, so missing the point.

[20] Compare this passage to the description at *Cael.* 4, cited at note 2, and to the beginning of the *Laelius*, cited at note 3.

the undertones of Greek homoeroticism, Sulpicius ends his request with an ample measure of *philellenismos*: he refers to his "beloved's" Tusculan villa as a *palaestra* and a *gymnasium* "preferable by far" (*longe . . . anteponam*) to the Academy and Lyceum. By rewriting the relationship between the youths (Sulpicius and Cotta) and the elders (Crassus and Antonius) into one of lovers and beloved, Cicero underlines both the intimacy and the obligation of the request, and establishes that as much as his dialogue recognizes its Platonic and Aristotelian forebears, it is a definitively Roman, and definitively Ciceronian, venture.

As soon as Sulpicius falls silent, Crassus remarks that he has always retreated from discussions on the nature of oratory while on Italian soil – words that serve as another sign that we are moving from Plato to Cicero and from Athens to Rome – in spite of the youth's exuberant insistence (*tibi cupienti atque instanti*, 1.22.99).[21] His shyness originates not in snobbery (*superbia*) or lack of affection, but because he felt incapable of engaging in discourse on a topic about which he knew so little (*insolentia, inscita*). Finally convinced to speak, Crassus interrupts himself yet again with a reference to his anxiety over the discussion as a whole and publication in particular:

Dicam quidem, quoniam institui, petamque a vobis, inquit, ne has meas ineptias efferatis . . . nam quid est ineptius, quam de dicendo dicere, cum ipsum dicere numquam sit non ineptum, nisi cum est necessarium? (*de Orat.* 1.24.111–112)

Well, I'll tell you, since I have already begun, but I ask that you not publish my *ineptiae* abroad . . . for what is more foolish than to speak about speaking, since speaking is itself always a foolish thing to do – except when one absolutely must?

In the course of these two sections (cited partially above), Crassus uses *inept-* lexemes six times (and in every imaginable configuration: *ineptias, ineptum, inepte, ineptus, ineptiarum, ineptius, ineptum*) to describe the very act in which he is participating. The adjective *ineptus* is usually translated as "foolish" (as I have chosen for convenience), "absurd," "silly," or the like. Its derivatives – *inepte, ineptia, ineptire* – are similarly understood: one might behave "improperly," publish one's "trifles," or "play the fool."[22] Certainly, such approaches to the term are not in any sense wrong or misleading, but I think that they fall short of getting at the "literary" importance of the term. Cicero's emphasis on these words, via the voice of Crassus, warrants a brief consideration of their use and significance in late Republican literature.[23]

---

[21] On this, see especially Hall 1996: 95–120.   [22] *OLD* s.v. *inepte* etc.
[23] On *ineptiae*, see Bower 1974.

First let us consider Catullus. On only one occasion does Catullus refer to his own writing as *ineptiae* (c. 14b);[24] on another, he commands himself to "get over" the Lesbia affair with the words *desinas ineptire* (c. 8.1). He calls his friend Flavius' sordid fling with a low-class hussy *aliquid ineptiarum* (c. 6.13–14),[25] and addresses both Asinius and "Faggot Thallus" (*Cinaede Thalle*) with the vocative *inepte* when he complains of their inopportune thievery of the poet's cherished belongings.[26] Finally, he applies the term to the unfortunate and irrepressible grin of the "urine-swilling" Egnatius (c. 39.16): *nam risu inepto res ineptior nulla*. When Cicero uses *inept-* words in the speeches or in the context of public display, and he does so with some frequency, they are strongly negative in tone and appear with words denoting effeminacy (*deliciae*, *Cael.* 67) or idiocy (*stultitia*, *Brut.* 67.236). In each case *ineptia* (and its cognates) is a matter of public opinion; of the way one's behavior is judged by those around one. These words appear also in the private correspondence and the above passage of *de Oratore*; in these texts the tone is milder – and almost jovial – but again I suggest that public opinion provides the touchstone upon which one's behavior is tried.

The basic linguistic shape of these words is simple: *in-* + *aptus*. Not fitting; inappropriate; out of (or without?) place. Within the display and exchange context of the late Republic, we see that Catullus and Cicero invariably use *inept-* words to denote not just something that is broadly "silly" or benignly "ludicrous," but something that is socially askew, an action or attitude that defies acceptable or recognized social norms. These words signal that a man's actions do not match the expected codes of behavior for any given situation. When Catullus, using a similar extra-poetic voice to that which we noted in the final stanza of c. 51, admonishes himself *desinas ineptire*, what he means is that it is time to "get with it"; to recognize the demise of his unhappy affair. When Crassus refers to the Tusculan conversation as a matter of *ineptia*, his concern is not so much the substance of the discussion as the *fact* of it, and with the public reception of that fact, should speech – his display – enter the textual record. Cicero's

---

[24] 14b: *sequi forte mearum ineptiarum lectores.*

[25] 6.13–14 *non tam latera effututa pandas, / ni tu quid facias ineptiarum*: "You wouldn't be looking like she's fucked you in half, / unless you've been slumming it a bit." The idiom here is nearly untranslatable, but the coarseness of the description is meant to shock. Flavius is an unknown, but was clearly a youth of the upper class; Thomson 1997: 221 suggests that he may have been pursuing the *tirocinium fori*, and notes (p. 222) that *inambulatio* (l. 11; here of the bed) is a technical term for oratorical movement. On these lines see also Fitzgerald 1995: 53.

[26] Thomson 1997: 266 notes that Thallus (in Greek "sprig" or "shoot") should be the name of a freedman. Its pairing with the crude adjective *cinaedus*, however, suggests that it may be an off-color nickname for one of the poet's friends.

Crassus is aware that his participation in the discussion might seem "out of place" to patronal-class men of the early part of the century. But by having Crassus raise this objection and then ultimately ignore it (he goes on to speak at great length), Cicero implies first that the conversation is not *ineptum* but indeed *necessarium*, and second that the private discussion of rhetorical *praecepta* has a noble Republican pedigree.

Cicero is no *homo ineptus*, however, and we can do more with this scene. For in Crassus' almost comical repetition of cognates (*inept-, inept-, inept-*), Cicero summons the specter of the Platonic ἄτοπος, a term closely linked in the dialogues to Plato's characterization of Socrates as "out of place" or "strange."[27] Socrates was, of course, ἄτοπος in every respect. Here it is not Crassus, but Crassus' agreement to "speak about speaking," that is characterized as *ineptum* – out of place, unfitting – so that Cicero might properly situate himself and his "textual Crassus" in relation to Plato and Plato's "textual Socrates" in order to point up the dynamic of what it means to textualize, and in textualizing to remake, "out-of-place" display.

Whereas for Crassus, and the social and political context of 91, the *otium*-facilitated discussion of oratory may have been viewed as *ineptum*, the late Republican textualization of that discussion – the grand act of patronal-class display that constitutes not only *de Oratore* but also indeed all of the dialogues – is altogether *aptum*. Leisurely patronal-class discussion is therefore not merely textualized in *de Oratore*; it is redeemed in its textualization: the dialogue provides precisely the *oti ratio* Cato had demanded more than a hundred years prior. In this short passage, then, Cicero not only deflects potential criticism of his own endeavor, he actually confronts elite opinions of behavior and display and turns them, through the very textualization of that display, on their head.

Although Cicero is subtle in his suggestions that *de Oratore* contains a mimesis of social initiation, his representation of the dynamic between the elders and youths would have resonated with his readers, the "textual audience" of the dialogue's display. Just as in fifth-century BCE Athens the image of a recumbent man and youth suggested instantly a *symposion*, and following immediately upon that, the interplay of *erastês* and *erômenos*, the audience of *de Oratore* would have recognized in the description of our group the unmistakable elements of the *tirocinium fori* – a ritual each audience member would have likely experienced during his own youth. We are given experienced elders, inexperienced youths, an eroticized desire for

---

[27] Cf. Plat. *Symp.* 174a, 215a, 223d; *Phaed.* 229c, 230c. The bibliography on Plato's use of ἄτοπος in the characterization of Socrates is extensive. Representative studies include Clay 1975; Ferrari 1987 (on ἄτοπος in *Phaedrus*; cf. esp. pp. 13–14); and Schenker 2006.

initiation into the unknown, and a transfer of spheres from the public to the private. In a sense, the only thing missing from the dialogue's description is the forum itself. In a bold move, Cicero has freed a social practice from the social context in which it was created, and has transplanted that practice into an abstract and textual venue. Display that Republican tradition had restricted to the public sphere Cicero has liberated into his private texts: he has replaced the forum of bricks and stone with a forum of paper.

FROM CURIA TO CONVIVIA: NATURALIZING THE
TEXTUALIZATION OF DISPLAY

D'Arms has argued that in the Roman banquets of the late Republican and Imperial periods, the emphasis lay in the theatrical as much as the culinary enjoyment.[28] Indeed, the convivia of the Empire had become full-fledged spectator events in which wealthy guests may have brought with them small "audiences" of followers to witness their convivial display.[29] Although we know little of the formal structure of a convivium at the time Cicero wrote *de Oratore*, the early sections of the dialogue suggest that the display contained therein is to be considered something of a convivial one. I noted above Cicero's introduction of Crassus' Tusculan villa as a means of retreating from the *negotium* of the forum and into the *otium* of the convivium (*ut dies inter eos Curiae uideretur, conuiuium Tusculani*, 1.7.27); shortly after this passage, Cicero expands the convivial imagery:

Et quod ille durissimis pedibus fecit, ut se abiceret in herbam, atque ita illa, quae philosophi diuinitus ferunt esse dicta, loqueretur, id meis pedibus certe concedi est aequius. tum Crassum: immo uero commodius etiam; puluinosque poposcisse, et omnes in eis sedibus, quae errant sub platano, consedisse dicebat. (*de Orat.* 1.7.29)

" . . . And what tough-soled Socrates did, when he threw himself down on the grass and embarked on that discourse the philosophers say was inspired – surely such can be granted more fairly to my own feet." "Not just more fairly," said Crassus, "but more *fittingly*!" And he called for pillows (as Cotta tells it) and they all sat together on those benches that were under the plane tree.

---

[28] D'Arms 1984; 1990; 1999.
[29] D'Arms cites Lucian, *On Salaried Posts*: οἱ μὲν γὰρ τῶν συνδείπνων ἀκόλουθοι ὁρῶντες ἐκπεπλ-
ηγμένον εἰς τὴν ἀπειρίαν τῶν δρωμένων ἀποσκώπτουσι. On the "public convivium," see also Sen. *Con.* 9.29: *Quid? si per deos inmortales, nullo sollemni die populo inspectante in foro conuiuium habuisses, non minuisses maiestatem imperii nostri? atqui quid interest conuiuium in forum an forum in conuiuium attrahas?*

Although *de Oratore* is the only one of the *technica* that situates itself in explicitly convivial space, Cicero imbues many of his later dialogues with a convivial tonality that is, I suggest, meant to evoke the private, leisurely, and intellectually charged space of the convivium. References to leisure-time, to eating, to drinking, to the promotion of Latin literature and philosophy, and to the similarity between poetic performance[30] and rhetorical display (a detail of particular importance to the early sections of *de Oratore*[31]) appear in more than half of the later *technica*.[32] Several of the dialogues (or books therein) begin with images of one or more of the interlocutors being found "at rest" (*otiosus* vel sim.), sitting or reclining in a quiet location where he is joined by the others (cf. *Brut.* 3.10; *de Orat.* 3.5.17; *DND* 1.6.15; to this cf. Tac., *Dial.* 3.1). In what is a probable echo of the end of Plato's *Symposion* (a text suspiciously absent from Cicero's own professed Platonic influences), the first and third books of *de Oratore* conclude with the participants rising up and parting (*exsurgeret*, 1.62.265; *surgemus*, 3.61.230; cf. Plat. *Symp.* 223D), while the late-night close of *Tusculan Disputations* makes reference to an early-morning departure of the participants. When the location of a dialogue is given (as it is in ten of the surviving nineteen treatises, fourteen of which are dialogues), it is without fail that of a private villa (Tusculum figures especially large in this capacity) or home (so Cicero's Palatine house in *Brutus*).[33] Even in those texts in which a location is not specified – as in *de Republica*, from which we are missing the preface, and in *Cato* and *Laelius*, in which Cicero has turned to a more theatrical style of

---

[30] Cicero's insistence that Cato approved of patronal-class performance of poetry in the convivium has been noted above (cf. *TD* 1.3; 4.3); his *Brutus* lends support to this in its discussion of early convivial songs celebrating the *laudes clarorum uirorum*: *atque utinam exstarent illa carmina, quae multis saeclis ante suam aetatem in epulis esse cantitata a singulis conuiuis de clarorum uirorum laudibus in Originibus scriptum reliquit Cato* (*Brut.* 19.75). Cf. also Val. Max. 2.1.10.

[31] Cf. 1.3.11 and, esp., 1.16.70: *est enim finitimus oratori poeta, numeris astrictior Paulo, uerborum autem licentia liberior*... Oratory and poetry are thematically coupled at *Brutus* 10.40 (where Homer is called "*plane orator*"), and the friendship between Ennius and the orator M. Cornelius Cethegus is emphasized at 15.58; that between Q. Catulus and the poet A. Furius – a friendship that included textual exchange – is noted at 35.132. *TD* begins with a review of Greek and Latin poetry before it introduces the setting of the dialogue itself. The kinship between orator and poet is noted also in *Brutus*, at 50.187 and 51.191. *Hortensius* included in its opening sections a similar comparison of poetry and history, the former championed by "Catulus" and the latter by "Lucullus."

[32] Cf. too *Ep. Fam.* 9.26, addressed to Paetus: *conuiuio delector; ibi loquor, quod in solum, ut dicitur, et gemitum in risus maximos transfero.*

[33] Tusculum is the site of *de Orat.* (the villa is Crassus'), *de Fin.*, *TD*, and *de Div.*; it is mentioned also at *de Rep.*, *Brut.*, *Orator*, and *Top.* Arpinum is the site of *de Leg.*; Hortensius' villa at Bauli the site of *Acad. Prior.*; Varro's villa at Cumae the site of *Acad. Post.* Cicero's villa at Cumae shares honors with Tusculum in *de Fin.*, and his place at Puteolanum provides the setting of *de Fato*. Cotta's house hosts the discussions of *DND*. That Cicero's dialogues are so deeply contextualized in the private villa makes Varro's choice of the *Villa Publica* as the site of the third book of his *DRR* somewhat subversive.

dialogue – it is clear that the conversation occurs at a private residence (even if the discussion itself is often held out of doors) rather than a public venue.

Most telling, however, is that the subject matter of these treatises, and especially the dialogues, is suggestive of what may be termed a "convivial (or if we have Plato in mind, *sympotic*) aesthetic." In their defenses of philosophy, literature (especially the transformation of Greek themes into Latin prose), and retreat from the state and renewed engagement with private intercourse, these dialogues transform the traditional intellectual display of the convivium into the unexpected intellectual display of the text. It is the text that is also a villa (or the villa that is at the same time a text) into which – Cicero tells us – patronal-class writers of the late Republic have been forced to retreat; it is in such "textual *uillae*" that they will now reside; and it is through such conflations of word and world that they will be able to continue to serve the state to whatever degree they are able.[34]

What of this display? We know that convivial display regularly included the performance of poetic works, either written in advance and delivered on the spot, or delivered ex tempore and (if Catullus 50 is evidence) later set to paper and circulated among participants. But the dialogues would suggest that rhetorical display (and the later circulation of this display, cf. *TD* 5.61.121) had also long been a component of such gatherings. Cicero's letters (not exactly an unbiased witness) corroborate this claim:[35] of Atticus' frequent and literary soirees Nepos remarks, *neque umquam sine aliqua lectione apud eum cenatum est* ("he never hosted a dinner without a show," *Ep. Att.* 14.1–2), and in a discussion of the great success and expanding textual circulation of his *pro Ligario*, Cicero likens the private dinner party to a *theatrum*, so greatly have these secondary performances contributed to the popularity of his text:

. . . ad Ligarianam de uxore Tuberonis et priuigna neque possum iam addere (est enim peruulgata) neque Tuberonem uolo offendere; mirifice est enim φιλαίτιος. theatrum quidem sane bellum habuisti. (*Ep. Att.* 13.20 (45 BCE))

---

[34] Cf. *Ep. Fam. 9.2*, to Varro: *sed hoc tu melius; modo nobis stet illud: una uiuere in studiis nostris, in quibus antea delectationem modo petebamus, nunc uero etiam salutem; non deesse, si quis adhibere uolet, non modo ut architectos, uerum etiam ut fabros, ad aedificandam rem publicam, et potius libenter accurrere; si nemo utetur opera, tamen et scribere et legere* πολιτείας; *et si minus in curia atque in foro, at in litteris et libris, ut doctissimi ueteres fecerunt, gubernare rem publicam et de moribus ac legibus quaerere*; and *Ep. Fam. 9.26*, to Paetus: *uiuas, inquis, in litteris. an quidquam me aliud egere censes aut possem uiuere, nisi in litteris uiuerem? . . . sic igitur uiuitur: quotidie aliquid legitur aut scribitur; dein, ne amicis nihil tribuamus, epulamur una . . .* The theme of "Tusculan life" as a retreat from the state appears again in *Ep. Fam. 9.6.4*.

[35] See Cic. *Ep. Att.* 16.2. fin., 16.3.1, 13.2.2.

I can't add anything to my "pro Ligario" about Tubero's wife and stepdaughter (for the thing has been published); nor do I want Tubero to be ticked off at me – the fellow's a terrific *épilogeur*. But that was certainly a nice little theater you had there![36]

Catullus frequently identifies the private dinner as a locus for the sharing and recitation of verse (so cc. 12 and 50, both discussed in Part I, and to the second of which we shall return in Chapter 7). But c. 44, a poem addressed to Catullus' own *suburbana uilla* (ll. 6–7), provides us with perhaps unexpected – and all the more tantalizing – evidence for a late Republican kinship between the convivium and the *oratio* in the production and publication of texts:

> ... Malamque pectore expuli tussim,
> non immerenti quam mihi meus uenter,
> dum sumptuosas appeto, dedit, cenas
> nam, Sestianus dum uolo esse conuiua   10
> orationem in Antium petitorem
> plenam ueneni et pestilentiae legi.

> ... and I got rid of that nasty cough,
> Which my belly gave me (and I deserved it!),
> While I was chasing after fancy feasts.
> Since I wanted to be invited to a convivium at Sestius'   10
> I read an *oratio* of his against the candidate Antius – the
> venomous beast practically did me in.

Whether or not this *Oratio in Antium* is to be performed at the convivium to which the poet seeks entrance – an attractive interpretation, though others are available – the implication is that the poet has been invited to dine with the expectation that he will have read the *oratio* before the event. The acceptance of an offered *oratio* (and probably the post-delivery rehearsal of such, cf. *Ep. Att.* 13.12.2–3) likely being polished up for textual distribution[37] serves as a kind of entry token into subsequent display

---

[36] On the use of *bellus* here to indicate subjective judgment, see Krostenko 2001: 51–59. Krostenko notes that *bellus* – originally the diminutive of *bonus* – normally expresses a level of subjectivity. It indicates a situation or circumstance that is favorable or well suited in reference to a particular individual: "The circle drawn by *bell(us)* may describe those of a certain intellectual character or literary taste. The 'fit readers but few' before whom Atticus gave a reading of Cicero's *pro Ligario* were a *bellum theatrum*. They were 'a nice bunch' or 'a good group,' as literary men like Cicero and Atticus would agree." On the implications of circulation for the philosophical text, see Murphy 1998.

[37] So Sandy 1978: 70, although Sandy supposes that Catullus was in some way Sestius' "client," a supposition that can be borne out by nothing in this poem (or indeed any other in the corpus). For the patronal-class request for a dinner invitation, cf. Plut. *Luc.* 41.3–5, in which we are told that

that the convivium will provide. But what sort of display is this? Poetic, perhaps; but in the case of Sestius' convivium, it is likely that rhetorical display – the rehearsal of forensic *orationes* that had already had a public audience – would have also figured large. This is important to our reading of *de Oratore*, and indeed to our understanding of both Republican textual culture as a whole and Cicero's literary and social program in the later dialogues, because it argues that the *orator in conuiuio* would have been a character familiar to Cicero's reading audience. If the "real" convivium is a place for both poetry and oratory, then the "textual" convivium might just as easily be imagined a place for literature, philosophy, and rhetoric.

Although poet and orator might seem strange social bedfellows at first glance, we need to remember that many men of the time engaged simultaneously in the political and poetic world, and the offhand remark of Catullus at c. 44.10 ("Since I wanted to be invited to a convivium at Sestius'...") suggests that poet and orator would have attended convivia in common as a matter of course; they would have shared not only food and drink, but also works of literature and acts of display. Indeed, both Catullus' joking reference to Cicero's skill in c. 49 (*dissertissime Romuli nepotum...*) and Cicero's wry (and vastly over-interpreted) comment about the *spondeiazon* of "hoi Neoteroi" at *Ep. Att.* 7.2.1 (*ita belle nobis flauit ab Epiro lenissimus Onchesmites. hunc spondeiazonta si cui uoles ton neoteron pro tuo uendito*) suggest shared, or at least overlapping, circles of poetic and rhetorical interaction and friendly competition far more than they do any kind of dark-hearted, seething enmity between bitter old orator and irreverent young rake (though to be sure the latter is a more amusing scenario). The poison tip on Catullus' poetic barb, of course, is that Sestius' *oratio* was so wretched[38] it made him physically ill. But even here, it is the quality of the oration that is criticized, not the fact that the orator and poet might dine – and display – in common. We saw in Part I that Catullus and Cicero intersect in their use of terms signifying leisure, reciprocity, literary obligation, and textual exchange. We should expect that the sharing of both text and display between the individuals of these groups would have been more of a rule than an exception.

Cicero certainly recognized an innate link between poetry and oratory, and he promotes this link repeatedly in his *technica*. He compares the

---

Cicero and Pompey caught Lucullus idling in the forum (shades of Catullus?) and requested that he invite them to dinner (on this cf. Wiseman 1982: 41). The Sestius of this poem is to be identified with Publius Sestius, Cicero's friend, and not his son, who was born in 73 and so clearly not the "host" Catullus had in mind.

[38] Alternatively, the poet's point may be that the oration made an excessively vicious attack on Antius. This is certainly possible, but the punchline (the poet's own illness) would be weakened.

two in the introduction of *de Oratore* (1.3.11–12), emphasizes their shared origins in *eloquentia* early in *Brutus* (cf. esp. 15.57–59),[39] and in *Tusculan Disputations*, after offering a brief review first of Greek and then of Latin poetry (1.3.3), he shifts to the claim that he will now Latinize philosophy by making it more like (his) oratory – that is, in his dialogues, which were by 44 a form of written discourse for which he can claim both recognition and respect in a textual community. Cicero emphasizes the many similarities between poetry and oratory, I suggest, in order to naturalize his own shift into the textualization of display and the subsequent dedication of such "display texts." And yet his at times heavy-handed comparisons of poetry and oratory suggest that although he recognizes that he is moving into a preexisting poetic model – one which locates textual generation in the doubtless often fictional discussions held in private homes, and which uses the dedication of texts to negotiate social relationships – he wants to make the case that *his* endeavor will carry greater authority in its desire and ability to "do things" in the extra-textual, and even political, world.[40] Catullus' dedications do not display such desire, and yet it is precisely this impulse – the impulse to use the text to interact with the non-textual world – that would become a fixed aspect of later textual dedication for authors who felt that the textual voice was the only one they had.

Conuiuium Tusculani (*de Orat.* 1.7.27) – the whole first book and, in a sense, the whole of Cicero's literary program revolve around – and truly "begin with" – these words and their suggestion that "the Latin dialogue begins here." Placed where they are, they signal on the one hand simply the close of the introductory portions of Cicero's narrative and all talk of the political crisis. The delights of literary conversation silence the sorrows of the forum. But coupled, as they are, with the imagery of Roman men reclining on pillows, displaying their erudition on matters of poetry, philosophy, and politics (for in *de Oratore* oratory is a combination of all three), these words introduce the characters – and us – to the atmosphere of urbane performance around which the remainder of the treatise is constructed. By invoking the social and literary expectations of the elite convivium, Cicero transforms his text into an intellectual feast and his readers into the invited guests to an intellectual "private party." Just as Cotta and Sulpicius are initiated into the elite rhetorical discourse, so too all of Cicero's young readers – Quintus, specifically, but by extension the whole of the Roman

---

[39] Tacitus suggests that poetry is a form of *eloquentia* at *Dial.* 10.4.
[40] This sentiment is echoed by Tacitus at *Dial.* 9.1 (poetry gains its author neither *dignitas* nor *utilitates*); 9.4 (poetry cannot accrue *amicitia*, and its fame is fleeting); and 10.1 (oratorical fame surpasses the poetic sort).

youth[41] – are initiated by him into the novel realm of elite textual exchange through the established doorway of elite convivial display. Pull up a chair – or rather, a pillow – and enjoy the party.

In *Brutus*, a text deeply concerned with the importance of writing and the orator's need to turn away from the forum and toward the sphere of private textual production, Cicero devotes much of his time to the discussion of each orator's reception by, and relationship to, his forensic audience.[42] As noted above, Cicero's discussion of the audience in *Brutus* makes clear the problems inherent in the orator's dependence upon his public and its judgment; and yet, as we saw, of only two orators throughout the history of Roman oratory – C. Visellius Varro and L. Gellius – does Cicero state that the opinion of the audience had been in direct contrast to his. And yet in *Brutus* Cicero's primary emphasis is that throughout most of the Republic the critical assessments of the audience were precisely identical to those of the most rhetorically trained. A question posed in the voice of Atticus:

Ex his Cotta et Sulpicius cum meo iudicio tum omnium facile primas tulerunt. hic Atticus: quo modo istuc dicis, inquit, cum tuo iudicio tum omnium? semperne in oratore probando aut improbando uolgi iudicium cum intellegentium iudicio congruit? an alii probantur multitudine, alii autem ab iis qui intellegunt? (*Brut.* 49.183)

"... of these, Cotta and Sulpicius – both by my judgment and by the judgment of all – easily take top honors." Atticus interrupted: "What do you mean 'by your judgment and by the judgment of all?' In deciding whether an orator is talented or not, does the judgment of the crowd always ally itself with the judgment of the few? Or is it the case that some men appeal to the multitude, and others just to the educated?"

is answered in that of Cicero:

Denique hoc specimen est popularis iudici, in quo numquam fuit populo cum doctis intellegentibusque dissensio. cum multi essent oratores in uario genere dicendi, quis umquam ex his excellere iudicatus est uolgi iudicio, qui non idem a doctis probaretur? (*Brut.* 50.189)

In this sort of popular judgment [of oratorical success] there is never disagreement between the opinion of the crowd, and that of the expert. For though there have

---

[41] On the young Quintus as representative of the Roman youth, see Leeman 1978.
[42] Cf. *Ep. Fam.* 9.6.4–5, written to Varro.

been many orators practicing every sort of style, has there ever been one who was judged exceptional by the people, and who was not similarly approved by the learned?

What is the meaning of this? If Cicero is trying to free himself and his colleagues from their dependence upon the unstable sympathies of the forensic audience, and to create instead a new kind of wholly textual display, why does he emphasize that the judgments of the audience had only rarely been in conflict with the judgments of the orator's peers? Why does he imply that, for the most part, the orator's audience had always been his most capable judge, when it seems a man arguing for the authority of a textual audience should do precisely the opposite?

Cicero's position here is a difficult one. He is unable to deny that the audience has always been an immensely powerful critical force in the orator's pursuit of public glory. Nor, indeed, would he want to. Questioning the historical judgment of the crowd would undermine not only the traditionally received opinions of Rome's oratorical past, but also the very source and substance of the orator's fame – and identity – in the arena of public display. But his insistence that the judgment of the "untrained" audience – the approval of the masses, the traditional source of an orator's "sellability" – will almost always ally itself with the judgment of the *docti*, involves a sleight of hand. If the crowd's judgment of ability can stand in for that of the learned, then the judgment of the learned can stand in for that of the crowd. In making this equation, the crowd – a crowd that, like a horse, might cease to "giddy up" when spurred – is made effectively obsolete: a nice thing if you've got it, but no longer particularly necessary as long as orators are writing and circulating their voice among a smaller and more stable circle of learned readers. And indeed, Cicero hints at places that the judgment of the learned, if it really comes down to it, will always trump that of the crowd. About halfway through the dialogue, he tips his hand:

At uero intellegens et doctus audiens Scaeuolam sentiret esse quoddam uberius dicendi genus et ornatius. ab utroque autem causa perorata si quaereretur uter praestaret orator, numquam profecto sapientis iudicium a iudicio uolgi discreparet. qui praestat igitur intellegens imperito? magna re et difficili; si quidem magnum est scire quibus rebus efficiatur amittaturue dicendo illud quicquid est, quod aut effici dicendo oportet aut amitti non oportet. praestat etiam illo doctus auditor indocto, quod saepe, cum oratores duo aut plures populi iudicio probantur, quod dicendi genus optumum sit intellegit. nam illud quod populo non probatur, ne intellegenti quidem auditori probari potest. (*Brut.* 53.198–4.199)

Indeed, a discerning and educated fellow, on hearing Scaevola speak, would have marked his rich and highly decorated style; but if at the end of the proceedings he were asked which of the two [who had spoken] was the better orator, the decision of this expert would never have differed from that of the crowd. So what is the advantage of the discerning critic over the man on the street? An immensely important one if, that is, it is a matter of any import to ascertain by what means the real gist of speaking – what is to be obtained or discarded – is actually obtained or discarded. The learned critic trumps the unlearned in this way as well: when two or more orators have gained public approval, as often happens, he will perceive which style is the better. For what the public dislikes must be equally rejected by the learned.

The end point of the passage is again that the judgment of the expert and that of the crowd will normally be in alliance; but the suggestion that the judgment of the learned – of Cicero, of Brutus, of Atticus and of all intended readers of the dialogue – carries with it the ability to get at "the real gist" of speaking is an important one. If the crowd has ceased to behave as it should – if, like a flute, it ceases to respond to an orator's breath[43] – then it has ceased to be of value. Cicero would never deny that the orator needs an audience; the question here is what audience shall he seek?

It is one of the more forceful points of *Brutus* that the orator's audience has always been a bifurcated one: that of the *imperitus* "listening crowd," on the one hand, and the *doctus* "reading expert," on the other. By first collapsing, and then carefully separating, these two categories, and by demonstrating (more than arguing) that only the orator who writes will be able to be judged by the critics who "really matter" (and these are the critics who read), Cicero's terse little history of Roman orators would seem to turn Roman oratory on its head. The *corona* of listeners is usurped by a *corona* of readers and critics (we think again of Catullus' textual rehearsal of "someone" from the forensic *corona* who seized on the opportunity to heckle Calvus, cf. 53); public speech is transformed into a written affair; and the forum in which Republican oratory was born is now to be made entirely of "paper."

It is to this "paper forum" that the orators of Rome's future must turn:

Tu tamen, etsi cursum ingeni tui, Brute, premit haec importuna clades ciuitatis, contine te in tuis perennibus studiis et effice id quod iam propemodum uel plane potius effeceras, ut te eripias ex ea, quam ego congessi in hunc sermonem, turba patronorum. (*Brut.* 97.332)

---

[43] In an interesting echo of the *tibicen* passage cited earlier in this section, in what immediately follows this discussion of the fallibility of audience judgment Cicero likens the audience to a musical instrument played by the orator: *ut enim ex neruorum sono in fidibus quam scienter ei pulsi sint intellegi solet, sic ex animorum motu cernitur quid tractandis his perficiat orator.*

Nevertheless, Brutus, although this ill-timed public disaster rests heavily on your career, hide yourself within your ageless pursuit of literature and do that which you have almost – rather *already* – done: tear yourself from that crowd of *patroni* I have just piled so high.

Brutus as a whole both mimics and alters the traditional structure of forensic display in its implied structure of the written and circulated *oratio*. Traditional display (as it is represented in the dialogue) consisted of a primary performance, via the spoken *oratio*, followed by several repeated performances, via the circulation, rehearsal, and subsequent critique of the written *orationes*. But at the same time, and through a suppression of both the primacy of speech and the authority of the "listening" audience, *Brutus* makes redundant the prerequisite of the primary performance; or rather, it suggests that because the secondary performance is the one that "really counts," it may stand in for the primary without diminution of oratorical status. For whereas the forensic audience had had its sensibilities dulled by the glut of Roman spectacle and the assault of Caesarian politics, the audience to which Cicero urges Brutus to turn will be one of impeccable and irreproachable taste and judgment; it will be an audience that will never confuse oratorical excellence and vulgar popularity. The orator who does not write is heard once and then silenced. But when the orator transports this voice to the text, when he privileges the secondary performance to the (for Cicero, ultimate) exclusion of the primary, he is then able to transcend the traditional boundaries of time, space, and social order and to enter a textual world in which he could survive, as Catullus and Nepos recognized, for "more than one generation."

As many have noted, for a text ostensibly concerned with Rome's oratorical "voice," *Brutus* is oddly interested in Rome's oratorical "text." Although writing (and reading) as a whole is highlighted throughout, one of the most pressing themes of *Brutus* is that only orators who have left behind their written orations are able to enter the historical record in full: only "writing orators" can be truly remembered for their skill.[44] The dialogue begins with a discussion of literary exchange between the three interlocutors (3.14–5.21) that includes pointed reference to the written rehearsal of speech: a discussion in Tusculum (5.20) is given as the model of the dialogue itself, and an oration of Brutus both heard and judged by Cicero "after the fact"

---

[44] Cf. *Brut.* 13.52: *ueniamus ad nostros, de quibus difficile est plus intellegere quam quantum ex monumentis suspicari licet*; and 23–24.91: *quid igitur, inquit, est causae, Brutus, si tanta uirtus in oratore Galba fuit, cur ea nulla in orationibus eius appareat? quod mirari non possum in eis, qui nihil omnino scripti reliquerunt. nec enim est eadem inquam, Brute, causa non scribendi et non tam bene scribendi quam dixerint.*

(5.21; Brutus' defense of Deiotarus did not succeed in the courts, but is given high honors by Cicero) is offered as valuable evidence for the general degradation of forensic opinion and the importance of the "reading judge." In the early sections of the work, Cicero notes that unless an orator has also written, his excellence can be merely surmised (cf. *Brut.* 13.52, cited above); he emphasizes shortly thereafter that the eloquence of Ti. Coruncanius is known only from his pontifical *commentarii* (14.55). The entire issue of whether or how well orators write their orations – and why they should do so – receives lengthy discussion (23.91–24.94, cited in part at the head of this section): the skill of Curio is known from his written orations (32.122), as is Scaevola's mastery of language (44.113); the importance of reading such orations as a key to judging this skill is mentioned on numerous occasions (cf. 35.132–133 and 89.305).[45]

It is impossible to conclude how many orators in the middle Republic had circulated their *orationes* as Cicero describes (I suspect that it was a fairly common practice; we shall return to this in Chapter 8), just as it is impossible to determine how frequently such orations were rehearsed, in the late Republic, in private convivial settings. But it is clear that some transmission of written *orationes* did occur, just as it is clear that oratorical recitation was not a particularly unusual component of elite leisure activity, and I think it is likely that the activity of these years is what may have fixed the later use of *oratio* to designate (as it did for Cicero and Tacitus) the dialogue qua a text that "speaks" to the extra-textual world. Cicero's claim in *Brutus*, as noted above, is that all he knows of the history of Roman oratory depends upon just such texts (fitting irony, then, that almost all we know of the history of Roman oratory depends on *Brutus*), and by the time of the publication of *Brutus*, we hear of great numbers of such circulated volumes.[46] And although the claim is a pointed one, and one repeated in various guises throughout the text, it is never accompanied by the "semantic signposts" – *tamquam, ut ita dicam*, and the like – that Cicero typically uses to key his readers in to an especially risky, ironical, or anxiety-filled assertion. In promoting this early ideal of the "writing" orator, and by claiming that the august orators of the past had always looked to their reading audience – and the "secondary performance" of which this audience is the judge – as a means of securing lasting oratorical renown,

---

[45] Such references run throughout the dialogue; see esp. 20.80–21.82 and 26.99.

[46] At *Brut.* 32.122–123 "Atticus" and "Brutus" are made to refer to the great number of available written speeches as *turba nouorum uoluminum*. "Brutus" implies that Cicero is no small contributor to the cause; *uir ipse* concedes: *praeclare, inquit Brutus, teneo qui istam turbam uoluminum effecerit. et ego, inquam, intellego, Brute, quem dicas . . .*

Cicero suggests to his readers, as much as to his dialogic interlocutors, that the orators of Rome's future will be able to secure their fame through a reading audience alone.

It is worth pointing out that the middle and late Republican circulation of written *orationes* constitutes a form of the textualization of display – forensic display. Catullus, a man whose only forensic display was that of *otium*, speaks to a late Republican textualization of display that, if not utterly unconcerned with forensic display, nevertheless pushed such display into the background and promoted in its stead the private display of the home. An important aspect of Catullus' textualization of private display – and an aspect that will become especially important to Cicero's textualization of such – is that because private display is private, and because the audience of such display is restricted, controllable, and potentially in collusion, textualized private display becomes textual display alone, with no expectation of a "real" prototype in the "real" world.[47] In Cicero's creation of a "paper forum" he taps into a preexisting late Republican praxis and – all evidence suggests this was a predominately Ciceronian innovation – shifts that praxis into the realm of politically interested prose dialogue. As early as the *Actio Secunda* of the trial against Verres, Cicero must have begun to suspect that the primacy of original display might be challenged by a text that presented itself as the record of that display – even if such never occurred. With *de Oratore, Brutus,* and the *technica* of his final years, Cicero introduced his reading audience to the notion that the oratorical – and, by extension, political and philosophical – text need not be predicated on the primary "real-world" display of the orator's voice, and that in addition to the epideictic display of the declamation halls (which function as another retreat from the forum in later periods, and to which certain aspects of the dialogues might be compared) the rhetorical display of the dialogues provided a profitable outlet for oratorical ability and social negotiation.[48] Cicero's textual display, though he continued in the dialogues to "pretend" (with a wink at the reader) to record prior spoken display, was finally freed from its prior dependence upon forensic display. Cicero had attacked the primacy of forensic display; and though it was an attack made out of

---

[47] These "plausible fictions" will be discussed below.
[48] Declamation functioned similarly as a retreat from the forum in later years, and similarly offered a form of "private" and "literary" oratory to those for whom the forum was out of reach. To Tacitus' Messalla, however, such empty displays had little to do with the "real" oratory of the later Republic (*Dial.* 31.1–4). On Roman declamation (and rhetoric) in the later period, see most recently Boomer 2007 (on Seneca and Quintilian) and Dominik 2007 (on Tacitus and Pliny), both with further bibliography.

desperation, he had struck a solid blow and one that would resound for centuries.

Thus, what seems at first to be a dialogue about speaking and the parity of vulgar and learned judgment slowly becomes a dialogue about writing and the ultimate redundancy of the forensic crowd. It is no small mark of the orator's skill that this paradoxical little gift-text (a *libellus*, through and through) does not offer merely *a* history of Roman orators, "when they arose, who they were, and of what sort" (*Brut.* 5.20); for modern scholars, it has come to offer *the* history of Roman orators. In Cicero's strange revision of the whole of Roman history (and some of Greek history as well) according to oratorical act rather than consular year, and in his casual privileging of the "writing orator" over the one who merely orates, he has made lasting oratorical fame – participation in the creation and propagation of oratorical *memoria* – inescapably contingent upon the ability and willingness to write. For the orators of Rome's past, this had meant the writing and circulation of their speeches. For the orators of Cicero's present, this means the writing, dedication, and circulation of intellectually engaged texts – the entry into the textual community. In his occasionally bumbling and almost apologetic claim that he who writes, wins, Cicero has scripted for himself the role of greatest victor of them all.

CHAPTER 6

The poetics of literary obligation

OBLIGED TO SPEAK: WHY AN ORATOR CAN'T HELP HIMSELF

In order to impose a strong sense of obligation and reciprocity on his written political voice, Cicero needed to adapt the unwritten system of rules, duties, and presumptions of the forum into the new medium of the exchanged literary text. There is no perfect term to describe this system, this understanding of expected social performance in the forum and between recognized orators, but we might designate it as a kind of "forensic obligation." It is forensic (as opposed to domestic, for instance, or martial) both in terms of geographical orientation – it is the obligation of the forum – and in terms of context – it is the principle that governs forensic practice. It is an obligation (as opposed to a habit or an expectation) because the actions required by this system were taken to be compulsory and binding (neither optional, nor a matter of preference); when an orator claims that he speaks only because he is under a forensic obligation to do so, he means that his voice is not passively expected – it is actively required.

It can pass without remark that Cicero and those with whom he habitually exchanges his texts were well conversant in the language and subtleties of forensic obligations; and indeed, this is the subject of many of Cicero's *technica*. For the most part, however, and if Cicero's apparent insecurity in the early stages of his project is any evidence (the relative timidity of *de Oratore*'s introductory sections stands in stark contrast to the increasing boldness of the *prooemia* to the later dialogues), this sort of obligation was traditionally considered as primarily oral even when the ultimate product of this obligation was the written, "post-production" version of the speech. As many have recognized, the textualization not only of display, but also of the language of social obligation, functioned as an important aspect of Catullus' dedicated texts: even the man who did not participate in the political sphere understood and incorporated the linguistic currency of its negotiations. What we see in the case of Cicero is that, in the mid 50s

BCE, when he conceived that the form of the dedicated dialogue might satisfy both his need to retreat from the forum and his desire to expand – or at least maintain – his social, political, and intellectual authority, he too sought not only to transform social form into written substance, but to turn the *oral* obligations of the forum into the *written* obligations of an established, and in these years especially vibrant, textual community.

To a certain extent, the literary structure of the dialogue resembles the oral form of rhetorical discourse. And although the dialogues, which combine witty off-the-cuff exchange and intimate innuendo with longer pieces of rhetorical "display," resemble epideictic oratory (the one branch notably absent from the discussion of *de Oratore*) rather than, strictly speaking, the forensic sort, they nevertheless provide a pleasing echo of an established form of display.[1] But as much as oratorical display – whether epideictic or forensic – provides an unmistakable backdrop for the dialogues, rather more compelling are the ways in which the dialogue form mimics precisely the relationship of ongoing textual and social reciprocity as enacted between author and dedicatee.[2] In *de Oratore*, the relationship of rhetorical reciprocity between Antonius and Crassus (the "conversation" itself) mirrors the relationship of textual, and indeed intellectual, reciprocity between Marcus and Quintus. It pantomimes the dedication and receipt of this "conversation" as much as it predicts the "conversation" between siblings that will provide the textual substance of *de Divinatione* some ten years later and suggests, in the relationship of the elder interlocutors to the younger, the relationship of textual producers to all subsequent recipients.

In *Brutus*, the conversation between the three protagonists – Brutus, Atticus, and Cicero himself – is also a conversation between three partners in textual reciprocity. The prologue to the dialogue provides a meticulously drafted road map to precisely these exchanges as if to specify for both the "real-life" interlocutors (the Brutus, Atticus, and Cicero who exist outside of the text), and indeed subsequent readers of the dialogue (the extended Society of Patrons), the precise rules of the game. In this latter text, as I will discuss below, it is especially difficult to distinguish the original from the

---

[1] Although I would locate the primary source for the dialogue style in epideictic oratory, Cicero draws out a judicial resonance in the good-natured disagreements between Antonius and Crassus. See esp. *de Orat.* 1.10.41: [Antonius speaks] *quod uero in extrema oratione, quasi tuo iure sumpsisti . . . id, nisi in tuo regno essemus, non tulissem, multisque praeessem, qui aut interdicto tecum contenderent, aut te ex iure manu consertum uocarent, quod in alienas possessiones tam temere irruisses*; to this cf. 1.14.61; 1.17.4.

[2] On this mirroring of textual and social form, cf. Stewart 1993: 7: "Rooted in the ideological, the literary genre determines the shape and progress of its material; but, at the same time, the genre itself is determined by the social formations from which it arises. The relation between literary producer and consumer will be reflected in the form of the genre."

mimesis, and we end up with a funhouse effect of mirror images: *Brutus* is a written "record" of an oral mimesis of written reciprocity; it is a rehearsal of an earlier conversation on precisely the topic of how important it is for speakers to write.

Indeed, reciprocal mirroring of literary and social form is an important feature of the majority of Cicero's dedicated treatises. The eponymous *Laelius* and *Cato* reflect, in their vibrantly theatrical dialogues, the underlying social interaction of donor and dedicatee (in each case, Atticus; we lack the bulk of *Hortensius*, but we know it was at least partially dialogic in form and would likely have displayed a similar dynamic); the vaguely epistolary *de Divinatione* and the non-dialogic *de Officiis* suggest long-distance communication between brothers and friends or father and son, and even the strangely "anonymous" interlocutors of the *Tusculan Disputations* are suggestive of the schoolhouse atmosphere Cicero seemed to have in mind in the construction of dialogues as "villas" that would serve as houses of learning to future generations. In each case the dialogue provides a didactic model for the relationship of reciprocity between the author and his audience. It teaches a lesson in urbane and isonomic turn-taking, and when the dedicatee reaches the end of the dialogue, and if he has learned his lesson well, the message is clear. *Now it's your turn: write something…*

That the form of the dialogue mimics the form of the social relationship is not to ignore or lessen the influence of Cicero's literary predecessors in this genre – Plato, of course, but also Aristotle and Theophrastus[3] – but there is an important novelty to Cicero's decision to write dialogues and, indeed, to his dialogue project as a whole. Simply put, and whatever we might suppose about what Cicero does in his appropriation of a Greek literary form for the propagation (if not invention) of his own Latin dialogue, he did not have to do it. Appropriation is not a passive process: Cicero was not obligated to select the dedicated dialogue for his rhetorical, political, and philosophical treatises; and yet, and as we have noted, for fourteen of the nineteen that have survived, he did.[4] There were

---

[3] Plato's dialogues are the usual suspects when it comes to Ciceronian *Quellenforschung*, and especially in the case of *de Oratore*. Although *de Oratore* is partially in dialogue with Plato (and most specifically *Phaedrus*), it is not, by any stretch of the imagination, a Platonic dialogue. Although both *Phaedrus* and *Gorgias* are invoked by the elder protagonists at the start of the discussion (1.7.28; 1.11.47), these references emphasize Cicero's appropriation of the dialogue form and and Plato's defense of writing (the first reference; on *Phaedrus* as a defense of writing, cf. Burger 1980) and his ability to make clever references to rhetorical criticism (the second). In the preface to book 2 of *de Divinatione*, Cicero mentions not Plato, but Aristotle and Theophrastus as his influences. See *Ep. Fam.* 1.9.23 on Aristotelian influence in *de Oratore*.

[4] The dialogues include: *de Orat.*; *de Rep.*; *de Leg.*; *Brut.*; *Part. Orat.*; *Acad. Prior.*; *Acad. Post.*; *de Fin.*; *TD*; *DND*; *de Div.*; *de Fato*; *Cato*; and *Lael.*; of the later *technica*, only *de Opt. Gen.*; *Orator*;

certainly non-dialogic exempla from which to choose, such as the *annales* of the middle Republic, which served as family records of genealogical accomplishment and affiliation.[5] The annalistic form is later adopted by historiographers and the *literati*; it would have been a literary genre both familiar to Cicero and well established by the 50s BCE, and one that is echoed, if dialogically, in the oratorical "histories" of *Brutus*. But *annales* were properly the stuff of intrafamilial and intergenerational circulation, and the tacit presumption of objectivity upon which they were predicated made them a poor choice for the implicitly subjective interests of dedicatory material – that is, it made them a poor choice for the extrafamilial publication required by Cicero – precisely because to dedicate a text to an extrafamilial individual is to make oneself at least potentially subject to that individual's desires. The memoir, a kind of private version of the more politically – and certainly textually – interested *commentarius*, was suitable for extrafamilial dedication, and we noted in the Introduction that Sulla dedicated his own memoirs (ὑπομνήματα) to Lucullus early in the first century BCE.[6] Cicero includes elements of the memoir – a reflective summary of his past is coupled with thoughtful advice on the recipient's future[7] – in the prefaces, and occasionally conclusions, to several of his dialogues. But even when he does, it is the dialogue form that structures the work as a whole; for though the memoir admitted the voice of just a single man, what Cicero needed was a way of speaking in the voices of many. What he does, then, is innovate: he writes not just his words, but

---

Parad. Stoic.; *Top.*; and *de Off.* are non-dialogic in form. On the evidence of the surviving *technica*, in which eponymous treatises are without exception also dialogues, it is likely that the eponymous *Hortensius* was written as a dialogue. Cicero's choice of the dialogue form has occasionally led to attacks on his (lack of) originality. Clarke 1996: 51 is skeptical of Cicero's rhetorical originality, and notes Aristotelian influence: "How far can we consider these ideas as Cicero's own? He himself said of *De Oratore* that it embodied the principles of Aristotle and Isocrates and of the ancients generally . . . for all of his lively receptiveness, his competence and his charm of manner Cicero often disappoints us . . . " We have lost the Aristotelian dialogues to which both Cicero and Clarke must refer, and so cannot judge the degree or expression of claimed influence. See further Fortenbaugh 1989.

5 On this see most recently Feldherr 1998: 20 19–25; Feldherr follows the prosopographical overviews of early historians provided by Badian 1966 and Frier 1999: 201–224. Conte 1994: 86–87 discusses Cato (himself a possible innovator in annalistic form) and the aristocratic tradition of Roman historiography. It appears that Cato did rewrite some of his own political speeches into *Origines*, but it is difficult to determine to what extent, if any, this choice influenced Cicero's further innovations in the genre.

6 Cf. Plut. *Sulla* 6.6: ἔτι δὲ Λευκόλλωι μὲν ἐν τοῖς ὑπομνήμασιν, ὧν ἐκείνωι τὴν γραφὴν ἀνατέθεικε . . .

7 On such elements at the beginnings of the dialogue, cf. e.g. *de Orat.*; *Brut.*; *de Fin.*; *TD* 1.1; *DND* 1.1; for such elements at the conclusion, cf. *Brut.* 96.330–end and *Lael.* 104; the dedicated and epistolary, but non-dialogic, *de Officiis* contains such elements at both the beginning and end of the text (cf. esp. 3.33.121). On select prefaces, cf. Habinek 1994.

his *voice*; and indeed, not just his voice, but the voices of Rome's most cherished and respected individuals; and indeed, not just his voice and the voices of Rome's *maiores* (and occasionally *iuniores*), but these voices engaged in lively pantomime of recognizable rhetorical – and often epide-ictic – form. The orator's voice was both an invaluable commodity in the late Republic and an unparalleled tool in facilitating homosocial alliances and obligations. Cicero, more than anyone, recognized the importance of controlling it, manipulating it, and – by containing it within the text – making every voice Roman, and every Roman voice his own.

De Oratore is the dialogue most closely allied to its oral – and oratorical – foundations. In the years that follow its publication, however, the dialogue project really gets going, and the dialogic form resides at the center of Cicero's sociointellectual agenda. For even if it is in the *Epistulae* that Cicero will find his ultimate legacy,[8] he chooses the dialogue for almost all of his exchanged or dedicated texts. As favored as the form was, however, this transformation of the oratorical voice into a token of elite reciprocity, this textualizing and objectifying personification of the ideal Republican subject, this creation of an oratorical voice that only underlined the reality of increasing oratorical silence, all were a clear source of anxiety.

This was an anxiety most evident in the dedications that introduce and explain these texts. The dedicatory sections of many of the dialogues – *de Oratore* and *Brutus* especially, but others as well – are acutely concerned with the difficult translation of public and oral authority (and obligations) into a private and non-oral form. Although Cicero does not name the difficulty outright, we can locate it, as I argued above, in the economically fraught orality of Roman forensic obligations and rhetorical performance. The very social power that made the orator's voice a nearly irresistible force at the height of Cicero's political career became a liability in its decline.

The social power of the orator's voice, and the close relationship between orator and audience, are recurrent themes of *de Oratore* and *Brutus*. In discussions of the successful and memorable orator, Cicero teaches that it is important for the orator to regulate his display in response to his audience's expectations. At the same time, however, he emphasizes that – at least in the case of forensic oratory – an orator's professional skill may be judged by

---

[8] I am thinking here primarily of Seneca and Pliny but also, perhaps, of the poetic epistles of Horace, Juvenal, and Ovid. Needless to say, there is a tradition of post-Ciceronian dialogists in the years following his death; and yet Tacitus' *Dialogus*, in which the final sections present a typical Ciceronian request for future discussion (and future dialogues), followed by laughter on the part of everyone but Tacitus and then the departure of all (*cum adrisissent, discessimus*, 42.2), seems to annul any possibility for the survival of the dialogic voice.

the tone and tenor of his voice alone. This emphasis gets at the problem of translating oral authority into written form. Forensic speech is as socially powerful as it is socially fraught. The orator's voice was considered not merely a trustworthy representation of his native intelligence, rhetorical education, and moral character. It was a sign of the orator's social standing and identity.

The forensic voice, we might say, finds its social and political meaning only in the presence of its complement: a non-oratorical, non-speaking, audience. The orator must not only win his case, he must win over his listeners. An early passage of *de Oratore* is illustrative of the problem. Crassus comments on the grave implications of public speech:

> magnum quoddam est onus atque munus suscipere atque profiteri se esse, omnibus silentibus, unum maximis de rebus magno in conventu hominum audiendum. (*de Orat.* 1.25.116)

> It is a great burden, if you will, and a *munus*, for a fellow to step forward and – as all stand silent – to claim in crowded assembly that when it comes to matters of the greatest importance, *he alone is the only man worth hearing.*

A passage like this tells us that – as far as Cicero was concerned – the orator's identity resides in his voice and everything it stands for. The successful use of this voice, his ability to speak as all stand silent, is an important source of forensic authority. And yet, how can he claim that he alone is worthy to be heard? How can he both diffuse the danger of his public speech, and present himself as safe, and indeed authoritative, enough to "stand alone" and address the audience?

It is a commonplace in Cicero's *orationes* that the source of his oratorical authority is predicated on the implicit fulfillment of the forensic obligation that has required him to speak in the first place. He is sure to remind the audience, either explicitly or implicitly, that his speech – or more precisely, the act of his speaking – is the inevitable outcome of a complex social equation. His voice is both requested and required; it is an elite *munus*, owed either his client or the Republic as a whole, to which he is bound to respond. In order to get at both the underlying meaning of this expressed obligation, and the form that it takes, it will be good to consider a somewhat peculiar, although by no means "original," rhetorical technique of which Cicero is most fond: an initial profession of reluctance to speak followed by a detailed *apologia* of social compulsion or obligation and, finally, by an urbanely reluctant assumption of the oratorical authority through which his case may be made. The technique is played out, in the *prooemia* to many of the forensic orations, as follows. First, Cicero makes the claim that he is deeply reluctant to speak to the case at hand: he professes to lack the age, the *auctoritas*, and the desire to presume that he alone should be heard. He next excuses his presence in the forum by referring to a specific social, political, or personal obligation or expectation under which he has been compelled to speak: perhaps his *cliens* is a family friend or someone to whom he owes a good turn, or perhaps he has been cajoled into giving the defense by an individual whose request he cannot politely refuse. Only then, when he has explained his reason for speaking in public as a matter of respectful submission to the rules of social behavior, does he "resign himself" to the burden of oral authority, and begin the speech proper (as he does, finally, at *Cael.* 2.5–6). Cicero's technique transforms an otherwise possibly presumptuous, socially problematic, and at least potentially over-proud display into the ultimate act of urbane – and even modest – Republican politesse.

A fine early example of this technique occurs in the orator's defense of S. Roscius of Ameria in 80 BCE. He begins with a brief declaration of his reluctance, and unsuitability, to speak to the case at hand:

credo ego uos, iudices, mirari quid sit quod, cum tot summi oratores hominesque nobilissimi sedeant, ego potissimum surrexerim, is qui neque aetate neque ingenio neque auctoritate sim cum his qui sedeant comparandus . . . (*Rosc.* 1.1)

I am sure, judges, that you are wondering why it is that, with so many outstanding orators and influential men yet seated, I above all should stand – I, who am to be compared to those seated neither in age, nor talent, nor authority . . .

But the young orator's protestations of reluctance to speak turn quickly into an oddly unconvincing *apologia* of why he must speak nonetheless. He is neither especially bold (*audacissimus . . . ex omnibus*, 1.2), nor eager to gain praise for his public duties (*officiosior quam ceteri? ne istius quidem laudis ita sum cupidus . . .*, 1.2). Indeed, the orator speaks not because he wishes to at all, but because he is obliged to: the special circumstances of his age and status – each one inferior to those men who "remain seated" – are precisely what require him to speak when, and where, and *as* these others cannot. His youth and relative public obscurity, so far from working against him in this prosecution, are what will protect him, and what allow him to speak more freely – *liberius* (1.3); the implication is "more honestly" – than other more mature and established *patroni*.[9] Finally, he admits, he is

---

[9] 1.3: *Deinde quod ceterorum neque dictum obscurum potest esse propter nobilitatem et amplitudinem neque temere dicto concedi propter aetatem et prudentiam. ego si quid liberius dixero, uel occultum esse propterea, quod nondum ad rem publicam accessi, uel ignosci adulescentiae meae poterit.*

simply required to speak out of personal obligation to those who requested that he do so:[10]

A me autem ei contenderunt, qui apud me et amicitia et beneficiis et dignitate plurimum possunt, quorum ego nec beniuolentiam erga me ignorare nec auctoritatem aspernari nec uoluntatem neglegere debebam. (*Rosc.* 1.4)

But those men who asked me [to defend this case] are those whose *amicitia*, kindnesses, and rank carry great weight with me; I could neither ignore their goodwill toward me, nor discount their influence, nor neglect their wishes.

This technique of "reluctance and resignation" occurs, in various guises, throughout the corpus of orations. In the *prooemium* to *pro Caelio*, a defense delivered in 56 and not long after the orator's return from exile, Cicero's emphasis on the ludicrous nature of the case (1.1–2)[11] suggests that he – and his audience – would rather be spending their time otherwise entertained; it is his personal connection with both Caelius and his father (4.9–10) that requires him to do so. In *pro Balbo*, delivered later that year, Cicero questions his role (*partes*, 1.1) in the trial, and responds that he is there to defend Balbus (in whose defense Pompey and Crassus had both spoken) not because of his great influence, experience, or ability, but by his strong personal obligation to the defendant.[12] The words with which he will defend Balbus are presented as a social currency with which he can repay with (his) speech a debt incurred through (another's) action.[13]

In every instance of this rhetorically tense process of reluctance, apology, and resignation, there is one constant. The orator's act of speaking does not originate in an unbridled, autonomic desire for forensic fame or political and personal authority. It is located, rather, in the subtle intersection of an appropriately modest reluctance to speak in so public a setting (likely a deflection of criticisms that he is eager to perform) and those social obligations or expectations which require that the orator speak nonetheless. The orator has no choice but to speak, and so no choice but to build increasingly and endlessly on his public and personal fame – to gain influence and authority with every word spoken. It is not his will: it is his *duty*. And

[10] To this passage cf. Plut. *Sulla* 1.2, of the request of L. Torquatus.
[11] On New Comedy elements in *pro Caelio*, see Geffcken 1973 and 1995.
[12] 1.1: *Quae sunt igitur meae partes? Auctoritatis tantae, quantam vos in me esse voluistis, usus mediocris, ingenii minime voluntati paris; nam ceteris, a quibus est defensus, hunc debere plurimum video; ego quantum ei debeam, alio loco.* We learn later that Cicero's debt to Balbus lies in the latter's kind service to Cicero's associations during the orator's recent period of exile, cf. 26.58: *Non modo non exsultauit in ruinis nostris uestrisque sordibus Cornelius, sed omni officio – lacrimis, opera, consolatione – omnis me absente meos subleuauit.*
[13] *Balb.* 1.2: *principio orationis hoc pono, me omnibus, qui amici fuerint saluti et dignitati meae, si minus referenda gratia satis facere potuerim, praedicanda et habenda certe satis esse facturum.*

indeed it is this sense of forensic obligation – this perfectly crafted social dead-end from which the only escape is a continued accrual of status – that an orator who had for the first time in his life begun to experience a marked and ongoing decrease in such status would have sought to translate into written form. But if the orator locates the *auctoritas* of his public speech in his personal and forensic obligations, how does he introduce a written obligation that will leave him no choice but to "speak" in private?

OBLIGED TO WRITE: MAKING THE OFFER
THAT CAN'T BE REFUSED

As we turn to the textualization of social obligation, and the affectively and textually productive systems in which Catullus and Cicero contextualize such obligations, it will be helpful to consider briefly the fifth-century BCE *rhetor* and elegist, Dionysios Chalcous.[14] Dionysios, born in Athens but identified as a founder of Thurii, is best known for his symposiastic elegies and, most especially, a poem that describes the game of *kottabos* and the activities of the *gymnasion* (fr. 3). The fragment we are interested in, however, is fr. 1; similarly symposiastic in setting and theme, this fragment describes not a game of *kottabos* but one of poetic production, dedication, and awaited reciprocation:

> [Ὦ Θεόδωρε][15] δέχου τήνδε προπινομένην
> τὴν ἀπ᾽ ἐμοῦ ποίησιν· ἐγὼ δ᾽ ἐπιδέξια πέμπω
> σοὶ πρώτωι, Χαρίτων ἐγκεράσας χάριτας.
> καὶ σὺ λαβὼ ν τόδε δῶρον ἀοιδᾶς ἀντιπρόπιθι,
> συμπόσιον κοσμῶν καὶ τὸ σὸν εὖ θέμενος.
>
> Dionysios Chalcous, fr. 1 (IE²: 59; PE, vol. 2: 1)

> [O Theodoros]: Receive – here's to you! – this toast
> Of my poetry; I rightly send it right over
> To you first of all, Graces blended with graces.
> And you, then: take this gift and give songs in return,
> Adorning our symposion and adding to your own glory.

This dedication is a simple one, but rich in the imagery of isonomic sympotic culture. "Theodoros" is instructed to receive the poem as a "toast"

---

[14] On Dionysios "ὁ Χαλκοῦς," see *RE* 97; an interesting suggestion on possible economic associations of his name is found in Ath. *Deipn.* (669d; cf. Callimachus, Pf. fr. 430), where Dionysios "the Brazen" is identified as the individual who urged the Athenians to adopt bronze coinage.

[15] "Theodoros" would not have been the original dedicatee, but this is the name supplied by Democritus when quoting the poem, as recorded by Athenaeus (cf. Ath. 669e); it is included above only to indicate the likelihood of first-position dedicatee in the vocative (as per Democritus' supplementation of it) and in order to avoid the excessively awkward repetition of "the dedicatee."

(προπινομένην, l. 1)[16] produced specifically by Dionysios (ἀπ᾽ ἐμοῦ, l. 2), and now "sent rightly" (ἐπιδέξια, l. 2; "to the right," but also "cleverly"; the pun is difficult to translate)[17] to its recipient, thus blending graces with the Graces (Χαρίτων ἐγκαράσας χάριτας, l. 3), which is to say, poetry with poetry[18] in terms suggestive of an ongoing cycle of production and reciprocation. And indeed, the next line advises "Theodorus" to "take up" the textual gift (δῶρον; this is the first use of δῶρον to refer explicitly to a poem created by its author),[19] and dedicate (ἀντιπρόπιθι) a song in return, both for the pleasure of group and for his own poetic fame.

As it stands, the elegy is an important piece of evidence for what we know to have been an ongoing tradition of sympotic poetic production and performance.[20] In addition – because Dionysios was a *rhetor* as much as an elegist – it attests to a similarly ongoing tradition of the symposion as a locus of rhetorical and poetic display: a textually productive space in which orators, poets, and philosophers might meet, as equals, and share not only discussion and dining but indeed produce, perform, and dedicate their poetic works. But it is the third line of this fragment that is of greatest interest here, for I would like to suggest that in Dionysios' σοὶ πρώτωι ("to you first of all") at the beginning of line 3, we have a suggestive forerunner – we can never go so far as to say "model" or even "inspiration" – to Catullus' *Corneli, tibi*, which appears at precisely the same point in his dedication of poetry to Nepos (c. 1, 1.3), and similarly following a description of the textual gift. Where Dionysios asks his dedicatee for a return of poetry, however, Catullus asks Nepos for nothing – it is a dedication written in the context of textual exchange, but so too is it one deeply concerned with alliances that move beyond the textual world.

[16] The verb προπίνω, "to drink before," is used more specifically to mean "to drink to a toast to" another person, drinking first oneself, and then passing the cup to the individual thus honored. Because the cup used for the toast would then frequently be given as a gift to the honoree (cf. Xen. *Cyr.* 8.3.35), the verb itself comes to signify simply casual or light-hearted giving.

[17] The core meaning of the adjective ἐπιδέξιος is "from left to right," and signifies the order in which wine is served at a symposion; the adverbial ἐπιδέξια comes to mean more specifically "dexterously," or "cleverly"; in the above poem, surely both nuances of the term are intended.

[18] Dionysios' χάριτες are of course his poems. For χάρις as poem, cf. Callimachus (*Ep.* 51): Τέσσαρες αἱ Χάριτες; ποτὶ γὰρ μία ταῖς τρισὶ τήναις / ἄρτι ποτεπλάσθη κῆτι μύροισι νοτεῖ. / εὐαίων ἐν πᾶσιν ἀρίζηλος Βερενίκα, / ἇς ἄτερ οὐδ᾽ αὐταὶ ταὶ Χάριτες Χάριτες; here the "fourth Grace," Berenikê, refers to Callimachus' recently completed *Plokamos*. Cf. Mel. *AP* 5.148.2, νικάσειν αὐτὰς τὰς Χάριτας Χάρισιν.

[19] Certainly the poetic dedication is prefigured in Pindar (cf. *N.* 3.76–9), but there, as in Hesiod's *Works and Days*, the poet refers to the poem as a gift of the Muse (cf. *N.* 3.1), and not of the poet himself.

[20] *Pace* Janson 1964: 18 n. 14, who cites Ruppert 1911: 12–21 and remarks – for reasons that remain unclear to me – that "even if" this fragment "is an instance of real dedication," it "is of little interest."

The first poem of the Catullan corpus has long been noted for its somewhat unusual tone.[21] Unlike Meleager's Μοῦσα φίλα, τίνι τάνδε φέρεις πάγκρατον ἀοιδάν; (*AP* 4.1.1; the closest chronological match for Catullus) or Martial's *cuius uis fieri, libelle, munus* (*Ep.* 3.2.1), the tone of Catullus 1 is casual and intimate, devoid of flashy "bookishness" or any anxiety as to whether the gift will be accepted. Catullus is aware that his dedication marks a kind of publication for his poetry – his *libellus* – but he is concerned not with Nepos' reception of the gift but – and here the onus is shifted to the Muse – with the ability of his poems to enjoy an extended existence. Similarly, whereas Meleager asks his Muse to whom she will give his song, and Martial – in an obvious Catullan echo – playfully asks his *libellus* whose *munus* it would like to be, Catullus, like Dionysios, makes the choice himself – and addresses only his dedicatee. Dionysios, it seems, starts with a vocative and then moves quickly to an imperative δέχου – take it! Catullus' c. 1 begins somewhat more coyly – we are invited to imagine him gazing around a room of companions, new volume in hand, as he asks with a smile, "To whom do I give . . . ?" But by the start of the third line of each dedication, σοὶ πρώτωι and *Corneli, tibi* (if Catullus was familiar with the poem, is the vocative *Corneli* a delayed echo of Dionysios' first line?), respectively, we are invited into a moment of textual display that encapsulates, in its pantomime of a moment of sympotic or convivial poetic display, the process whereby poetry is produced and shared within a society of equals in which the refusal of an offered poem would be out of the question. Dionysios' poem is steeped in the world of sympotic poetic production; Catullus' poem speaks to the world of convivial textual exchange. But whereas Dionysios wrote a "poem as a toast" and thus emphasizes the orality of the dedication, Catullus produces an emphatically textual and material dedication in Nepos' honor, cleverly instructing his readers, and his dedicatee, that the sphere of social obligation into which his *libellus* will now enter is one that has emerged from a long tradition of isonomic and reciprocal textual play. Even if Catullus never read this poem, we sense he would have enjoyed it. For in the space of five lines, Dionysios has created a gift-poem that is the work of a man and not a Muse (and thus it is the author of the poem who shall decide its destination); he has created a poem that will forever echo the author's voice at the very moment he has transferred ownership; and he has created (for

---

[21] Cf. Zicàri 1965.

us, at least) a dedicatory poem that embodies in language and imagery the textual world in which it was created and is intended to move about.

Tore Janson has observed that Latin prose authors looked to various Greek prototypes – Hesiod, Isocrates, Archimedes – for the basic structure and style of their dedicatory prefaces,[22] but he argues that beyond mere "structure and style," two distinct prefatory types, developed by the Greek technical writers of the fourth century BCE and expanded in the Hellenistic period, were especially influential on Roman prose practice: the rhetorical type, which has its origins in public speech, and the epistolary, which has its origins in dedicatory letter-writing.[23] Of the first, he notes that Greek prose authors were influenced by the *rhetores* who began speeches with an explanation or reason for their presence in court. This explanation frequently took the form of a general claim of rhetorical and political ignorance coupled with the statement that the speaker has been forced, against his will and by the issue at hand, into the position of speaking publicly. As such, the *apologia* of "ignorance and compulsion" provided a simple way of sidestepping – or at least, assuaging – the standard suspicion of treachery that accompanied clever or persuasive speech and playing to the audience's own anxieties about loss of liberty: "I don't want to be here, I don't know what I am doing, but I have been robbed of choice in the matter – I must defend myself." This maneuver makes perfect sense in the context of public speeches that were actually delivered before an audience, and it was likely an effective one.

But the powerful justification for personal expression provided by this protestation of rhetorical *naïveté* and concomitantly "forced" speech, though it has its origins in the law courts, was not confined there. As Janson has noted, Isocrates retains this practice in "speeches" that were written with no expectation of performance in the present or future, but constituted in their entirety a gift given or honor rendered to the addressee, effectively

---

[22] Janson 1964: 14–24. In the fourth century, the dedicatory preface becomes more common, and is for the first time attached – like a gift tag on a birthday present or, more to the point, an inscription on a gift book – to an otherwise thematically unrelated piece of extended prose. Both Isocrates and, much later, Dionysios of Halicarnassos refer to their written work as a δῶρον. See Isocr. 1.2 (the preface to *ad Nicoclen*): ἀπέσταλκά σοι τόνδε τὸν λόγον δῶρον, and D. Hal. *Comp.* 1.1: δῶρόν τοι καὶ ἐγώ, τέκνον φίλε, τοῦτο δίδωμι. The pseudo-Isocratean *ad Demonicum* makes a similar reference. Theognis' dedicatory lines to Kurnos (ll. 19–20) specify his poem as a δῶρον, but the attachment of the "seal" (σφρηγίς) serves as a verbal invocation of physical materiality, a "gift tag" contained completely within the words of the poem.

[23] Janson 1964: 24 sees rather sharper distinctions than would I between the rhetorical and the epistolary preface, and between what he identifies as the "poetic" and the "rhetorical" style of introduction.

translating the oral authority of the courts into the written authority of
the text.[24] And as suggested above, we can see traces of a similar transfer
of oral authority in Cicero's prose dedications, but I think that the Greek
practice cannot be the orator's primary influence. The standard claim of
the Greek *rhetores* and logographers is one of rhetorical ignorance or lack
of expertise, experience, and learning, an utter *naïveté* in the area of judicial proceedings, and dangerously persuasive speech.[25] This sort of claim,
however, never forms part of Cicero's *apologiai*. He might apologize for
seeming too bold, or eager, or haughty, or proud – but this speaks to
anxieties concerning public propriety and social obligation, not, strictly
speaking, professional or intellectual ability. It is surely the case that the
Greek anxieties over excessive rhetorical expertise are to no small degree
social in their nature; the distinction lies, however, in the Greek focus
on the fear of excessive learning and deceptive expertise as opposed to
the Roman highlighting of inappropriate or inopportune public address.
While there is no question of the influence of Greek rhetorical form on
the Latin Republican oratory, then, Cicero's concern over propriety and
obligation are essential clues to the dynamics of Republican display and
textual reciprocity.

On the other hand, the *prooemia* to the dialogues are clearly reminiscent
of the introductions to Cicero's speeches, and his written apologies bring
to mind the Roman rhetorical practice of professing incompetence or
lack of ability. This sort of defense is a usual element of the *exordium* or
praemunitio – the orator must try to anticipate and circumvent others'
criticisms, and to gain for himself the goodwill of his listeners – and it is
easy to see why this maneuver is important to the "real time" display of
the forensic oration. But as we shall see, Cicero's apologies in the dedicated
technica are much more than literary shadows of the forensic orations.
When Cicero seeks to translate the oral authority of the forum (and his
speeches) into the written authority of textual reciprocity (and his *technica*),
he appropriates the "reluctance and resignation" technique of the forum,
but is not constrained by it. Even if Cicero's *prooemia* are meant to recall
the forensic oration, they are too literary – too poetic – for the speeches
to have been his main inspiration. He does not simply transplant his

---

[24] Janson 1964: 17: "It is evident that he regards his writings as speeches: certainly speeches of a special
character, speeches that for some reason have never been performed, but still speeches." I would
place a somewhat greater "text value" on these "speeches," as they seem deeply aware of their textual
existence, but Janson's emphasis on the intense orality of these texts is well placed.

[25] Plat. *Gorg.* 459b–c, 463a. On the profession of rhetorical inability, see Volkmann 1885: 130; Janson
1964: 18 discusses Isocrates' pretense of rhetorical inability in the *ad Nicoclen*; to this cf. Lysias 12.

forensic authority from spoken to written form; he translates the entire social language of the forum into a dialect of obligation perfectly suited to textual reciprocity. The rhetorical *prooemium* must have influenced Cicero's dedications, then, but it cannot be the primary source.

Janson's proposal of a second primary source of inspiration for the Latin prose preface, the epistolary dedication, is of rather greater value. This type of dedication was developed first by the Hellenistic mathematician Archimedes, who dedicated numerous technical treatises to his friend and colleague Dositheus.[26] It takes the form of a brief letter which introduces the text and is addressed to its dedicatee and which lays out the basic theme of the main text but does not itself address the content. In contrast to the technique of the rhetorical *prooemium*, the profession of incompetence is not a normal element of the Greek epistolary salutation. What such dedicatory letters do provide, and what seem likely candidates for influence on late Republican prose (and indeed, poetic) dedication, is the standard inclusion of, first, a reference to private social obligation and, second, the claim of death or personal tragedy as a source for the present composition.

First let us consider the reference to private social obligation. Hellenistic Greek prose authors are the first to use an epistolary preface to claim that their compositions are the result of the ceaseless requests of the recipient. Archimedes, for instance, prefaces both *de Spiralibus* and *de Sphaera et Cylindro* with brief references to Dositheus' repeated requests for information, specifying, in the latter case, the recipient's "incessant" requests for such writing.[27] In each of these prefaces, the reference to the request is unadorned; Janson suggests that it is mentioned only to provide a reason for the present work.[28] But there seems to be more at work here, for in creating a text that functions as an item of affective social reciprocity ("you keep on asking me to write about this . . ."), rather than of a royal or courtly commission, Archimedes may represent an important stage in the evolution of textual dedication, circulation, and reciprocity.

---

[26] The standard form consisted of (1) the sender's/author's name (in the nominative); (2) the recipient's/reader's name (in the dative); (3) the salutation proper; and (4) the remaining details of the dedication. Thus Archimedes (287–212 BCE; b. Syracuse) begins an epistle: Ἀρχιμήδης Δοσιθέωι χαίρειν. The books of his *Quadratura Parabolae* were each preceded by brief letters of dedication; see further Janson 1964: 21–22.

[27] *De Sphaera et Cylindro* 2: ἐπέστειλάς μοι γράψαι τῶν προβλημάτων τὰς ἀποδείξεις and *de Spiralibus*: τῶν θεωρημάτων, ἅπερ ὧν ἀεὶ τὰς ἀποδειξίας ἐπιστέλλεις μοι γράψαι.

[28] Janson 1964: 21: "Dositheus had written to Archimedes, evidently several times, and asked for explanations of certain theorems."

The excuse of social obligation as a factor in textual production and exchange appears as a dedicatory topos from the late Republic on. Catullus and Cicero provide our earliest Latin evidence for this practice (we might imagine Varro had done the same in his earliest dedications to Pompey, but his *DRR* shows no trace of such), and both use the excuse that they have written only because of the "incessant request" of a dear friend or colleague;[29] variations on this theme are further developed by the textual communities of the Principate and Empire, and indeed it becomes a core part of the formal idea of all later textual dedication. Catullus uses this technique to "give" a poem that claims that writing is impossible (c. 68b), to introduce a Latin rendering of a Greek original (so c. 65 introduces c. 66), and to "repay a favor" with a recollection of established Greek mythic themes (c. 68b).[30] Cicero uses a version of the request technique in his private letters – the exchange of writing at its most basic and personal level – at times making the request an explicit one (*quod rogas ut mea tibi scripta mittam*, *Ep. Fam.* 1.9.23; *uelim* σχόλιον *aliquod elimes ad me*, *Ep. Att.* 16.7), but for the most part referring rather more casually to the expectations of ongoing reciprocal correspondence.[31] But he also adapts this epistolary intimacy to introduce and dedicate both his "remembered" conversations and the more blatantly fictitious of his dialogues: *de Oratore* (a pseudo-memory) begins with a pointed reference to Quintus' repeated request for the text (*uis enim, ut mihi saepe dixisti… aliquid eisdem de rebus politius a nobis perfectiusque proferri*, 1.2.5), while *Laelius* (a theatrical

---

[29] The theme of literature as a response to incessant comment calls to mind the incipit to Callimachus' poem against the Telchines (*Aetia* 1.1), the first word of which, it is now agreed, reads πολλάκι (on which reconstruction cf. Pontani 2000).

[30] C. 65 introduces and dedicates c. 66, the poet's rendering of Callimachus' *Plokamos*. Catullus claims that he has written in response to his friend's request: *sed tamen in tantis maeroribus, Hortale, mitto / haec expressa tibi carmina Battiadae / ne tua dicta uagis nequiquam credita uentis / effluxisse meo forte putes animo* (ll. 15–18). C. 68a is clearly written in response to a friend's request: *id gratum est mihi, me quoniam tibi dicis amicum, / muneraque et Musarum hinc petis et Veneris* (c. 68b. 9–10), even as it serves as the poetic gift it claims it cannot give. Poem 68b, which is discussed further in Chapter 7, brackets a brief lament over the death of the poet's brother with short references to Troy and more expansive ones to Laodamia, and ends with a reference to a debt paid by the poem: *hoc tibi, quod potui, confectum carmine munus / pro multis, Alli, redditur officiis, / ne vestrum scabra tangat robigine nomen / haec atque illa dies atque alia atque alia* (ll. 149–152).

[31] On the latter, cf. *Ep. Att.* 1.6: *non committam posthac ut me accusare de epistularum neglegentia possis*; 1.9: *nimium raro nobis abs te litterae adferuntur, cum et multo tu facilius reperias qui Romam proficiscantur quam ego qui Athenas*; 4.2 *si forte rarius a me quam a ceteris litterae redduntur, peto a te ut id non modo neglegentiae meae sed ne occupationi quidem tribuas*. Well over half of the letters begin with an explicit reference to epistolary reciprocity, and frequent mention is made of a letter recently received (see, e.g., *Ep. Att.* 10.4; 10.9; 11.2; 12.12; 12.37; 13.17).

fiction) is dedicated to Atticus with the reminder *cum enim saepe mecum ageres ut de amicitia scriberem aliquid.*[32]

Whether such (presumably written) requests for dedicated literature were a spontaneously or formally functional part of the process of isonomic dedication, or whether they exist as a rhetorical fiction of the dedication alone, is difficult to say. Was the process a purely pragmatic, if somewhat disingenuous, one, with colleagues in the Society of Patrons "urged" or expected to write and circulate such requests as a way of giving "advance notice" for a dedication they expected to be headed their way? Was the process one of genuine, if casual, generosity, with the requests for textual dedication made both frequently and spontaneously as a way of providing one's allies with an ongoing excuse to write under the claim of textual obligation ("if you're looking for a dedicatee for that, I'll take it")? Were the requests taken at face value? Were feelings hurt if they were denied? Was it more important that a "real" request was received, or that the author includes reference to such a request in his dedicated text? In the case of Cicero, at least, we know that he both made requests of his own and received such requests from his *familiares*. As we saw, Caelius requested – but did not, apparently, receive – from Cicero the dedication of a "treatise of some sort" (aliquod . . . σύνταγμα, *Ep. Fam.* 8.3) as a lasting testament to their *amicitia*. Following the assassination of Caesar, C. Trebonius – a former Caesarian ally turned co-conspirator (he delayed Antonius outside the Senate house as the attack occurred) – asks Cicero to write him into one of his dialogues, as if by way of prearranged (if irresistibly creepy) remuneration for his role in the murder:

Tu, sicut mihi pollicitus es, adiunges me quam primum ad tuos sermones; namque illud non dubito, quin, si quid de interitu Caesaris scribas, non patiaris me minimam partem et rei et amoris tui ferre. Vale et matrem meosque tibi commendatos habe. (*Ep. Fam.* 12.16 (44 BCE))

Now, just as you promised me, I would that you write me into one of your dialogues as soon as you can. For I don't doubt but that if you write anything about the death of Caesar you'll be sure I get my fair share of both the deed and your lasting affection. Well, so long – my mother and my family are in your care.

---

[32] See too the prefaces of *Acad. Post.* (cf. *Ep. Fam.* 9.8); *Brut.* 5.20: *quem ego sermonem cum ad Brutum tuum uel nostrum potius tulissem, magnopere hic audire se uelle dixit; Top.* 1: *qua inscriptione commotus continuo a me librorum eorum sententiam requisisti; Part. Orat.* 1: *studeo, mi pater, Latine ex te audire ea quae mihi tu de ratione dicendi Graece tradidisti*; and *TD* 1: *rettuli me, Brute, te hortante maxime ad ea studia . . .*

The suggestion that Trebonius took on the role as (partial) hit man in return for the honor of being included in (and possibly receiving the dedication of) one of Cicero's dialogues is both massively impressive and deeply troubling. On the one hand, it suggests that Cicero's plan to transport his forensic *auctoritas* onto the dedicated dialogue was, as of 44, a smashing success. The phrase "worked beyond his wildest dreams" (we are reminded of Caelius' letter at *Ep. Fam.* 8.3.1) is hard to resist, and it seems the man who felt the forum had destroyed him has done his best to repay the favor. On the other hand, if we can take the letter at even partial face value, the blatant bartering of life for literature speaks of a generative textual economy that had become so identified with the political one from which it originated as to have adopted all of its dangers – and as it seems, much of its madness. Books for murder: talk about literary intrigue. Trebonius was remunerated for his role in the tyrannicide, although not by Cicero and not as he would have desired. Proconsul of Asia in 43, Trebonius was murdered by the turncoat Dollabella after Dollabella had been refused entry into Smyrna (cf. *Ep. Brut.* 2.3).[33]

Just as various individuals did indeed request that Cicero either dedicate a work to them or include them in an upcoming dialogue, so too do we know that Cicero made such requests of others: an early letter to Atticus expresses disappointment in Archias' failure to render a poetic account of his consular years (cf. *Ep. Att.* 1.16). In 56, as we noted in the Introduction, he asks the orator-turned-historian L. Lucceius (*Ep. Fam.* 5.12) to "make his name famous" and "render him immortal"[34] by writing of his exploits in Lucceius' soon-to-be completed History of the Italian and Civil Wars. The letter in which he does this is telling: Cicero offers suggestions as to how Lucceius might "weave him into" (*contexere*, 5.12.2; cf. *intexere* at *Ep. Fam.* 13.12) the historical narrative as a whole or perhaps produce a monograph on Cicero's consulship in particular; he insists that his own reputation is not particularly at stake (*ad nostram laudem non multum uideo interesse*, 5.12.2); and he admits that he is behaving somewhat *impudenter* in both making the request (*onus*) that might be refused and asking outright that Lucceius "bedeck" (*ornare*) his deeds by writing about them. Cicero then

---

[33] We may have a similar case of textual commendation of the murder of Caesar from the same period. Plut. *Brut.* 2.4 tells us that Empylus, a rhetorician and friend of Brutus (Marcus, not Decimus) wrote a history of the death of Caesar entitled *Brutus* and, as we should expect, dedicated to him.

[34] *Ep. Fam.* 5.12.1: *ardeo cupiditate incredibili, neque ut ego arbitror, reprehendenda, nomen ut nostrum scriptis illustretur et celebratus tuis... neque enim me solum commemoratio posteritatis ad spem quandam immortalitatis rapit, sed etiam illa cupiditas, ut uel auctoritate testimonii tui, uel indicio beneuolentiae, uel suauitate ingenii, uiui perfruamur.*

pulls out all the stops: he confesses to asking Lucceius "repeatedly" (*etiam atque etiam rogo*, 5.12.3) for this eulogy; he suggests the historian praise his deeds with more fervor than he might actually feel (*uehementius etiam quam fortasse sentis*, 5.12.3) and with details that speak more to personal affection than absolute fact (*amorique nostro plusculum etiam quam concedat ueritas largiare*, 5.12.3). Lucceius is assured that Cicero is the stuff of which gripping histories are made; his rendition of the consular years will add to the glory of each man; Cicero will be Themistocles to Lucceius' Herodotus. He finally admits that if Lucceius does not accept the request to write of his consulship, he will have to do it himself (as he did, trebly; as I suggested in the Introduction, Lucceius' refusal to write about Cicero may have had a role in spurring on the textual project of his final years),[35] but states that if the request is granted, he will quickly throw together some *commentarii* to serve as primary source material. One has the impression, of course, that such *commentarii* have long been at the ready.

The letter to Lucceius is a tantalizing one; it aids our effort to retrace the negotiations whereby an individual sought either the dedication of a text, or inclusion as a literary figure within it (a kind of "secondary dedication," as I discuss below). No grand arguments can be made on the basis of one letter, especially one that did not produce the desired effect, but it seems safe to say that as much as written requests were, in fact, exchanged between colleagues in the textual communities of the late Republic, and as much as these requests were sometimes accepted and sometimes denied, it is the inclusion of the request within the dedicated end-product that seems to have been almost more important than the actual tone (or manner) of the original solicitation. By prefacing their dedications with elaborate examples of the polite (and often-repeated) request for literature on the part of their dedicatee, these authors turn writing into a matter of obligation and *gratia*. By presenting their composition as the product of that request, orator and poet create an unassailable justification for their literary activity.[36]

---

[35] On Cicero's various efforts to record the details of his consulship in every possible form, cf. *Ep. Att.* 1.9.10; 1.20.6; and 2.1.1; *Ep. Fam.* 1.9.23; and *Ep. Frat.* 2.13.2 and 2.15.5.

[36] In comparing his act of literary prestation to Helen's treatment of Telemachus, Dionysios of Halicarnassos writes: καθάπερ ἡ παρ᾽ Ὁμήρωι φησὶν Ἑλήνη ξενίζουσα τὸν Τηλέμαχον … πλὴν οὔτε χειρῶν δημιούργημα πήμπω σοι τῶν ἐμῶν, ὡς ἐκείνη φησὶ διδοῦσα τῶι μειρακίωι τὸν πέπλον, οὔτ᾽ ἐς γάμου μόνον ὥραν, καὶ γαμετῆς χάριν εὔθετον, ἀλλὰ ποίημα μὲν καὶ γέννιμα παιδείας καὶ ψυχῆς τῆς ἐμῆς κτῆμα δὲ σοὶ τὸ αὐτὸ καὶ χρῆμα πρὸς ἁπάσας τὰς ἐν τῶι βίωι χρείας ὁπόσαι γίνονται διὰ λόγων ὠφέλιμον (*de Comp. Verb.*, preface). The work is dedicated to the son of a friend; it is represented not as a creation *ex nihilo* (οὔτε χειρῶν … τῶν ἐμῶν) but as the product and offspring of the author's learning.

The late Republican claim that the production and dedication of literature is predicated primarily on the "incessant request" of a friend had
long-lasting effects. This is nowhere more evident than in the vibrant epistolographic habit of the early Empire, a genre that seems to have evolved
out of the textual dedications of the late Republic – but in a way that
suggests either an even greater silencing of the authorial voice, or perhaps
simply the increased belief than *no* form of literary activity could ever be
truly "private" when the emperor was always looking (and reading) over
your shoulder. Thus Seneca, writing under – and inevitably for – Nero,
uses the request-topos frequently in his *Epistulae Morales*,[37] and indeed
claims that both *de Providentia* and *de Ira* were written primarily as a result
of a friend's request or inquiry.[38] Writing under the somewhat relaxed (or
so we are led to believe) textual world that emerged under Trajan, Pliny
predicates many of his letters on a friend's demand for their composition,[39]
and Tacitus begins his *Dialogus*, the last Imperial dialogue and itself in clear
dialogue with the Ciceronian tradition, with a reference to the frequent
demands of social obligation: "You have often asked me, Fabius..."[40]
Whatever its sources in the Hellenistic technical and poetic authors, it is
clear that the Republican incarnation of the request technique continued
to be favored in the exchanged and dedicated literature of the Empire.
And each time it is used, it is social obligation, a sense of favor or *gratia*,
that packs the punch.[41] The incessant request becomes a sure-fire means
of validating one's own literary endeavors: *I have only written this because
of your request...*
    A second characteristic of the Hellenistic epistolary dedication espe-
cially evident in the dedications of Catullus and Cicero is the tendency

[37] See especially *Ep. Mor.* 38, which begins *merito exigis, ut hoc inter nos epistularum commercium frequentemus...* and ends with a familiar formulation: *multa inuicem et ipsa generabit et plus reddet quam acceperit.* Similar references occur at 39 and 40; Lucilius' supposed questions are given as the starting point for composition in *Ep.* 9, 29, 43, 71, 72, 106, 108, 109, 111, 113, 114, and 117.
[38] *De Providentia* is dedicated to Lucilius and begins with the words *quaesisti a me, Lucili, quid ita, si prouidentia mundus regeretur, multa bonis uiris mala acciderent. De Ira*, dedicated to Novatus, makes the request even more explicit: *exegisti a me, Nouate, ut scriberem quemadmodum posset ira leniri...* The dating of the *dialogi* is controversial and no solid date can be assigned to *de Providentia* (though cf. Waltz 1909: 7, who assigns a date in the early years of exile, ca. 41–42 CE); *de Ira* was probably written shortly after the death of Caligula – that is, early in Claudius' reign – and at any rate before 52 CE.
[39] So Pliny *Ep.* 9.2.1: *facis iucunde quod non solum plurimas epistulas meas uerum etiam longissimas flagitas.*
[40] 1.1 *saepe ex me requiris, Iuste Fabi, cur, cum priora saecula tot eminentium oratorum ingeniis gloriaque floruerint, nostra potissimum aetas deserta et laude eloquentia orbata uix nomen ipsum oratoris retineat.* Cf. too Frontinus Balbus, writing contemporary to Tacitus, in his *Expositio et Ratio Omnium Formarum* (*notum est omnibus, Celse, penes te studiorum nostrotum manere summam...*, 1.1).
[41] So Hall 1996: 97 identifies *gratia* as the "coin" in "the currency of Roman favors and obligations."

to "double" the dedication by claiming that the death of a dear friend or colleague has inspired the writing. In this sort of preface, death is used as the creative impetus for the text, a means of memorializing the deceased with a technical work that is dedicated to a living person. Perhaps picking up on the tradition of the *laudatio funebris*, the silencing of one voice, in a sense, prompts the speech of another and the "new" dedication is placed *in medias res*, in which the affective reciprocity shared with the deceased is transferred, by means of the text, to a new partner in exchange. Archimedes uses the double dedication in his *Quadratura Parabolae*. Although the text is itself dedicated to Dositheus, the recent death of the astronomer Conon is given as the impetus for the writing. Dositheus, then, we can call the "primary" dedicatee; but Conon is a no less important "secondary" dedicatee, a posthumous recipient of the author's goodwill, who will receive the gift in the form of a publicly expressed *munus mortis*. While this sort of dedication stretches its influence into the past, it does so with shrewd cunning and thus provides a telling example of elite liberality: when you give a gift to a dead person, he cannot help but "accept" it even as there is no chance of making an equitable return. This kind of textual gift writes its own reception and assures a warm welcome from the primary dedicatee. It was good enough for *Conon*, after all . . .[42]

I am wont to agree with Janson's claim that the epistolary preface was a distinctly Hellenistic invention. It provided for writers of technical literature a means of communication with each other throughout a geographically scattered community of readers and thus filled a sociotextual need that had not previously existed.[43] I would add that it is used in the Hellenistic period only of textual gifts exchanged between friends; never, that is, of literature produced under a system of hierarchical patronage, and seemingly never as a means to initiate broader publication. Janson notes that Archimedes never uses dedicatory letters when sending a composition to a friend in his own town, but saves this technique for treatises that are sent to friends far away. This suggests that although Archimedes recognized the literary potential of the epistolary dedication as a textual form, he still considered it closely connected to the idea of actual epistolary practice. In other words, and *pace* the culture of email and "text messages," you don't send a letter to someone in your own town (much

---

[42] Isocrates uses an early form of double dedication when he claims that his rhetorical gift should serve as witness to his goodwill to one man, and as a sign of his intimacy to another: ἀπέσταλκά σοι τόνδε τὸν λόγον δῶρον, τεκμήριον μὲν τῆς πρὸς ὑμᾶς εὐνοίας, σημεῖον δὲ τῆς πρὸς Ἱππόνικον συνηθείας.

[43] Janson 1964: 20.

less the next office over). In the late Republic, however, this connection between form and practice dissolves; both Catullus and Cicero use versions of the epistolary dedication for all manner of compositions, few instances of which (*de Officiis* is an exception) conjecture a great deal of physical space actually separating author and dedicatee.[44] If Janson is correct, as it seems he must be, about the utilitarian reasons for the development of the epistolary preface, what are we to think of the Republican innovation on the form, and how do we map this innovation onto the continuum of dedication that would continue into the Principate and early Empire? What does it mean when key elements of the epistolary preface (the incessant request, the theme of death, the double dedication) are applied in the late Republic to compositions dedicated not to distant colleagues, but to friends and allies in the selfsame city – partners in an exclusive circle of textual reciprocity?

I noted earlier that Cicero's dedications show the marks of the Hellenistic prose preface. As Janson has suggested, however, these prose prefaces also show the influence of a much earlier tradition of textual dedication, and one with which we are certain Cicero was well acquainted: that of archaic Greek poetry.[45] In *Works and Days*, a poem Cicero clearly admired,[46] Hesiod locates the authority for his work within the dedicatory sections of the poem itself;[47] while his invocation of the Muses establishes them as the "source" of his poetic content,[48] his harsh apostrophe to his brother[49] fixes his (reluctant) impetus for writing. Although Cicero dedicates his dialogues to his co-producers of exchanged literature rather than a named or unnamed "Muse," he marks his awareness of poetic textual heritage even as he subverts it. His composition of *de Oratore* is fashioned as a return to the "gentler Muses" (*mansuetiores Musae*) – that is, literature – that nourished his youth and would provide sustenance to his advanced

---

[44] Similarly, while Seneca writes his *Epistulae Morales* as though they were "real" letters, we have no reason to suspect that Lucilius (also the dedicatee of *de Providentia* and *Quaestiones Naturales*) lived at any great remove from the author. Although Lucilius held various procuratorships under Claudius and Nero, and so would have at times been away from Rome, it is clear that the form of the *Epistulae* was chosen for stylistic, not practical, purposes.

[45] On the influence of Greek prefaces, see Janson 1964: 14–24.

[46] On this, see my discussion of Cicero's use of Hesiod in Chapter 2.

[47] I read as dedicatory lines 1–41. These first lines are divided thus: 1–10 invocation to the Muses and establishment of the theme of the poem (the δίκη of Zeus); 11–26 the two *Erides*; 27–41 apostrophe to Perses, description of his brother's wrongdoing, and a general lament over the crooked state of affairs. At line 42 the poet turns to the reason for just behavior: κρύψαντες γὰρ ἔχουσι θεοὶ βίον ἀνθρώποισιν.

[48] Ll. 1, 2: the Muses are asked to tell of the justice of Zeus.

[49] L. 27: ὦ Πέρση, σὺ δὲ ταῦτα τεῷ ἐνικάθεο θυμῷ.

age, even as it is aggressively dedicated only to individuals who could pay back the favor with interest.[50]

Because Cicero's dialogues claim to be the written recollections of private conversations set in the past, they are supremely flexible in their form and content.[51] Sometimes, indeed, the dialogues are set in the distant past – *de Oratore*, of course, but all the more so *Cato* and *Laelius* – and this temporal retrojection seems a definitively "Ciceronian" twist on both the prose dialogue and the dedicated text.[52] The textualization of display tends, in both the late Republic and the periods that follow, to be set in a *de facto* past; the display must first occur before it is textualized (the pressing immediacy of c. 1 stands out as an exception to this rule), but the temporal distance between "original (fictitious) act" of display and the textualization of that display is either minimalized or simply unspecified. In their attractive conflation of the reader's present and the interlocutors' (and Rome's) past, Cicero's dialogues meld reality (the characters, the places, the social and political concerns of the day) and fantasy (the dialogue itself, the particular circumstances under which it takes place); death and life (not only do Cicero's readers get to "encounter" the voices of Rome's past; in both *Lucullus* and *Hortensius* Cicero is the only one of the interlocutors alive at the time of publication);[53] history and the future. The *prooemia* to these dialogues, in which Cicero talks in his own literary voice, move smoothly into the early stages of the dialogue proper, in which the author introduces the characters, their problems, and their voices into the made-up world of

---

[50] Of *de Oratore* and his "Muse," Cicero writes at *Ep. Fam.* 1.9.23: *scripsi etiam (nam me iam ab orationibus diiungo fere referoque ad mansuetiores Musas, quae me maxime sicut iam a prima adulescentia delectarent) scripsi igitur Aristotelio more . . . tris libros in disputatione ac dialogo 'de Oratore,' quos arbitror Lentulo tuo fore non inutilis.* For Varro's "Muses" see *Acad. Post.* 1.2: *silent enim diutius Musa Varronis quam solebant, nec tamen istum cessare sed celare quae scribat existimo.* To this, cf. *Ep. Att.* 2.6: *quae copio deponere et toto animo atque omni cura* φιλοσοφεῖν? *sic, inquam, in animo est; uellem ab initio, nun uero, quoniam quae putaui esse praeclara expertus sum quam essent inania, cum omnibus Musis rationem habere cogito.* A similar sentiment of returning to the studies of one's youth is found at Sall. *BC*4.

[51] What I mean by this is that the form of the narratological dialogue (the historical present *inquam*: "and then I said . . . ") describes events that have already occurred – whether the fictional interval is a period of fifty years or fifty minutes. When Cicero turned in 45 to the form of the dramatic dialogue (e.g. the name of an individual "Laelius," followed by a direct quote), he could have set a contemporary stage, but in each of his three endeavors of this sort (*TD, Cato* and *Laelius*) he sets the drama in the past.

[52] This retrojection appears to be spoofed by Varro's *DRR*, in which there is no chronological continuity between the three books of the dialogue.

[53] *Lucullus*, or *Acad. Prior.*, published in 45, was set sometime in the mid 60s; the interlocutors are Lucullus (d. 56), Catulus (d. 60), and Cicero. *Hortensius*, similarly published in 45, is set between 65 and 60; interlocutors are Lucullus, Catulus, Hortensius (d. 50), and Cicero.

his composition. These plausible fictions,[54] precisely because they are so plausible (even as they were certainly never meant to be taken as *factual*), are an apt tool for his literary and social aspirations. Although he veers from the truth now and again – a point made cheerfully in *Brutus*, where Atticus is made to give *carte blanche* to Cicero's blatant fictions[55] – Cicero seeks to present his characterizations as "believable enough" to make both the words of the dialogue, and (as we saw in *Laelius*) the innuendo couched within these words, a reasonably attractive and persuasive whole.[56]

Cicero's transmutation of his "forensic voice" into a "textual voice," capable of being contained within the dedicated dialogue, is significant at two levels. First, because it transforms the genre of oratorical writing, it transforms the social – and of course, textual – function of oratory as a whole. By arguing, and moreover by displaying, that the written voice can be a suitable – even superior, if no other options remain – replacement for the spoken, Cicero locates himself in provocative opposition to everything for which he, and his forum, had once stood. Indeed, in introducing oratory into the textual world – one that can, as we see with poetry, contain the oral via mimesis and so partake of its authority while giving nothing in return – he set himself at an irreconcilable distance from the world of its origins. As likely as it is that Cicero would have welcomed, to the end, a successful return to forensic oratory (though both the Caesarian speeches and the *Philippics* suggest he did not see one on the horizon), his hard-sell replacement of a public, forensic elite with a private, literary one would forever change the face of textual and intellectual culture.[57] Second, and this is a theme to be discussed more fully in Chapter 8, his suggestion that the text is a safer locale for the orator's voice than is the forum introduces the

---

[54] At *de Orat.* 2.2.7–9 Cicero emphasizes the importance of making his dialogue believable. Kirby 1997: 16 ff. follows Kennedy 1972: 215–217 in the belief that "Cicero is at pains to stress that the opinions expressed by the interlocutors in the dialogue are consonant with those held by the historical people" and remarks that "[a]ll of this leaves us with the conviction that, if such a conversation ever occurred, it would have gone something very like what we read in *De Oratore*" (Kirby 1997: 16–17). Kennedy 1972: 215 n. 95 provides bibliography for the questioned historicity of *de Oratore*. Clarke 1996: 50 says of the text, "[it] is a discursive dialogue on oratory in general, based on the scholastic doctrine, but treating it in the elegant humane manner of a cultured and experienced man of letters and man of affairs." For Cicero's own take on the "historicity" of *de Oratore*, see 3.4.16.

[55] Cf. *Brut.* 11.42–3: *quoniam quidem concessum est rhetoribus ementiri in historiis*; to this, compare *Lael.* 3 (dedicated to Atticus): *quasi enim ipsos induxi loquentes . . . ut tamquam a praesentibus coram haberi sermo uidetur*; and 4: *tu uelim a me animum parumper auertas, Laelium loqui ipsum putes.*

[56] Writing to Varro about *Academica*, a fictional conversation between himself, Varro (to whom the dialogue is dedicated), and Atticus, Cicero tips his hand: *puto fore ut, cum legeris, mirere nos id locutos esse inter nos quod numquam locuti sumus, sed nosti morem dialogorum* (*Ep. Fam.* 9.8.2).

[57] Zanker 1995: 197 notes that purely literary communication "creates [a] private world, distant from the public life of . . . society."

idea that mainstream social relations can be projected onto, and negotiated through, the physical object of the book. He has transformed the oratorical text from a passive mimesis of the orator's voice to a stealthy, and almost irresistible, replacement for it.

In sum, and as Cicero would express it, the orator does not *want* to speak so much as he is required to. When he addresses his audience, he is fulfilling an obligation to his client or the Republic; the fulfillment of this forensic obligation, this request for and payment of oratorical speech, gives an orator's voice its authority. By combining, however, the expectations of the Republican forum and Republican society with elements of social expectation as they emerged in the Hellenistic prose preface, Cicero translates the dynamics of oral, social, and forensic obligation – the claim of reluctance, the excuse of obligation, and the assumption of the authority to "speak" – into a newly textual, and so almost inevitably "*movable*," form. The orator who was once obliged to speak is now, in Cicero's world, obliged to *write* and, because the written voice must transfer hands to pay back the debt for which it was composed, he is obliged to *give*. By drawing upon established dedicatory and rhetorical prototypes and translating the forum's standard cries of reluctance into a kind of charming literary shyness, Cicero has projected an urbane hesitancy onto his decision to engage in something as intellectually indulgent – as markedly *otiosus* – as writing. The figure of the orator, when Cicero is through with him, has been transformed into a *uir bonus scribendi peritus*.

The dedication and reciprocal exchange of "object" poetry and scientific treatise had promoted the interests of textual publication and social negotiation for centuries before either Catullus or Cicero set in upon their tasks. But in the intersection of Catullus' use of the text to capture, control, and critique the private world of display and obligation and Cicero's adaptation of isonomic dedicatory prose to the intellectual mainstream of the late Republic, we see evidence for a late Republican textual practice that is as engaged with the traditions of the past as it is influential upon the developments of the future. In the case of Cicero in particular, we also see what was in essence the invention of the practice of academic publication.

OBLIGED TO TWO WORLDS AT ONCE: DOUBLE DEDICATION
IN CICERO AND CATULLUS 65

Because the overarching social goal of traditionally hierarchical literary patronage is the location of the dedicatory honor in one man alone, it is not surprising that the Hellenistic prose practice of "double dedication" never really found favor with the primarily poetry-based patronage communities of either the earlier Republic or the Augustan and Imperial periods. But precisely because the double dedication "divides the honor" (or at any rate, the recognition) of the given text it was an attractive and exceptionally useful dedicatory maneuver for the Society of Patrons. For whereas the traditional dedication "to one man" fixes the unequal social (and literary) relationship between patron and client, the double dedication "to this man and that" (and by extension to the reader) masquerades as an act of shared beneficence, thus deflecting any suspicions that the dedicator is naturally or circumstantially subservient to the dedicatee and reorienting the act of textual prestation as one of almost excessive generosity.

Like their Hellenistic models, the double dedications of the late Republic are usually distributed between living and deceased dedicatees. What I would call the "primary" dedicatee – the individual to whom the text is explicitly given as a physical object – is in all cases the former: the author's living ally in the ongoing process of textual exchange of which the text at hand is the latest installment. What I would call the "secondary" dedicatee – the individual to whom the text is implicitly given as a means of memorializing a relationship past, adding authority to the present literary product, or making strong claims as to the relationship with the primary dedicatee – is in virtually all cases the latter: the author's deceased relative or friend, or the ideological ancestor with whom the author would wish to share some degree of the social obligation or intellectual aesthetic through which the obligation to produce the text arose. Thus Catullus dedicates to (Hortensius?) Hortalus his reworking of Callimachus' *Plokamos* (c. 66), first with the statement that he will "never stop singing" of his brother's untimely death (*semper maesta tua carmina morte canam*, l. 12) – a reference to both c. 65 and the fraternal death commemorated in c. 66 – and then with several lines carefully outlining the connections between death, grief, memory, friendship – and writing. Thus does Cicero posit the death of perhaps this same Hortensius as the impetus for writing *Brutus* (cf. *Brut.* 1.1: *cum e Cilicia decedens Rhodum uenissem et eo mihi de Q. Hortensi morte esset adlatum . . .*),[58] as much as he gives the deaths of Crassus and Antonius

---

[58] Thomson 1997: 525–526 discusses the problems that surround (1) a positive identification of the "Hortalus" of c. 65 with the Hortensius referred to at c. 95.3, and (2) the identification of either of these personae with the Q. Hortensius Hortalus mentioned in Cicero's *Brutus* and the secondary dedicatee, presumably, of the lost rhetorical work *Hortensius*. Plutarch (*Luc.* 1.5) and Pliny (*Ep.* 5.3.5) identify Hortensius the orator as a writer of poetry; Ovid (*Tr.* 2.441–442) and Aulus Gellius (19.9.7) mention the poems of a Hortensius, but there is some question as to whether this character is to be identified with the orator. The highly rhetorical effect of c. 65, however – as identified by Charles Murgia, and as I discuss in Chapter 2 – suggests that we might reasonably identify Catullus' Hortensius with that of *Brutus*.

(or at least, the recollections of these deaths) partial credit for the orator's decision to write *de Oratore*[59] and, in *Cato* and *Laelius*, effectively splits the dedication between Atticus, who will receive the text as a physical object, and the deceased and eponymous *maiores*, who will receive the fame that adheres to having an entire text created as a *conformatio* – personification – of one's being. In each case, the double dedication increases the author's symbolic circle of reciprocity – he can dedicate to the past as well as the future and thus dislocate himself from the pressing concerns of the political present – and maximizes the social value of his textual *munus*. From their affective and intellectual alliances with the past (Catullus' brother, Crassus and Antonius, Hortensius, Laelius, Cato) these authors claim social and literary pedigree for the substance of their texts; from their alliances with the future (Quintus, Brutus, Atticus, Varro) they assure social support and, presumably, subsequent textual exchanges.[60]

The primary dedicatee of a text is expected to take an active role in the promotion of that text as well as any subsequent textual exchanges, and Cicero chooses his dialogues' recipients with extreme care.[61] When texts are dedicated to adult males other than his son,[62] two underlying expectations often accompany the textual gift: first, that the recipient should aid in the text's reception and publication; and second, that the recipient should eventually write and dedicate a textual return.[63] Because any gift circulated in an economy of ongoing reciprocity (whether isonomic or hierarchical) is also a request for future gifts, the social and literary standing of the recipient come into play.[64] We have little evidence of the behind-the-scenes

---

[59] *Laelius* and *Cato* have similarly doubled dedications: to the eponymous and deceased Republican, on the one hand, and to the very much alive and very literary Atticus, on the other. In *Laelius*, Cicero is moved by the death of Q. Mucius Scaevola – the young Cicero's public "mentor" and Laelius' son-in-law – to retell a *sermo* of C. Laelius that Scaevola had told him (*Lael.* 1); the "original" sermo was also prompted by the death of an important figure: *exposuit nobis sermonem Laeli . . . paucis diebus post mortem Africani*. In this text, both Laelius and Scaevola serve as "secondary" dedicatees in the memorium to the departed.

[60] Certainly Cicero expected and received such exchanges from Brutus – as he did from Atticus, Varro, and Caesar; his expectations from Quintus and Marcus *filius* are more difficult to determine, but the latter was no stranger to literary production.

[61] Murphy 1998 addresses some of these problems in a recent article on epistolary evidence for the exchange of the *philosophica*. Richardson 1999: 50–51 makes a similar argument for the dissemination of Renaissance manuscripts.

[62] Cicero dedicates the three books of *de Officiis* to his son, but does not seem to expect from him the usual obligations of such an exchange, asking him only to care for the texts with the personifying *tamquam hospites*. Perhaps the innate social hierarchy between father and son disallowed their entering into an exchange-relationship as social equals.

[63] See esp. *Ep. Fam.* 9.8.1, in which Cicero makes explicit his request for a return from Varro.

[64] So Catullus, in his dedicatory poem, turns from a second-person address to Cornelius Nepos to a bold invocation of the Muse, asking that his *libellus* outlast, as it were, the paper on which it is written. Auson. *Ecl.* 1.1 identifies the dedicatee as the historian Cornelius Nepos, and it

deliberation that led Catullus to dedicate c. 66 to Hortalus or c. 51 to Calvus (though it is possible that c. 65 and c. 50 are meant to rehearse some of this for us), but Cicero, in his letters to Atticus – especially those concerned with writing a text suitable to be dedicated to Varro[65] – discusses his exchange strategy with all the intensity and anxiety of a general readying for war. Although the language of the dedications is often casual and charming, the message of the letters is clear: this is no game.

The lengthy dedicatory sections of *de Oratore* give us much to go on by way of analyzing the choices crucial to such dedication. The primary dedicatee – the individual most easily recognized as the dedicatee "proper" – is his younger brother Quintus, a man of considerable learning and some literary talent, if not as prodigious an author as his brother. The secondary dedicatee, I suggest, must be none other than Crassus, the dialogue's virtual personification of Republican *auctoritas* and style and, not surprisingly, the figure most commonly identified as the textual representative of Cicero's own views (and thus Cicero also subtly dedicates *de Oratore* to *himself*). Next to *de Oratore*, discussed further below, *Brutus* offers a dedicatory structure that is more complex, but so too more brilliantly calculating, for although the text seems primarily dedicated to Brutus, the introductory sections of the dialogue indicate that the dedication is a double one. Both these sections, and indeed the dialogue as a whole, present a careful balance of politics and textual production, and Cicero's choice of dedicatees reflects this balance. Brutus, representative of Cicero's "new oratory" and the political scene, is the recipient proper; the text is published "in his name" (cf. *Parad. Stoic.* 5) and he speaks the first words in the dialogue (3.10). But if the text is explicitly given "to" Brutus, it is also written "for" Atticus, Cicero's late Republican *litteratus* par excellence and, as we have seen, an established publicist of his orations. To a certain extent, Cicero seems to

---

is surely no mistake that the poet chooses a historian to ensure that his poems "make it into the history books." See further Thomson 1997 *ad loc.* Fitzgerald 1995: 39 notes of Catullus' gift, "[Catullus] acknowledges that Nepos, by seeing something in Catullus' bits and pieces, is responsible for their publication"; but he also recognizes the fact that what this book *is* depends on how its future readership receives it. On Atticus' brilliant political promotion of *pro Ligario*, see *Ep. Att.* 13.12.3 (45 BCE): *Ligarianam praeclare vendidisti. Posthac quicquid scripsero, tibi praeconem deferam*; and 13.19.3: *Ligarianam, ut video, praeclare auctoritas tua commendavit. Scripsit enim ad me Balbus et Oppius mirifice se probare ob eamque causam ad Caesarem eam se oratiunculam misisse.*

[65] On Cicero's anxiety over what to dedicate to Varro, see *Ep. Att.* 4.16.2, 13.12.3: *ergo illam* Ἀκαδημικήν, *in qua homines nobiles illi quidem sed nullo modo philologi nimis acute loquuntur, ad Uarronem transferamus. Catulo et Lucullo alibi reponemus, ita tamen si tu hoc probas; deque eo mihi rescribas uelim*; 13.13 + 14.1 (a change of mind): *commotus tuis litteris, quod ad me de Uarrone scripseras, totam Academiam ab hominibus nobilissimus abstuli, transtuli ad nostrum sodalem . . . tu autem mihi peruelim scribas qui intellexeris illum uelle*); 13.14 + 15.1; 13.16.1; 13.18.1; 13.19.3.

be taking out a double insurance policy on the reception of his dialogue. Because *Brutus'* concerns are both political and textual, Cicero directs it toward well-known representatives of each of these concerns, placing himself, qua the man in whom political and textual interests combine, squarely in the middle.

The position of secondary dedicatee is likewise expanded. At one level, the text is dedicated "secondarily" to the deceased Hortensius, but because the death of a Hortensius becomes an allegory for the death of Cicero's voice – and indeed, the death of Republican oratory as a whole – *Brutus* becomes an exchange-gift offered to the countless array of Republican orators who fill its pages. The dedications of *de Oratore* and *Brutus* are in many ways different, and I do not mean to imply that *Brutus* simply warms-over the formulae of the earlier text. When taken together, however, these dialogues transform Cicero's forensic voice into a textual and literary one; they do not merely distance Cicero's voice from the orality of the forum – they help his voice rise above it.

In *de Oratore* Cicero situates his vision of the future within a recollection of the past. As is so often the case with his exchanged dialogues, Cicero uses the memory of the golden Republic as a destabilizing foil for his literary revisions: its presence in the text only underlines its absence to the reader.[66] Of course, we may suppose that the Rome he describes in these sections, a Rome of *honor* and *gloria*, a place where man and Republic flourished in tandem, is more of a rhetorical merman – a quack relic dragged from the vaults of some dusty Republican curiosity shoppe – than a historical or political reality.[67] Nevertheless, the language of the dedication is seductive, and Cicero's vision of Rome's past suspends the reader in an odd and definitively textual time and space. The Tusculan world of Cicero's *de Oratore* seems strangely backwards, or at least darkly intangible.[68] The layers of narrative time telescope; the text resists moorage in either the past or the future, but points coyly to both even as the dialogue as a whole avoids the present. The recipient (even now) is made to ask: Does the dialogue pre-date the text, or does it exist only within it? Is it dedicated to Quintus, or to Crassus? Or to Rome? Are the memories Cicero's and Cotta's, or Crassus' and Antonius'? Is the text a memory hidden in

---

[66] In her discussion of the Catullan aesthetic, Janan 1994: 5 notes: "boundary *ipso facto* implies transgression as its antithesis." Here I suggest that the "Golden Republic" is presented by Cicero precisely to underline – and suggest – the social and political decline of the reader's present.

[67] To this imagery, cf. *de Orat.* 1.30.

[68] On the geographical background of *de Orat.*, see Goerler 1988.

dialogue, or a dialogue masquerading as memory?[69] Is there, really, any difference?[70]

To a certain extent, most of these questions collapse in upon themselves. *De Oratore* as a whole resists the expected political content of Republican (oral) discourse. It is extra-urban, non-forensic, non-political, and of indefinable time and place. More than anything else, I suggest, *de Oratore* is about *itself*. It is a discourse on the topic of discourse; a recollection of orators discussing their oratorical recollections;[71] dedicated to one man but written for another. It is an exchanged text set in a time when social obligations and the boundaries of public behavior were well defined, but written for a world in which these boundaries and obligations have become – at least for Cicero – seriously threatened.

De Oratore is a self-enacting text. By this I mean that *de Oratore* (as much as the other dedicated textualizations of display we have considered in Part II) simultaneously actualizes and promotes the social structures and relations with which it claims to deal.[72] It is a text about the patronal exchange of information, but it is also the planned product of just such an exchange. The dialogue between Antonius, Crassus, and their various interlocutors is fashioned as a pseudo-historical recollection: each man retells what he "heard" once while traveling abroad, or during a previous extra-forensic conversation.[73] But at the same time the text as a whole

---

[69] On memory in the *technica*, cf. *Top.* 5: *Itaque haec, cum mecum libros non haberem, memoria repetita in ipsa nauigatione conscripsi tibique ex itinere misi, ut mea diligentia mandatorum tuorum te quoque, etsi admonitore non eges, ad memoriam nostrarum rerum excitarem.*

[70] Cf. Butor 1961: 20–21 on the reader's temporal relation to the text: "As soon as we can speak of a literary 'work,' and hence as soon as we approach the province of the novel, we must superimpose at least three time sequences: that of the adventure, that of the writing it, that of reading it." Cicero complicates this narrative structure by clothing his dialogue (Butor's "adventure") in layers of memories and earlier conversations. On the odd temporality of the narrative, see also Connery 1998.

[71] Cicero is fond of choosing "experts" for his dialogues, cf. *Lael.* 4: *sed ut in Catone Maiore, qui est scriptus ad te de senectute, Catonem induxi senem disputantem, quia nulla uidebatur aptior persona quae de illa aetate loqueretur quam eius qui et diutissime senex fuisset et in ipsa senectute praeter ceteros floruisset . . .* ; and 5: *sed ut tum ad senem senex de senectute, sic hoc libro ad amicum amicissimus scripsi de amicitia tum est Cato locutus, quo erat nemo fere senior temporibus illis, nemo prudentior; nunc Laelius et sapiens . . . et amicitiae gloria excellens de amicitia loquetur.*

[72] So Feldherr 1998: 23 notes of the erection of Republican *monumenta*: "The continuities between act and commemoration also emerge from the dedicatory inscriptions that accompanied these memorials, which record not only the victory but the erection of the *monumentum* itself."

[73] The geographical settings of the interlocutors' previous discussions are always pointedly non-Italian: Crassus and Antonius took part in rhetorical discussions while in Athens (1.11.45; 1.28.82), and Scaevola happened upon a meeting with Apollonius when he came as a praetor to Rhodes (1.17.75).

is imagined to be the product of such recollection: of what Cotta once told Marcus, what Marcus now tells his brother – and us.[74] Because the dedication orients the text both to the past and to the future it holds a middle position in the cycle of textual reciprocity. From the past Cicero seeks an implicit authority for his present endeavor; from the future – Quintus – he looks presumably for subsequent textual exchanges and continued promotion of his literary vision.

Shortly after the publication of *de Oratore*, Cicero wrote two more dialogues on political topics, *de Republica* (written in 54–51) and *de Legibus* (52–51[?]; unfinished at the time of the orator's death). In the years that followed, he used the dialogue, and variations on the dialogue, for the overwhelming majority of his philosophical and rhetorical treatises. It is perhaps no surprise that of all the dedicated dialogues, the eponymous *Brutus*, with which Cicero resumed his literary endeavors in 46 after a five-year hiatus, most closely resembles *de Oratore* in both dedicatory form and oratorical concerns; it is also the only dialogue to be set within the walls of the *urbs*, and the first of many dialogues that were to become increasingly literary and – in the case of the latest of the dialogues – increasingly theatrical. *Academica Posteriora*, also called *Varro*, was written a year after *Brutus* and functioned as the return-dedication for Varro's *de Lingua Latina*.[75] *De Finibus* and *de Natura Deorum*, also written in 45, were both dedicated to Brutus. *Hortensius*, now lost, is a product of the same year; it seems to have been half dialogue and half exhortation to philosophy, and likely would have been dedicated to Atticus, as it was composed at his house. *De Divinatione*, the entire first book of which is devoted to the view of "Quintus" and the second to that of "Marcus," is a dialogue only under the loosest of definitions. If the text has any sort of dedication, and it is not clear that it does, it is in the beginning sections of the second book, which was written in 44 immediately following the tyrannicide of Caesar. In *Partitiones Oratoriae* (written in 46–45 and seemingly dedicated to his son), *Disputationes Tusculanae* (written in 45 and dedicated to Brutus), and *Cato* and *Laelius* (both written in 44 and dedicated to Atticus), Cicero abandons the last narratological vestiges of the dialogue, and writes in a

---

[74] The myriad and complex social and literary implications of Cicero's manipulations of memory are beyond the scope of the present work. For now, I would like to consider the ways in which the language and structure of the dedication create in *de Oratore* a textual tool with which to forge and strengthen social relationships of exchange, expectation, and reciprocity.

[75] Varro's role in the community is discussed more fully in the Introduction; his textual activity is outlined in the Appendix.

fully dramatic form – *inquam* and *inquit* are replaced by simple tags of speaker identification.[76]

But this all starts – for Cicero, and for us – with *de Oratore*. On the whole, the structure of this dialogue's dedication is a simple one and, because of its chronological primacy in the corpus, a good place to look for early indications of the orator's textual aspirations. The dialogue aims to be a wholly Roman discussion of Roman rhetoric and, as such, initiates Cicero's creation of his distinctly "Roman voice."[77] It starts with a straightforward address to Quintus and a sentimental reference to the golden past of the Republic (1.1.1–1.2.3), and then makes explicit reference to Quintus' request for the text and Cicero's own initial reluctance to engage in rhetorical writing (1.2.4–5). The next sections refer more generally to Cicero's frequent reflections on the problems of oratory, and why it is that Rome has seen so few orators of any ability or worth (1.2.6–1.6.22). The dedication then returns subtly to the task at hand and the author's specific literary choices: dialogue form, geographic and temporal setting (91 BCE, Crassus' Tusculan villa), and *dramatis personae* (1.6.23–1.7.29). These final sections move almost seamlessly from dedication to dialogue: narrative speech-markers become shorter in length: *oratio obliqua* and simple narrative are replaced by *inquit*-introduced *oratio recta*, and as we venture ever more deeply into Cicero's textual Tusculum, the voice of Cicero seems to fade into the background.

The theme of "request and resignation" runs throughout these early sections and is recalled at two places in the dialogue proper. Cicero emphasizes that his dialogue is written not only as a textual product but also, and even more significantly, as a tool of social obligation and negotiation. In its repayment of preexisting obligation – this is marked by Quintus' request – the dialogue establishes an obligation in return: the benefaction of asking for subsequent production of literature. At the beginning of the dedication, Cicero sets the stage for his composition. The turbulent state of the Republic has deprived him of his recently renewed enjoyment of literary studies,[78] and has thrown him once again into the fray of political

---

[76] *Lael.* 3: *quasi enim ipsos induxi loquentes, ne 'inquam' et 'inquit' saepius interponeretur, atque ut tamquam a praesentibus coram haberi sermo videretur.* On this, compare what Cicero says about the effects of the dialogue in *Lael.* 4: *genus autem hoc sermonum positum in hominum ueterum auctoritate, et eorum inlustrium, plus nescio quo pacto uidetur habere grauitatis; itaque ipse mea legens sic afficior interdum ut Catonem, non me loqui existimem.*

[77] Kirby 1997: 16 notes that *de Oratore* differs from the "typical rhetorical handbook" in certain important ways (dialogue form, nationality of the interlocutors). Cicero emphasizes these innovations at 1.6.23. Kirby follows Kennedy's belief (1972: 215–217) that the dialogue is meant to be believable.

[78] The literary studies of Cicero's youth are referred to three times in the first chapter: *ac fuit quidem cum mihi quoque initium requiescendi atque animum ad utriusque nostrum praeclara studia referendi*

combat. Cicero complains to his brother that he has been worn out by the demands of the state, and has little time (*otium*)[79] for the pleasures of literature. In language that speaks of intimate epistolarity rather than formal rhetoric (some of the dialogic portions of *de Oratore* are epideictic in form, but the tone of casual intimacy with which it is dedicated is reminiscent of Catullus 1),[80] he casually introduces his brother's repeated requests for a discussion on the matter of public speech:

Tibi uero, frater, neque hortanti deero, neque roganti, nam neque auctoritate quisquam apud me plus ualere te potest, neque uoluntate. Ac mihi repetenda est ueteris cuiusdam memoriae non sane satis explicata recordatio sed, ut arbitror, apta ad id quod requiris... (*de Orat.* 1.1.4–1.2.4)

And indeed, my brother, whether you demand or ask [for my writings], I will not fail you – for no man's influence or desire affects me more than yours. And so now I must seek again the recollection of a certain ancient memory – not, it is true, as clear as it could be, but, if you ask me, well suited to what you are after...

The language is simple and pointedly Republican (*auctoritas... uoluntas*),[81] but this passage is plainly reminiscent of the Hellenistic dedication. Cicero takes a simple request and transforms it into a matter of private obligation and social grace. In what is by all accounts a brief reference to his brother's request, Cicero speaks for the first time of a distinctly Roman, distinctly literary, obligation. Regardless of his "public" troubles, he must devote whatever time and energy he has to this "private" task. He does not want to write, but he must.

The textualization of social obligation appears also in Catullus, most extensively in c. 65,[82] the poem that introduces and dedicates his

---

fore iustum et prope ab omnibus concessum arbitrarer (1.1.1); *neque uero nobis cupientibus atque exoptantibus fructus oti datus est ad eas artis, quibus a pueris dediti fuimus, celebrandas inter nosque recolendas* (1.1.2); *sed tamen in his uel asperitatibus rerum uel angustiis temporis obsequar studiis nostris et quantum mihi uel fraus inimicorum uel causae amicorum uel res publica tribuet oti, ad scribendum potissimum conferam* (1.1.3).

[79] As noted in Chapter 1, Cicero makes *otium* a requisite aspect of the flourishing Republic: *ut [qui] uel in negotio sine periculo, uel in otio cum dignitate esse possent* (1.1.3). To this cf. *Sest.* 98: *id quod est praestantissimum maximeque optabile omnibus sanis et bonis et beatis, cum dignitate otium*; *Ep. Fam.* 1.9.21: *id quod a me saepissime dictum est, cum dignitate otium*; *Phil.* 10.3: *cur cum te et uita et fortuna tua ad otium ad dignitatem inuitet.* On this theme see also Balsdon 1960: 43–50, and Boyancé 1941: 172–191.

[80] The conversational tone of *tibi uero, frater* (1.1.4) and the parenthetical *ut mihi saepe dixisti* (1.2.5) evoke casual intimacy rather than rhetorical finesse.

[81] *Voluntas* and *auctoritas* are often paired in the speeches and seem generally to belong to the language of public conduct and oratorical expectation. See, e.g., *Rosc. Amer.* 4 (with *beneuolentia*); *Verr.* 2.1.136 (in a list with *ius, aequitas, misericordia, oratio* and *gratia*); 2.1.153 (with *oratio*); 2.2.122; *Caec.* 65; *Mur.* 47, *Balb.* 39; *Mil.* 91; and *Phil.* 9.13.

[82] C. 65 is cited in full in Chapter 2, because of its use of *munus*. In addition to c. 65, poems predicated on tragedy (even if the tragedy is spoofed, as I think must be the case at c. 3) run throughout the

"translation" of Callimachus' *Plokamos*. If we read the whole of c. 65 next to
the dedicatory sections of *de Oratore*, there emerge intersections of rhetoric
and form that point to a cross-generic late Republican dedicatory practice.
First, Catullus and Cicero introduce their dedications with images of or
references to personal tragedy, described in terms of emotional shipwreck
or political tempest, to explain why they find the requested composition
difficult, overwhelming, or seemingly impossible.[83] In Catullus' case, the
tragedy is his brother's death; in Cicero's, it is the political disaster of the
Republic. Second, each author says that he will honor the requests of the
dedicatee lest he disappoint or frustrate the personal relationship upon
which the request was predicated.[84] Catullus worries that he will seem
to have forgotten his friend's request for literature (c. 65.17–21); Cicero
turns his brother's request for a textual *munus*[85] into a supreme test of
fraternal affection (*tibi uero, frater, neque . . . deero, de Orat.* 1.1.4). Finally,
in each case the offered "payment" of the obligation takes the form not
of an original textual composition, but of the author's clever translation
(*haec expressa . . . carmina Battiadae,* c. 65.16) or recollection (*ueteris cuiusdam memoria . . . recordatio, de Orat.* 1.11.4) of an authoritative original: a
Hellenistic court poem on the one hand, a conversation of the Republic's
maiores on the other.[86]

The first shared element of these dedications, the reference to personal
tragedy, is an important one. Catullus and Cicero were both likely aware
of the Hellenistic dedicatory practice, but whether either of them chose
to mimic this practice consciously is of course impossible to say. What

corpus: in addition to the "love gone wrong" series in which Catullus uses his mourning over the
lost relationship with Lesbia as a spur to poetic production, cf. cc. 96 and 101.

[83] Cat. 65.3–4: *Etsi me assiduo confectum cura dolore / seuocat a doctis, Hortale, uirginibus, nec potis est
dulcis Musarum expromere fetus / mens animi – tantis fluctuat ipsa malis*; Cic. *de Orat.* 1.1.3: *et hoc
tempus omne post consulatum obiecimus eis fluctibus, qui, per nos a communi peste depulsi, in nosmet
ipsos redundarunt.* See too Cat. 68a. 1–4: *quod mihi fortuna casuque oppressus acerbo / conscriptum hoc
lacrimis mittis epistolium, / naufragum ut eiectum spumantibus aequoris undis / subleuem et a mortis
limine restituam . . .*

[84] *Sed tamen in tantis maeroribus, Hortale, mitto / haec expressa tibi carmina Battiadae, / ne tua dicta
uagis nequiquam credita uentis . . .* (c. 65.15–17); *sed tamen in his uel asperitatibus rerum, uel angustiis
temporis, obsequar studiis nostris . . . tibi uero, frater, neque hortanti deero, neque roganti, name neque
auctoritate quisquam apud me plus ualere te potest, neque uoluntate* (*de Orat.* 1.1.3–4).

[85] *de Orat.* 2.3.11.

[86] We possess enough of Callimachus' *Plokamos* to interpret Catullus' *expressa carmina* as, loosely
speaking, a "translation" (on this see Pf. fr. 110, also Thomson 1997 *ad loc.*), though terms such as
"adaptation" or "reworking" speak more closely to the process. Cicero, conversely, claims literary
primacy in his written memory of the past: although the dialogue form may have been inspired by
Greek prototypes, the content of *de Oratore* is purely Roman.

is important is that they have each made the text, and textual production, a locus for the negotiation of affective relationships. By referring to a personal tragedy, Catullus and Cicero both gain the reader's sympathies and underline the intimacy of the exchange. Because the textual gift – c. 65, *de Oratore* – has been given at a time when writing is difficult, it is all the more valuable. The emphasis on the difficult circumstances under which the author is compelled to write dissolves the line between the destructive and productive elements of loss and tragedy, and suggests that personal (or in Cicero's case, personally political) disaster can provide a strong incentive to literary creativity. Catullus has lost his brother, and Cicero his Republic. Catullus nevertheless "translates" a story of separation and longing, and Cicero "retells" a conversation on the nature of Republican oratory. Whereas both Catullus and Cicero fulfill their textual obligations in spite of a personal tragedy, the frequency with which they – and of course especially Cicero, because he both wrote and dedicated far more than did Catullus – cite tragedy as the starting point for textual composition suggests that they have located it as a textually productive force.

In both c. 65 and *de Oratore*, the reference to personal tragedy is followed by the second shared element of these dedications, a very "Roman" emphasis on the precise nature of the social relationships at stake in the exchange. Whereas Archimedes refers to the request and the social obligation this implies only in passing (ἐπέστειλάς μοι γράψαι τῶν προβλημάτων τὰς ἀποδείξεις[87]), Catullus frames the social motivations behind his dedications in the highly fraught language of textual reciprocity (*dicta . . . credita*, l. 17; *furtiuo munere*, l. 19), and Cicero mixes throughout his dedication the theme of private textual reciprocity with the terms of judicial obligation (*auctoritas, uoluntas*, 1.1.4). Both late Republican authors tap into the tonality of social obligation and expectation to emphasize the affective intimacy upon which the request and its fulfillment are based. They bring the importance of the exchange, and the text as the social object through which that exchange is enacted, to the foreground.

In short, Catullus and Cicero emphasize the private and textually generative relationship between dedicator and dedicatee in markedly different ways. This is not especially surprising. For if Catullus and Cicero do not differ significantly in their social status (they were both in the upper ranks of society) and textual activity (they both wrote texts for, and exchanged

---

[87] Introduction to Archimedes' *de Sphaera et Cylindro* 2; cf. Janson 1964: 21.

texts with, men of similar rank), we must imagine that they would have differed in terms of how each man wanted his "social texts" to function in a social world. What is of use here is not merely the observation that they are different, but that a closer look at the differences may tell us more about the motivations and expectations of the broader textual world – of politically active and textually interested writers of poetry and prose – in which Catullus' motivations would likely have been the exception, and Cicero's more representative of the rule.

Catullus' dedication to Hortalus is tonally affectionate, rhetorically elevated (as discussed in Chapter 2) and, at times, strangely coy in its terms of expression. The somewhat jarring poem-end conflation of Catullus and Hortalus' relationship with that of Cydippe and Acontius shifts both the theme – from homosocial to heteroerotic affection – and the register – from that of lofty Roman rhetoric to that of carefully wrought Hellenistic *aition*. The translation of Roman male intimacy and textual obligation into mythologized and Greek heterosexual – and deeply textual – courtship is the sort of poetic nod to the *carmina Battiadae* (l. 16) that Catullus would have expected Hortalus to recognize and, even if it produced a wry chuckle, to appreciate. At one level, the Acontius and Cydippe reference – which marks a strongly poetic shift from the highly rhetorical structure with which c. 65 begins – connotes the relationship between donor and recipient as one informed by the language and customs of the forum, but situated solidly outside of it. At another level, however, both Callimachus' *Acontius* and his *Plokamos* are poems about the power of the text to rewrite, and remake, affective relationships. In the *Acontius*, it is the inscribed apple that remakes flirtation into a marriage oath; it is writing, in other words, that establishes a long-term affective relationship. In the *Plokamos*, surely a requested that (a request that Callimachus could not have easily refused), the poem itself functioned as an element of the Ptolemaic propaganda whereby a politically driven royal marriage was recreated as one predicated on young love and true affection.

In the painfully private – if carefully "published" – emotional tempest of c. 65, Catullus' brother is presented as the secondary dedicatee; in Catullus' claims – claims surely not disingenuous, but perhaps slightly distant – that he can't write anything at all, he produces a brilliantly original and provocative composition. His brother's death provides Catullus with a means of connecting with and honoring the past even as it serves as the impetus for producing textual relationships aimed at the future. At the same time, however, the somewhat odd reference to the story of Procne and Itys at lines 13–14 – whereby Catullus fashions himself a Procne and his brother her slaughtered son Itys – might give us a clue to the textual reconstruction of family alliances that runs through this poem.[88] Procne betrayed her relationship with her son Itys in favor of showing allegiance to, and establishing an ongoing relationship with, her sister Philomela – a woman who had been first violated and then silenced by Tereus' complete lack of recognition for family relations. Philomela could not, of course, relay Tereus' crimes to Procne with her voice; she had no voice, and was at any rate imprisoned by Tereus. What the woman who is to be transformed into the bird of poetry[89] does instead is send her sister the female structural equivalent of a text. She weaves the tale of Tereus' violence, her imprisonment, and her request for help into a tapestry the code of which Procne is both able to read and ready to act upon. Catullus did not (let us assume) have any hand in his brother's death; but the Procne reference suggests both that Hortalus' request was one made in writing and, perhaps – if we push the "nightingale as poetry" angle – one made in verse and prior to the brother's death. It may well be that c. 65 points to the form and source of the request, even as, in Catullus' decision to put his grief aside in order to respond to the request, it suggests that his brother's death has forced a shifting – or expansion – of allegiance and affection; a poetically inspired reconfiguration of affective bond. For almost as soon as the poet has claimed that he will sing forever of his brother's death, his story breaks off (. . . *absumpti fata gemens Ityli* –, l. 14) and turns quickly to a precise description of the gift he sends now to Hortalus (*sed tamen in tantis maeroribus, Hortale, mitto / haec expressa tibi carmina Battiadae*, ll. 15–16): it is a gift that "sings forever" the sorrow of filial loss. The reference to Callimachus nicely sets up the Acontius and Cydippe episode with which the poem ends. It is similarly a tale of shifting allegiance, this time not from husband to sister but – and here is where Cydippe and Catullus meld into one – away from family and toward the outsider who has offered a textual gift (*tua dicta*) that, in the obligations it invokes, functions as a tool of social negotiation.

---

[88] I am grateful to Christina Franzen for first suggesting this approach to c. 65 in a seminar I taught on late Republican textual reciprocity.

[89] On the nightingale in Greek and Latin poetry, see Chandler 1934. It may be especially the tendency for a nightingale to be understood as a poet or his poetry that is behind Catullus' use of this myth. Hesiod, at *WD* 202–212, tells of a hawk that threatens a nightingale, a passage Chandler (p. 81) suggests refers to a tyrant threatening the poet. Call. *Ep.* 2 might give us something more to go on. This epigram, written upon the death of Heraclitus, refers to the poems of Heraclitus as "nightingales." Heraclitus' death is located in Asia Minor (as is that of Catullus' brother), and *Ep.* 2 is in many ways reminiscent of Cat. 101.

Cicero's dedication of *de Oratore* similarly collapses what would seem traditional distinctions between public and private spheres. Although his dedication uses the basic structure and nuance of the epistolary (and thus implicitly private) dedication, it is also shot through with the language and concerns of oratorical and political practice. Cicero takes the image of the private tempest and gives it a delightfully Republican twist: he has been devastated not by the sudden death of a beloved brother, but by the slow destruction of a beloved political system. In the pathetic image of the old man (Cicero himself) devastated by the political storm, Cicero brilliantly manages to do three things. First, he makes Republican politics a matter of intimate sorrow: he grieves for the *Respublica* as a man would grieve for his friend – or brother. Second, by interweaving private concerns with public language, his dedication invites a larger audience: it seems to have one eye on Quintus, so to speak, and one on all subsequent readers. Third, and perhaps most remarkably, the image of the political shipwreck – and of the textual gift that results – introduces the idea of the text as an intentionally social object: a text written so as to initiate, promote, and revise social interaction.

The third shared element of these Republican dedications, and an element entirely absent from the Hellenistic treatises, is that the content of the dedicated text is in each case explicitly, surprisingly, unoriginal. In Chapter 2, we saw that *munus* is applied in the late Republic to objects (or acts) of reciprocity that are circulated in an unending cycle. There can be no beginning to this reciprocity and no end; the *munus* becomes an "instant" heirloom, a valuable that embodies its own history and tradition and that is possessed by necessity of a pedigree, inherited or manufactured.[90] Thus the value of the *munus* qua text may (and often does) lie not in the originality of the content but in its status as an heir to, and often a transformation of, an established tradition or primal archetype. The pedigree value of the new composition is heightened by its relationship with the past.

One way to do this is through imitation that singularizes. Both Catullus and Cicero write these texts in order to mimic the social form, and not just the content, of the original. Just as Cicero, in *de Oratore* – and indeed many of his dialogues – goes to great pains to claim that his text represents

---

[90] The material expression of a pedigree is important for the authority it implies: the crest, the coat of arms, the bust or portrait, the written genealogy or manuscript. Kopytoff 1986: 73 calls such objects the "symbolic inventory of society," and includes "public lands, monuments, state art collections, the paraphernalia of political power, royal residences, chiefly insignia, ritual objects . . . [p]ower often asserts itself symbolically precisely by insisting on its right to singularize an object, or a set or class of objects."

the "faithful reproduction" of an altogether fictitious oral original (only the later and increasingly theatrical dialogues – *Laelius* and *Cato* – drop this fiction), Catullus' choice of the *Plokamos* as his "gift" to Hortalus is to be located in the fact that the Callimachean original was itself a dedicated and requested poem. But the choice to translate the *Plokamos* is not unproblematic. On the one hand, the *Plokamos* is itself a tale of the death of a brother – it is the lock of hair "cut off" from its brother-locks that gives voice to the poet's words – and so Catullus' promise never to stop singing of his brother's death is reified in his choice of translation. But if the *Plokamos* is a tale of brotherly sorrow, it is also a highly ironic – and, as I suspect, utterly disingenuous – piece of court poetry dedicated to Berenike II and, by extension, to her husband Ptolemy III Euergetes. I find it difficult to believe that the irony of the original would have been lost on Catullus. There is nothing in c. 65 that suggests Catullus is being disingenuous in the affection he expresses for Hortalus, and indeed the "gift" of Greek verse transformed into Latin seems to have constituted a special category of late Republican textual exchange (cf. c. 51 and Cinna, fr. 1). Yet deep in mourning, Catullus sends a poem of mourning – but he does so in the dedication of a piece of extreme (or even doubled) poetic artifice: even as he claims he cannot write, the irony of the model is brought to bear on Roman textual politics. He seems to understand that the expectations and obligations of the textual world were such that the request for writing might trump private concerns; but in his choice to translate a poem written at the order of the Ptolemaic court, and to offer a poem that manages yet to orient itself to his brother's death, he offers a wry commentary on the social obligations implicit in the request that cannot be refused even as he maintains full control over the way in which that request will be honored.

The practice of dedicating and circulating a text that claims to be, and seeks value precisely from its status as, a recycled product – a cross-cultural and cross-linguistic transformation of artifice – is a late Republican innovation (even as it has its roots in the middle Republic). In the textual reciprocity of the late Republic the recycled and dedicated text carries a value that is disproportionate to the social codes of literary production. The method and means of this recycling varies, and so the force of the "revision" functions at different levels. Catullus offers both "transformations" of original Greek texts and, as we have seen, textualizations of remembered "real" acts of convivial and poetic display. Cicero similarly engaged in a great deal of transformation of Greek poetry, but when he aims at a textual reproduction, he chooses instead the Latinized reproduction of elite conversation – consisting in large part in philosophical and rhetorical display – and of Greek intellectual thought. Although Catullus' *Coma* seems to vary little from its Callimachean model, verbatim rendering appears to have been the exception rather than the rule. In his transformation of Sappho 16, and in his and Cicero's textualization of patronal-class discourse, and in Cicero's reproductions of Roman discourse on the topics of Greek learning, the authority of the model – be it a text or a conversation – elevates the pedigree of the new composition[91] even as the author's deviation from the model – his Roman reworking of tone and style – is an advertisement of his ability to remake the past and improve upon it.

These dedications point to a late Republican aesthetic in which textual gifts were more valuable – more singularized – if they were written as recognizable or believable rehearsals of established textual or performative models.[92] Perhaps not surprisingly, these "rehearsals" are not only more valuable than the model, but also more valuable than an altogether original composition. Just as an act of reciprocity is never discrete or terminal, but always looks Janus-like to the obligations of the past and of the future, so too the exchangeable revision of an earlier "model" straddles the social and textual divide between then and now, old and new: it is a textual embodiment of social reciprocity. The exchanged textual rehearsal, then, speaks to both utilitarian and didactic concerns, and the recognition of these concerns aids in explaining the purpose served by dedications through which such texts were presented. Even such recognition, however, cannot account completely for the significant textual allure of the exchanged rehearsal. For this we need to turn to the third main intersection between Catullus and Cicero, and one of the characteristics of late Republican textual production that would find its greatest expression in the Principate and Empire: the materialization of the text.

---

[91] Themes of oratorical and textual pedigree, expressed by terms such as *antiquitas* and *uetustas*, run throughout *de Oratore* and *Brutus*. See also *Lael.* 4: *genus autem hoc sermonum positum in hominum veterum auctoritate*, and *Cato* 2: *hunc librum ad te de senectute misimus. Omnem autem sermonem tribuimus non Tithono ut Aristo Cius (parum enim esset auctoritatis in fabula), sed M. Catoni seni, quo maiorem auctoritatem haberet oratio*; Dupont 1997.

[92] This is not to say, of course, that Callimachus' *Coma* would have functioned as a "commodity" in any useful sense of the word; rather, that it would have been unthinkable for Catullus to respond to his friend's request for poetry with a mere edition of the Greek original.

PART III

The materialization of the text

Intersections of rhetoric and social practice (2): The dedicated text as "acting object"

> For when I open a medieval manuscript, and this is different from opening a printed book, I am conscious not only of the manu-script, the bodily handling of materials in production, writing, illumination, but also how in its subsequent reception, the parchment has been penetrated; how it has acquired grease stains, thumb-marks, erasures, drops of sweat; suffered places where images have been kissed away by devout lips or holes from various eating animals.[1]

If Freud's Shoe was never merely a shoe,[2] and Marx's Table was never merely a table,[3] it is safe to say that, for the late Republic, the patronal-class dedicated text was very rarely merely a patronal-class dedicated text. The phenomenon of a text being, at least potentially, more than just a text – the phenomenon of the received value of the whole (volume) transcending in value the sum of its material and intellectual components – is one likely naturalized by most readers of *this* text. But as the fact of this naturalization might be considered to be the single most important contribution of the textual community of the late Republic, it will be useful to finish our study with those aspects of the late Republican community that speak most strongly to those periods that follow, from the obsessively textual worlds of the Principate and Empire to the social and intellectual engagement with textual materiality as it continues into our time.[4]

Chapters 7 and 8, then, focus on the third major intersection of Catullus and Cicero's textual practice: the various ways in which each author began to imbue his dedicated texts with a sense of physicality or materialism. Because each author's "textual materialisms" (I shall get to exactly what I

---

[1] Camille 1997: 41.
[2] For Freud, the shoe – for instance – was a fetish object that took its value as a replacement object for the mother's lost penis; for more of this wacky theory, see in general Freud 1953–1966, vol. 21: 149.
[3] Marx 1981: 81–82 on the idea of the table as a commodity and the way values issue from commodities.
[4] What I have in mind here is primarily the western phenomenon of the book and book culture, but there is a wealth of literature on similar phenomena in non-western literary cultures; for ancient parallels, Connery 1998: 63–70 provides an excellent and useful discussion of textual materiality in early imperial China.

mean by this and what it means for each author below) are related to their textualizations of *display* – once a text has been made to contain the social display of the "real world," it shifts, if subtly, into the realm of the physical – there will be some overlap between the texts we consider in these chapters and those considered previously. But because the textual materialisms of Catullus and Cicero do not overlap precisely with their textualizations of display – this is especially the case with Catullus – and because Catullus and Cicero endow their texts with physicality in different ways and, as it seems, to decisively different ends, it will be most useful to consider this intersection separately from that discussed in Part II.

Just as the intersection of textual materialism seems conceptually related to that of the textualization of display, my identification of this intersection grew out of my recognition of the "display function" with which these texts were endowed. Both Catullus and Cicero, especially in compositions that are predicated on the understanding of the text as a receptacle for display and social negotiation, endowed their texts with various forms and degrees of "materiality" that suggest that each man imagined his text as an "acting object" that was distinct from, and eternally connected to, his own textual motivations. That each man chose to do this may suggest the emergence of a late Republican cross-generic awareness of the power of the book – and now, I think, we might move from the scriptural category of "text" to the more purely social category of "book" – as a distinctly material "acting object." But there is more to it than this. For as much as the textual materialisms of Catullus and Cicero are asymmetric in terms of the form they take and the apparent intent with which they were produced, each man's practice seems to have made its mark on the textual materialisms that emerge in even greater quantity in the literary world of the Principate and early Empire.

As much as Catullus and Cicero intersect in their textual materialisms, they express these materialisms in tellingly different ways. Thus under the rubric of "textual materialisms" as addressed in the following chapters, I have in mind two distinct but interrelated phenomena. I discuss these phenomena in terms of "weak" and "strong" materializations of the textual product, the relative "weakness" or "strength" of which is determined by the degree to which the materiality is forefronted by the text itself. Catullus' materialisms, I argue, are primarily of the "weak" sort, and consist mainly of textual "fetishizations." The representative poems I discuss in this category are of two varieties: first, those poems that seem to have dislocated themselves from their author in order to serve as the physical representative of his social and textual negotiations; and, second, those that seem to have become fully distinct from their authorial origin in order to function as physical entities endowed with poetic volition and voice and capable, in the poetic imagination, of autonomous movement and action. Cicero's materialisms, by contrast, are primarily of the "strong" sort, and consist overwhelmingly of the aggressive and explicit personification of both oratorical voice and the dedicated treatise (usually, but not inevitably, the dialogue) in which it is housed. In this category, it will suffice to focus on one extraordinary example of such personification, and indeed the first example of such personification in the *technica*: it is the personification of the Republican voice – *eloquentia* – as advanced in the deeply textually interested *Brutus*. I will discuss in conclusion the ways in which the dedicated dialogues as a group function as *conformationes* – "invocations" and quite nearly "resurrections" – of both Rome's deceased *maiores* and the late Republic's yet-living participants in the textual world.

I noted in the Introduction that the textual story of the late Republic is a difficult one to tell, and in some ways our consideration of the formal and intentional distinctions of our authors' practice of textual materialization is the most difficult part. But as asymmetric as our authors appear to be in this practice, it is more important here than anywhere else that we consider them in concert. For when Catullus and Cicero engage in textual materialism, whether in the "weak" materialism of the fetishized poem, the "strong" materialism of a personified voice, or the rhetorically compelling historical *conformatio*, they each create texts that, because they are imbued with both materiality and motion, function as social – and in Cicero's case at least, political – objects. Catullus' single instance of addressing his own verses as a poetic entity separate – or at least separable – from its authorial source (and, as we shall note, separated from this source in order to move beyond the world of homosocial textual exchange) is the one that may point most tellingly to the practice adopted by some of the most prolific poets of the later periods. We may think especially of the poetic offspring of Ovid and Martial, cunningly crafted poems that scamper madly into and about the *urbs*, negotiating return, or welcome, or protection. And yet the Ciceronian drive to extend authorial influence outside of the purely textual realm – the text that is never fully separate from its author, but always drags him, and his interests, along with it – is evident in the works of later periods that sought to use the text and its status as a "gift" – if it is now almost exclusively a gift offered up hierarchically and with little expectation of textual return – as a means of negotiating not merely the textual world but the social and political ones.

But the textual materialisms of the late Republic, as innovative and subsequently influential as they seem to have been, did not arise *ex nihilo*, so before we look more closely at the emergence of this practice in Catullus and Cicero, it will be useful to return briefly to the periods that preceded it in order both to locate the late Republican materialisms on the broader continuum of textual materiality and to suggest how and why this materialism continued to evolve in the periods that followed. It has long been recognized that the Hellenistic period as a whole is marked by the centrifugation of political and social power from the core of Athens to the eastern and southern periphery of the Greek world; some of the epistolary implications of this centrifugation were discussed in Chapter 6. The establishment of new centers of power and learning in, for example, Pergamon and Alexandria brought changes not only in the social and political structure of the Greek world but also in the overarching nature of scholarship and study, and the collection, housing, and use of written materials throughout the Mediterranean. As the written text became an increasingly important tool in the transmission and circulation of intellectual activity (we think again of Archimedes' prose prefaces), the physical text acquired a powerful new socioeconomic valence.

The private libraries that had become so important an element of late Republican textual culture (we have read of Cicero's pained negotiations to acquire such) had of course existed, even in large-scale form, long before the Hellenistic period proper; and the small-scale circulation and enjoyment of the written word qua written word (that is, not as a text recording an earlier lyric, choral, or dramatic performance) is likely to have been a commonplace among the *literati* by at least the late fifth century BCE. Indeed the physical text (whether stationary stele or portable book roll), as well as the acts of reading it solicited, seems to have been imbued with identifiable, if limited, social and erotic functions almost as soon as writing entered the playing field of intellectual and aesthetic discourse.[5] Even in the earliest periods, writing is figured as seduction; reading is figured as surrender; and the book in particular is figured as a suggestively sexual object. For whereas the fifth-century reading of a public stele or inscribed sympotic vessel invites the passerby (or guest) to engage in a public and performative seduction, the book roll lures its reader into a

---

[5] On this see especially Svenbro 1993: 187–216, on vase inscriptions of the early fifth century, in which the writer of the inscription is figured the active sexual partner (*erastês*), and the reader the passive (*erômenos*). Svenbro also discusses the category of "schoolboy" vases, in which young men are depicted, with various degrees of eroticization, in the act of reading (*CVA*, Germany [Adolphseck, Schloss Fasanerei] 16.2, no. 62 is perhaps the most famous example).

private courtship between two men alone.[6] The book roll, evolving its contents in a slow striptease and vacillating seductively between the world of thought and the world of stuff, underlines the inevitable distance between writer and reader even as it provides – we can consider this more fully in our consideration of Catullus 50 – a physical point of contact between the two.

The erotic connotations of early acts of reading have been attributed to the physical shape of the book roll itself, to the practice of the oral reading of written discourse, and to the deeply affective and socially exclusive settings in which early texts were most frequently crafted and shared. In the Hellenistic period, however, the previously intimate eroticism of the privately circulated text is imbued with broader and more powerful social and political valences. As Pfeiffer noted,[7] it is this period that invents the "Classics" with all of the cultural and intellectual fetishism that this implies. It is in this period that we first see the birth of the canon, the creation of anthologies, hypotheses, glossaries, the critical and authoritative editions, and the beginnings of advanced literary criticism that are not only adopted and expanded in the middle and late Republic, but that seem largely responsible for the second-century BCE emergence of a textual culture in Rome. It is also this period that invents, practically speaking, a book as such: it is in the Hellenistic period that the physical text, qua original or authoritative version, becomes the object of political and social interest – and even desire – that it remains today. We know to raise our eyebrows at Ptolemy III Euergetes' arrogant confiscation of original texts at the Alexandria docks (copies were returned to the owners), and uniformly condemn his theft of the official copies of the three tragedians given on loan from Athens.[8] But anyone who has sought out a first edition or rare old volume is apt to empathize, if secretly, with his appetite for "the real thing."

The Ptolemaic practice of large-scale book "acquisition" (for which let us read, "theft") appears to have brought with it a second, similarly important

---

[6] Thus note the erotic connotations of the "textual" meeting of Socrates and Phaedrus at the beginning of Plato's dialogue: Δείξας γε πρῶτον, ὦ φιλότης, τί ἄρα ἐν τῇ ἀριστερᾷ ἔχεις ὑπὸ τῷ ἱματίῳ. τοπάζω γάρ σε ἔχειν τόν λόγον αὐτόν (Plat., *Phaed.* 228D). This passage is discussed usefully by Svenbro 1993, cf. pp. 198–201.

[7] Pfeiffer 1968: 87–104 esp.

[8] The bibliophilic drive of the Ptolemies is well documented. For the tale of Euergetes' thefts, see Galen 17 (1) 607 (on the confiscation of originals and return of copies) and Galen *Comm. in Hipp. Epidem.* 3 (reproduced *in extenso* by Fraser 1972, vol. 2: 480–481). Green 1990: 87–91 esp. discusses the project of the Library's planned acquisition of every known work ("The scholars who staffed the Library saw their mission as nothing less than the rescue of all past Greek literature") and remains an invaluable source for the political and intellectual background of the Hellenistic period.

and perhaps further-reaching, social and intellectual by-product: the small-scale collection and ostentatious display of books as indicators of upper-class citizen status. In what had been an ongoing and evolving aesthetics of citizen-status accoutrements – a process not restricted to, but most traceable through, funerary reliefs and vase paintings – the visual art of the Hellenistic period suggests a subtle reconfiguration of the visual means through which upper-class men contested and advertised their identity. Whereas upper-class male citizenship tended to be marked in the archaic period by the spear (δόρυ / δόρος),[9] and in the classical period by the speaker's staff (βακτηρία),[10] in the Hellenistic period such citizenship is expressed in terms of representations of learning in general and the book roll, and related literary paraphernalia, in particular.[11]

Zanker has discussed this phenomenon at length, and there is no need to replay his argument here.[12] What we see, in short, is that from the late third and early second century on the male citizen becomes ever more visually "intellectualized," choosing to have himself represented, usually on grave monuments, as a collector, displayer, and user of books.[13] These

[9] The examples of this type are too numerous to list in full; representative are the stele of Aristion, ca. 510–500 BCE, in the National Archaeological Museum at Athens (funeral stele no. 29); the black-figure amphora in the British Museum signed by Exekias and depicting a battle between Achilles and Penthesilea (1836, 0224.127; vase B210); and the amphora showing Ajax and Achilles playing draughts, also by Exekias (though many versions of this theme exist), ca. 550–540 BCE and in the Vatican museum, no. 16757.

[10] The speaker's staff – βακτηρία – was used to help secure a fold of the *himation* under the armpit in order to free up the two hands required for the proper choreography of political address. Some of the earliest sculptural examples of this are the stele from Orchomenos by Alexenor, ca. 500–490 BCE (National Archaeological Museum at Athens, funeral stele no. 39), and the Kouros base representing youths at play, ca. 510 BCE (National Archaeological Museum at Athens, no. 3476). The βακτηρία appears as an element of upper-class citizen dress on numerous sympotic vessels (cf. Toledo, Ohio 64.126 [kylix]; Brussels R 259 [same, by Scheurleer painter]; West Berlin F2279 *ARV* 115,2 [kylix by Peithnios]), and is often "put to work" in scenes of monetary negotiation with, or seduction of, *hetairai* (cf. Rome, Villa Giulia 27254 [kylix]; Chicago 1911.456 *ARV* 572,88 [hydria by the Leningrad painter]; Adolphseck 41 *ARV* 566,6 [pelike by Pig painter]); it is frequently depicted off to the side in scenes of copulation or revelry, in which the result of not using a βακτηρία – the unveiling of the male body – is made explicit (cf. London E 68 *ARV* 371,24 [kylix, by Brygos painter]; London E 44 *ARV* 318–9 [kylix, by Panaitios painter]; and Würzburg 479 *ARV* 372,32 [kylix, by Brygos painter]).

[11] It is true that the book roll appears in some earlier depictions, such as the funeral stele of a youth, ca. 420, now in an abbey in Grottaferata, but such depictions do not gain broad currency until the third century and later. Although depictions of book rolls always retain minority status on Attic vases, they do appear, cf. Immerwahr 1964 and 1973.

[12] Zanker 1993 and, esp., 1995: 188–197.

[13] Thus on a collection of *stelai* from this period typical of the Ionian coast (many of which are located in the Anadolu Medinyetleri Muzesi in Ankara), individuals of all classes begin to be represented as members of the *intelligentsia*. These reliefs – there are some 20,000 of them in the Ankara museum, though only a handful are on display – are marked first and foremost by the conspicuous presence of

funerary representations of the east mark, I think, an emergent aesthetic in which an upstanding citizen came to be recognized by his interest in, and ability to procure, display, and interact with, the objects of the textual world. Whereas before a good citizen was "made" by the ability to fight with valor or speak with eloquence, in the Hellenistic period and beyond (we need think only of the Pompeian "Sappho," or any one of numerous funerary statues from the Augustan and Imperial periods)[14] such a citizen was designated increasingly by his (and, for the first time, her!) ability to read, to write, and to own – books.

In what follows, Chapter 7 investigates Catullus' relatively casual materialisms in terms of three distinct varieties of textual "fetishizations." The first is the fetishization of the poem as a physical means of social contract and payoff. As I consider this the weakest form of textual materialism, if the one that appears to be most closely related to Catullus' textualization of display, I shall deal with these poems somewhat briefly. The second is the fetishization of the poem as an "object of affection" – both the physical entity upon which homoerotic textual play is projected and the material and erotic object that has resulted from the textual play. The third category of fetishization, one that may indicate a late Republican textual form influential on the practices of the Principate and early Empire, is found in a selection of poems (cc. 35 and 42, but we shall also consider c. 36) in which the poet addresses the poem – the poem, that is, as a physical object – and orders it to journey into the textual world either with, or on behalf of, its creator; as a conclusion to this chapter, I consider Catullus' *Coma* as a poetic personification that will be useful to keep in mind as we turn to the personifications functioning in the dialogues. Catullus' expressions of textual materialism are interesting in their own right. They fall in line with the emergence of text as social object in the Hellenistic period,

---

large numbers of book rolls and writing implements (cf. Zanker 1993 and 1995: 190–193). Apparently ordinary citizens (the majority of the Ionic *stelai* are of relatively low quality and are likely pre-, rather than custom-, made: not the *stelai* of the poorest members of society, but nor are they those of the very upper crust) begin to appear in the guise of scholars, philosophers, men of science, and the collectors and displayers of texts.

[14] The so-called "Sappho" portrait, Naples 9084, depicts a young woman with writing tablet in hand and stylus rested suggestively on her lips; the provincial "literary couple," Naples 9058, depicts what is likely a non-aristocratic duo "done up" in aristocratic manner: like "Sappho," the woman holds tablet in hand and stylus to mouth; the man is togate, with a book roll held just under his somewhat scraggly beard. From the Augustan period, a funerary statue (now in Buffalo, at the Albright Gallery) of a man with chest exposed and book roll in hand, speaks to a literary chic of the period. Zanker 1995: 214–215 identifies the individual as a professional poet ("a member of the aristocracy could hardly have had himself so depicted"), but this is an identification I feel we should not make too hastily; cf. the statue of Posidippus with the head reworked (after ca. 50 BCE) into that of a Roman senator (cf. Zanker 1995: 211).

and so a "materializing" consideration of these poems will expand our understanding of the evolution and expansion of textual materialism as it continued into the Empire. Yet their greatest value to this study is precisely their contrast with the more aggressive materialisms of Cicero. For as much as Catullus' poetic *praxis* appears to have been anomalous for the period (Lucilius offers our only convincing forerunner), it seems likely – based on what little we have in the fragments – that his "weak" materialisms present not only an alternate late Republican tonality but perhaps the more pervasive one at the time. As much as Catullus was anomalous in his rejection of the world of prose and (for the most part) political activity, it may well be that in his aggressive promotion of textual personification it is Cicero who is to be considered the anomaly. Indeed, it is precisely because textual fetishization (the "weak" materialisms of Catullus) and textual personification (the "strong" materialisms of Cicero) occupy two points on a broader continuum of what it means to "make a book more than just a book" that the distinctions in our authors' practices, when considered in concert with the operative conditions under which each man wrote, will inform our understanding of what each author sought from his materialisms and to what extent he saw them as a matter of aesthetic choice, social statement, or political necessity. Beyond this, however, and perhaps even more tantalizingly, it may inform our understanding of the broader Society of which Catullus and Cicero are our primary representatives.

It will not be surprising to see that Catullus' fetishizations restrict their interests – for the most part – to the negotiations of the textual realm, while Cicero's personifications seem to extend beyond that realm and negotiate relationships on behalf of their author in a broader social and political world. If textual history ended with the late Republic, it would be easy enough to remark that because Catullus (anomalous though he was) seemed never to have been especially politically active, he did not need to remake his texts as "little bodies" that could move about the city – intellectually speaking – in a way he was no longer able to do. Catullus was neither politically uninformed nor politically disinterested. He was, by contrast, deeply politically engaged (and as one senses, frequently deeply politically concerned); but as a man who seems to have restricted his textual negotiations to the textual sphere, his interest in textual materialism seems primarily an aesthetic or purely sociotextual one. Because the materialization of the text continues, with interesting variations, in the textual productions of later periods, it will be useful to note that although the form of such later materializations – the text as an object of poetic address – follows most closely that which we see in Catullus, the function of such materializations – the text as an object that moves into and through the city concerns itself with extra-textual matters – is in greater alignment with what we see in Cicero.

Cicero's textual materialisms, as I argue in Chapter 8, are both more forceful and more developed. I first discuss *Brutus* as a text that "gives voice" to a Cicero who had long been silent, move next to a consideration of the social and textual power of personification, and finally analyze the careful process through which Cicero transforms *eloquentia* into *Eloquentia*: from the abstract concept of "spoken eloquence" to the concrete concept of a young girl who is to be safeguarded "at home." In the final pages of the chapter, I shall suggest that the recognition of Cicero's Brutine *Eloquentia* as a personification of Republican voice invites us to go a step further and read all of Cicero's dialogues as *conformationes* – "personifications" – of their characters. What we have in the dedicated dialogues, then, are not merely the prose embodiments of Cicero's oratorical voice, but the resurrected voices of Rome's Republican past. In their containment within a dedicated text, these voices – Republican voices, now fully co-opted by Cicero – are able to move beyond the textual world to which Catullus seemed to restrict himself and into the social, political, and intellectual ones in which Cicero had always placed his interest and to which the authors of later periods were constrained perforce.

CHAPTER 7

An object of Catullan affection

MORE THAN JUST TEXTS: FETISH AS "ACTING OBJECT"

That Catullus is an author deeply invested in the variously figured homosocial relationships between reader and poet has been well established, as
has his use of exchanged *uersiculi* in the poetics of both an elite Roman
manhood and his own self-positioning in the lyric construction of such.[1]
The studies of, for example, Fitzgerald, Janan and D. Wray have greatly
advanced our understanding of a late Republican "literary masculinity,"
and have established Catullus as an author of wide-reaching import and
influence for later modes of poetic communication and homosocial negotiation. These studies have helped to reconstruct the homosocial aesthetic
of the late Republican textual world and have provided much of the theoretical foundation upon which my discussions in the following sections
are constructed. What I want to do in this chapter, however, is to take
poems that have been noted for their function as creators (and challengers,
and products) of "literary masculinity," resituate them in terms of the late
Republican textual world, and consider how they functioned in this world
qua their status – one that is often emphasized by Catullus – as variously
materialized, "givable" objects.

The theme of poetic materiality and textual exchange – of giving the
"textual gift" – runs intermittently throughout the Catullan corpus, and it
might reasonably be argued that any of the poems that address or allude to
a second party might be seen as contributing to the ongoing creation of the
late Republican textual world. In the sections following this one, however,
I limit my discussion to those poems that appear to embody a specific
"exchange function" in an ongoing cycle of textual production, then to
those that make explicit their material function within that exchange,
and, finally, to the one that represents the strongest form of Catullan

---

[1] On these themes see especially Fitzgerald 1995, esp. 34, 58; and Wray 2001: 64–112 (on the use of
Lesbia in the construction of manhood in the shorter poems).

materialism, as it shifts out of the normal sphere of straight-up dedication or address and is imagined to be the primary addressee of the poet's words or a full personification of an absent poet and poem. Because these poems underline their existence as social (and often, material) objects within a social world – they are polished or crude, they attack or arouse, they repay or request a favor, build or destroy an affective bond – they transgress the physical boundary of their textuality and actually, or at least putatively, "do things" in the textual world in which Catullus writes.

In emphasizing the materiality of his poems but confining the interests of this materiality to an erotically charged textual world, Catullus constructs his poems as objects of cultural – most specifically, textual – fetish. In these poems' ability both to represent the "distant presence" of their author, and to blur the boundaries between performative world and performative text, they contain and, in some cases, nearly embody impulses of the affective relationship through which they are exchanged. No merely objectified forms of desire, these poems become a telegraph of action and emotion: a slap or a kiss, a handshake or a rape.

As I shall suggest in the pages that follow, in the precise moment that Catullus makes specific the materiality of his poetic exchanges (and assaults), these poems are transformed into something other – "more" – than words on the page. His emphasis on the text as an object, in short, dissolves the traditional boundaries between word and world and displaces on to the text the psychic fixations and erotic impulses through which the text is imbued with social value. It turns text into fetish: a category of social meaning as inherently unstable as it is potentially powerful. Once the poem has been transformed into materialized "fetish text" – a textual object through which desire and value are constructed – it must continually question, and in some cases contradict, its own nature, identity, and value.[2]

Fetish is a contestable object category by nature, and no less contestable is the concept of fetish in theoretical discourse.[3] As Matt Wray remarked, if critical theorists have a fetish at all, it is probably fetishism itself. The concept of fetishism is one that has become increasingly attractive to investigations into spectacle, materialism, eroticism, and indeed any aspect of social or economic reciprocity. But as "fetish" and its related terms are used as many ways as there are disciplines to adopt them, it will help first to narrow the definition of the term, and the category of social meaning in

---

[2] Marx 1981: 85 "Value . . . does not stalk about with a label describing what it is."

[3] Wray 1998: "Clearly, we derive a certain perverse pleasure from using the term, enjoying its cachet and the way it wryly suggests a sexual, libidinal energy at work in everything from shopping to sport, from celebrity worship to public humiliations."

which it operates, to one with the greatest applicability to the textual world with which we are concerned. In charting the social meaning of fetish, as a cultural category applicable to the textual world of the late Republic, I have found the work of Apter and Pietz, among others[4] who advance a fairly flexible approach to the concept of cultural fetishism, to be of greatest use. Along these lines, the fetishization of the Republican text, as I discuss it, sits at a crossroads of two of the more traditional configurations of fetish, the Freudian and the Marxian. Although we shall see that neither Freud's nor Marx's configuration of fetish will be sufficient to our purpose in and of itself, a quick review of the "object category" of fetish will help us get at why both category and term will be useful in discussing the textual materialisms of Catullus.

The Freudian fetish revolves, generally speaking, around the idea of castration anxiety and the male urge to locate his desire for the missing female penis in objects that represent at some level his first awareness of female lack.[5] Because the Freudian fetish is a psychological phenomenon of particularity rather than universality, and because his fetish is one that is subject to stasis and hoarding rather than exchange and circulation, a strictly Freudian approach cannot account fully for the social phenomenon of textual fetishization, as it is at work in the late Republic. And yet, precisely because Freud endows the fetish of the "maternal phallus" – the object of the fetishist's lack – with a form of autonomy and potential for action, and because his use of the term carries with it an awareness of displaced and substituted desire, we will find it helpful for our investigation into texts that functioned as the receptacles for just such poetic displacement and substitution.

Marx, by contrast, uses fetish to describe a kind of magical thinking in commodity-driven societies. This fetish is not sexual in nature, but economic; Marx focuses on the idea of the "hidden value of commodities" and the properties we project upon the objects of everyday life. According to this configuration, the value of any commodity is encoded in our own assignment of that value; value is not inherent in an object but is always a matter of social relations, a subjective property that is first arbitrarily assigned to it and then completely naturalized. When ordinary

---

[4] See esp. Apter 1993: 1–2; Pietz 1993: 115–151 (on fetishism and materialism); and Foster 1993: 251/265 (on fetishism in Dutch still-life paintings); see also Apter 1991 and Krips 1999.

[5] Although I will refer to this kind of fetish as the "Freudian," Freud (in his *Three Essays on Sexuality*) was only popularizing an early notion of fetish, adopting a term current in psychoanalysis to describe a particular type of male behavior. Alfred Binet, in 1887, was the first to apply the term "fetish" to certain types of unusual or "abnormal" male sexual behavior, in 1887.

objects – the table, the hat, or the automobile – are turned into commodities, they gain a hidden value, a value "above and beyond" the object itself: in Marx's terminology, they gain the character of the fetish. Because the Marxian fetish is an interpretive category restricted to recognizable commodities, it does not address the idea of erotic displacement on to the fetishized object per se. And yet, precisely because the texts with which we are concerned function as a type of commodity, even if it is a type that was restricted to the exchanges of a world that kept their texts at a remove from cash transactions, Marx's understanding of the socioeconomic value of the fetishized object will prove useful to our understanding of Catullus' textual fetishizations as conceptual composites of erotic and economic value.

THE POEM AS CONTRACT, ASSAULT, AND PAYOFF: CC. 1, 16, 49, 68b

Catullus 1 neatly embodies the characteristics of what we might call the "composite" fetish. Some of the more "materialistic" aspects of this poem have been discussed previously, but it will be useful to return briefly in order to situate it within the broader context of fetish text. Because it introduces the *libellus* as much as it introduces itself, and because it is as much a gift as the poems it gives, c. 1 – in whatever form this *libellus* took, and whatever it originally contained – embodies the dedicated collection, at the moment of its giving, as an object of homosocial affection and social contract:

> Cui dono lepidum nouum libellum
> arida modo pumice expolitum?
> Corneli, tibi; namque tu solebas
> meas esse aliquid putare nugas
> iam tum, cum ausus es unus Italorum   5
> omne aeuum tribus explicare cartis
> doctis, Iuppiter, et laboriosis.
> quare habe tibi quidquid hoc libelli
> qualecumque; quod, <o>patrona uirgo,
> plus uno maneat perenne saeclo.   10

> To whom do I give this delightful new book –
> Just now rubbed smooth with the dry pumice-stone?
> To *you*, Cornelius; for you have always thought
> That my little trifles were worth something,
> When you alone of all Italians dared   5

To detail the whole of history in three volumes –
Learned they were, by god, and laborious.
So then, have for yourself this little book, whatever its worth
And however you find it; and, O patron virgin,
May it survive ever-fresh and for more than one generation.   10

As noted at the start of this study, the very question with which the poem begins is one of deceptive simplicity: the words that create the gift problematize the concept of what it means to *give one's words*. Although we know that it is Catullus who is writing, c. 1 is written in such a way as to invite us to imagine that it is the poem that is speaking. Both poet and poem muse playfully about the choice of dedicatee; both poet and poem recognize in Nepos a good partner in textual prestation; both poet and poem close their dedication by shifting its focus, and indeed the responsibility for the reception and promulgation, away from Nepos and onto the Muse (and all subsequent readers).[6] The personifying force of the diminutive *libellus* invites us to imagine that both the poetic collection and indeed c. 1 have identities distinct from that of their author; the volume is Catullus' creation, but c. 1 captures it at the moment it becomes something more like his *creature*.

I want to suggest that the voice of the poet in c. 1 gives birth to, but is not identical with, the voice of the poem; the effect is that of a fusion of textual voices, a rhetorical vacillation between the "poetic" and the "poematic." What the poet has written (and perhaps spoken; as noted in Chapter 6, c. 1 plays awfully well as poetic dedication introducing an intimate poetry reading) but once, the poem repeats at each reading. But even this repetition is inexact, for it depends upon whether we imagine it is Catullus or the *carmen* making the dedication. If we listen to the "poetic" voice (that is, the voice of "Catullus the poet"), then the dedication is framed as an exchange between textual allies: men of different age and literary aesthetic, perhaps (although Pliny *Ep.* 5.3 indicates that Nepos wrote light-hearted verse as well), but compatriots in a larger world of textual circulation. Dionysios Chalcous "toasted" "Theodoros" in a sympotic

---

[6] There is a metrical problem in line 9 as it stands. Thomson 1997: 198–199 notes, "the metrical defect in the line . . . caused the Humanists either to restore 'o' (later adopted by most editors) or to substitute *quidem* for *quod*. Presumably the second of these remedies prompted Bergk's rewriting of the line (*qualecumque quidem est, patroni ut ergo*), which however is unconvincing for several reasons . . . the word *ergo* absolutely cannot mean, and nowhere comes close to meaning, 'by the agency of <a person>,' as it would have to do on Bergk's interpretation. On the contrary, in every instance quoted in *TLL* it means 'for the sake of,' or 'in consequence of' a thing or aim . . . Clausen 1976: 38–48 ('the evidence against Bergk is clear and damning')." Thomson also notes that "patron cannot be reasonably applied to the sense of this poem and the poet's own interest in retaining autonomy in the dedication." On this see also Cairns 1969.

context; Catullus "passes the book roll" (or perhaps begins to read from it) to Nepos in what is a suggestively convivial one. If we read the poem this way – and in some ways the poem directs us to do just that – Nepos is the sole or primary recipient of the *libellus*, an intimate gift given in a context of intimacy (cf. *tibi* at ll. 3 and 8: "I give it *to you*, Cornelius; have it *for yourself*"). Whoever else may receive the poem in the future, the poet's dedication makes certain that only Nepos can identify with the *tibi*: the poem is the property of Catullus and Nepos alone. If, on the other hand, we listen to the "poematic" voice – the voice of the poem that has arisen from that of the poet – c. 1 is written in such a way that it seems to give itself, and the *libellus* it represents, to all subsequent readers, to each individual who, for a moment, can identify with the *tibi* of l. 3 (*to me?*) even as, in the subsequent moment, this identification is ruptured (*Oh. To Cornelius*). Because it at once records and enacts its own exchange (and the exchange of its poetic siblings) the poet's question – "to whom do I give (or refuse) my delightful new book?" – becomes the poem's question – "to whom do I give (or refuse) *myself*?" The poematic voice is able to express a question that is above and beyond that of the poet; because it is not just given, but also actively gives, it becomes more than a poem and, in some ways, aspires to the social function of its author.[7]

Exchange, bartering, and trade rituals are an inherent part of the idea (and linguistic shape) of "fetish" in many cultures, and in Catullus it is often precisely the exchange of a poem (or a book of poetry) that sets it apart as especially powerful or valuable.[8] The language and sense of c. 1 emphasize the importance of the poem's exchange, of the fact that it is given, under precisely such circumstances. It is through the exchange of the poem, the symbolic separation of the poetic voice from its source, that the poem gains its ability to act – to continue to give itself and "its" *libellus*, and to negotiate its ongoing reception in an ideally circumscribed, but ultimately unknowable, community of recipients.

---

[7] Even when the poem has been given, its questioning nature remains immediate and active – "to whom *do I give* myself?" and never "to whom *have I been given?*" – and keeps it from ever being completely and utterly received. Fitzgerald 1995: 39 comes to a similar conclusion but via a different route: "so the object that Catullus is giving to Nepos is both a delightful physical object and a polished work of art that is not confined to any one of its instantiations, and this duality is what complicates the gesture of giving, because the book as a work of art cannot actually be given." Fitzgerald later remarks, "but [in the case of poem 1] it is the same thing that is both given and retained" (p. 40).

[8] Apter 1991: 5; Apter describes the Portuguese *fetisso* (fetish) as a word that "stood not just for the native idol but also for the 'small wares' or trinkets that European merchants used for barter or upon which they would swear an oath to honor a commercial transaction." Apter cites also Pietz 1987: 45; see also Pietz 1985.

Even as the poem is valued for its role in the exchange, however, it is also valued as a piece of literature that is distinctly material, an object that is delightful to look upon, a suitable focus for the scopophilic gaze. For in the very first line of the poem (and before we even know what is being given) the gift is described as *lepidus* – a word that is usually rendered "delightful" or "charming." As Krostenko has argued, though, there is more to *lepidus* than mere charm and delight: he notes that the structure of *lepidus* is difficult to model, but suggests that the word "had, or came to have, an element like 'decadent,' 'indulgent,' or 'erotic' as part of its semantic core."[9] If *lepidus* carries erotic undertones, it also carries the connotations of visual light, of a literal – as well as figurative – brilliance.[10] When the poem establishes the *libellus*[11] of which it is a part as a sparkling, brilliant object (an image that is picked up by the *expolitum* – smooth or polished – of line 2), it does two things. First, it emphasizes its status as a material gift, a "continually fresh" aesthetic object that deserves to be maintained in this state and protected from the ages (*plus uno maneat perenne saeclo*).[12] Second, by emphasizing its visual and aesthetic qualities (sparkling, new, and polished) the *libellus* fashions itself as the point of contact between the giver and the recipient, a material reminder of the expectations that accompany a dedication.[13] The *libellus* sparkles *for* Nepos, as it draws his gaze and desire and willingness to ensure its fame; but it sparkles *because of* Catullus, for it is through the poet's labors and affections that the *libellus* gains its visual as well as literary qualities. The poem, then, makes the exchange; it becomes a physical, movable object on to which the poet can displace his affections for and expectations of the recipient.

If the fetishized gift-poem may function as a socially binding contract, a physical manifestation of gratitude, or an elevated substitute for erotic contact, so too may it function as a virtual act of physical communication between the author of the poem and the poem's intended recipient. That

[9] Krostenko 2001: 67. On *lepidus* see also Seager 1974.
[10] Krostenko 2001: 67: "A further peculiarity is that the lexeme seems to have partly become reliteralized as a light term, a sense of which there are clear instances later, and which, if it was sensible to Plautus, may have induced him to use *lepidus* for the Greek New Comic λαμπρός, whose range is similar to that of Plautus' *lepidus*." Krostenko punningly cites as "clear instances" Lucr. *DRN* 2.502; 5.1257–1259 (to which compare 4.83–85, of the *lepos* of light entering a theater) and Cic. *Ep. Att.* 2.3 (of light entering windows).
[11] The appropriative value of this term is discussed at greater length in Chapter 1.
[12] On which cf. Fitzgerald 1995: 40; "Nepos, though he gets this attractive little book because he made something of Catullus' *nugae*, can't really have it because the virgin sees to it that the book will remain fresh for future generations."
[13] Fitzgerald 1995: 41 remarks on the sexual connotations of *expolitum*. On Latin words of smoothness or depilation, see also Putnam 1982: 32.

Catullus both recognized and tapped into the power of dedicated poetry to "act virtually" – a power I identify as the "action function" of such poems – is clear enough. But the poet does not limit his use of this "action function" to the exchange of amorous physical affection between himself and his beloved; if poems can "function as" kisses, so too can they "function as" acts or threats of violence against individuals who have interfered with – or perhaps simply criticized – his literary or social activity.

The "action function" of textual exchange as it is enacted in c. 16 provides one of our most vivid examples of the depth and variety of textual generation and reciprocity – and indeed, literary criticism – in the late Republic. In approaching the action function of poem (its function, that is, as a poem fetishized in terms of its imagined dislocation from its author) and in resituating this poem in the textual world in which it was created, I would like to suggest that we keep in mind the modern genre of the "musical response piece" or "musical feud."[14] This vibrant musical genre, one that is predicated on both an ongoing published exchange of lyrical invective and its capacity as an artistic (and thus artificial) tool of calculated, and often emotionally "dislocated," aesthetic critique (the lyrical insult is personal, but the underlying critique issues from artistic differences), may help us avoid the biographical fallacy against which c. 16 cautions, and may reveal more about the textually generative role of Catullan invective. The point behind artistic feuds (the Gellius cycle, especially c. 116, may speak to a similar such feud), as they operate in modern terms, is precisely that they provide artists with the excuse – indeed, almost the "obligation" – to compose and publish artistic responses to artistic insults received. In c. 16, as we shall see, Catullus appears to be engaging in precisely such a publication, as he presents a sexually violent and self-actualizing attack on his *sodales* in response to published,[15] and doubtless

[14] Among the most famous examples of "response-piece" feud cycles is that of Neil Young and Lynyrd Skynyrd. Young's "Southern Man," a deeply critical and anti-Southern racism song, spurred the southern band Lynyrd Skynyrd into angry response with "Sweet Home Alabama," which responded to Young's critique: "Well, I heard Mister Young sing about her / Well, I heard ol' Neil put her down / Well, I hope Neil Young will remember / A Southern Man don't need him around anyhow." Record sales increased for both artists. The feud (which was always a purely artistic one; Skynyrd's Ronnie Van Zandt and Young were close friends) was further memorialized in the song "Ronnie and Neil," from the band Drive-By Truckers. The "response piece" is an especially powerful genre in the world of hip-hop and rap, where "trash-talk" poetic responses trace back to early MC "battles" which required *ex tempore* oral composition. Many musical "response pieces" center around either foundational aesthetic differences or the accusation that one artist has stolen the rhymes or lyrics (napkins?) of another.

[15] Although c. 16 contains no reference to the form of critique that incited its production, Catullus' general practice of returning a poetic "gift" with one of his own makes this a logical assumption; cf. Thomson 1997: 249.

poetic, aesthetic critiques of his poetry expressed (as here) in terms of his masculinity:

> Pedicabo ego uos et irrumabo,
> Aureli pathice et cinaede Furi,
> qui me ex uersiculis meis putastis,
> quod sunt molliculi, parum pudicum.
> nam castum esse decet pium poetam   5
> ipsum, uersiculos nihil necesse est;
> qui tum denique habent salem ac leporem,
> si sunt molliculi ac parum pudici
> et quod pruriat incitare possunt,
> non dico pueris, sed his pilosis   10
> qui duros nequeunt mouere lumbos.
> uos, quod milia multa basiorum
> legistis, male me marem putatis ?
> pedicabo ego uos et irrumabo.

> Fuck you, boys, and suck my dick,
> Aurelius you pussy and Furius you fag:
> You judge a man from his verse, and think
> That just because I write love poetry, I'm not man enough?
> A good poet should be restrained   5
> Himself – but no need for his verses to be!
> At any rate they are loaded with charm and wit,
> If perhaps they are lovey-dovey and a little soft
> – And they can really turn you on:
> I'm not talking about the kids, but those geezers   10
> Who can scarcely get it up!
> But just because you read of my endless thousands of kisses,
> You think I'm no kind of man?
> Well, fuck you, boys, and suck my dick!

Whereas c. 50 makes the exchange of poetry as intimate as a kiss, c. 16 explores entirely different connotations of putting the words of another "in one's mouth."[16] The sexual connotations of reading another's words

---

[16] The first two lines of this poem have been notoriously difficult to render in English, precisely because they are making use of crude Latin idiom. While an antiseptic translation ("I shall penetrate both of you anally, and I shall then force you to perform fellatio on me") will clearly not do, the more common "British schoolboy" rendering of "bugger and stuff" (so Lee's 1990 translation, but common elsewhere), though idiomatically apt, creates for American ears an odd fetishization of language in which one knows that the obscenity is there, but it remains strangely obfuscated (as noted in the Introduction, I have yet to teach an American undergraduate for whom these terms carry the shock value they should). First of all, these lines are meant as an insult, not a detailed description of the poet's intended sexual assault on his friends. Second, the lines are intended both to shock and to amuse. Furius and Aurelius have apparently criticized Catullus' poetry for its use

have long been recognized,[17] and Fitzgerald has argued persuasively for this poem as a dramatic portrayal of the power relations between the poet and his reader.[18] This is correct, but if we recognize that c. 16 is also likely dedicated to individuals who had published first their own critiques of Catullus' poetry – if we recognize that it is a text written and given not only to readers, but also to *writers* – then we see that its invective, and especially the "materializing nature" of this invective, is partaking of a textually productive genre of literary criticism in which like is exchanged for like in an ongoing "conversation" of and, quite likely, dispute over, aesthetic judgments.[19]

C. 16 surely threatens textual violence represented sexually (and is thus a fitting response to what was likely the original critique); and yet it can be read not only as a threat of violence, but – especially as we think of its subsequent reading by its dedicatees – as the physical accomplishment of that violence as well. For because the threat takes the form of dedicated poetry, and because the poem's recipients are presumably imagined to read the poet's words themselves, the pair will in their reading reify Catullus' threat of anal and oral rape: Catullus has taken what they have produced (poetic critique of poetry), and, remaking it into his own, he has forced it back into their own mouths.[20] In its dislocation from its authorial source – a dislocation underlined by the self-actualizing nature of the first and final lines – c. 16 rises above its inherent social and material value.[21] Furius and Aurelius have criticized Catullus' choice of poetic theme in terms of a sexualizing attack on his manhood;[22] by responding in kind, Catullus

of intimate language and theme, so here he plays the macho man who cannot help but put even his profanity into verse. In my own translation, I have clearly chosen coarse idiom over clinical detachment; on this poem, and with a very good translation of it, see further Krostenko 2001: 277–282.

[17] See especially Richlin 1981; Fitzgerald 1995: 50 notes of this poem: "the identification of the reader with the pathic in [poem 16] has its precedents"; he cites a graffito from the Roman world (*CIL* 4.2360): *amat qui scribit, pedicatur qui legit, / qui auscultat prurit, pathicus est qui praeterit. / ursi me comedant et ego uerpa<m> qui lego.* Svenbro 1993 discusses Greek parallels to this configuration, in which the writer is figured the *erastês*, the reader the *erômenos*; see especially Svenbro 1993: 190, on the so-called "Porkos skyphos," and the Latin inscriptions cited there.

[18] Fitzgerald 1995: 49: "[Catullus] begins with a phallic threat that reverses the position that Furius and Aurelius, as readers of Catullus' titillating verse, have adopted in relation to the poet who speaks in the style of an effeminate."

[19] On *sal* and *lepos* as terms of aesthetic judgment in this poem, see Buchheit 1976b.

[20] Both the language of this poem and the sentiments of literary criticism contained therein are echoed, if in less caustic terms, by Martial in *Ep.* 1.35: *uersus scribere me parum seueros / nec quos praelegat in schola magister, / Corneli, quereris.*

[21] Cf. Camille 1997: 37: "[The] split between what the fetishist really wants to do with the object and the actual social status of that object is one of the crucial dynamics of the fetish. In the Middle Ages . . . it was seen as quite normal to have an intensely personal response from books."

[22] Kinsey 1966 suggests that the *versiculi* of this poem indicate effeminate poetry in particular.

underlines the raw physicality – and veiled sexuality – that underlies all textual discourse.

In c. 1 Catullus presents his *libellus* as an object of affection and social contract, and in c. 16 he uses his poem to comment harshly on the poetic criticisms of others. In cc. 49 and 68b, he engages his poems in similar social negotiations, each time creating an "acting object" that at once professes gratitude and – either implicitly or explicitly – settles the debt of that gratitude with the poem itself. C. 49, a mock-serious expression of thanks for an unnamed gift or favor, is addressed to Cicero and constitutes the only contemporary textual evidence of any relationship between the two men:[23]

> Disertissime Romuli nepotum,
> quot sunt quotque fuere, Marce Tulli,
> quotque post aliis erunt in annis,
> gratias tibi maximas Catullus
> agit pessimus omnium poeta   5
> tanto pessimus omnium poeta
> quanto tu optimus omnium patronus.

> Most eloquent of the descendants of Romulus,
> As many as are and were, Marcus Tullius,
> And as many as shall be in the years to come,
> To you, heartfelt thanks, from Catullus
> The worst of all poets   5
> So the worst of all poets
> As you are the best of all – *patroni*.

The nature of c. 49 – or more specifically, the nature of the gift or favor for which it enacts repayment – has always been a puzzle. Whereas Tatum viewed the poem as an "urbane taunt"[24] that need not respond to a specific gift from the orator, Kroll[25] argued that a copy of Cicero's *in Vatinium* may have prompted the poem (on Catullus' famed *odium Vatinianum*, cf. c. 14.3). Both Thomson and Laughton[26] have suggested, and to my mind considerably more convincingly, that a gift of one of

---

[23] There are some (so Collins 1952) who have argued that c. 49 does not – cannot – point to such a relationship; but such views are predicated on the assumption that no two such "different" men (as Collins puts it, "as we know them"!) could have shared empathies or interests. There are no other poems in the corpus for which a relationship between Catullus and the addressee is brought seriously into question and I have found no fair argument for doing so here. C. 49 need not be indicative of deep friendship, but it speaks to a relationship of some familiarity.

[24] Tatum 1988: 184.   [25] Kroll 1989: 88.

[26] Thomson 1997: 323 and 1967: 225–230; Laughton 1970: 1–7. Friedricksmeyer 1973 offers an excellent survey of the more influential studies of this tantalizing poem.

Cicero's own poems may have incited this poetic return. This suggestion is bolstered by both Catullus' joking poetic remunerations elsewhere in the corpus (cf. e.g. c. 14, discussed in Chapter 2, c. 42, of the theft of *pugillaria*, and c. 116, possibly of the epigrammatist Gellius' own literary attack on the poet) and the semi-formal tone of the third-person singular form of address, which it is tempting to take as a coy echo of Republican political *commentarii* and, perhaps more to the point, of the "poetic *commentarius*" that was Cicero's own *de Consulato Suo*.[27] In c. 49, then, the voice of the poem speaks for the voice of the poet as a kind of disinterested personal messenger, simultaneously revealing and concealing its creator in third-person reference at middle-point line-end. It both repays what was likely a poetic gift with its own poetic self, and offers as repayment its own humorously "subjective" opinion of the gift to which it responds: *Marcus, don't quit your day job.*

A fourth case of poetic contract and repayment worth considering, and one that shares with c. 1 a reference to poetic immortality (this time of the dedicatee rather than the text), is found in c. 68b, a cyclically arranged poem dedicated to an otherwise unknown Allius and professing to offer repayment for the kindnesses rendered the poet in his love affair with an unnamed *domina* (l. 156, generally and probably rightly assumed to be Lesbia).[28] After the briefest of invocations to the Muses (*deae*, l. 1), the poem presents its business with the claim that the poet is unable to "remain silent" (*non possum reticere*, l. 41) in the face of the *officia* rendered him, lest Allius' devotion (*studium*, l. 4) – and, indeed, Allius himself (cf. l. 48) – become forgotten in the course of time.

The introduction of the poem is vaguely reminiscent of both c. 65 (discussed in Chapter 6) and c. 68a, but whereas the former poems profess to respond with difficulty to a specific – and either specifically or implicitly written – request for poetry, c. 68b stakes its claim not as a written response to written request, but as a poetic repayment of "actual" favors (*officia*, l. 2) rendered. In its brief reference to the death of the poet's brother (ll. 91–100),

---

[27] Cicero refers to the Greek account of his consulship as a *commentarius, Ep. Att.* 1.19.10: *Commentarium consulatus mei Graece compositum misi ad te… Latinum si perfecero, ad te mittam. tertium poëma expectato, ne quod genus a me ipso laudis meae praetermittatur*; cf. *Ep. Att.* 2.1.1.

[28] On the issue of unity versus division between this poem and c. 68a, and for a summary of the arguments for or against such, see Thomson 1997: 472–474. Thomson, Wiseman 1974b (cf. too Wiseman 1974a), and Courtney 1985, take cc. 68a and 68b as completely separate poems collocated perhaps because of certain shared themes (not the least of which is textual repayment), but written at different times and for different individuals. Contra this view, see Sarkisan 1983; I have chosen to refer to c. 68b following the arguments for division, but I find such division anything but certain.

c. 68b shares characteristics with c. 65 and c. 68a (65.5–15; 68a.19–26);[29] in its "gift" of a Greek source revised according to *au courant* linguistic and social aesthetics and within a cycle of explicitly textual exchanges, it might be compared to c. 51 or c. 66, but while cc. 65 and 68a use the brother's death to claim that creative writing cannot occur (a claim contradicted not only by the poems themselves but also by c. 66), and cc. 51 and 66 offer careful and nearly whole-cloth reworkings of specific Greek *poemata* (Sappho 31; Callimachus' *Plokamos*), fraternal death is rather notably *not* credited with poetic silencing in c. 68b, and indeed the refusal of the poem to align itself with any singular Greek text suggests that the contractual exchange it signifies exists more in the realm of spoken *muthos* than written *poëma*.

Indeed, a rather outstanding characteristic of c. 68b is precisely the emphasis placed on the non-textual nature of Allius' favors. Not only are they described as *officia* at both the beginning of the poem and the end (ll. 2, 150), but the precise nature of these *officia* (Allius had provided Catullus and his *domina* with a love nest) is described deliberately – and in the first case, mythically – both early in the poem (ll. 67–72) and again at its conclusion (ll. 155–156). In a world in which gifts and return gifts are almost inevitably textual in nature (when they are specified or alluded to), one of the most unusual arguments of 68b is precisely that a textual, material, gift can offer fitting payback (that is, payback with interest accrued) for a non-textual, immaterial, favor. At the close of the piece, Catullus collapses the spheres of the material and the immaterial, and suggests that a textual gift offers respectable remuneration for his friend's actions:

> Hoc tibi, quod potui, confectum carmine munus
> pro multis, Alli, redditur officiis,
> ne uestrum scabra tangat robigine nomen
> haec atque illa dies atque alia atque alia . . .
>
> 68b. 149–152

> To you, this *munus* – the best I could manage – is wrought in a song
> And given in return, Allius, for your many kind favors,
> Lest this day, and the next, and the ones after that
> Sully your name with their creeping rust.

In these lines – one of the instances in which Catullus offers a poem in return for a non-poetic, although surely poetically charged, good – the imminently tangible poetic *munus* is placed on the balance with

---

[29] On the possibility that ll. 91–100 of c. 68b are a later addition, possibly in order to provide a neat stylistic juxtaposition of this poem with c. 68a, cf. Copley 1957.

the imminently intangible favors wrought for Catullus. The phrase *pro multis... redditur officiis* claims that the exchange completed (*confectum*) by the poem is a fair one; but in the lines that follow, it is suggested that the scale is weighted more heavily to Catullus' account. For as much as Allius' loan of a love nest was an action ascribed weighty social value by Catullus, the comparison of *munus* with *officium* (a comparison encouraged by parallel line-end position) and the following claim that it is through this poetic *munus* that Allius' name will gain eternal renown (an offer made first at ll. 48–50) provide a careful economic evaluation of the situation. The loan of a romantic getaway is as ephemeral a delight as the love affair it seeks to enable; the *munus* of a poem that is able to endow its recipient with immortality (even as it similarly immortalizes loan and love) is the essence of durability.[30] Allius' favors were the fleeting stuff of "real life." By projecting affective alliance on to the pages of the text, Catullus' textually "material" remuneration at c. 68b – a remuneration that comes closest to the practice of Cicero in its recognition of the concerns of the non-textual world – signals his understanding of a potential "real-world" value of the textual gift. Catullus only rarely uses his textual dedications to negotiate interests that are themselves part and parcel of the textual world; but it is clear that he knew he could.

HOC POEMA FECI – EROTIC STAND-IN AND EROTIC PRODUCT: C. 50

In cc. 1, 16, 49, and 68b, Catullus offers his poems (or has a poem offer itself) as objects capable of fulfilling the requirements of a social contract. In cc. 50 and 51, the poet builds on the idea of the text as a mechanism of homosocial interaction, but endows that interaction with a more explicitly erotic tonality. We examined c. 51 in Chapter 1, in our discussion of the time during which patronal-class individuals engaged in textual production. Let us now turn to c. 50, in which we learn more about the erotic physicality of those texts they produced:

> Hesterno, Licini, die otiosi,
> multum lusimus in meis tabellis,
> ut conuenerat esse delicatos:
> scribens uersiculos uterque nostrum
> ludebat numero modo hoc modo illoc,   5

---

[30] On the power of poetic durability to trump the ephemeral gift, see my discussion of Martial's *Xenia* and *Apophoreta*, Stroup 2006.

reddens mutua per iocum atque uinum.
atque illinc abii tuo lepore
incensus, Licini, facetiisque,
ut nec me miserum cibus iuuaret
nec somnus tegeret quiete ocellos,   10
sed toto indomitus furore lecto
uersarer, cupiens uidere lucem,
ut tecum loquerer simulque ut essem.
at defessa labore membra postquam
semimortua lectulo iacebant,   15
hoc, iucunde, tibi poema feci,
ex quo perspiceres meum dolorem.
nunc audax caue sis, precesque nostras,
oramus, caue despuas, ocelle,
ne poenas Nemesis reposcat a te.   20
est uemens dea: laedere hanc caueto.

Yesterday, Licinius, we took our time
And fooled around quite a bit – in my notebooks –
As it seemed a good idea to give ourselves over to pleasure:
We each took turns writing little poems
Playing with the meter – now this one, now that,   5
Making fair exchanges soaked in wine and wit.
And I went away so aroused
By your charm, Licinius, and your cleverness,
That neither could I find any joy in food
Nor could sleep set my eyes to rest,   10
But I spent the whole night overflowing with passion,
Tossing and turning, counting the seconds until sun-up,
So I could talk with you and rejoin your company.
But after I lay spent from my labors,
My whole body half-dead on the bed,   15
I wrought for you this poem, my darling,
Clear evidence of the pains I suffered.
Now don't you be brazen, and my prayers,
My dear, don't you dare reject them,
Lest Nemesis demand in return – punishments.[31]   20
She's a crazy goddess: don't you dare mess with her.

In c. 50, the description of luxurious convivial composition forges an
image of the exchanged text as erotic go-between, a physical manifestation

---

[31] The pun here is difficult to render. As Nemesis is the goddess of violent retribution – the flip side
of affective reciprocity – the *poema* of l. 16 may set up the expectation that *poenas* at l. 20 is to be
poemata (I am grateful to Jim Clauss, who first pointed out to me the resonance between *poema*
and *poena*). It is thus tempting to render *poenas* as "poemishments," but I am not so bold.

of the poet's affection for his friend.[32] This happens at two levels. First, the physical intimacy implicit in the friends' erotic textual play[33] (*lusimus*) is entirely displaced on to the physical exchange of the *uersiculi* themselves.[34] Catullus and Licinius share not kisses or caresses, but polymetric – and so in all likelihood erotic or blatantly sexual – verse. The effect is an odd one. C. 50 both tantalizes and disappoints its reader, and the description of poetic interchange is all the more erotic precisely because it withholds sexual detail. From the first line on, the poem is full of the imagery of intimacy, luxury, and desire;[35] so much so, I suggest, that both poet and reader (here, Calvus) are encouraged to engage in a kind of fantastic voyeurism, to read into the act of textual exchange an act of sexual intimacy. The exchanged poem becomes the physical object of the friends' affection, and the two are recast as bibliophiles who adore their poems not just for what they contain but also for the social meaning of their circulation.[36] At one level, we might say that Catullus is just playing around with his poem (*ludere in tabellis*) and the idea of poetic arousal: c. 50 is meant to arouse the reader as much as the *uersiculi* of the day before aroused the poet. At another level, however, Catullus promotes the exchange of literature as a social action: if textual intercourse can be a representation of social interaction, then perhaps it can also be its substitute.

---

[32] On the relationship between cc. 50 and 51, see Buchheit 1976a, Burgess 1986; Hallet 1988; Thomson 1967; Woodman 1966 (with rather more emphasis on c. 51); and Wray 2001: 88–109, who argues for an "epistolary" tone in both c. 50 and c. 65.

[33] In Catullus the verb *ludere* frequently carries erotic connotations: see especially cc. 2.2 (of Lesbia's intimate play with her sparrow, on which see further Thomas 1993), 2.9 (of the poet's desire to mimic Lesbia's "play"), and 99.1 (of Iuventius: *surripui tibi, dum, ludis, mellite Iuuenti / sauiolum dulci dulcius ambrosia*). Pliny uses the term also of his hendecasyllables, *Ep.* 4.14.1–3: *lusus meos tibi prodo . . . his iocamur, ludimus*; *Ep.* 8.21.2: *lusus et ineptias nostras legis*; *Ep.* 7.9.9: *fas est et carmine remitti . . . ; lusus uocantur*. On the semantic weight of *lusus, ineptiae*, and *ioci*, see further Bower 1974; Burgess 1986: 577 n. 3 notes that *ludere* is used by Catullus of poetic production (cf. 61.225) and remarks that Vergil uses the term at *Ec.* 1.10 and 6.1 of agonistic bucolic competition. On *otium* in this poem and c. 51, see Clack 1976.

[34] See for comparison Camille 1997: 41 in a discussion of Richard de Bury's *Philobiblon*: "For most literates in the culture, however, the very act of reading was a libidinal experience, of penetrating the bound volume, that dangerously ductile opening and shutting thing . . . the result was a promiscuous interpenetration of books, not only with the bodies that read them, but also with those that were excluded from them."

[35] L. 1: *otiosi*; l. 2: *lusimus* (see note 33, above); l. 3: *delicatos*; l. 4: *uersiculos* (on this aspect of the diminutive, see Part I); l. 5: *ludebat*; l. 6: *per iocum atque uinum* (language of the poetic convivium); l. 7: *lepore* (on which see Krostenko on *lep(idus)* as cited above, note 9); l. 8: *incensus . . . facetiis* ("aroused by your cleverness"); l. 9: *me miserum*; ll. 10–15 (the description of the poet's nighttime "labors"); l. 11: *iucunde*. See further Burgess 1986; Scott 1969; and Wray 2001: 96–109.

[36] Camille 1997: 35: "The limits of the bibliophile's desire are problematic precisely because his objects are everywhere, circulating in the culture as powerful symbols of knowledge and power."

The friends' metrical play (*ludebat . . . modo hoc modo illoc*) echoes Lesbia's eroticized intimacy with her sparrow (*circumsiliens modo huc modo illuc*, 3.8). But just as the sexual implications of the *passer*-poems (cc. 2 and 3) are cloaked in the innocent interaction between a young woman and her pet,[37] the implications of c. 50 are cloaked in the terms of a homosocial exchange. In spite of their (apparently, or at least ideally) shared desire, Catullus and Calvus can find only textual outlets for their flirtations; for all of their intimacy, the two friends are denied physical realization of their act.

But what, exactly, is the nature of this denial? As much as c. 50 cheats its participants of physical consummation (and us of our lascivious predictions), it also offers itself as an advertisement for the exchange of erotically charged literature as the purest form of love-making.[38] Indeed, the non-fulfillment of sexual desire (either Catullus' or our own) brings us to the second way in which c. 50 functions as a physical manifestation of Catullus' affection for his friend. Once the textual game is finished, Catullus returns home aroused (*incensus*) but unfulfilled; and the homoerotic play of afternoon turns into the autoerotic labor of evening. He finds no comfort in food or sleep, he tosses and turns, counts the hours until dawn, wears himself out. In the image of a poet lying alone in bed – at textual play no more with Licinius but now only with himself – we get at an important aspect of textual production and exchange. Writing is lonely work, and it is only in its circulation – in its exchange – that the rift between author and reader ("donor" and "recipient") can ever be healed. As much as c. 50 is inspired by the poet's arousal for Calvus, it is the only physical evidence, the sole material product, of the poet's solitary labors: indeed, it is only through this "object of affection" that a poet's thoughts may ever

---

[37] On this see further Fitzgerald 1995: 43.

[38] Some 1400 years later, similar erotic qualities are attributed to another book shared between lovers, Dante *Inferno* 5.127–138: " . . . Noi leggevamo un giorno per diletto / di Lancialotto come amor lo strinse; / soli eravamo e sansa alcun sospetto. / Per più fïate li occhi ci sospinse / quella lettura, e scolorocci il viso; / ma solo un punto fu quel che ci vinse. / Quando leggemmo il disïato riso / esser basciato da cotanto amante, / questi, che mai da me non fia diviso, / la bocca mi basciò tutto tremante. / Galeotto fu 'l libro e chi lo scrisse: / quel giorno più non vi leggemmo avante." Dante's *Commedia* was completed by 1321. Francesca was the wife of Gianciotto Malatesta of Rimini; she entered into an affair with Giancotto's brother, Paolo; Giancotto murdered the pair upon their discovery. See further Pinsky 1996 *ad* 5.65. The "Lanciolotto" of line 128 must refer to the Arthurian romances (which the lovers would have read in Latin), in which Lancelot betrays Arthur's trust and enters into an affair with the king's wife Guinevere. See Pinsky 1996 *ad* 5.122: "Galeotto, or, in French, Gallehault, acted as a messenger between Lancelot and Guinevere. The French version of his name has become a synonym for "pander" or "go-between.""

successfully reach his object of desire. Even in a system of isonomic and homosocial reciprocity, the poet remains fiercely independent and retains for himself full credit for and control over his work.

The words *poema feci* (l. 16) complete the picture of solitary textual production. Although the Greek term *poema* appears three times in the corpus, Catullus applies it to his own writing only here, preferring in general the natively Latin terms *carmina* and *uersus/uersiculi*. The Greek term appears elsewhere only twice, in c. 22 (ll. 15, 16), a description of Suffenus' artistically clumsy, if visually pleasing, literary endeavors: as soon as Suffenus "touches" (*attigit*) *poemata*, he is made "more uncouth than the uncouth boonies" (*infaceto est infacetior rure*, l. 14), and yet he is never more pleased with himself than when he writes one. The application of *poema* to both the (presumably) approbative situation of c. 50 and the definitively derogative situation of c. 22 may seem puzzling, but the etymological associations of the word might provide a clue as to Catullus' choice. For whereas the *carm[en]* (< *cano* + **men*) has the core sense of a song or spoken proclamation and *uers[us]* (< *uerto* + **tus*) conjures the turning lines of written text, ποίημα (as well as the related ποίησις and ποίεω)[39] signifies the tangible product of physical labor. In c. 22, the strongly "tangible" *poema* plays nicely off Catullus' elaborately visual description of Suffenus' upmarket book rolls (ll. 6–8) that prove themselves all show and no (poetic) substance. His choice here to apply a Greek word to the product of his nighttime textual efforts reveals two interlocking concerns. First, if we take *hoc poema* to refer internally to c. 50 but also – as it must – externally to c. 51,[40] the use of *poema* points nicely to the "transformed" Greek ποίημα that follows, even as it provides a clever lexical resonance with, and hint as to the nature of, the *poenae* (l. 20) Nemesis shall seek if the poet's gift is rejected.[41] Second, in drawing attention not only to the physical elements of his labors (the somewhat forced *feci* rather than the more expected *scripsi*), but also to the luxury and artifice of a text that is itself offered in the hopes of a return,[42] the poet's overarching

---

[39] To these words compare πράττω and πρᾶξις, which signify action but without specifying a physical product of that action.

[40] So Wray 2001: 107, *pace* Sandy 1978: 73, who suggests that these words refer not to c. 50, but to another poem in the corpus that has not survived.

[41] Wray 2001: 107 compares *Nemesis* in c. 50 to *Fides* in c. 30, and suggests that both invocations allow Catullus to "adopt the stance of an abandoned lover."

[42] Burgess 1986: 584 (followed by Wray 2001: 107) rightly notes that the *preces nostrae* (l. 18) refer to Catullus' request to continue in a cycle of reciprocal poetic exchange. Burgess 1986: 577 cites Theoc. *Id.* 5 and 8 as prototypes for this kind of reciprocal composition.

poetic message is driven home. Exchange is a game for two, but a poem
through which this exchange is enacted is the masterpiece of one man
alone.

HOWLING *HENDECASYLLABI* AND OTHER MATERIAL MOMENTS: CC. 35, 36, 42, 66

By way of both closing this chapter and looking ahead to the one that
follows, I will consider in brief four poems in which Catullus engages
in his "strongest" acts of textual materialization. These materializations –
although what we have by now are really personifications – are, if yet
asymmetrical in form to those produced by Cicero, quite compellingly
similar in terms of their apparent function.

In the first three poems (cc. 35, 36, and 42), this materialization consists
of direct poetic address to – that is, personification of – the pages or
contents of the text. This textual address becomes fairly conventional in
the poetry of later periods (cf. e.g. Hor. *Ep.* 1.8.1; Ovid *Trist.* 1.1; and Mart.
Ep. 3.2), but c. 35, in which a papyrus page is instructed (*uelim Caecilio,
papyre, dicas*, l. 2) to take a message from one poet to another (indeed, a
poeta tener), constitutes the first instance in all of Latin poetry of a poet
addressing his text and asking that text to transport a message to another
individual.[43] A similar form of address occurs in c. 36, although this time
Catullus addresses not his own page, but the *annales* of Volusius. The
work is personified by means of both direct address (*Annales Volusi, cacata
charta*, l. 1) and imperative (*uotum soluite*, l. 2), and in their materialization –
a materialization reversed at poem-end by their imagined destruction (*at
uos interea uenite in ignem*, l. 18; to this cf. the antepenultimate line of
c. 14, which similarly personifies and addresses physical texts: *uos hinc
interea ualete abite*) – they are envisioned capable of discharging a vow
made by Catullus' girl.

In c. 42, the form of address is rather different. This time the personification arises not from the material status of the pages on which words
are inscribed, but rather the social function of poetry that is able to move
aggressively out into the streets of the city and engage actively with individuals outside of the homosocial textual sphere:

---

[43] Thomson 1997: 293–294 notes the novelty of this maneuver, but most scholarship on this poem
focuses more specifically on the relationship between Catullus and Caecilius (so Friedricksmeyer
1985) or the role of the "Sapphica puella" (so Forsyth 1984).

> Adeste, hendecasyllabi, quot estis
> omnes undique, quotquot estis omnes.
> iocum me putat moecha turpis,
> et negat mihi nostra redditturam
> pugillaria, si pati potestis.
> persequamur eam et reflagitamus . . .
>
> 42. 1–6

> Come here, all you hendecasyllables, as many as you are
> And wherever you be – every last one of you!
> A filthy slut is playing me for the fool,
> And says she's not going to return
> Our writing tablets – if you can believe it.
> Let's chase her down, and demand them back . . .

The strong imperative *adeste* in first position underlines the personification of Catullus' hendecasyllables. As we saw of cc. 1, 16, 49, 68b, and 50,
discussed in this chapter, and of c. 14, discussed in Chapter 2, this poem
functions as a self-actualization of the social act it is charged to perform.
In c. 14 Catullus' "promised" hendecasyllables are actualized in the poem
that delivers them. In c. 42, the hendecasyllables are similarly actualized,
but this time they are also actively personified: they are summoned to the
poet's side in order to aid him in an act of poetic *flagitatio*,[44] as they attempt
to rescue the textual paraphernalia (*pugillaria*, l. 5; *codicilli*) in which they
might normally reside. Early in the poem, Catullus and his verses move
and act as one (*persequamur eam et reflagitemus*, l. 6). But in the lines that
follow, the verses dislocate themselves entirely from their author, while he
addresses them independently from himself (*quaeritis* and *uidetis*, l. 7) and
directs their movement (*circumstite* and *reflagitate*, l. 10) and metrical voice
(*moecha putida, redde codicillos* / *redde, putida moecha, codicillos*, at ll. 11–12
and 19–20; *conclamitate . . . altiore uoce*, l. 18), as if from the side. At the end
of the poem, Catullus and his verses rejoin in his remark that in speaking
the truth, they've made no headway (*nil proficimus*, l. 21), and so in the
final lines of the poem and, I think, in a tip-off to the poetic irony at work
in many of the invectives, the verses are advised to change their approach
and frame their attack in terms of affection that are quite the opposite of
those first, and perhaps more honestly (?), expressed.

Perhaps Catullus' most compelling and, to my mind, most demonically
clever act of textual personification occurs in – or rather, is constituted

---

[44] On this poem as a *flagitatio*, Thomson 1997: 311 notes that Usener 1901 was the first to recognize its
function as such.

by – Catullus' "translation" of Callimachus' *Plokamos* at c. 66. At one level, of course, this poem's personification is that of the lock of hair – the *coma* – from the "mouth" of which the entire poem issues. But there is more. Precisely because the original "talking lock" was that produced by Callimachus, and thus the original voice of the poem was not Catullus' own, in his representation of the Greek *Plokamos* with the Latin *Coma* (a representation that shifts the grammatical gender of the original voice), and in his representation "as if present" of the voice and form of the absent and indeed historically distant poet, Catullus does not merely "translate" Callimachus: both he, and his poem, actively *personify* a poet and poem of the past.

CHAPTER 8

Brutus: *the dialogic personification of the Republican voice*[1]

CICERO, *WRITE SOMETHING*

As I discussed in Chapter 6, Cicero inserts the unmistakable echoes of elite performance into *de Oratore* in order to introduce into the isonomic exchanges of his elite readers a new type of text that served as a venue of secondary and private display. In this chapter, I argue that *Brutus* too embodies a kind of social display, a recognizable textual echo of elite and private ritual. However, instead of a ritual concerned with the education of Roman youth and the sharing of erudite wit, *Brutus* presents an array of interlocking rituals that speak both to Cicero's own pressing political circumstances and the ultimate inevitability of his textual endeavors. In crafting a strangely gendered image of both the "death" of Republican oratory and the subsequent "life" of private textual circulation and collection – what de Bury would describe in the fourteenth century as the "community of books" or *librorum municipium*[2] – Cicero fashions in *Brutus* a boldly procreative model for the writing of rhetorical histories and historical dramas in prose.[3]

Composed and published in 46 BCE,[4] the dialogue is set in the immediate present. Pompey's humiliating defeat at Pharsalus in 48[5] is a fresh

---

[1] The bulk of this chapter appeared first in Stroup 2003.

[2] *Faciendi plures libros nullus est finis. Sicut enim librorum corpora, ex contrariorum commixtione compacta, suae compositionis continuum sentiunt detrimentum, sic per prudentiam clericorum reperiri debet remedium, per quod liber sacer, soluens naturae debitum, haereditarium obtineat substitutum et simile semen fratri mortuo suscitetur uerificeturque statim illud Ecclesiastici tricensimo: Mortuus est pater illius et quasi non est mortuus, similem enim sibi reliquit post se. Sunt igitur transcriptiones ueterum quasi quaedam propagationes recentium filiorum, ad quos paternum deuoluatur officium, ne librorum municipium minuatur* (de Bury 1903: ch. 16).

[3] See Dugan 2005: 172–250 for an excellent discussion of many aspects of this dialogue.

[4] On the dating of *Brutus*, see Douglas 1966: ix–x and Narducci 1997: 104 n. 27; Gowing 2000 provides a thoroughgoing discussion of the dating of *Brutus* in the appendix to his article (pp. 62–64), *pace* Fantham 1996: 45 who seems to suggest that the dramatic date of the dialogue should coincide more closely with the death of Hortensius in 50: "*Brutus* [is] dated to the outbreak of the civil war."

[5] Caesar crossed the Rubicon and marched on Rome in January 49 BCE; the ensuing turmoil lasted some two decades. Although it would be anachronistic to establish a date for the definitive "death

wound on Cicero's mind, and although he had gained pardon by Caesar in the autumn of 47, Caesar's recent victory at Thapsus in April of 46 had left the orator's position anything but secure.[6] The continued conflicts between Pompey and Caesar, and Cicero's own failed attempts at successful social triangulation in the dispute, had left the orator at an unarguable dry spell in his oratorical and literary career, all but deprived of the forensic popularity and social status he once enjoyed. Cicero had not delivered an oration since the anxiously reworked *pro Milone* in 52; in that same year he brought into circulation his *de Optimo Genere Oratorum* (the fourth of his rhetorical treatises), followed by *de Re Publica* in 51, but seems to have published nothing of substance between this and *Brutus* in 46.[7] The man who once considered himself the very voice and body of the Republic has found himself a virtual exile[8] from the forum that had so long been his home and at a loss, or so he suggests, as to how to reinstate himself in the "oratorical *ciuitas*" of the *urbs*. *Brutus* is represented both as a breaking of

of the Republic" – a finality of transition that I suspect would not have been fully comprehended until as late as the end of Augustus' reign – upon the conclusion of the civil war it seems clear that the Republic had given way in part to an incipient monarchy and the eventual rise of a new imperial structure. On these years and the difficulty of establishing any single moment of "collapse," see further especially Gruen: 1974, pp. 1–5.

[6] It has often been supposed that *Brut.* 3.10 (*quid uos, inquam, Brute et Attice? Numquid tandem noui? Nihil sane, inquit Brutus, quod quidem aut tu audire uelis aut ego pro certo dicere audeam*) refers to the outcome at Thapsus on 6 April (so Douglas 1966: ix–x), and so it has been argued that the dialogue (or this part of it, at any rate) was written before the news of Thapsus had reached Rome. However, it is entirely possible that the orator, himself aware of the outcome of the African campaign, wished to set the dialogue either in the days before the news of Caesar's victory had reached Rome or, and as Gowing 2000: 62–64 convincingly argues, after the news of Thapsus had reached our interlocutors, in which case 3.10 might refer to Caesar's plans in the wake of his victory (for which reading Gowing cites *Ep. Fam.* 9.2.4 as evidence).

[7] It is likely that some work was completed on *de Legibus* (started in 52) in this year, and it has been suggested that the work begun on this text was picked up again in 46 at around the same time as the composition of *Brutus* (Gowing 2000: 40 and MacKendrick 1989: 77, among others, cite *Ep. Fam.* 9.2.5 in support of this chronology); it seems to have been worked on from that point until, perhaps, the author's death in 43. Evidence suggests that *de Legibus* remained unpublished during the orator's lifetime and can at any rate be identified as a very late composition. All of Cicero's rhetorical and philosophical works of the early and mid 40s contain stated or implied dedications. In his final, highly productive years of literary activity (45–44) the orator begins to move away from formal dedications or addresses, and toward the subtle assertion that the characters of his dialogues are themselves to be understood as the dedicatees. *De Legibus*, however, lacks any sort of extra-dialogic dedicatee whatsoever. Further, Cicero's dialogues evolve somewhat steadily from the "narratological" (so *de Orat.*, of 54) to the "theatrical" (so *Cato* and *Laelius*, both of 44) as the author becomes, I contend, increasingly interested in character formation and the textual embodiment of the living voice. Of all the orator's surviving prose works, *de Legibus* is the most purely theatrical: imagined as a conversation between Atticus, Quintus, and Marcus, it lacks any introductory narrative or authorial explanation, and is structured rather in terms of a dramatic script.

[8] So Bloomer 1997: 54 notes of Cicero's rhetorical, political, and philosophical treatises of the late 50s and 40s: "These Latin dialogues with Roman characters, however anachronistic, are complex texts, the publication of a professed, not legal, exile."

Cicero's textual silence (*iam pridem enim conticuerunt tuae litterae, Brut.* 5.19) and as the prologue of his reentry into the intellectual, and as I shall contend, textual, life of the city.

The details of this reentry are made explicit early in *Brutus*, where in a pointed discussion of the economics of textual exchange Atticus is made to describe in novel and definitively textual terms the "debt" of which the present dialogue is imagined fitting repayment:

Itaque quoniam hic [inquit Atticus] quod mihi deberetur se exacturum professus est, quod huic debes, ego a te peto. Quidnam id? inquam. *Ut scribas*, inquit, *aliquid*; iam pridem enim conticuerunt tuae litterae. nam ut illos de re publica libros edidisti, nihil a te sane postea accepimus . . . (*Brut.* 5.19)

"And thus, [said Atticus,] since this fellow has claimed that he will exact what you owe me, I come to get payment for what you owe him." "Whatever do you mean?" I said. "*That you write something*," said Atticus, "for it has been too long now that your pages have held silent. I've received essentially nothing from you since you published those books *On the Republic* . . .

The blatantly economic tones of an elite discussion of textual reciprocity are indeed surprising – nowhere in any of the orator's earlier technical treatises does such language or imagery appear – but have been little discussed by critics and commentators in the past.[9] Yet even before we get to Atticus' remarkable suggestion that the orator's text (in lieu of his voice) might function as a kind of social currency, the dialogue establishes itself on a subtle theme of public silence and its cure in private literary memory and recollection. The treatise begins with a narrative that recalls the details of the autumn of 50, shortly after the orator received the news of the death of Q. Hortensius[10] but presumably before the definitive start of civil war. In the death of Hortensius, as soon becomes clear, Cicero has lost not just a friend and esteemed colleague but all of his hopes for the future of Republican speech and the political freedoms of which this speech is the expression. Indeed, and as we told at the end of the dialogue, the orator sees in the death of Hortensius an allegory for his own particular fate: *Hortensi uox exstincta fato su' est, nostra publico*, "Hortensius' voice was silenced by his own death, mine by that of the state" (*Brut.* 96.328).

---

9 The response of Douglas 1966: 10–13 is representative: "In this difficult passage, in which it is hard to determine how far the metaphors should be pressed for precise references, C[icero] promises to repay his debt to Atticus, and in § 19 his debt to Brutus, by some published works" (p. 10).

10 Q. Hortensius, cos. 69, died in mid June 50 BCE; Cicero learned of this death on ca. 10 August, upon his return to Rhodes: *Brut.* 1.1; cf. *Ep. Fam.* 3.12; 2.15; *Ep. Att.* 6.6. Hortensius, born in 114, was eight years older than Cicero (*Brut.* 64.230) and held undisputed oratorical preeminence until the rise of the latter; political rivals early in Cicero's career (cf. *in Verrem*, of 70, and *pro Lege Manilia*, of 66), the two were on the same side in trials from 63 onward (cf. Douglas 1966: 3 *ad* 15).

We saw in Chapter 6 that from the Hellenistic period on it had been a
standard feature of the dedicated text that it should begin with a reference
to the death or loss of a loved one and use this death as the affective impulse
for the "life" offered by the subsequent composition and prestation, but as
has been noted by several scholars,[11] the funereal imagery of *Brutus* is limited
neither to the introduction of the dialogue nor to the orator's discussion
of Hortensius. For after a brief but moving eulogy for his colleague (1.1–5),
Cicero expands the scope of his lament to include both the Republic and, as
an implied corollary, the whole of Roman oratory (2.6–9). His only solace,
as the final lines of the introduction tell us, is engaging in the recollection[12]
of Rome's great oratorical lineage (2.9). It is with this sentiment that the
introduction – and Cicero's solitude – comes to an end, and the imagined
sermo is brought to the stage with the arrival of Atticus and Brutus at
Cicero's Palatine[13] residence. Cicero's two interlocutors happen upon the
orator strolling in his private garden,[14] quietly lamenting the worsening
fate of the Republic (3.10). The very sight of his beloved comrades eases
Cicero's troubled heart, and after a brief reference to the ills of the state
(a likely echo of *de Oratore*, which itself began on such a note), Atticus
asks of Cicero whether they might enjoy a bit of *de re publica silentium*
(3.11) and hear something from Cicero himself (*aliquid audiremus . . . ex
te*) rather than be the bearers of news that might only add to his worries.
After a jovial chat over the circulation and exchange of *litterae* in which
the three participate with clear enthusiasm (3.11–5.21),[15] Cicero agrees to

---

[11] Recognized by modern critics first by Haenni 1905: 52 ("Ciceros, Brutus' ist in gewissem Sinne
die grosse politische Grabrede an die eloquentia Romana"; cited also by Gowing 2000: 58); cf. too
Douglas 1966: xi; Fantham 1996: 45–46: "[The] dialogue opens with an obituary and reflects the
feeling that political oratory, like the orator and the free republic, has been silenced. The history
of oratory, that most public and political literary form, is itself dangerously close to an obituary";
Narducci 1997: 98: "giustamente si è parlato del *Brutus* come di una *Grabrede*, di un epitafio
dell' eloquenza romana; il tono funereo è presente fino dal proemio, una lunga felicitazione per
la tempestiva morte che ha impedito a Ortensio . . ."; and Gowing 2000: 58–59. The approach to
Brutus as a kind of *laudatio* for the public life of *Eloquentia* is discussed more fully below.
[12] *Quorum memoria et recordatio in maxumis nostris grauissimisque curis iucunda sane fuit, cum in eam
nuper ex sermone quodam incidissemus.* For an excellent discussion of the themes of memory and
silence as they run throughout this dialogue, see Gowing 2000.
[13] This is clearly the dramatic location of the dialogue, as indicated by the phrase *cum . . . essem otiosus
domi*, "when I was . . . in a state of *otium* at home" (3.10), cf. Douglas 1966: 7 *ad* 10 and Gowing
2000; *pace* Fantham 1996: 45, who places the dialogue at Tusculum, the site of the orators' earlier
conversation: *quod mihi nuper in Tusculano inchoauisti de oratoribus* (5.20).
[14] *Nam cum inambularem in xysto et essem otiosus domi, M. ad me Brutus, ut consueuerat, cum T.
Pomponio uenit . . . .*
[15] Cf. Gowing 2000: 48, who notes rightly of sections 3.13–4.16: "His reading of it, Cicero responds,
brought him *salus* (13), and once again following the principle of poetic reciprocity – citing in this
instance Hesiod – Cicero insists on repaying Atticus in kind." I discuss Cicero's citation of Hesiod
at *Brut.* 4.15–5.16 in Chapter 2.

Atticus' request to discuss Rome's oratorical past (5.20: *quod mihi nuper in Tusculano inchoauisti de oratoribus: quando esse coepissent, qui etiam et quales fuissent,* "[I'd like to return to] that which you recently began telling me about the orators: their origins, and who they were, and what they were like"). The rest, as they say, is history.

Or is it? For even as *Brutus* is a dialogue ostensibly intent on a presentation of Rome's oratorical past,[16] it is similarly a text deeply concerned with the future role of the orator in a Republic that had come increasingly under the stifling power of an autocrat.[17] As noted above, it has long been recognized that *Brutus* (a text aptly identified by Gowing as a literary "anomaly")[18] plays an important role in the orator's attempt to write himself back into the intellectual life of Rome. So too, critics have somewhat more recently noted that the oratorical biographies of which *Brutus* is composed may mark a kind of turning point from primarily oral to primarily written rhetorical practice – a newfound or at any rate reinvigorated interest in the literary history of Rome.[19] But as much as the literary interests of the dialogue have been recognized, I would argue that even the excellent recent studies of *Brutus* have tended to view Cicero's literary and textual interests as secondary to his oratorical or historiographical ones.[20]

---

[16] As Marco Zangari has suggested to me, *Brutus* refashions the whole history of the Republic according to a definitively oratorical worldview. It reclaims the growth and preeminence of the *urbs* as one imminently dependent upon the successes of its orators, and reckons time not according to consular year so much as oratorical milestone. Thus the whole of the text can be read as a kind of alternative history of Rome in which the ebb and flow of the state is measured only according to the oratorical time frame. Gowing 2000: 41 calls *Brutus* "a history of sorts;" see further Rawson 1972 on this dialogue in the context of the orator's historical endeavors.

[17] As Alain Gowing has remarked to me, the tone of *Brutus* works more effectively if the orator has, indeed, already received news of Thapsus at the time of composition. The finality of Caesar's victory leaves the orator with little reason to mull anxiously over political uncertainties; now is the time for him to plan instead his strategy for the ultimate survival of the orator – and his eloquence – under the rule of the autocrat.

[18] Gowing 2000: 40: "In a literature as genre-bound and precedent-driven as Roman literature, Cicero's *Brutus* is an anomaly. While exhibiting characteristics of a philosophical treatise, a dialogue, a rhetorical handbook, an historical narrative, biography, and even a speech . . . this account of Roman orators and oratory set in the immediate aftermath of Caesar's victory at Thapsus . . . resists firm categorization." For the literary motives of *Brutus*, see further esp. Kytzler 1973 and Narducci 1997: 157–160.

[19] Narducci 1997 discusses the role of *Brutus* in this process in chapter 5 (*Dal Discorso Pronunciato al Discorso Scritto. L'eloquenza come Prodotto Letterario*, pp. 157–173); see too Kytzler 1973. Elsewhere, the literary leanings of the dialogue are recognized, but the textual aspirations of its author rarely noted: thus Rathofer 1986: 158–160 limits his discussion of such to "literarische Kritik" in *Brutus*, whereas Fantham 1996: 46 remarks upon the dialogue's utility as a source-piece for our own investigations into the early history of the Republic: "The *Brutus* is as near as surviving Roman texts will bring us to literary history."

[20] For an early investigation into the literary concerns of *Brutus*, see Haenni 1905; somewhat later see Kytzler 1973 and Rathofer 1986; and most recently Narducci 1997 and Gowing 2000. Fantham

That Cicero's composition of stylistically varied and thematically wide-ranging technical treatises attests to his pervasive literary interests is at this point beyond question. As I argue, however, Cicero's literary interests had by 46 come to extend forcibly into his own work, as well as into his own aspirations for textual production and explicitly literary renown. Indeed, Cicero's choice to write *Brutus* at a time of extreme personal and political destabilization should incite us to look beyond the stated themes of the dialogue and to plumb more deeply the social and textual implications of this rich treatise. There are of course manifold potential starting points for a productive "textual" exploration into *Brutus*. The following pages address one of the most prevalent, and yet least discussed themes of the dialogue: Cicero's peculiar and progressively complex personification of Republican eloquence – *Eloquentia* – in terms of a gendered physical being – a young woman, to be precise – who can move throughout, and be manipulated within, his textual world.

WHY PERSONIFY?

Before we get to the process of personification as it unfolds in *Brutus* it will be useful to review the form and function of personification as a literary and rhetorical topos in the textual world with which Cicero (and indeed, Catullus) was in dialogue. The cultic, artistic, and literary personification of cognitive abstractions (the process by which variously "non-human" attributes acquire recognizably human characteristics[21]) and the invocation of dead or absent individuals (the Latin term for both practices is *conformatio*) occupy a prominent position in the social and intellectual life of antiquity. So too, as I shall argue, Cicero's choice to use *conformatio* in his dialogues – the "personification" of *Eloquentia* in *Brutus* and the invocation of Rome's *maiores* in a great many of his dedicated dialogues – is an important clue to the ways in which he imagined his dedicated texts functioning as "acting objects" in the social and intellectual world. However,

---

1996: 45–46 refers to *Brutus* as alternatively (and rightly) a "cultural history" and a "literary history"; La Penna 2002: 3 confesses a predilection for *Brutus* "non solo per la galleria di ritratti, ma ancora più per la capacità di calare la storia dell' oratoria romana nella storia politica e culturale di Roma." Habinek 1998: 96 notes that *Brutus* demonstrates "interest in literary as well as political history."

[21] Stössl (*RE* 1042–58) describes the phenomenon neatly: "*Von Personificationen kann gesprochen werden, wenn einem Unpersönlichen, also Seelenlosen die Merkmale der Persönlichkeit verliehen, ihm Eigenschaften, Gedanken, Gefühle, Bestrebungen, Handlugen zugeschrieben werden, die sonst nur beseelter Persönlichkeit – menschlicher oder göttlicher – zukommen.*" On personification in the Greek world, in a work that is also helpful in approaching the Roman conceptualization of the phenomenon, see Stafford 2000.

both the designation of any particular personification as such and, within the realm of personification, the production of a meaningful distinction between "cultic deification," "anthropomorphic characterization," and "literalized lexical effect"[22] are consistently fraught issues. On the deification end of the spectrum is what I would term the "strong personification" of abstract civic *desideranda* (for example, *Tyche/Fortuna*, *Hygeia*, *Concordia*, and *Pax*) that come outfitted with physical attributes, topographical associations, and family trees, and tend to be more a matter of cultic practice and, in turn, artistic representation than they do of poetic device.[23] In opposition to these figures, I posit as "weak personification" both the literalizing lexicality of passing phenomena or human concerns (*Phobos* and *Aidos* in Homer; *Fortuna, Salus*, and *Spes* in Plautus; and *Fama* in Virgil) and the self-contained mythopoetic pedigrees that are emotionally effective at a world-order level but rarely exert narratological force outside of the passages in which they occur (so *Atê* is the daughter of Zeus at *Il.* 19.91; the progeny of *Nux* are given at Hes. *Theog.* 211–232).[24] For whereas each of these maneuvers functions as a powerful literary device within a particular passage or work, in each case the *Personifiziert* is rarely characterized with more than a simple epithet and in any case tends to function at the rhetorical sidelines – rather than thematic center – of a text. But if the vividly personified *Tyche* of Rhamnous stands at one pole, and the scarcely personified *Fortuna* in Terence (*Phorm.* 203) stands at the other, then the

---

[22] I adopt this term from Quilligan's discussion of female allegory in Pizan's *Cité des Dames*: "personifications of abstractions such as Philosophy and Nature take the feminine form primarily because allegory always works narratively by literalizing lexical effects. The gender of abstract nouns made from verbs in Latin is always feminine – *auctoritas* itself, for instance, is feminine – and so the personifications embodying these concepts take on the gender of the words: Lady Philosophy, Lady Nature, Lady Fortuna" (Quilligan 1991: 24–25; cited also in Paxson 1998: 149–179, see esp. pp. 160–161). Although Quilligan is misdirected in her apparent implication of a verbal source for *philosophia, natura*, and *fortuna* (as opposed to *auctoritas*, which derives from *augere*), her recognition of the grammatically linked "lexical effect" is nonetheless useful for this investigation. For a helpful summary of modern theories of personification and gender, see Paxson 1998: 158–162; Paxson is incorrect in his early statement that "in Hellenic, Roman, and much medieval art and allegorical literature, personified abstractions ... were exclusively *female*" (1998: 149; italics in original) – there are of course a fair number of masculine personifications in antiquity (e.g., *Phobos, Thanatos, Ploutos* and *Demos* in Greek authors; *Amor* and *Furor* in Latin). Nevertheless, he provides an interesting discussion of the (predominately) feminine gendering of personification and makes the attractive suggestion that "Individual personifications are women because Personification is a woman" (p. 175). Paxson 1994: 8–34 provides a helpful survey of the definitions of personification from antiquity to the medieval period.

[23] On the deification of abstract ideas in Rome, Axtell 1907 remains an important resource.

[24] So *Atê* is named daughter of *Eris* at Hes. *Theog.* 230, and the mother of *Peitho* at Aiskh. *Ag.* 385–386. Pindar gives *Hybris* as the mother of *Koros* at *O.* 13.10, and Euripides lists *Alastor, Phonos, Thanatos*, and *Phthonos* as possible fathers of Helen at *Tro.* 768–769.

majority of what are casually referred to as Greek and Roman "personifications" are situated somewhere on the highly literary continuum between
strong cultic abstract and weak grammatical invocation.

It is in this category of "middling personification," the detailed and
literalizing endowment of an abstract concept with variously human characteristics (for instance, heredity and appearance, thought and sensation,
intention and action), that we find the boundaries of the abstract and the
materialized most vibrantly tested. Thus in Prodicus' fable of Herakles'
choice between *Eudaimonia/Kakia* and *Aretê* (Xen. *Mem.* 2.1.21–34), in
Aristophanes' bickering *Logoi* (Ar. *Neph.*), and in Callimachus' comically
mournful *Plokamos* (Cat. 66, discussed in Chapter 6), we have personifications that reside not in the pale grammatical margins of a text so much as
at the vibrantly discursive core. So when I refer to *Eloquentia* as "personified" in *Brutus*, what I mean is that the abstract concept of *eloquence* – the
refined speech of the public male voice – is transformed in the text into an
increasingly human, identifiably female character.

In her personified state, *Eloquentia* is subject to many of the freedoms,
attentions, and restrictions of a "real woman," but in the hands of Cicero
this "real woman" possesses such attributes always and only with the understanding that she acts as the physical embodiment of the Republican –
which is to say, Ciceronian – voice.[25] Thus she is capable of speech (though
quite significantly she does not speak in the text), silence, movement, stasis,
learning, unlearning, romantic overture, and – most importantly – protection from these overtures at the hands of her idealized "fathers." At no place
in this dialogue would I suggest that Cicero endows his *Eloquentia* with
divine status, or offers her up as an object of cultic worship in anything
more than the most abstract or poetic of terms (though a later fragment of
his *Hortensius* might indeed point to such: . . .]*ca eloquentia tueri, quam tu
in caelum, Hortensi, credo, ut ipse cum ea simul ascenderes, sustulisses*, fr. 19),[26]
but neither can his highly literary construction of *Eloquentia* be dismissed
as weak grammatical abstraction or mere rhetorical effect. As I argue in the
following pages, the personification of *Eloquentia* in *Brutus* is nothing so
much as an intensely *literary* and textually interested maneuver. As such, it
is not only a powerful embodiment of the orator's own hopes and plans for

---

[25] Cf. *Dial.* 30.3; 32.4; and 40.2; Tacitus' use of Cicero will be discussed briefly in the Epilogue.
[26] The context is of course unclear (would that we had more of this text than we do!), but as *Hortensius*
likely dates to 45 – the year after the publication of *Brutus* and yet within the period of the orator's
greatest literary production – I find it not unlikely that Cicero is even here pursuing the theme of
Eloquentia as a kind of politico-literary "Muse" intimately connected to the interests of Republican
oratores.

the distinctly textual future of the Republican voice, but indeed a blueprint for the literary expression and textual exchange that would presage much of what becomes the accepted norm for poetic production in the Augustan and Imperial periods.

If the lion's share of ancient literary personifications falls into the category of this "middling" type, then even in the case of such middling personifications there is the strong tendency to resist, if not reject, a standardization or consistency of form and degree of characterization. So in the earliest poetic examples of personification – figures such as *Dike*, *Hypnos*, *Thanatos*, and *Atê*²⁷ – the personifications vary from passage to passage and author to author²⁸ in terms of the degree to which they are endowed with anthropomorphic physical, intellectual, or emotional characteristics. Even in the case of later authors a single word will often vacillate – rapidly and within the same text – between vivid personification and unmarked abstract, and I would suggest that it is the very lexical and stylistic flexibility endowed by this "middling personification" that seems to have been its greatest source of appeal for authors interested in exploring the poetic and rhetorical potentialities of this landscape of abstraction.

In his own use of personification we find Cicero no more or less consistent than, and at least as enthusiastic as, his Greek and Roman predecessors. Cicero's acquaintance with the dialect and literary tradition of personification, in its many forms, is evident throughout the corpus. He knew of Prodicus' seductive moral apologue; his reference to it in *de Officiis* is a primary source for Roman knowledge of the fable,²⁹ and although his

²⁷ For *Dike*, cf. Hes. *WD* 219–224, 256–262; for *Hypnos*, cf Soph. *Phil.* 827 ff.; for *Thanatos*, cf. Eur. *Alk.*; for *Atê*, cf *Il.* 9.505–507; 19.91–96, 126–133; Hes. *WD* 216, 231, 352, 413; Aiskh. *Ag.* 355.
²⁸ So Greene (*OCD* s.v. "Personifications"): "A single figure, such as Atê, varies from passage to passage and from poet to poet, being now a physical or psychological phenomenon, now a moral force, now a full-fledged divinity with family connections . . . even a given poet within a single work often vacillates between the genuine personification of a vividly characterized abstraction and a 'grammatical apotheosis' to the despair of modern editors who would like to be consistent in the matter of capital letters." Greene's summary of personification in ancient art, literature, and culture is certainly a useful one, although I would perhaps disagree with the author on some of his points of definition.
²⁹ *Nam quod Herculem Prodicus dicit, ut est apud Xenophontem, cum primum pubesceret, quod tempus a natura ad deligendum, quam quisque uiam uiuendi sit ingressurus, datum est, exisse in solitudinem atque ibi sedentem diu secum multumque dubitasse, cum duas cerneret uias, unam Voluptatis, alteram Virtutis, utram ingredi melius esset . . .* (*de Off.* 1.118). Cicero's utter silence here on Prodicus' highly eroticized personifications of Eudaimonia/Kakia and Aretê is indeed surprising, though one wonders whether the orator might have considered that kind of detail excessively lascivious (!) for a book on moral duties dedicated (in 44) to his son. Cicero mentions Prodicus elsewhere at *Brut.* 8.30 (in the early history of rhetoric in Greece) and *DND* 1.118 (in a discussion of the "cultic personification" of moral goods: *quid Prodicus Cius, qui ea quae prodessent hominum uitae deorum in numero habita esse dixit, quam tandem religionem reliquit?*)

citation of it eschews mention of the sophist's hypersexualization of the
young Herakles' "moral choices," it is clear that he had acquaintance with
the text of Xenophon. As is perhaps unsurprising, Cicero theorizes more
than any other prose author on the enthronement of civic good as a means
of influencing public behavior.[30] He argues in the technical treatises for
the personification of *uirtutes* (though never *uitia*, cf. *de Leg.* 2.19, 28) as
a means of encouraging proper behavior among the *boni*,[31] and represents
the voice and character of absent (or deceased) individuals and abstracts –
through the process of *conformatio* – in many of his public orations and with
notorious success. To the modern critic the philosophical "personification"
of, for example, *Fides* and the forensic "voicing" of a deceased ancestor (so
Appius Claudius Caecus in *Cael.* 33–34) may seem like inherently – and
perhaps even significantly – divergent rhetorical maneuvers. A discussion
of *conformatio*[32] by the *auctor* of the *ad Herennium*, however, suggests that
the two were not, for a man of the late Republic, as functionally distinct
as they might seem to us:

Conformatio est cum aliqua quae non adest persona confingitur quasi adsit, aut
cum res muta aut informis fit eloquens, et forma ei et oratio adtribuitur ad
dignitatem adcommodata aut actio quaedam . . . haec conformatio licet in plures
res, in mutas atque inanimas transferatur. Proficit plurimum in amplificationibus
partibus et commiseratione. (*Her.* 4.53.66)

Conformatio entails the fashioning of an absent individual as if present, or *when a
silent or unformed thing is made eloquent*, and both form and speech are attributed
to it, or a certain type of movement suited to its character . . . This *conformatio*
may be applied to a variety of things, both silent and inanimate; it is especially
effective in the techniques of "*amplificatio*" and "*commiseratio*."

---

[30] In addition to *DND* 1.118 (cited above), see 2.61: *res ipsa in qua uis inest maior, sic appellatur, ut
ea ipsa nominetur deus, ut Fides, ut Mens, quas in Capitolio dedicatas uidemus.* Cicero explicates the
moral good of personification at *de Leg.* 2.19 and 28: *bene uero quod Mens, Pietas, Virtus consecrantur
humanae, quarum omnium Romae dedicata publice templa sunt, ut illas qui habeant (habent autem
omnes boni) deos ipsos in animis suis conlocatos putent.*

[31] It is unclear, of course, where else in the Republican and early Imperial corpus we might expect
to see such theorizing. It would be unlikely for this kind of discussion to appear in the historians,
and indeed it does not; Quintilian theorizes on *prosopopoeia* at *Inst. Orat.* 12.10.61 and (more fully)
9.2.29 and 11.1.39, but it is clear that what he has in mind is the representation of absent individuals
rather than the attribution of *Persönlichkeit* to abstract concepts. The letters of Pliny and Seneca
would be more probable suspects for such inquiry into "true" personification, but it does not occur.

[32] Cicero himself uses the term throughout the *technica* in both its most basic sense, as an indication
of physical or "semi-physical" fashioning, shape, and form (*DND* 1.18.47; *TD* 1.22.50; *de Orat.*
1.25.114), as well as its more metaphoric, as an indication of expression, mental notion, verbal
arrangement and even, in *Brutus*, something like "figure in speech" (*de Orat.* 1.5.18; 3.52.201; *DND*
1.38.105; *Top.* 5.27; *Brut.* 37.140).

In the passage above, we have the inclusion of two apparently distinct rhetorical maneuvers (the Greek *ethopoeia* in the first case and *prosopopoeia* in the second) within one and the same conceptual and linguistic category. The first technique of *conformatio*, one we might call "animate personification" (the "voicing" of an absent but theoretically animate *persona*), is rarely included in modern surveys of either "personification" or rhetorical figure but was indeed used by the orator frequently and with great success.[33] The second technique, one we might specify as "inanimate personification," (the "voicing" of, or attribution of *Persönlichkeit* to that which is naturally mute, unformed, or inanimate) is similarly a common enough element in Ciceronian oratory: if it appears with somewhat less frequency than the first, it arguably carries with it even greater rhetorical power. Thus Sicily is made to speak at *Caec.* 11–27, *Res Publica* at *Planc.* 12–13, and *Patria* [et al.] at *Cat.* 1.18 and 27; *Patria* is made to "hate and fear" at *Cat.* 1.17.[34] As distinct as these two techniques may seem to the modern critic, the *auctor*'s explanation of the term, in concord with Cicero's own free use of both "types" of *conformatio*, would suggest that both the voicing of the absent animate and the voicing of the mute inanimate were considered identical (or at least comparable) rhetorical processes. In either case, the orator is attributing speech – *oratio* – and physicality – *forma*[35] – to *aliqua persona* not actually present. Whether or not that *persona* was, or had ever been, an actual person (as opposed to an abstract concept) seems of little or no import to the oration or – as I shall argue – text at hand.

The technique of *conformatio* as described above ("animate" or "inanimate personification") might at first seem to be applied only rarely in the technical treatises. Certainly it is my argument that the personification of *Eloquentia* in *Brutus* represents the orator's most complex, and peculiar, *conformatio* within the whole of the corpus. But it is far from the only one, for according to the *auctor*'s description of *conformatio* – a description utterly in accord with Cicero's own practice – we might say that all of the

---

[33] Surely one of the more famed examples of such is at *Cael.* 33–34, in the orator's over-the-top dramatization of Appius Claudius Caecus' imagined horror at the events wrought by his descendant; an imagined speech by Milo functions similarly at *Mil.* 93–98 (on which see further May 1988: 137–140). Quintilian discusses this technique at *Inst. Orat.* 12.10.61 (and elsewhere), where he identifies it as a component of the "grand style" of oratory; at 9.2.31, he distinguishes between *prosopopoeia* (in the case of the deceased) and *ethopoeia* (in the case of the living).

[34] Just as Cicero had personified *Res Publica* and *Patria* while under attack, and as a means to "save" them, I suggest that his Brutine personification of *Eloquentia* functions as an attempted rescue of an embattled "foundation" of Roman culture.

[35] Of the *auctor*'s description in this passage, Paxson 1998: 153 rightly notes: "the significant polyptoton ... in the definition (*Conformatio ... informis ... forma*) evokes the traditional word for trope or figure in Roman rhetoric – forma ..."

orator's dialogues, and the eponymously titled ones perhaps most vividly, function as extended, and highly literary, *conformationes*: representations of the voice and character of absent *personae* for a specific rhetorical – and in the case of the dialogues, textual – purpose.[36] There is surely something Platonic in Cicero's choice to write named dialogues – a *Brutus*, a *Lucullus*, a *Varro*, a *Catulus*, a *Hortensius*, a *Laelius*, and a *Cato*. In his dramatic introduction of the voices – and indeed, identities – of Rome's *maiores* onto his new textual stage, he is beating the forum at its own forensic game.

As the *auctor* makes clear, *conformatio* was thought to be especially effective for the purposes of *amplificatio* (the stirring of indignation) and *commiseratio* (the stirring of pity), each of which may adduce the authority of the past or the fears for the future as a means of strengthening the argument at hand.[37] This is, of course, exactly what Cicero does in his choice and presentation of "characters" – *personae* – in his many dialogues. He imputes to the august authorities of the past (Crassus and Antonius in *de Oratore*; Laelius, Scipio, and Cato in *Cato*) or the "learned men" of the present (Atticus, Varro, and Cicero in *Academica*; Atticus, Brutus, and Cicero in *Brutus*) the intellectual attitudes of the late Republic as well as, in many cases, his own biting anxieties over the perceived degradation of social and professional freedoms.

If the dialogues are themselves understood as literary exercises in the forensic practice of *conformatio* then, I contend, what we have in the case of *Eloquentia* is not so much an *unheimlich* intrusion of poetic or rhetorical figure into dry historiographical treatise as it is, in effect, the perfectly natural – and indeed, delightfully clever – containment of one "type" of *conformatio* within another. She is a personification that has entered into a personifying dialogue, a rhetorical "figure" perfectly at home in Cicero's figurative rhetorical world.

---

[36] On Cicero's personification of his dedicated texts, cf. *de Off.* 3.121: *Habes a patre munus, Marce fili, mea quidem sententia magnum, sed perinde erit, ut acceperis. Quamquam hi tibi tres libri inter Cratippi commentarios tamquam hospites erunt recipiendi.* To this, cf. Pliny *Ep.* 4.26, in which the author refers to the *libelli* he sends to Maecilius (the recipient also of the letter) as *comites . . . commodissimos.*

[37] Of *amplificatio* the *auctor* writes: *amplificatio est res quae per locum communem instigationis auditorum causa sumitur . . . primus locus sumitur ab auctoritate, cum commemoramus quantae curae ea res fuerit dis immortalibus aut maioribus nostris, regibus, civitatibus, nationibus, hominibus sapientissimis, senatui* (*Her.* 2.30.47–48). Of *commiseratio*, he writes: *misericordia commovebitur auditoribus si variam fortunarum commutationem dicemus; si ostendemus in quibus commodis fuerimus quibusque incommodis simus, conparatione; si quae nobis futura sint nisi causam obtinuerimus enumerabimus et ostendimus . . .* (*Her.* 2.30.50).

The orator's recognition of the stylistic and rhetorical power of the personified abstract, as well as his obvious comfort with the idea of this "personification play," are made apparent in his marvelously ekphrastic personification of Pleasure and the Virtues in the second book of *de Finibus*, a dialogue dedicated to Brutus in return, or so it seems, for Brutus' dedication to Cicero of his own *de Virtute*:[38]

Pudebit te, inquam, illius tabulae quam Cleanthes sane commode uerbis depingere solebat. iubebat eos qui audiebant secum ipsos cogitare pictam in tabula Voluptatem pulcherrimo uestitu et ornatu regali in solio sedentem; praesto esse Virtutes ut ancillulas, quae nihil aliud agerent, nullum suum officium ducerent nisi ut Voluptati ministrarent, et eam tantum ad aurem admonerent (si modo id pictura intellegi posset) ut caueret ne quid faceret imprudens quod offenderet animos hominum, aut quidquam e quo oriretur aliquis dolor. 'nos quidem Virtutes sic natae sumus ut tibi seruiremus; aliud negoti nihil habemus.' (*de Fin.* 2.21.69)

"You will blush," I said, "at the image Cleanthes used to draw so skillfully in his lectures. He would advise his listeners to imagine for themselves a painting of Pleasure in the most elegant raiment and sitting on a marvelously decorated throne. Beside her should stand the Virtues as her handmaidens; they should have nothing to do, no business of their own, other than to minister to Pleasure, and merely murmur in her ear (if only a painting could be imagined to murmur) that she should avoid ill-advisedly doing anything that might offend the sensibilities of the public, or anything from which any pain might arise: 'We are the Virtues, and born thus to serve you – we have no other task.'"

De Finibus, published the year after *Brutus* and conceived as a dialogue between L. Torquatus, C. Triarius, and Cicero himself, purports to provide a newly Roman examination of Greek philosophical themes. The tone of the above passage is clearly negative. But it is important to note that the criticism is aimed at the substance of Cleanthes' teachings, and indeed Epicurean ethics as a whole, rather than his use of personification per se. Cicero was no more required to engage in such an extensive description of Cleanthes' pedagogical style (as noted above, he recounts Prodicus' fable of Herakles with no reference to the original "inanimate personification") than he was to cast the whole of this inquiry into dialogue form. And indeed, nowhere else in this dialogue are the abstracts *uoluptas* or *uirtus* imbued with such strong *Persönlichkeit*. His choice to do so here, then, points to the orator's recognition of the "inanimate personification" as a semantic marker of authorial interest and appropriation. In its capacity as such,

---

[38] *Voluptas* is briefly personified again at the start of the third book of *de Fin.*

we might imagine the personification to function along the ideological lines of the Latin diminutive, itself a polysemic appropriative category of which Cicero is remarkably fond. Just as the semantic structure of diminutive is such that it carries both an evaluation (be it ameliorative or pejorative) and a reference to the evaluator (the author's suggested decoding of the descriptive display of his words), so the personification is able to transfer a discussion of abstract ethical concepts into the realm of authorial subjectivity and, more to the point, affective possession or rejection. The representation of Cleanthes' original "inanimate personifications" is no vapid mimesis of Greek prototype; on the contrary, the orator's pointed reiteration of Cleanthes' lecture serves precisely to undermine the authority of the original. It is a deft projection of the orator's own harsh critique of the philosopher's ethical precepts onto his description of the teaching of these precepts itself. In his unexpectedly vivid description of *Voluptas* and the *Virtutes* as figures of corrupted female luxury, Cicero stirs up in his textual audience a carefully constructed reaction against Cleanthes' philosophical stance.

As an appropriative marker of authorial critique, then, the "inanimate personification" (to which I shall from this point on refer to simply as *personification*) carried with it a vast literary potential for a strengthening of argumentation. It is the recognition of this potential, I contend, that moved Cicero – one year earlier and in a very different sort of dialogue – to forge in his discussion of the abstract *eloquentia* a source of literary power and persuasion. The theme of eloquence runs throughout the dialogue and is referred to in terms ranging from unmarked abstraction (which instances will not, for the most part, be brought into the discussion) to strong and, as we shall, see progressively evolving personification.

In the next two sections of this chapter I focus on three major points of transition in the dialogue – from the introduction to the Greek biographies, from the Greek biographies to those of Rome, and from Rome's past to Brutus' future – in which Cicero develops the "character" of *Eloquentia* (henceforth capitalized when in reference to the *Personifiziert*) by means of progressively detailed and complex personifications. First, I read the dialogue's initial reference to *Eloquentia* "in the present" (6.22) as an introduction to the orator's own unnatural positioning in the interstices between traditional Republican "speech" and the "silence" that has been imposed upon it under the rise of Caesarian autocracy. I then turn to Cicero's description of the *Eloquentia* "of the past" (13.51) and examine the orator's use of traditionally Atticist criticisms in his unmistakably gendered description of her early years and near-destruction as a result of wayward

Eastern travels. Finally, I analyze one of the penultimate sections[39] of *Brutus* – surely the most compelling and important personification in the text – in which *Eloquentia* "of the future" (96.330) is referred to in terms of an orphaned intellectual daughter-figure who must be rescued from the forum and brought back within the confines of the home, that she might be circulated exclusively at the hands of her oratorical guardians. By the end of *Brutus*, Cicero has transformed the abstract concept of Republican *eloquentia* from a poorly defined catchword for rhetorical ability into a vibrantly personified promise of social and literary resurrection for the producers of written *eloquentia* – in the form of rhetorical, historiographical, and philosophical treatises as well as, of course, poetic ones – themselves.

WHEN SPEECH FELL SILENT (AND PICKED UP A PEN)

The first personification of *Eloquentia* in *Brutus* – indeed, the first reference to *eloquentia* in the text as a whole – occurs in the early sections of the dialogue, in which Cicero's previously expressed sorrow over the death of his colleague is subtly rewritten into a lament for the loss of something far greater. Shortly after the three interlocutors have met, and following quickly upon a lament over Brutus' own truncated oratorical career, Cicero introduces the theme of eloquence as he summarizes the whole of the Republican decline in the haunting collocation of speech and silence:

Nam mihi, Brute, in te intuenti crebro in mentem uenit uereri, ecquodnam curriculum aliquando sit habitura tua et natura admirabilis et exquisita doctrina et singularis industria. cum enim in maximis causis uersatus esses et cum tibi aetas nostra iam cederet fascisque summitteret, subito in ciuitate cum alia ceciderunt tum etiam ea ipsa, de qua disputare ordimur, *eloquentia obmutuit.* (*Brut.* 6.22)

For when I gaze upon you, Brutus, I am often made to worry whether your wondrous natural ability, your flawless learning, your remarkable devotion will ever have their day at the races. For whilst you were busying yourself in cases of the utmost importance, and my own advanced age was giving way and laying down the scepter, suddenly everything went to hell in our state and even *Eloquentia* – the very topic of our discussion – *fell silent.*

---

[39] All manuscripts break off at section 97.333 (following *oportunorum*) and before the dialogue's formal conclusion. It is unlikely, however, that we are missing more than one or two sections of the text, the equivalent of perhaps one half of a Teubner page; so Fabius Blondus writes at the end of B, *non erat amplius in exemplari, a quo abscisse sunt charte due. quamquam ut mihi uidetur nedum charte sed pauca admodum uerba deficiunt.* This conclusion probably included a very brief description of the end of the dialogue and – perhaps – a valediction to Brutus or promise for future discussion.

Eloquentia obmutuit. Of course, we need not posit even a "weak person-ification" of *Eloquentia* in order to make this phrase comprehensible. It is a fairly unremarkable literalized lexical effect, and if the semantic collocation creates a nicely unsettling frisson – "Speech stopped speaking" – it does not in and of itself qualify as a convincing *conformatio*. Indeed, far from "voicing" *Eloquentia* in this passage, Cicero is positing a lack of voice[40] – a mouth opened as if to speak, but robbed suddenly of its freedom to do so. It will be good to remember that this is a dialogue itself precipitated by the death of the orator Hortensius, who was a very real "voice of the Republic" and certainly a participant in the textual world of the late Republic. So if we read *eloquentia obmutuit* to signify not an actual silencing (as indeed it cannot), but a metaphorical death of *Eloquentia's* public voice (qua the "virtue" that is Republican speech[41]), it is interesting to note what the author does next. Far from abandoning *Eloquentia* to her silence, Cicero develops the theme of wordlessness through the language and imagery of the formal funeral:

hic ego: laudare igitur eloquentiam et quanta uis sit eius expromere quantamque eis, qui sint eam consecuti, dignitatem afferat, neque propositum nobis est hoc loco neque necessarium. (*Brut.* 6.25)

And I said, "But to praise *Eloquentia*, to display the magnitude of her strength, to tell of the great dignity she bestows upon those who follow her – neither is this my intention right now nor is such necessary."

Indeed, after these words the orator leaves off from discussing *Eloquentia* herself for several chapters. What follows instead, as we know, is an exhaus-tive presentation of Greek, and especially Roman, oratorical nobility: a virtual funeral parade, we might say, of *Eloquentia's* family tree.[42]

---

[40] As Alain Gowing has pointed out to me, Ovid creates a similar – if inverted – effect in his silent personifications of *Tacita* and *Muta* at *Fast.* 2.571 and 583. Tacitus' personification of *eloquentia* in *Dialogus*, a personification that I think must have come straight from *Brutus*, is not merely silent, but almost pathetically powerless.

[41] *Eloquentia* identified as a *uirtus* in the first book of *de Oratore*: [*Mnesarchus dicebat*] . . . *oratorem autem nisi qui sapiens esset, esse neminem; atque ipsam eloquentiam, quod ex bene dicendi scientia constaret, unam quamdam esse uirtutem, et qui unam uirtutem haberet, omnes habere* . . . (*de Orat.* 1.18.83).

[42] Gowing 2000: 41 counts some 250 orators named in *Brutus*; Kytzler 1973: 461 gives the count at 275. For a full prosopography of characters in this dialogue, see Sumner 1973. However, even before we get to the biographies of the individual orators, Cicero gives two brief biographies of, as it were, *Eloquentia* herself. The first (6.26–9.38) presents a "biography of the *res*," that is, the evolution of oratory as an oral form; the second (10.39–13.52) presents a "biography of the *ars*," that is, of oratorical theory and its relationship to the written text. For the biography as an essential component of the *laudatio*, cf. *RE* 922–994; see also Kierdorf 1980. Although recent scholarship has recognized the apparent duplication of these biographies, the content of these passages (*res* vs. *ars*) has received little notice.

Several years and at least one dialogue had intervened between the composition of *de Oratore* and that of *Brutus*, but these two texts are remarkably similar in a variety of ways. The former dialogue is set on the eve of the Social War; the latter is both set and composed at the end of the Civil War.[43] Each dialogue tells a story of education and initiation, each looks to the past as a way of arguing for the future, and – above all – each underlines in its telling the importance of the written and circulated text as a weapon of elite autonomy and its resistance to political destabilization. Whereas the pedagogical displays of *de Oratore* seemed an optimistic first effort in the orator's entry into the community of textual reciprocity, *Brutus*' mimesis of the *laudatio funebris* reads like the morose plea of a man acutely aware of the extent to which his own social survival has become incontrovertibly linked to that of his fellow writers.

Surely modern critics have been right to note that the funereal tones of the early chapters of *Brutus* (beginning, of course, with the introductory description of the death of Hortensius) are so pervasive as to suggest that the entire dialogue might be read as a literary rehearsal of the *laudatio funebris*.[44] But what are the implications of this stylized *pompa*? What might the orator have in mind in his textualization of oratorical death? Is this, indeed, his intention at all?

The origins of the *laudatio* are obscure. Although we have no detailed descriptions of the funeral procedure written by a Roman author, Polybius' (6.53) account of the funeral practices of the Republican elite are exceedingly helpful in developing an outline of the ritual as a whole. Beginning in the atrium of the deceased, the *pompa* would reach its rhetorical and spectacular climax in the forum itself[45] with the *laudatio funebris*, a meticulous biographical display of the deceased's own accomplishments carefully interwoven with those of his (or her)[46] predecessors, delivered before the assembled crowd from (in most cases) the political and visual

---

[43] A point noted too by Narducci 1997: 98: "il lettore che seguiva con assiduità la produzione ciceroniana, non sarà sfuggito all' impressione di un angosciante ritorno di vecchie tematiche: meno di dieci anni prima, il *de oratore* aveva celebrato in toni non tropo diversi la scomparsa di Crasso alla vigilia degli sconvolgimenti della guerra sociale."

[44] The full term *laudatio funebris* does not appear until Sen. *Suas*. 6.21; before then, as in Cicero, *laudatio* alone is enough to signify the funeral context. Gowing 2000: 58 notes: "the funeral oration or *laudatio funebris*, as defined by Cicero in the *Brutus*, fulfils two functions: to serve as a record or *memoria* of the family's achievements and to provide the means to verify one's ancestry," and compares Polybius' description of the Roman funeral (6.53) to Cicero's presentation of Rome's orators in *Brutus*. Flower 1996 provides the definitive modern study for the Roman funeral and the standards of the *laudatio funebris*, and provides at p. 97 n. 34 a list of passing literary references to various funeral practices. See further Vollmer 1892, *RE* 1925 and Kierdorf 1980.

[45] Cf. *de Orat*. 2.341; Flower 1996: 98.

[46] On the form and content of funeral speeches delivered for women, see Flower 1996: 122–124.

focal point of the Republican *rostra*. On structural and rhetorical grounds, the ritual seems to have arisen from a combination of the formal and public orations of the forum and the informal and private lamentations of the graveside; indeed evidence would suggest that both the stylistic and political ambitions of the Republican *laudatio* developed alongside those of the Republican forum. If we are to believe Cicero's Brutine narrative (and we must do so with caution, as the passage in question contains a subtle attack on Clodius), the late Republican *laudatio* had become a politically informed, "characteristically Roman"[47] spectacle, a means for powerful families to present fictional accounts of their collective past and thus recreate the public memory of elite pedigree.[48] Charges of biographical falsification aside, there is little doubt that throughout the Republic an important concomitant to the funeral procession of the noble family was the ritual presentation of the *imagines maiorum*, wax portrait-masks[49] created in the image of male ancestors who had held high magistracies or were otherwise renowned for their service to the Republic. In practice, actors were hired to wear these masks – often displayed in the family home when not in use[50] – during both the *pompa* and the *laudatio*, thus invoking via a *conformatio* of the deceased not only the memory but also the presence and authority of the departed *maiores*.[51] This provided a vibrant mimesis of the ancestors of the deceased as well as a powerful visual complement to the rhetorical performance of the *laudatio*, a performance that would itself be "repeated" in the circulation of a written version of the speech following the events.[52] An encomium of the glory of the deceased through a vibrant rehearsed biography of family ancestry, the funeral offered the descendants

---

[47] Flower 1996: 129, cf. 124, where Flower notes the highly political nature of several Republican *laudationes*, focusing most heavily on Caesar's daring funeral for his aunt Julia, for which cf. Plut. *Caes.* 5.

[48] Cf. *Brut.* 16.62, in an attack on Clodius' falsified transfer to the plebs: *et hercules [mortuorum laudationes] quidem extant: ipsae enim familiae sua quasi ornamenta ac monumenta seruabant et ad usum, si quis eiusdem generis occidisset, et ad memoriam laudum domesticarum et ad allustrandam nobilitatem suam. Quamquam his laudationibus historia rerum nostrarum est facta mendosior. Multa enim scripta sunt in eis quae facta non sunt: falsi triumphi, plures consulatus, genera etiam falsa et ad plebem transitiones, cum homines humiliores in alienum eiusdem nominis infunderentur genus.* On this see further Ridley 1983.

[49] Flower 1996: 32–43 discusses the substance, form, and use of the Republican *imago*.

[50] So weighty was the social capital associated with the possession and presentation of the *imagines* that the right to display an ancestor's *imago*, as well as the right to have one's own *imago* preserved and displayed, could be revoked as a result of criminal conviction, proscription, or *damnatio memoriae*.

[51] Flower 1996: 128–129 notes that the presence of the *imagines* at the funeral created for the speaker of the *laudatio* a kind of private and authorizing audience of his predecessors.

[52] Flower 1996: 129 makes clear that the publication of the *laudatio* would have been an expected concomitant to the delivered oration; see also Gruen 1992: 152–182.

a way to connect the deceased's accomplishments with the family's past, the survivors' present, and the descendants' future.[53]

If *Eloquentia*'s sudden silence is understood as a "death of Republican speech,"[54] we can read Cicero's biographies as a literary presentation of Rome's oratorical *imagines* (itself constituting a kind of *conformatio* of the deceased's ancestors[55]) in conscious mimicry of the public funeral. In his stylization of Rome's oratorical masters as the "ancestors" of Republican *Eloquentia*, Cicero transforms the abstracted silence of the Republican voice into a personal family tragedy – a tragedy for which he, as the eldest surviving son of the oratorical family, will deliver the eulogy.[56] If *Eloquentia*'s life in the forum has come to an end, then, *Brutus* is both a *laudatio* for its passing and, as Gowing has argued, an important literary record of the "family" memory.[57] I think that this cannot be the end of the story, however. In an excellent article on memory and silence in *Brutus*, Gowing suggests that Cicero's idealized concealment of *Eloquentia* (96.330) contains a reference to the domestic containment of the *imagines*.[58] But just as the *laudatio* praises the ancestors of the deceased and the accomplishments of the family's past, it must necessarily (and at the same time) stake a claim for the family's future. The "death" of *Eloquentia* in these early sections is intended only as a public one (with apologies to William Goldman, she is only "mostly dead"[59]) and carries with it tantalizing hints

[53] On the function of the *laudatio* as a link between the past and the future, see Flower 1996: 128–158. In his discussion of the funeral tones of *Brutus*, Gowing 2000: 59 notes: "the impetus behind the funeral and the funeral oration and the *Brutus* is precisely the same: the preservation and transmission of memory." Flower 1996: 104 argues: "one important function of the funeral procession was to present and hence to define the community of past family members and Roman citizens, while showing their close connection with those still living."

[54] Although Fantham 1996 does not discuss *eloquentia* per se (much less in terms of a personification), her statement that *Brutus* was "written in part as a eulogy of the lost art of free speech" (p. 56) is closely in line with my present argument.

[55] Flower 1996: 128–129 hints at the connection between the forensic and funereal *conformatio*: "The actors wearing the *imagines* re-enacted past events and personalities and illustrated the subject-matter of the eulogy. During the delivery of the speech itself they formed a special audience. Ancestors were also treated in several other types of rhetoric, in both political and judicial contexts."

[56] As was the common practice in the Republic, cf. Flower 1996: 130–131.

[57] Gowing 2000: 59: "The impetus behind the funeral and the funeral oration and the *Brutus* is precisely the same: the preservation and transmission of memory, in the belief that a knowledge of the past is the most secure means to ensure wisdom in the future."

[58] Gowing 2000: 58, in an illuminating comparison of Polybius' description of the funeral and the structure of *Brutus*. "The deceased's image is then placed in the family's house to serve as a constant reminder of the man's virtues... much as Cicero admonishes Brutus to keep *eloquentia* shut up 'in the house.'"

[59] The reference here is to the character Miracle Max, in Goldman's novel *The Princess Bride*. Upon inspection of the apparently deceased Wesley, Max informs Inigo that there is a substantial difference between "sort of dead, mostly dead, and all dead." (1973: 276).

that there may yet be a way to resuscitate the oratorical pedigree. *Eloquentia* has fallen silent in public – but might there arise an alternate venue for her voice?

FROM GREECE TO ROME; FROM FORUM TO HOME

Nam ut semel e Piraeo eloquentia euecta est, omnis peragrauit insulas atque ita peregrinata tota Asia est, ut se externis oblineret moribus omnemque illam salubritatem Atticae dictionis et quasi sanitatem perderet ac loqui paene dedisceret. (*Brut.* 13.51)

For as soon as *Eloquentia* set out from Piraeus, she wandered about all the islands and so traveled the whole of Asia that she ended up smearing herself with foreign practices and destroyed the vigor – and health, if you will – of her Attic diction and almost forgot how to speak.

The second major personification follows shortly upon the first and, as if gaining life force from the descriptions of *Eloquentia*'s Greek ancestors, is all the more vivid. It is yet early in Cicero's oratorical biographies. He has twice reviewed the development of refined speech in Greece (7.26–13.50), and prepares to move to the rise of eloquence in Rome. The transition from East to West is marked by both an abrupt shift in tone and a remarkable account of the Eastern adventures of a young *Eloquentia* who left her birthplace, wandered the isles, and ended up nearly losing her voice – and herself – in the East.

The description is a striking one, and presages a description of the orator's own youthful journeys at the end of the dialogue.[60] In these lines we have neither a dry summary of the evolution of Greek rhetorical theory, nor a simple grammatical invocation of *eloquentia* qua public speech, but rather a vivid travelogue of a young girl's departure from Athens and near-destruction of herself – and her reputation – through the unchecked abuse of Eastern luxuries. The image of *Eloquentia* "setting out" on her oratorical journey is not the first such in Cicero – a similar abstraction occurs in the early sections of the orator's youthful *de Inventione*.[61] But whereas there the language was relatively uncolored and only incidentally "gendered," *Brutus* provides the detailed innuendo of a distinctly female danger. In Greece, *Eloquentia* was allowed to travel abroad without a male guardian; as a result she fell victim to the naïve over-application of the unnecessary "cosmetics"

---

[60] Cf. the language and imagery of *Brut.* 91.314–315.
[61] *Ac primo quidem sic et nata et progressa longius eloquentia uidetur et item postea maximis in rebus pacis et belli cum summis hominum utilitatibus esse uersata* (*de Inv.* 1.3); Daly 1950.

of foreign rhetorical practice (*se externis oblineret moribus*).[62] The orator's suggestion that *Eloquentia* "almost forgot how to speak" as a result of her childish misuse of Eastern luxury anticipates his transition to the more salubrious nature of mature Roman oratory: the ills *Eloquentia* encountered in Greece, it is implied, will be cured upon her arrival at and cultivation in Rome. Taken as a whole, and coupled especially with the echoes of Cicero's own youth, this description provides both a meaningful turning point for the progression of the dialogue and a subtle parallelism of *Eloquentia*'s "life" with the orator's own present literary endeavor. *Eloquentia* has left Athens; she (and Cicero) can only arrive in Rome.

If we also understand personification of this sort to function as a strongly appropriative maneuver, then Cicero's description of *Eloquentia* in these lines functions at two further levels. First, and as we saw was the case in his rehearsal of Cleanthes' *Voluptas*, the personification of *Eloquentia* at this point of transition enables the orator to insert into an otherwise straightforward account an acute (if modestly cloaked) authorial critique: that Asianist rhetoric is a distinctly, even necessarily, "immature" predilection. It is a forgivable impulse in the young (and so we think of Cicero's own youth), but must be guarded against in the speech of the mature. Second, by referring to *Eloquentia* in personified and distinctly gendered terms – men used unguents as well, but the sloppy overuse implied by *se . . . oblineret* is feminizing – the orator is able to "claim her as his own", to underline both his personal interest in her subsequent reception at Rome and (in anticipation of the end of the dialogue) her continuing, and increasingly textual, interaction with the orators with whom she comes into contact.[63]

The critique of literary production and reception via the representation of a sexually suspect personification is far from unique to Cicero or the Republic. In his second *Isthmian*, Pindar personifies the poems of Terpsichore with his cynical claim that they are sold with "silver-glinting faces" now that the Muse has learned to sing in exchange for payment.[64] In

---

[62] The verb *oblinere*, here understood as "daub" or "smear," is used frequently in the case of cosmetics (though also paint and mud), and as such often carries with it an extended implication of moral or ethical corruption or degradation. Cf. Cic. *Verr.* 3.31 (*Apronius . . . unguentis oblitus*, of a dissolute official, coupled with the use of perfumes); Mart. *Ep.* 6.93.9 (*acida latet oblita creta*, of a strumpet's make-up, coupled with bean paste perfumes, etc.); Ovid *Ep.* 11.2 (of a *libellus*); Tac. *Ann* 2.17; Sen. *Ep.* 123.7 (of face ointment); Hor. *Ep.* 2.1.204; 1.19.30; Suet. *Gram.* 10 (of "sullied" literature).

[63] The importance of writing is addressed in the case of the Greek orators, but Cicero's emphasis on the importance of textual eloquence – the written *oratio* in particular as primary evidence for rhetorical skill – is even more heavily underlined in his Roman biographies. On this, see further Gowing 2000: 43–44.

[64] Pindar *Isth.* 2.6–8: ἁ Μοῖσα γὰρ φιλοκερδής / πω τότ᾽ ἦν ἐργάτις· / οὐδ᾽ ἐπέρναντο γλυκεῖ- / αι μελιφθόγγου ποτὶ Τερψιχόρας / ἀργυρωθεῖσαι πρόσωπα μαλθακόφωνοι ἀοιδαί, "the Muse

a somewhat more culturally and temporally relevant example, Dionysios of Halicarnassos, in his treatise *On the Ancient Orators*, personifies Asian rhetoric as "some crazed prostitute" (ἑταίρα τις ἄφρων) who has expelled the Attic Muse from her rightful domain and is bent on destroying her own livelihood:

[ἑτέρα δὲ ῥητορική] . . . ἦν φορτική τις πάνυ καὶ ὀχληρὰ καὶ τελευτῶσα παρα-
πλησίαν ἐποίησε γενέσθαι τὴν Ἑλλάδα ταῖς τῶν ἀσώτων καὶ κακοδαιμόνων
οἰκίαις. ὥσπερ γὰρ ἐν ἐκείναις ἡ μὲν ἐλευθέρα καὶ σώφρων γαμετὴ κάθηται
μηδενὸς οὖσα τῶν αὑτῆς κυρία, ἑταίρα δέ τις ἄφρων ἐπ᾽ ὀλέθρωι τοῦ βίου
παροῦσα πάσης ἀξιοῖ τῆς οὐσίας ἄρχειν, σκυβαλίζουσα καὶ δεδιττομένη τὴν
ἑτέραν· τὸν αὐτὸν τρόπον ἐν πάσηι πόλει καὶ οὐδεμιᾶς ἧττον ἐν ταῖς εὐπαιδεύ-
τοις (τουτὶ γὰρ ἁπάντων τῶν κακῶν ἔσχατον) ἡ μὲν Ἀττικὴ Μοῦσα καὶ
ἀρχαία καὶ αὐτόχθων ἄτιμον εἰλήφει σχῆμα, τῶν ἑαυτῆς ἐκπεσοῦσα ἀγαθῶν,
ἡ δὲ ἔκ τινων βαράθρων τῆς Ἀσίας ἐχθὲς καὶ πρώιην ἀφικομένη, Μυσὴ ἢ
Φρυγία τις ἢ Καρικόν τι κακόν, Ἑλληνίδας ἠξίου διοικεῖν πόλεις ἀπελάσασα
τῶν κοινῶν τὴν ἑτέραν. (*On the Ancient Orators*, 1)

[This other Rhetoric] . . . was altogether vile and foul and finally made Greece resemble nothing so much as the houses of the profligate and wicked. For just as in such houses there resides a wife, freeborn and prudent but with no authority over her own affairs, while some crazed prostitute, set on the destruction of her livelihood, thinks herself fit to control the entire estate, terrifying the [wife] and treating her like filth; thus in every *polis* and in the exceedingly civilized ones no less than elsewhere (and this was the straw that broke the camel's back), the ancient and autochthonous Attic Muse lost both her rank and her possessions, while the upstart, arrived only yesterday or the day before from the god-forsaken depths of Asia – a Mysian or Phrygian or Carian beast – thought herself fit to rule over Greek *poleis*, ousting her opponent from public affairs.

Although the simple personification of *Eloquentia* qua "eloquence" would not have been problematic for Cicero, the distinctly textual nature of this Brutine *Eloquentia* makes her all the more suitable to be imagined as a gendered variety of "movable property." Cicero bases his estimation of prior oratorical excellence in *Brutus* on the preservation and circulation of the written text (be it the epic *poema*, the historical *monumentum*, or the formal *oratio*): from her very birth, *Eloquentia* is recognizable only when she has entered the textual record – a fairly obvious point, but one crucial to Cicero's textual interests in *Brutus*.[65]

was not then greedy for gain, nor a working-girl; nor were the sweet, soft-murmuring songs of honey-voiced Terpsichore put up for sale, with their silver-glinting faces."
[65] Cicero makes explicit the importance of the written record in the case of, e.g., Pericles and Thucydides (both at 7.27), Themistocles (known *ex Attici monumentis*; 7.28), Alcibiades, Critias, and Theramenes (known *ex Thucydidi scriptis*; 7.29), Lysias and Demosthenes (both 9.35); at both 10.41 and 13.50 Homer is adduced as "evidence" of *honos eloquentiae* in the early period. The

Certainly, the gendered personification of texts or textual concepts had become increasingly common in the literary and visual production of the late Hellenistic period, during which time the physical text and literary paraphernalia moved to the forefront of the lexicon of social and political status.[66] For the late Republican audience, such personification on Cicero's part would have been considered, if not a commonplace (again, I suspect Cicero may have been anomalous in this regard), at least a recognizable stylistic topos and one that is indeed later developed in the literature of the Augustan and Imperial periods.[67] In his image of a wandering *Eloquentia* who is subject to the damaging moral influences of foreign practice, Cicero both underlines the potential dangers of insufficiently guarded public speech and foreshadows his ultimate plan to safeguard against such dangers – now manifest in the oratorical practice of Rome.

The theme of *Eloquentia*'s reception and development at Rome runs intermittently throughout the remaining biographical portions of the dialogue. We learn that although she had been raised in Athens,[68] it is the forum for which *Eloquentia* had been born:

Itaque [Calui] oratio nimia religione attenuata doctis et atttente audientibus erat inlustris, <a> multitudine autem et a foro, *cui nata eloquentia est*, deuorabatur. (*Brut.* 82.283)

Thus [Calvus'] language was attenuated due to his excessive scrupulousness; experts and those who listened carefully noted its quality, whereas the crowd and the forum – *for which Eloquentia was born* – simply ate it up.

Roman biographies are introduced with a direct reference to the importance of the written record (*optime, inquam, sed ueniamus ad nostros, de quibus difficile est plus intellegere quam quantum ex monumentis suspicari licet*, 13.52–14.53); textual evidence is emphasized in the biographies of, e.g., Ti. Coruncanius (*ex pontificum commentariis*; 14.55), M. Cornelius Cethegus (Ennius *Ann.* 303–305), Cato (*Catonem uero quis nostrotum oratorum . . . legit?*; 17.65; see also 19.75), A. Albinus (21.81), and C. Laelius and P. Africanus (*quorum extant orationes*; at 21.82). This emphasis on the written record is echoed by Sallust at *BC* 8.

[66] As noted above, Callimachus' *Plokamos Berenikes* is surely nothing if not a detailed, and humorously extended, *conformatio*; the poem itself seems to have been subsequently personified at Epigram 51 (52 Schn.), in which the author refers to a *Berenika*, "lately fashioned and yet moist with perfume," who has been added as a "fourth Grace." On visual personification of the text, cf. the relief of the Apotheosis of Homer by Archelaos of Priene (ca. 125 BCE, now in the British Museum (1819, 0812.1; sculpture 2191), which shows the poet seated and flanked on either side by young female figures of the *Iliad* and *Odyssey*. Svenbro 1993: 187–216 discusses a kind of Greek personification of the text that expands upon the homoerotic bond between reader (as *erômenos*) and author (as *erastês*).

[67] On the personification of texts in the Augustan and Imperial periods, see Connor 1982: 145–152; Oliensis 1997: 151–171; 1998: 174–181; Pearcy 1994; and Wyke 1987. Camille 1997: 50 notes of the gendered mediaeval text: "If books are male through their grammatical gender, their authors, and their voices . . . desire for them can only be mediated through the female, through mother or woman, with a gaze that is penetrative and phallic."

[68] Of *Eloquentia*'s birth and youth in Athens, Cicero writes: *uidesne igitur uel in ea ipsa urbe, in qua nata et alta sit eloquentia, quam ea ero prodierit in lucem?* (10.39).

As Cicero would have it, *Eloquentia*'s arrival in Rome constitutes the ultimate fulfillment of her birthright. The rising threat of a Caesarian autocracy, and the concomitant weakening of oratorical freedom, have meant – for Cicero – that the city that was to be the house of *Eloquentia*'s maturity has instead become the tomb of her silence.[69]

If the erstwhile Muse of the forum has turned into the ultimate victim of Republican decline, Cicero's final personification of *Eloquentia* is all the more exceptional for its literary force and social implications. For after Cicero has treated his guests to the whole of oratory's family tree, and as he moves toward the concluding sections of the dialogue, he abruptly transforms *Eloquentia* from a sexually suspect wandering Muse into an orphaned daughter-figure who must be returned to the home and protected from the ham-handed advances of ignorant suitors:

> Nos autem, Brute, quoniam post Hortensi clarissimi oratoris mortem orbae Eloquentiae quasi tutores relicti sumus, domi teneamus eam saeptam liberali custodia, et hos ignotos atque impudentes procos repudiemus tueamurque ut adultam uirginem caste et ab amatorum impetus quantum possumus prohibeamus. (*Brut.* 96.333)

> But Brutus, since the death of Hortensius – that most brilliant of orators – has left us as the guardians (if you will) of an orphaned *Eloquentia*, let us keep her within the home, shielded by our noble protection: let us send away these shameless and good-for-nothing suitors, let us keep our full-grown virgin chaste, and let us repel from her – as much as we can – the advances of her lovers.

The personification here is a powerful one, and more detailed, explicit, and socially charged than any other in the Ciceronian corpus.[70] Yet even when this scene has been noted in critical inquiries into *Brutus* – and in the vast majority of cases, it is not – it has received only glancing interest, dismissed, in Douglas' words, as merely an "elaborate simile."[71] Nevertheless,

---

[69] Cf. Narducci 1997: 97–98: "dopo la guerra civile, il foro è practicalmente deserto... molti tra i migliori oratori sono scomparsi, in sequito al conflitto o per inesorabile necessità di natura; i pochi rimasti sono ridotto al silenzio: il dominio di Cesare ha decretato l'estinzione di ogni libero dibattito."

[70] *Pace* Douglas 1966: 232 *ad* 96.330, who considers this image to be effectively the "same" as those at *Ep. Fam.* 3.11.3, *tanta penuria est in omni uel honoris uel aetatis gradu ut tam orba ciuitas tales tutores complecti debeat*, and *Orat.* 64, which refers to the *mollis oratio philosophorum* as a *casta, uerecunda, uirgo incorrupta quodam modo (itaque sermo potius quam oratio dicitur)*. There are of course similarities: the former passage personifies the *ciuitas* as an orphaned child, and the latter philosophical speech as an untouched *uirgo*. However, in neither case does Cicero advise or imagine personal – much less gendered – interaction with these personifications (cf. *domi teneamus eam... procos repudiemus tueamurque ut... ab amatorum impetus... prohibeamus*) as an allegory for extra-textual political or literary activity, nor does he pursue these personifications with any formal purpose through the remainder of these works.

[71] Douglas 1966: 232 *ad* 96.330; Dugan 2005: 232–233 notes the personification of *Eloquentia*.

in light of what I have argued as an extended and evolving personification of *Eloquentia* throughout this text, and especially at points of marked transition or emphasis, the text demands that we give this passage a second look. Certainly the image of a young woman who can retain her chastity only under the protection of an older man brings with it at least implicitly erotic undertones.[72] Unlike Herakles' eroticized "choice" between *Eudaimonia/Kakia* and *Arete*, though, Cicero and his interlocutors – indeed, the whole reading audience of *Brutus* – are imagined in terms that are paternalistic rather than romantic. The literary allies of *Brutus* are forged here as the mature and domestic protectors (*tutores*) of their young Muse, placed in opposition to her eager, if utterly inept and unworthy, lovers. What exactly does Cicero intend in this highly gendered image of a newly domesticated *Eloquentia*? What can it mean to keep this enticing figure locked within the home, shielded by the noble tutelage of her oratorical protectors? What, finally, are we to make of this startling suggestion that the place for public speech must now be the private home?

To get at these answers, we must reconsider the social and literary program of *Brutus* within the context of Cicero's personal and political fortunes in 46. As noted earlier, *Brutus* has been recognized as an early attempt by the orator to reinsert his voice into the intellectual consciousness of the Republic. If *Eloquentia* has fallen silent at the beginning of the dialogue, it is Cicero who now speaks on her behalf. In his personification of *Eloquentia*, Cicero has provided her with both a voice and a venue: he has done for her precisely what she has done for orators in the past.

This final personification encodes a meticulous, if brilliantly simple, blueprint for Cicero's planned textual, social, and political strategy. Cicero, a man who *retreated* perforce from the oral *negotium* of the forum into the textual *otium* of the home, creates in *Brutus* (his first "named" dialogue and the first of those completed in his lifetime to contain living Roman interlocutors) the image of a young girl *rescued* from the forum, brought within the "private home," and placed under the protection – and until the forum should be redeemed, it will be a textual protection – of the men of the textual world. In this image, we have a striking allegory for his own shift of activity and influence from the long-established *corona* of the forum to the relatively untested convivial *theatrum* of elite textual circulation – that Society of Patrons, in other words, for which *Brutus,* and indeed all subsequent *technica*, are intended. Cicero would not have turned his back

---

[72] As Hallett 1984: 138 has noted, there is often sexual tension in the triad of a young woman, her father, and her suitor.

on public oratory with any relish, nor indeed do I think that he would have imagined, even in 46, that his absence from the Republican forum would be irreversible.[73] But just as the orator likened his own silence to that of Hortensius (*Hortensi uox exstincta fato su' est, nostra publica*, 96.328), he would similarly have understood his own fate as inexorably intertwined with that of his Muse. If *Eloquentia* was "born for the forum," the orator considers himself no less entitled to this birthright, and so in his imagined rehabilitation of her powers of speech, he must surely have in mind his concomitant redemption.

Should the literary implications of a "domesticated *Eloquentia*" remain unclear, *Brutus* embodies the answer. Cicero frequently refers to rhetorical writing – the newly penned dialogue no less than the reworked *oratio* – as a distinctly *domesticus*, as opposed to *forensis*, *labor* (cf. *Brut.* 24.92). In his final image of *Eloquentia* made "domestic," Cicero interweaves the spheres of cultural and textual practice and relies upon his reading audience to recognize the implications. In Cicero's Rome (as in virtually all geographical and temporal intersections in the span of classical antiquity), a young woman's worth – her economic potential – resided preeminently in her use, by her father, as an object of marital exchange. An unmarried daughter was kept within the home and away from unacceptable suitors not that she might be eternally "hoarded" by her *pater familias* (indeed, such hoarding would constitute a destruction of exchange value), but precisely so that she could be "married off" in a match that would cement the bonds between the adult male exchange partners and their respective houses.

The personification and "domestication" of *Eloquentia* within *Brutus* seems to "recreate" her as a definitively, and even primarily, textual being – and to a certain extent it does. But Cicero knew better than anyone else that *eloquentia* had never been the possession of orators alone, but rather had always been the province of both orators and – the ongoing harangue of his *technica* – poets. *Eloquentia* had always been at least partially textual because it is only in the text that *eloquentia* can be appreciated with the learning and sophistication she demands. So when Cicero suggests that *Eloquentia* will now "reside in the home" of those who write, he knows of course that she has long resided in the homes of poets. When he suggests that she is to be traded between men "in marriage" and by means of precisely those dedicated texts that are written for, and circulated throughout, the

---

[73] Though essentially, of course, it was. The circumstances of the *Caesarianae* (46–45) were hardly those of the Republican forum; the *Antonianae* (or "*Philippics*") similarly reflect an anxious awareness that the orator has found himself playing a dangerous political game – the rules of which have suddenly, and ominously, changed. This sentiment is echoed in the character of Aper in Tacitus' *Dialogus*.

textual community of the late Republic – the *bellum theatrum*; the convivial gatherings of the Society of Patrons – he knows that this is precisely how she has been circulated, by means of poetic dedications, for decades. *Eloquentia* always lived in the home of the textual producers of the late Republic: when Cicero describes her domestication and textualization, her turn from the forum and retreat into the home, he is really describing his own.

It is *Eloquentia*, via Cicero's ongoing program of personifying and textualizing the voices of Rome's past, that will provide a lasting textual voice to those who have found themselves prematurely silenced by the Republic:

Equidem etsi doleo me in uitam paulo serius tamquam in uiam ingressum, priusquam confectum iter sit, in hanc rei publicae noctem incidisse, tamen ea consolatione sustentor quam tu mihi, Brute, adhibuisti tuis suauissimis litteris, quibus me forti animo esse oportere censebas, quod ea gessissem, quae de me etiam me tacente ipsa loquerentur uiuerentque mortuo . . . (*Brut.* 96. 330)

And although I have cause to grieve, since I set out on the path of my life so late that night has fallen upon this Republic before my journey has come to a close, I am nevertheless sustained by the consolation you offered me in that most pleasing treatise,[74] Brutus, in which you advised me to be stout of heart, since I have accomplished such things as will both speak of me when I am silent, and will live on, after I have died . . .

In the beginning of *Brutus*, Cicero portrayed an *Eloquentia* who had begun to threaten both her parents' reputation and society's accepted norms of behavior. In the final sections of the dialogue, the orator rewrites a "public" *Eloquentia* – the young woman who had corrupted herself with Eastern luxury – into a "private" *adulta uirgo*: an object of desire to those who perceive her, a coin of cultural value for the domestic protectors within whose domain she will reside until the forum be made safe once again. Thus, by styling *Eloquentia* a *uirgo* and the members of his intended literary circle noble *patres familias*, Cicero has forged a scheme of isonomic exchange in which textual embodiments of eloquence are to be traded back and forth in the manner of young women betrothed (*despondere*[75]) in

---

[74] This is a reference to Brutus' own "epistolary" treatise *de Virtute*, undoubtedly dedicated to Cicero and mentioned first at *Brut.* 3.11–12; cf. Douglas 1966: x–xii.

[75] Cicero uses *despondere* to describe the process of textual exchange or transfer on at least two occasions. At *Ep. Att.* 13.12, he discusses the "promising" of *de Finibus* in precisely such terms, as he searches frantically for a suitable text to dedicate to Varro: *nunc illam περὶ τελῶν σύνταξιν sane mihi probatam Bruto, ut tibi placuit, despondimus, idque tu eum non nolle mihi scripsisti.* At *Ep. Att.* 1.10.4, he writes: *bibliothecam tuam caue cuiquam despondeas, quamuis acrem amatorem inueneris.* Although the verb *despondere* can mean "pledge" or "dedicate," it also commonly means betroth, a meaning Cicero intends at least six of the twelve times he uses the verb: *Clu.* 179: *despondit ei filiam suam; de Orat.* 1.61.239: *quod Crassi filiam Caio filio suo despondisset; Ep. Fam.* 8.7.2: *Cornificius*

the self-interested agreements of their fathers. And if texts are exchanged in terms of elite marriage agreements, the progeny of these exchanges – the infinitely self-replicating "intellectual offspring"[76] of the union – will be subsequently promised, and exchanged, literary works. In a cleverly "personifying" maneuver that would find powerful textual resonance with the increasingly fraught poetic production of the Principate – we need think only of Ovid's frequent reference to his poems as variously behaved "children" in his works from exile[77] – the orator has created a remarkably domestic solution to an inherently political problem.

Brutus continues to be a text – and a tale – valuable to scholars for the wealth of information it provides on the oratorical, literary and, to a certain extent, political history of Republican Rome, but its aims can be read as no more strongly historical than they are painstakingly textual. *Brutus* is, in the end, a brilliant *apologia* for its own writing. So too is it an *apologia* for Cicero's textual future, and for the numerous dedicated and exchanged dialogues in which he would continue, until his death, to reproduce his voice. As such, it provides us with an almost disturbingly lucid snapshot of the conflicts that arise between political system and rhetorical practice and one man's distinctly textual response to his own imminent fate. *Brutus* begins with the image of an oratorical world that is out of the orator's control. By the end of the dialogue, Cicero has translated a dangerously destabilized Republican oratory into the terms of private, authoritative, and definitively controllable social exchange. By refiguring the voice of the Republic in the body of the orphaned daughter, he has created a novel way of containing his language, status, and character within a medium that can transcend the bounds of space and time. For just as Cicero has transformed Eloquence into his textual child, so too he has transformed himself into a

---

adulescens Orestillae filiam sibi despondit; *Ep. Att.* 1.3.3: *Tulliolam C. Pisoni L. F. Frugi despondimus*; *Ep. Frat.* 2.6.1: *dederam ad te litteras antea quibus erat scriptum Tulliam nostram Crassipedi . . . esse desponsam.*

[76] The notion of literary texts as the intellectual offspring of their "authorial parents" is not unique to Cicero or the Republic. Although it does not appear in the Republic prior to Cicero's usage (though as is often the case this may be a matter of extant sources), I would not be surprised if he found the inspiration for *Eloquentia* as his "intellectual child" in the Greek sources with which he was certainly familiar. The text-as-offspring formulation appears several times, if with nothing approaching even middling personification, in Plato (cf. *Phaed.* 257b; 274e; 275a; 276e–277a; 278ab; *Rep.* 330c; 534d; 599b–600b; *Symp.* 177d; 209a–e; *Tht.* 164e) and twice in Aristophanes (*Neph.* 137; *Batrakh.* 1059); on intellectual offspring in *Phaedrus*, see further Derrida 1981: 76–84; on writing as a form of reproduction, see Steiner 1994: 110–116 (I am indebted to Ruby Blondell for all of these references). Svenbro 1993: 147 figures the Sapphic poem similarly: "once [the poems] became written objects, they could circulate 'to the right and to the left,' separated from their 'mother.'"

[77] On the theme of "parents and children" in Ovid's exile poetry, see especially Davisson 1984.

new and powerful type of literary patriarch, and the whole of the Republic into the sort of *librorum municipium* that is recognizable yet today.

I suggested above that Cicero's dialogues, and indeed his dialogic program as a whole, may be profitably viewed as engaging in repeated acts of textual *conformatio*; they engage in the invocation of deceased or absent individuals for the purpose of heightening Cicero's rhetoric and swaying his audience – for Cicero, now, it is a reading audience alone – to his favor. Indeed, the materializing and personifying function of the dialogues, and especially the means through which they are imagined both to become and to house those individuals whose voices they remake for display, form the core of my next planned project with these texts. The end of one story is rarely the best place to start in on another (a dictum almost never followed by screenwriters) and yet, perhaps because it is natural for one story to lead to the next – as de Bury noted, *faciendi plures libros nullus est finis*; screenwriters call this the "sequel" – it will be useful here, I think, to say a few words about how I think this practice of *conformatio* may be operating in the dialogues, and why further investigation into this practice will help our understanding of what "happens" to the text, as object, as it moves out of the Society of Patrons I have argued for in the late Republic, and into the vibrant textual worlds of the Principate and early Empire.

"Speaking volumes" is of course also the title of Alessandro Barchiesi's collection of excellent articles on narrative and intertextuality in Ovid and other Imperial poets.[78] The title of the volume, Barchiesi tells us, is based on the somewhat startling and "prophetic image" (p. 8) of *Tristia* 1.1.105–120, in which the collection of Ovid's own books are personified as communicating *with each other* inside of his bookcases. As Barchiesi notes in his discussion of this poem, "new texts reread their predecessors" (p. 27), and I want to suggest that this is a point as useful for understanding Ovid as it is, I think, for understanding Catullus and Cicero. It is also a point that speaks to the process of textual publication from the late Republic to the modern academy, and one that, in its claim that texts must speak "to each other" across not just distance but time – by means of direct quotation,[79] cryptic echo, or anything in between – gets at the heart of what I think

---

[78] Barchiesi 2001.   [79] Thus my "sampling" of Barchiesi's book title at the head of this section.

Cicero is doing when he sets in motion a textual program of "talking texts."

The forensic practice of *conformatio* was one in which an orator would conjure up a deceased Roman – or an inanimate patriotism – and return to that Roman his voice – or give to the country hers – in a display of trans-temporal, or trans-substantial, ventriloquism. In remaking the voices of the distant past according to the political exigencies of the immediate present, the orator appears to be allowing the past to speak even as he is aggressively speaking for, and thus actively remaking, the past. The *conformatio* I see at work in the dialogues consists of the purely textual mimesis of absent or deceased individuals engaged in dialogue (sometimes the living and the dead meet in the text, ripping through the boundaries of life and death) and presented before the textual, rather than forensic, *corona* of readers. There is a functional and formal difference between *conformatio* that begins in speech and only later moves to text, and *conformatio* that was created for, and resides in, text alone. But the textual *conformationes* with which Cicero spends his final years constitute a reworking of Rome's past that trumps any he had endeavored in the forum. The dialogues are texts that are set in the past but dedicated to the future; they are in dialogue with their predecessors as much as they invite others into dialogue. Indeed, almost the only place Cicero's dialogues do not exist, and the only place to which they do not directly speak – the place they seem to avoid, the sight from which they must turn their heads – is in Rome's fragile, dangerous, and depressing present in the middle years of the first century BCE. In skirting the present in order to bind themselves to the past and the future, Cicero's *conformationes* – his dialogues – become "speaking volumes" that, because they are in eternal dialogue with the past, are able to continue to speak to Rome's future.

It is clear from the dialogues themselves that Cicero envisioned the forensic and textual *conformatio* to overlap in terms of both form and function. In the third book of *de Oratore* he describes the process of *conformatio* (he does not use the term) as the "impersonation of *personae*" (*personarum ficta inductio, de Orat.* 3.53.205). In this passage, it is clear that what Cicero has in mind is the activity of the "forum of bricks." Some ten years later, however, and in the opening sections of one of his last dialogues and indeed one of the most theatrical of his historical "prose dramas," Cicero introduces his decision to do away with *inquam* and *inquit* with the explanation that he wanted to "lead his characters" into the dialogue "speaking for themselves" in terms that echo his earlier description of the forensic practice:

Quasi enim ipsos induxi loquentis, ne inquam et inquit saepius interponeretur atque ut tamquam a praesentibus coram haberi sermo uideretur. (*Lael.* 1.3)

For I have, as it were, led out these speaking for themselves, so that I can avoid the excessively frequent interruptions of "I said" and "he said," and so that they might seem to be present and speaking in person.

In the passages that immediately follow Cicero's clear explanation of why he has decided to take his textual *conformationes* to a new level, he refers to his *Cato*, and *his* Cato, in similar terms (*sed ut in Catone maiore . . . Catonem induxi senem disputantem, Lael.* 1.4). In the final years of Cicero's career, and life, he turned not merely to the text, but to his textual *Cato* – perhaps the longest and most textually productive *conformatio* of them all – as well as to his textual *Brutus, Laelius, Catulus, Lucullus, Hortensius,* and *Varro* (it is worth noting again that although *de Officiis* was not a dialogue, Cicero personifies the books *tamquam hospites* when he dedicates them to his son). At the start of *de Fato*, the *conformatio* of Hirtius informs Cicero that he is used to "hearing" Cicero when he reads what he has written (*audiam te disputantem, ut ea lego qua scripsisti*, 1.4): the voice of the dialogue, "Hirtius" assures us, is a voice that speaks. Immediately thereafter, and with a jolly "let's sit down!" (*consediamus hic*) – an invitation that echoes the initiation of Cicero's first *conformatio*, "Crassus, why don't we pretend we are Socrates?" (*cur non imitamur, Crasse, Socratem?, de Orat.* 1.7.29), and one that comes to mark, in the dialogues, an entry into the dialogic textual world – "Hirtius" signals that he is ready to "become" the sort of *conformatio* he has only read about. He is ready to enter into, and to be remade as, text.

I think it is likely that the Society of Patrons I have hoped to uncover and, to a certain extent, to reconstruct in this study may have consisted, in large part, of the collection of textual *conformationes* created in, and housed by, the textual dedications upon which I have focused. When Cicero turned from the forum, he did not merely turn toward the text, nor merely toward the world of textual dedication: in professing that the Muse of oratory is also the Muse of poetry, and indeed that she always had been, Cicero transformed the oral forum into the textual villa, and subsequently populated these villas with the most powerful and reliable members of the intellectual world with which he was in dialogue. Catullus' dedicated texts, and especially his dedicated *conformationes*, engage in a recreation of the world of textual production – not perhaps in terms of the villa, but very frequently in terms of the private home – as vividly as do those of Cicero. And if he is less concerned with using his texts to negotiate relations that lay outside his textual world, it is likely because he was one of the few textually productive men of this period who may not have understood – who could, indeed, afford not to understand – everything that Cicero stood to lose. Catullus and Cicero use textual production as a means of shifting their textual legacy into the future. In writing and dedicating texts in such a way as to invite both present and future generations of writers into an ongoing cycle of discourse – be it poetic or rhetorical – our authors have allowed their Society of Patrons, now a Society of Books, to speak volumes.

Epilogue

In examining the terminological, rhetorical, and sociopractical intersections between Catullus and Cicero, we have been able to uncover a bit more of the textual story of the late Republic. And yet, mapping the textual practices of the late Republic onto the ongoing continuum of ancient textual culture and the "textualization" of culture as a whole, leaves us with one further question: *what happened next?*

There is of course no monolithic answer to such a monolithic question. What happened to the text and the textual world in later periods? To a certain extent I would respond that the Principate of Augustus, and the resultant blooming of textual culture in the Principate and early Empire, is what "happened" to the text and the textual community that fostered it. As isonomic textual prestation seems to have all but disappeared in this later period – it might indeed be argued that under the social and political structure of the Principate textual isonomy had become well-nigh impossible – there arose an immensely productive system of the sort of hierarchically organized literary patronage investigated by White and others. Yet as much as the textual efflorescence of the Principate and Empire may seem to have little in common with the practices of the earlier periods, the disjuncture between these two periods is not so great. Indeed, the Augustan textual world has its roots firmly planted in the soil of the Republic, and the points of contact and lines of continuity suggested in this study will, I think, be useful for ongoing investigations into these later periods.

What we have seen in this study is that when texts in the late Republic are dedicated – when they move into and partake of a textual world – they tend to talk about themselves "as texts," and to underline, especially in their dedications and subject matter, the textuality in which they are invested. When we look for contact and continuity between the late Republic and early Empire, it is perhaps not surprising to see that although the social and political conditions operative in the former period differ radically from those in the latter, the "textual talk," and to a certain degree the textual form, of later texts align themselves fairly closely to those of the former. Indeed, the three most noteworthy points of continuity are those three that relate most precisely to the three parts of this study – terminology, social function, and textual materialism – and so it will be good to end things here by reviewing how and to what degree the textual habits of the late Republic continue into periods that follow.

As noted throughout Part I, of the terminological markers at which Catullus and Cicero intersect, *otium* and *munus* function as especially important textually linked terms in the Principate and Empire. Although *otium* has, in the later period, become disjoined from its sense of autonomous time – the plural is used to refer to those hours a patron's favor *may* allow a poet to write (to a certain degree, the plural *otia* seems to stand in for the *carmina* produced in that period) – it continues to be used as the key term designating the most socially appropriate "time to write." The late Republican textual sense of *munus*, as argued in Chapter 2, adheres least to the "textual talk" of the later periods (although note Mart. *Ep.* 3.2). This rupture in argot may inform our understanding of how the expectations of the Roman textual world shifted as they moved from an isonomic structure to an almost exclusively hierarchical one. If *munus*, in later periods, ceases to be applied to isonomically exchanged texts, we must wonder whether the worlds of the Principate and early Empire considered isonomic textual exchange a thing of the distant (and quickly becoming "Golden") past. *Libellus*, finally, becomes an exceptionally important textual term in a world in which there was a great deal of textual dedication and publication. Both Pliny and Martial use *libellus* with great frequency (and both emphasize the physicality of the term, cf. Mart. *Ep.* 6.60 and Pliny *Ep.* 6.7); their usages are completely in line with the "published treatise sent into the world" sense of the term, and the term appears almost exclusively in contexts in which it is the real or imagined "motion" of a given or received text that is at question.

The textualization of display continues on, to some degree: Horace and Vergil come to mind especially, but so too Pliny in the letters and Tacitus in *Dialogus* – the text on which this text shall end. What we see more frequently than the mere textualization of display are the ways in which textual dedications of later periods view the dedicated text as a valuable means by which to negotiate social relationships outside of the purely textual world. As we saw above, Catullus seemed to restrict his use of the dedicated text to the interests and negotiations of the textual world, but even he recognized that the text had the ability to move out of the sphere of textual interactions and "do things" in the world at large. Of our two late Republican authors, however, it was Cicero who exploited this facet of the dedicated text to the greatest effect: his recognition that the dedicated text was a powerful tool in the negotiation of social relationships is one that seems to have proven especially useful for periods in which the textual voice was the only thing one had. Yet it seems likely that the ultimate legacy of Cicero's dialogic project turned out to be other than he may have imagined, for as much as the work of later dialogists – Varro, Seneca, and Tacitus – attests to a continued "dialogue" with Cicero's dedicated *technica*, Cicero's textual and literary legacy came to be realized predominately in the epistolary compositions of the early Empire to the early Christian periods, when it was the letter, rather than the dialogue, that was seen to most effectively negotiate the divide between privacy and publication.[1]

If the form of late Republican textual materialism fails to resonate strongly with the textual cultures of the later periods, the drive of textual materialism – the fetishization of the text and the personification of dedicated or "published" poems and books – is maintained and expanded. From Ovid's many and naughty poetic offspring[2] running about the *urbs* and chattering to each other on their bookshelves, to Martial's self-identification of self with textual body (*me manus omnis habet*, *Ep.* 6.60) and creation of two textual "collections" in which each poem claims to be precisely something other than it is (the varied distichs of the *Xenia* and *Apophoreta*),[3] to Pliny's remark that, in his absence, his wife places his *libelli* in the imprint he has left on the couch beside her (*Ep.* 6.7), the textual materialization of Catullus and Cicero is the characteristic of their work that would prove most important to a world in which the dedicated text became one of the sole means of communicating across spatial and social divide.

Both Catullus and Cicero wrote for the future. Each man wanted his books – his *libelli* – to last for more than one generation, and to our great pleasure each man got his wish. But by way of closing my thoughts on the late Republic and opening, I hope, some thoughts on the years that would follow, I want to take a moment to focus on Cicero's fears, and predictions, for those future years. I feel that if Cicero could have looked back on the Republic from the first century CE, he would have claimed not that his

---

[1] I am thinking of course mainly of Seneca and Pliny, although cf. too I. Frontinus Balbus' dedicated, and exceedingly "Ciceronian," *Expositio et Ratio Omnium Formarum* and the early Christian epistolographers. On later Roman declamation and its relationship to earlier practice, see, e.g., Bloomer 2007.

[2] On Ovid's "naughty offspring," especially as depicted in *Tristia*, cf. Davisson 1984.

[3] On this, cf. Stroup 2006.

voice died with the death of the Republic (the claim made in *Brutus* as a signal of his entry into the textual realm), but that the voice of the Republic died at the moment he did. Such a claim would have fit perfectly with the Ciceronian hyperbole to which we are accustomed, but in a sense I think our "Imperial Cicero" would have been right, at least according to men of his political interest and engagement. *Non solum Eloquentia obmutuit sed etiam Res Publica.*

Indeed, I think this is precisely the message of Tacitus' *Dialogus*, the only Imperial text to engage actively with Cicero's "speaking volumes," the only one that dares accept Cicero's ongoing offer to engage in dialogue with both past and future, and so a good place to start if we are to consider "what happened next," and how it came to happen. *Dialogus*, a dialogue especially in dialogue with *Brutus*, requires its reader to recognize the discourse of sameness and difference it establishes with that text. *Dialogus* invokes *Brutus* in its very first section, with a haunting verbal echo of the topic of the earlier dialogue (*deserta et laude eloquentiae orbata*, 1.1; cf. *Brut.* 96.330). Indeed, Cicero's personification of *Eloquentia* runs throughout *Dialogus*, but instead of speaking hopefully of an *Eloquentia* that can be preserved to speak the future, the *Eloquentia* of Tacitus sinks more and more deeply into a broody textual silence. First, the *persona* of Messalla invokes *Brutus* by name, and informs his interlocutors that in the final sections of the dialogue Cicero relays the story of "his *eloquentia*'s" education (*suae eloquentiae uelut quandam educationem refert*, 30.3). A few sections later, we learn that the orators of the Empire have "worn eloquence down" and expelled her from her kingdom; she who was once the *domina* of all the arts is now *circumcisa et amputata sine apparatu sine honore* (32.4). The final personification of *eloquentia* in *Dialogus* is the darkest, and bitterest, of all:

> Sed est magna illa et notabilis eloquentia alumna licentiae, quam stulti libertatem uocant, comes seditionum, effrenati populi incitamentum, sine obsequio, sine seueritate, contumax temeraria arrogans, quae in bene constitutis ciuitatibus non oritur. (*Dial.* 40.2)

> But the great and famed eloquence [of the Republic] is the foster child of license, which fools called freedom: the friend of sedition, the stimulant of a people out of control, with no sense of obedience or subjection, a haughty, reckless, and arrogant thing that does not arise in well-ordered states.

However, as much as *Dialogus* is concerned with what has become of eloquence – and what has become of *Eloquentia* – it is a text that speaks to what has become of the dialogue, and what has become of Cicero, and how we are to triangulate the relationship of man, voice, and text. The dialogue portions of *Brutus* began, we remember, with Atticus and Brutus coming to Cicero's Palatine home and finding Cicero strolling in his outdoor garden. The dialogic portions of *Dialogus* begin with the interlocutors coming upon Maternus – the orator who, like Cicero, has turned his back on the forum and dedicated himself to the writing of politically interested texts – sitting in the inner reaches of his home and holding in his hands a book – quite tellingly, his *Cato* – which he had recited in public the day before.

That *Dialogus* begins not with speech so much as with a book can tell us much about what became of the book in the Principate and early Empire. The presence of Maternus' *Cato*, a historical tragedy that engaged sufficiently with political criticism to have been criticized for precisely that, speaks meaningfully to the textualization of the political voice of the Republic. Maternus' "personified" *Cato* had endeavored to be a text that "did things" in the world at large; it is one that is meant to speak, and speak loudly, and if his Cato doesn't say it, Maternus grumbles, his Thyestes will (*quod si qua omisit Cato, sequenti recitatione Thyestes dicet*, 3.3). But perhaps precisely because his *Cato* is not a dialogue, its political critique, and political voice, has faltered and failed.

Indeed, the "nameless" *Dialogus* is a strangely silent text. Cicero's dialogues always located themselves in the continuum of past, and especially future, discussions and publications. The only "past" in *Dialogus*, however, is that of an increasingly distant Republic (Aper, indeed, dates the "new period" of oratory *ab interitu Ciceronis*, 17.3), and we are haunted throughout by the constantly and consistently silent Tacitus; the man who refused, in his life, to publish a single of his *orationes* contributes not a single word to a dialogue at which he was present. And when at the close of the dialogue a request is made for future discussions, this request is met merely with laughter – from everyone but Tacitus, who, silent until the end, waits until they have finished, and then departs with the group (*cum arrisissent, discessimus*, 42.2). His voice, we suspect, we must provide ourselves.

What "Society of Patrons"? A prosopography of the players

Although the focus of this study lies almost entirely on the dedicated and "dedication-minded" texts of Catullus and Cicero, it will be good to say a word about the scope of the broader Society in which these exchanges were taking place. In what follows I provide a brief survey of those individuals – first the "probable," then the "possible," and finally two likely influential forerunners – whom we might identify as participants in this Society, as suggested by our textual evidence from the Republic (this is especially the case for the "probable" participants) and that which would come later.

To attempt a concrete reconstruction of a textual Society that was by all evidence a highly plastic one – shaped and reshaped by artistic, social, and intellectual debates, inside jokes and real enmity, newly formed alliances and stiff competition (and thus not too foreign to the world of academia) – would be both artificial and misleading, and so is not my goal. The survey that follows is certainly not exhaustive, nor does it claim excessive detail in either its prosopography or bibliography. While many of the individuals included below are well-known figures from the Republic, little or nothing survives of their dedicated work, and our knowledge of titles and subject matter is often rather tenuous (the latter usually derived from the former). These individuals are included in this list – and indeed, I think it best to present this as a simple list, ordered alphabetically by cognomen (if known), with a brief notation of the scope of work or interesting intersections with other authors – for two reasons. The first is that no such list of a "writing patron class" has been produced previously (larger surveys of "Latin literature" distract from the overlaps), and it will be good to place this somewhat narrowly focused study with a clearer idea of the grand scale of the practice in which it must be contextualized. The second is that in bringing these individuals together, and in placing them – textually speaking – "side by side," we see the breakdown of imaginary boundaries of literary genre and social or political clique and the emergence of a larger Society of patronal-class writers who defined their texts in terms of function – the "cultural work" accomplished via dedicated literature – rather more than they did in terms of fashion – the aesthetic concerns with which each author engaged. As much as the late Republic witnessed a shift in the way the educated elite came to think about writing, it was more than anything else a time in which writing – poetry, history, philosophy, and letters – was something educated Romans simply *did*.[1]

As I am positing a relatively small community (large for Rome, that is, but small in a modern intellectual context) of learned individuals, I have proceeded tentatively along the path of both "inner nexus nomenclatorial shorthand" and, subsequently, Occam's razor. In short, and at the risk of aligning too closely the intellectual communities of the past with those of the present, I have assumed that members of a self-identifying "specialist" group will tend to refer to the most preeminent of its members by the briefest, and sometimes most hypocoristic, of names. In any casual conversation among a group of Latinists, for example, if the names Syme, Austin, or Winkler (with Pliny *Ep.* 5.3, I find it more tasteful not to include the names of the living – even if the parallel becomes a bit forced) are uttered within the context of classical scholarship but with nothing but surnames indicated, they are reasonably understood to refer to the most likely suspects at hand (Ronald, Roland, and John) rather than the least (Jennifer, Stone Cold Steve, and Henry). It is imperative that we keep in mind the rampant difficulties involved in untangling the messy web of Roman homonyms and the simple fact that much "specialist" group idiom of the late Republic will be entirely lost on us. In order to sketch in outline the likely breadth and scope of our late Republican group – the only goal of the section that follows – I have decided that when the context and readership of a text might be reasonably reconstructed or conjectured, we do not risk too much in identifying briefly or idiomatically named individuals on the basis of the most, rather than least, likely individuals of that name known from the period.

First, then, the list of individuals I consider certain – or at least highly "probable" – participants in a broadly defined Society of Patrons. Although we can reckon with some degree of likelihood that all of these men knew (or knew of) each other, we should suppose neither that they all necessarily (or at all times) liked each other, far less that any individual would have

---

[1] Quinn 1979: 2–3 notes the pervasiveness of writing and the variety of genre in the first century BCE.

dedicated texts to even a majority of others on the list – or to no others than those who appear here. I have included below only those individuals we can reasonably identify on the basis of the explicit literary evidence – the addressees and dedicatees of Catullus and Cicero, the frequent interlocutors of the latter, and claims made by later authors when the identification of the individual is unproblematic – and not those we might hypothesize as "possible" participants based on merely circumstantial evidence. In an effort to err on the side of caution, this list is a short one, but its membership is telling:

- *T. Pomponius Atticus* (110/109–32 BCE), dedicatee of Cicero (*Cato; Lael.; de Orat.*), recipient of numerous letters, and frequent interlocutor of the *technica*, who circulated both his histories (the most notable of which was the *Liber Annalis*) and his poetry (*Ep. Att.* 1.16.5), and seems to have dedicated to Cicero a *tractatio litterarum* (cf. *Brut.* 4.15) – a work I have come to suspect is not to be identified with the *Liber Annalis* but a rather more literarily oriented treatise from which Cicero gained inspiration. Friend of the obvious suspects, including Hortensius the orator (and possibly poet),[2] and a dedicatee of Varro Reatinus.

- *M. Iunius Brutus* (85–42 BCE), Cicero's most frequent dedicatee (*Orat.; Parad. Stoic.; de Fin.; TD; DND*), and recipient of numerous letters; Brutus was a "writing orator" who circulated both his *orationes* (Cic. *Brut.* 5.21) and his *carmina* (Tac. *Dial.* 21.6; Pliny *Ep.* 5.3),[3] and who dedicated his *de Virtute* to Cicero (cf. *TD* 5, *incip.*). Brutus and Varro are

---

[2] Note that at *Ep. Att.* 2.25.1, Cicero refers to a Hortalus who is a *familiaris* of Atticus; although John Morgan (via private correspondence) is of the opinion that this reference seals the identification of "Hortalus" as an individual from Reate and therefore not the orator Hortensius, the content of the letter does not make this certain.

[3] In the case of those not traditionally associated with a specific genre (most usually poetry), representative – though hardly exhaustive – citations are provided. Pliny *Ep.* 5.3, the "smoking gun" letter written to Titius Aristo and in defense of Pliny's own *uersiculi*, is especially useful in reconstructing the group of upper-class individuals who engaged in the writing of light verse. Part of this letter is worth citing in full: *An ego uerear – neminem uiuentium, ne quam in speciem adulationis incidam, nominabo –, sed ego uerear ne me non satis deceat, quod decuit M. Tullium, C. Caluum, Asinium Pollionem, M. Messalam, Q. Hortensium, M. Brutum, L. Sullam, Q. Catulum, Q. Scaeuolam, Seruium Sulpicium, Varronem, Torquatum, immo Torquatos, C. Memmium, Lentulum Gaetulicum, Annaeum Senecam et proxime Verginium Rufum et, si non sufficiunt exempla priuata, Diuum Iulium, Diuum Augustum, Diuum Neruam, Tiberium Caesarem?* Sherwin-White 1985: 317 offers an identification of these men, and rightly notes that the list "is confined to senators, mostly also distinguished for oratory." I agree for the most part with Sherwin-White's identifications, but as his list is both one that subscribes to a loose chronology and one of senatorial men who were known for writing prose – and so for whom verse composition would have been the more unexpected and noteworthy composition – I take Scaeuola not as the augur but as the tribune of 54 (so Blänsdorf 1995), and Messala as the consul of 53 and not the Augustan figure.

the only two of Cicero's dedicatees to have received a "named" dialogue (*Brutus* and *Varro*, the alternate title for the first book of *Acad. Post.*); all other "named" dialogues are named after individuals who have died. Brutus was similarly the dedicatee of Empylus' *Brutus*, an account of the death of Caesar (Plut. *Brut.* 2.4; *FgrH* 191 T1).[4]

- *C. Iulius Caesar* (100–44 BCE), a "writing orator" and author of *commentarii*, ἀποφθέγματα (Cic. *Ep. Fam.* 9.16), and poetry (Cic. *Ep. Fam.* 9.16; Pliny *Ep.* 5.3; Plut. *Caes.* 2.4; Suet. *Iul.* 56.7; Tac. *Dial.* 21.6). Caesar was an addressee of Catullus' *carmina* and the recipient of Cicero's *pro Ligario* (cf. *Ep. Att.* 13.19) and the second part of Varro's *Antiquitates* (47 BCE); he dedicated to Cicero his own *de Analogia* and was a friend of Brutus (we might suspect he reviewed the affective depth of this relationship late in life) and Cinna.

- *C. Licinius Calvus* (82 – ca. 47 BCE), a "writing orator" (cf. *Brut.* 82.283; Tac. *Dial.* 21.1), author of *commentarii* (Tac. *Dial.* 23.2), and respected poet (Hor. *Sat.* 1.10.17; Ovid *Trist.* 2.431–2; Pliny *Ep.* 5.3; Prop. *Carm.* 2.34.89; Sen. *Contr.* 7.4.7, etc.). He is a frequent and intimately represented dedicatee/addressee of Catullus (later grouped with this poet by Hor. *Sat.* 1.10.19), and was on apparently friendly terms with Atticus, Brutus, and Cicero.[5]

- *C. Valerius Catullus* (ca. 84–ca. 54 BCE), poet, who dedicates/addresses poems to, among others, Asinius Marrucinus[6] (brother of Asinius Pollio), C. Iulius Caesar, C. Licinius Calvus, M. Tullius Cicero, C. Helvius Cinna, "[H]ortalus" (possibly Hortensius), C. Memmius, Cornelius Nepos, L. Manlius Torquatus, and of course other lesser-known figures (Gallus, Egnatius, Veranius and Fabullus, Furius and Aurelius, a Caelius, etc.); shows acquaintance with, e.g., a Hortensius (if the figures of c. 65 and c. 95 are not the same man), Piso (usually identified as L. Calpurnius Piso Caesoninus, father of Calpurnia), Philodemus (if he is

---

[4] Quintilian mentions (apparently this) Empylus (*Inst. Orat.* 10.6.4) in a passage noting that Cicero wrote of Empylus' views of rhetoric (Empylus is identified by Plutarch as ῥήτωρ); but no trace of the name appears in Cicero's extant works. It is impossible to determine under which rubric Empylus made his dedication to Brutus. He was a Greek from Rhodes and, according to Plutarch, lived in the house of Brutus (a detail strongly indicative of hierarchical patronage, cf. Wiseman 1982: 32, though we should keep in mind the close relationship of Lucullus and Sulla); the *Inst. Orat.* passage groups him with Hortensius, which only problematizes the situation.

[5] Although some have suggested that Cicero's relationship with Calvus was one of enmity, cf. Frank 1919.

[6] With Thomson 1997: 12–13, and *contra* Kroll 1989 and others, I take Marrucinus as a proper name.

to be identified as the Socration of c. 47),[7] the orator Sestius, and other variously politically, philosophically, or literarily active men.[8]

- *M. Tullius Cicero* (106–43 BCE), orator and statesman, author of a large number of dedicated philosophical, political, and rhetorical treatises (the *technica*, dedicated variously to Atticus, Brutus, Q. Cicero, Varro, and others), epistolographer, and prolific poet (Gordian. 3.2; Plut. *Cic.* 2.3; Cic. *Ep. Frat.* 2.14; 2.16; 3.1, etc.; Sen. *Contr.* 3. *praef.* 8; Tac. *Dial.* 21.6; Mart. *Ep.* 2.89.3, Pliny *Ep.* 5.3). Cicero's poetic works included a *Marius*, a *Prognostica Aratea*, an *Alycones*, a *Limon*, light epigrams, the *de Consulatu Suo*, the *de Temporibus Suis* (dedicated to Lentulus; cf. *Ep. Fam.* 1.9.22), and numerous translations, of various lengths, of Greek poets (including passages from the *Iliad*, the *Odyssey*, and the dramas of Aeschylus, Sophocles, Euripides, Aristophanes, and Aratus) and philosophers.[9] Friend of and epistolary correspondent with, among the obvious suspects, Memmius (cf. *Ep. Fam.* 13.1, etc.) and Nepos (Macrob. *Sat.* 2.1.4; Suet. *Iul.* 55, etc.); an almost certain acquaintance of Cinna, Catullus,[10] and Calvus. Although we know something of the dedication of his poetry, and might extrapolate rather more, we have no dedicatory sections from the surviving fragments. Cicero certainly read Lucretius' poetry (*Ep. Frat.* 2.9.1), but there is no evidence that the two knew each other.
- *Q. Tullius Cicero* (102–43 BCE), brother of the orator, author of tragedies and annalistic works (Cic. *Ep. Att.* 2.16.4; *Ep. Frat.* 2.16.3; 3.1.13; 3.5.7; 3.7.6; Auson. *Ecl.* 25), frequent dedicatee of Cicero's *technica*, and frequent interlocutor in same. Although it is difficult to determine to what extent Quintus participated in this group, both Atticus' apparent commentary on his poetry and "Quintus's" off-hand comment at *de Leg.* 1.2 (*ut ait Scaeuola de fratris mei Mario*, an apparent reference to the tribune

---

7 On this question, see Nappa 1998: 387 n. 6; Nappa cites further Bongi 1943; Dettmer 1986; and Marcovich 1982.
8 Catullus, Calvus, and Cinna (the former two coupled by Horace at *Sat.* 1.10.19) are the only three of this list for whom we have no direct evidence of non-poetic writing. As the *only* of these three who appears to have rejected – for the most part – direct engagement with the political life of the city in favor of a purely "poetic career," perhaps Catullus is to be compared most closely with Lucilius (with whom, as noted in the Introduction, he was later associated by the fourth-century CE grammarian Diomedes). On the topic of "literary career," cf. esp. Farrell 2002. Although I do not agree with every element of his formulation of the Roman "literary career," especially with respect to the role of hierarchical patronage, Farrell provides a useful discussion of what it meant to be a "literary professional" in Rome.
9 For the fragments, cf. among others Blänsdorf 1995.
10 Although the only evidence for the personal acquaintance of Cicero and Catullus is the latter's c. 49, both that poem and what we know of the extended social circles of these two make the argument against their acquaintance Claudian in its clumsiness.

of 54 and author of light verse, cf. Pliny *Ep.* 5.3) points to some level of inclusion in the inner circles of textual production and circulation.

- *C. Helvius Cinna* (first half of first century BCE), tribune of the plebs and poet (Gellius *NA* 19.9.7; Suet. *Gramm.* 18; Ovid *Trist.* 2.435; Quint. *Inst. Orat.* 10.4.4; Verg. *Ecl.* 9.35, etc.).[11] Cinna was known to be friend of Caesar (Suet. *Iul.* 85; Plut. *Brut.* 20; *Caes.* 68) and Catullus (cc. 10, 95, 113) and an admirer of P. Valerius Cato (Suet. *Gramm.* 11); it seems he was acquainted with Cicero, though we know little of their relationship. One of his surviving epigrams (11; cf. Blänsdorf 1995: 222), a poem dedicating a translation of Aratus (note that Cicero also wrote such a translation) and echoing an epigram of Callimachus, is so heavily imbued with the language and tone of the late Republican textual world (the *carmina* are also called *munera*, and are specified to be contained in a *libellus*) as to place his involvement in this world beyond all doubt.[12]

- *Q. Hortensius [Hortalus?]* (114–50 BCE), orator, poet, and writer of *annales*[13] (Gellius *NA* 19.9.7; Ovid *Trist.* 2.441–2; Pliny *Ep.* 5.3; Plut. *Luc.* 1.5; Quint. *Inst. Orat.* 8.3.35; Serv. Dan. *Verg. Aen.* 11.496; Varro *DLL* 8.14; 10.78); Hortensius was an interlocutor – with Catulus, Lucullus, and Cicero – in Cicero's *Hortensius* (published ca. 45/44, with a dramatic date of ca. 65–60),[14] a dialogue I suspect was dedicated to Atticus. Hortensius similarly appears as an interlocutor in the third book

[11] With Wiseman 1974a: 44–58, I feel it certain that the tribune and poet are to be identified.

[12] On this epigram and its relationship with Catullus 1, see Flores 1976.

[13] The solid identification of the orator with either "[H?]ortalus" in c. 65 or "Hortensius" in c. 95 remains impossible. On stylistic grounds, I find the identification of the [H]ortalus of c. 65 and the Hortensius of c. 95 with the orator Hortensius both attractive and plausible; my approach to c. 65 proceeds, with prosopographical caveats in mind, from this angle. The note at Serv. Dan. *Verg. Aen.* 11.496, in which we are told that Hortensius' poetic preference for the archaic use of the singular *ceruix* over the plural *ceruices* influenced Cicero's choice of *ceruicula* should point to identification with the father. Morgan (again, via private correspondence) is of the opinion that c. 65 is addressed to one Marcius Hortalus (perhaps of Reate, son of Atticus' *familiaris* [*Ep. Att.* 2.25.1], and father of the *nobilis iuuenis* of Tac. *Ann.* 2.37.1), and that Pliny *Ep.* 5.3 refers to the lesser-known son of the orator, as does Ovid *Trist.* 2.441 ff. Morgan's arguments are well documented and interesting, and he makes many excellent points; as this is a study concerned with intra-class exchanges rather than intra-generation ones, however, the question of "father or son (or other)" is peripheral to my overarching argument.

[14] On the fragments of the dialogue, see both Plasberg 1892 and the review of Plasberg in Purser 1892. As with many of Cicero's dialogues, and especially the very late ones, *Hortensius* appears to have contained discussions of various sorts of literary activity (the character of Catulus covers poetry while Lucullus covers history) and would likely have included a defense of engaging in such activity in Latin. As the dialogue was probably composed during the orator's stay with Atticus in Nomentum (cf. Purser 1892: 448), Atticus is a credible choice for dedicatee. It is an interesting detail of this dialogue that Cicero would have been the only living of the interlocutors at the time of composition: Catulus had died in 82, and Lucullus in 56. To this, compare the *Academica Priora* of 45 – the first book of which had been named the *Catulus* and the second the *Lucullus* – which shares many characteristics with the *Hortensius*.

of Varro's *DRR*, and he was close friend also of Atticus (Nepos *Att.* 5.4). If this character is to be linked with the cognomen Hortalus, then he – or perhaps his son, about whom little is known – likely will have been the dedicatee of Cat. 65 and 66; the name "Hortensius" appears at c. 95.

• *L. Lucceius*, orator and writer of histories. Cicero approached Luccieus in 56 with the request that the latter write an history of his consulship, most specifically his role in exposing the Catilinarian conspiracy (*Ep. Fam.* 5.12); Lucceius agreed to the task, but never fulfilled his promise.

• *C. Memmius*, tribune of 66 (d. ca. 49 BCE), orator, and poet (Gellius *NA* 19.9.7; Pliny *Ep.* 5.3; Ovid *Trist.* 2.433, 439–40); Memmius, identified in Suetonius (*Gramm.* 14) as a patron (along with Cn. Pompeius) of Curtius Nicia, is the addressee / dedicatee of Lucretius' *de Rerum Natura* (and so is possibly to be identified as the latter's patron, though cf. the discussion of this in the Introduction) and an addressee of Catullus. Known for his interests in literature (Cic. *Brut.* 70.247) and rather loose character, Memmius is also one of Cicero's correspondents (*Ep. Fam.* 13.1–3), though at frequent odds with the Luculli.

• *Cornelius Nepos* (100–24 BCE), prose author (*Chronica, Exempla, Lives*, a work on geography, *de Viris Illustribus*, and a *libellus* in which he compared degrees of literary polish and learning; cf. Suet. *Gramm.* 4) and poet (Pliny *Ep.* 5.3); dedicatee of Catullus 1 (and possibly, though not certainly, of c. 102). Nepos is one of Cicero's correspondents (Macr. *Sat.* 2.1.14; Suet. *Iul.* 55) and surely a close friend of Atticus, at whose urging he wrote an expanded account of Cato's life and manners (cf. *Cato* 3: *huius de uita et moribus plura in eo libro persecuti sumus, quem separatim de eo fecimus rogatu T. Pomponii Attici*) and to whom I think it likely – based on the above reference to Atticus' "request" for the writing – his second *Cato* was dedicated.

• *L. Manlius Torquatus*, perhaps both the father, b. ca. 110 BCE and praetor ca. 69/68, and the son, b. ca. 90/89 BCE and praetor 50/49. The elder was a schoolmate of Atticus (Nepos *Atticus* 1) and the younger an intimate of Brutus (Cic. *Brut.* 76.266); both are referred to as writers of light verse at Pliny *Ep.* 5.3. While both are praised in Cicero's *Brutus* (*Brut.* 68.239 and 76.265), it is the younger Torquatus who is given rather more notice as a politically inclined and literarily learned "writing orator" (*Brut.* 76.265). It is probably the elder Torquatus who is our interlocutor in *de Finibus* (and likely the post-mortem dedicatee of the first book of that work, which was originally named for him, cf. *Ep. Att.* 13.5), if merely because C. Triarius and the younger Torquatus were coeval (*Brut.* 76.265) while the Triarius of *de Finibus* is specified as an *adulescens* in contrast to the elder Torquatus. With Thomson 1997: 348, I feel it is likely the younger Torquatus who is intended at Catullus 61 (ll. 16, 209, 215), and who may similarly be the Manlius – if there is a Manlius – of c. 68a.11.[15] We may say with some certainty that both men were highly literary in their interests and activities, both wrote poetry, and both were the addressees or dedicatees of the texts of others.

- *M. Terentius Varro*, of Reate (116–27 BCE), exceedingly prolific author of prose treatises, Menippean satires, tragedies, and various volumes of poetry (Cic. *Acad. Post.* 1.3; Quint. *Inst. Orat.* 1.4.4; Pliny *Ep.* 5.3;[16] Ovid *Trist.* 2.440–1). In addition to *de Re Rustica* (ca. 37 BCE) – which appears to have had three separate dedicatees, as noted in the Introduction, and in which Atticus was an interlocutor – Varro dedicated twenty books of *de Lingua Latina* (45–43) to Cicero, *Antiquitates* (47) to Caesar, *Ephemeris Naualis* (77) to Pompey, *de Vita Populi Romani* to Atticus and *de Antiquitate Litterarum* to Accius (date unknown, but perhaps mid 80s). Varro is the dedicatee of Cicero's *Academica Posteriora*, the first book of which was also called *Varro* (cf. *Ep. Fam.* 9.8) and is an interlocutor (with Atticus) in that dialogue.

Our list of "probable" participants in isonomic textual exchange, then, is as follows: Atticus, Brutus, Caesar, Calvus, Catullus, Marcus Cicero, Quintus Cicero, Cinna, Hortensius, Lucceius, Memmius, Nepos, Torquatus (or rather, the Torquati), and Varro. Each one of these men is known to have written poetry, and the overwhelming majority composed both verse and prose. Catullus is notable as the only one of the above to have eschewed both prose writing and involvement in the political sphere, but aside from him our group is representative of a wide spectrum of participation in political, social, intellectual, and literary spheres. These were men – all economically self-sufficient and many reasonably politically influential – who acted, thought, and wrote. If our list does not include all of the "powerful intellects of the Republic," it contains a representative sample of such

---

[15] The reading of the Codex Bononiensis MS is *Malli*; that of Biblioteca Riccardiana 606 is *Manli*; Lachmann, followed by Mynors and others, proposed *Mani*. Thomson 1997: 475 provides a reasonable defense of the reading of Bibl. Ricc., but the line is hopelessly problematic. Thus while I have noted the possibility of a Manlius (and so possibly Torquatus) at c. 68a.11, this reading is anything but certain.

[16] It is possible that Pliny *Ep.* 5.3 is referring to Varro Atacinus (so Blänsdorf 1995: 228). The whole point of Pliny's list, however, is that men known for somber prose were also avid writers of light verse; if the Varro of this list is Varro of Atax – a man known primarily for his poetry – his inclusion would be meaningless.

and argues for a vibrant patronal-class involvement in the production and circulation of texts.

The list of "possible" participants in a group of textual exchangers is rather longer. Although some of these individuals present us with just enough information to make them a puzzle, we may deal with many more briefly precisely because so little is known of who they were, or what they wrote, or whether or not they dedicated their texts or, if they did, under what rubric. At the risk of committing precisely the sort of *petitio principi* I sought to avoid in my exclusion of Lucretius from the core of this study, I have decided to be freer with my criteria for inclusion in this list, and so the individuals below appear either because the tone or language or context of the ancient reference to their person, or indeed what we know of the general character of their literary production, may be said to point to participation in the loosely sketched sphere of isonomic textual exchange suggested by the authors listed above. Surviving evidence renders it impossible to establish any of these individuals as "probable" members of this broader group, and such is not my argument. I feel certain both that some of the names given below were probably not considered active participants in the inner nexus of textual production and that I have chosen to omit, on the basis of my above criteria, some who might be included. It will nevertheless be good to get these names out on the table, if we are to hold in our mind both the likely scope of the group as a whole – that it surely contained many men beyond those fourteen listed above – and the very difficulty in trying to establish much when we move beyond our most solid evidence from the period.

• *Aurelius*, frequent addressee of, or character in, Catullus' *carmina* (cc. 11, 15, 16, 21); sometimes identified with Aurelius Cotta, but perhaps more likely one of the younger Aurelii mentioned by Cicero at *Ep. Fam.* 13.40.[17] With Thomson 1997: 235, I find it likely that both Aurelius and Furius (noted below) are to be included in the group of the poet's friends (the two are called *comites* at c. 11) if perhaps they represent a quarter of differing aesthetic orientation.[18] As I suggest in Part II, c. 16 points strongly to an engagement in some degree of literary reciprocity and criticism, and if we take the poet's use of *amores* as a term that collapses

---

[17] I thank John Morgan for this suggestion and reference.

[18] Wiseman 1982: 40 notes that the language with which the poet lampoons both Aurelius and Furius (the two are paired at cc. 11 and 16) is economic in tone and might suggest that these two belong to a social class rather beneath that of the poet (cf. esp. c. 21, on Aurelius, and c. 23, on Furius). As I argue in Part II, however, Catullus often uses accusations of economic interest or motive as a means of criticizing acts of poetic or social performance.

"real" affection with the erotic or affective verses that celebrate it,[19] the same might be said for cc. 15 and 21.

- *Furius Bibaculus*, of Cremona (b. first decade of first century BCE?), writer of both poetry and prose (Quint. *Inst. Orat.* 10.1.96; for his prose work – *Lucubrationes* – cf. Plin. *HN praef.* 24), known especially for biting epigrams against Augustus (cf. Tac. *Ann.* 4.34.5, in which Bibaculus is grouped with Catullus as those poets who attacked the Caesars); an apparent admirer of P. Valerius Cato (Suet. *Gramm.* 11). He is usually identified as one of the major "Neoteric" poets, and it has been argued that he is to be identified with the "Furius" of Catullus 11, 16, etc.;[20] this is surely an attractive suggestion, but the utter lack of evidence makes it totally unable to be proved.

- *Caecilius*, of Novum Comum, author of a *Magna Mater* and *sodalis* of Catullus (c. 35; cf. c. 67); nothing solid is known of this individual, but Catullus generally reserves the term *sodalis* for those poetic partners with whom he is closest in affection and class (cf. c. 10.29, in which Cinna is referred to by the same term, and c. 12.13, where it is used of Fabullus and Veranius).

- *P. Valerius Cato* (b. ca. 100 BCE?), grammarian, teacher, poet, and possible editor of Lucilius (cf. Suet. *Gramm.* 11); almost nothing is known of his social class – charged with being a *libertus*, he published an *Indignatio* in which he claimed to be freeborn but orphaned at an early age. This Cato is possibly to be identified with the addressee of Cat. 56.[21] Inclusion in the very inner circles of the group of isonomic exchangers may be unlikely based on what we know of Cato's socioeconomic standing (though he once held a Tusculan villa, he lost it to creditors and ended his life in extreme poverty) and status as a "professional teacher." The men of this group – insofar as we can determine it based on those we establish as "probable" participants – appear to define their participation in terms of the *otium*, or lack of formal economic obligation, that allowed them "time to write."[22] If Cato is to be included at all, I would place him at the extreme periphery: perhaps a respected professional, but likely not one of the "learned amateurs" of the inner nexus.

---

[19] Bernstein 1985 makes precisely such a suggestion (though in the context of c. 13) and cites Verg. *Ecl.* 8.23, 10.54 and Ovid *AA* 3.343; the *Amores* as a whole may be taken as a rather later development of this conflation of love with poetry.

[20] For a review of the argument and further bibliography, cf. Thomson 1997: 236.

[21] Another possible identification for the Cato of c. 56 is M. Porcius Cato of Utica; on this possible, and even attractive, but highly unprovable, suggestion, see Thomson 1997: 339.

[22] The implications of the term *otium* as "writing time" are addressed in Part I.

- *Q. Cornificius*, quaestor of 48 BCE, poet (Ovid *Trist.* 2.435–6; Hier. *Chron. a Abr.* 1976),[23] correspondent with Cicero (*Ep. Fam.* 12.17–30), and recipient of a copy of *Orator*. It is almost certain that it is this Cornificius from whom Catullus requests a poem (c. 38) in order to cheer him up and likely – if we take *meos amores* (l. 6) as "my verses" as well as "my affection" – in return for a poem sent by the poet to Cornificius.
- *Egnatius*, philosopher-poet (Macr. *Sat.* 6.5.2, 12; he is grouped with Lucretius and Cornificius), possibly to be identified with the Spaniard Egnatius of Cat. 37 and 39. If the Egnatius of the *carmina* is to be identified with Macrobius' Egnatius the poet, then the evidence for the man's likely rank – he is accused of being one of Lesbia's lovers in c. 37 – may gain him inclusion in a sphere of textual exchange. He is at any rate no friend of Catullus – not, at least, at the time of the writing of c. 37 (there is nothing in this poem that suggests it functions in a cycle of reciprocal poetic feud) – and any inclusion into the broader "group" for which we have evidence is exceedingly tenuous. He is perhaps to be grouped with the likes of Suffenus (cc. 14, 22), Sulla *litterator* (c. 14), and those whom Catullus would appear to attack and expel as "wannabe" participants even if social rank alone might allow them entry.
- *Fabullus*, apparently one of Catullus' most intimate friends and a social equal (cc. 12, 13, 28, 47)[24] and often grouped with Veranius; the name is otherwise unattested in the Republic. There is no direct evidence for poetic production on the part of Fabullus (or indeed Veranius), and we must emphasize that any inclusion in this group is purely circumstantial. Nevertheless, the tone and setting of c. 12 are intensely marked by the sort of elite dinner parties Catullus explicitly associates with the production and sharing of verse (for which cf. c. 50), and both Fabullus and Veranius are given pride of place. C. 13, Catullus' famously humorous invitation to a bring-your-own-dinner, carries similar implication of literary conviviality (*et uino et sale et omnibus cachinnis*, l. 5); and if we take *meros amores* (l. 9) as "erotic verse"[25] Fabullus is to receive from the poet – *suauius* and *elegantius* are terms suggestive of literary performance – we

---

[23] Although some have suggested that the Cornificius of Ovid's poem must be L. Cornificius, the citation of Hieronymus makes clear that the quaestor was similarly a poet.
[24] On the social status of both Fabullus and Veranius, cf. Wiseman 1982: 40–41.
[25] So Bernstein 1985, who argues for a "literary" reading of this poem and notes "as the epithet *uenuste noster* makes clear, this 'party' is for educated urbane people."

might see the entire invitation as a literarily minded one.[26] So too for cc. 28 and 47, as Nappa 1998 argues, we see in the persons of Fabullus and Veranius men of a rank like or equal to that of Catullus and men who – though they may angle for dinner invitations – do so not in the role of *clientes*.[27] Tempting evidence all, but purely circumstantial. Of this character we can say nothing definitive.

- *Flavius*, otherwise unknown addressee of Cat. 6. The tone and language of c. 6 make Flavius' participation in the sort of poetic exchange circles detailed elsewhere in the corpus (e.g., cc. 12, 50) both attractive and possible – note again here the suggestive use of *amores* (l. 10) – but little more can be said.

- *Furius*, frequent addressee of, or character in, Catullus' *carmina* (cc. 11, 16, 23, 26); see above discussion of Aurelius and Bibaculus.

- *Gellius*, apparent friend but frequent target of Catullus in the *carmina* (cc. 74, 80, 88, 89, 90, 91, 116), probably to be identified with L. Gellius Publicola, cos. 36, and likely an epigrammatist himself,[28] although not obviously a textual exchange partner with any of our other identifiable figures.

- *M. Messalla*, poet (Pliny *Ep.* 5.3). *Pace* Sherwin-White 1985: 317, I would identify this as Marcus Valerius Messalla Rufus, the consul of 53, rather than his son, Marcus Valerius Messalla Corvinus (64 BCE – 8 CE). In truth, Pliny *Ep.* 5.3 could refer to either figure, and to a certain extent the Augustan Messalla (64 BCE – 8 CE), a politically powerful and literarily interested individual, might suggest an attractive extension of the system as it is formed in the late Republic. The loose chronology of *Ep.* 5.3 makes the determination difficult. M. Messalla is preceded in the list by Asinius Pollio, a man closer in age to the Augustan figure; he is followed, however, by Q. Hortensius, who (if he is the elder Hortensius, as I believe he must be) was the uncle of Messalla Rufus – and so it may be this connection Pliny has in mind. Both men, at any rate, were literarily minded and highly regarded; Messalla Rufus was also the author of a prose treatise on the science of divination (Macr. *Sat.* 1.9.14; Pliny *Ep.* 5.3, etc.), and a man known to Cicero and his group. Messalla Corvinus'

---

[26] Nappa 1998 offers an excellent reading of this poem, including its likely literary nuances and its possible resonance with Philodemus 23, written to Piso. On this connection in particular, see further Marcovich 1982.

[27] A point made most clearly at Plut. *Luc.* 42, where we learn that Cicero and Pompey sought such an invitation from Lucullus.

[28] On this question see especially Wiseman 1974a: 119–129; on his status as an epigrammatist, cf. Thomson 1997: 497 and 554–555.

literary interests are well documented – a fact that might indeed make him a less likely candidate for Pliny's list of "unexpected" poets.

- *L. Papirius Paetus* (fl. first half of first century BCE?), a solid friend and epistolary correspondent of Cicero (see esp. the series at *Ep. Fam.* 9.15–26). It is certain that Paetus participated in at least one form of textual prestation, for we hear as early as 60 (cf. *Ep. Att.* 1.20 and 2.1) that Paetus has given Cicero the *munus* of a large library of books he had received from his brother. Much like Atticus, Paetus was an Epicurean and kept his distance from the political world, choosing instead to spend his time in discussions of philosophy and literature (cf. *Ep. Fam.* 9.25). He was apparently a frequent *conuiua* of Cicero's (*Ep. Fam.* 9.24 and 26) and the man who advised him to "live in his literature."[29] We have no evidence of direct textual dedication between the two. Paetus is the sort of character who lends tone and shadow to our textual world of the late Republic, but he gives us little in terms of its shape or form.

- *C. Asinius Pollio* (76/75 BCE – 5 CE), orator, poet, and historian (Pliny *Ep.* 5.3; Tac. *Dial.* 21.7; Verg. *Ecl.* 3.86), erudite younger brother of Marrucinus of Cat. 12. Although Pollio would have been one of the younger participants in the group (he is Catullus' junior by approximately 9 years), his acquaintance with Cicero, Caesar, and Hortensius, as well as Catullus' favorable estimation of his wit and style, make his a useful name to include here.

- *M. Caelius Rufus*, orator and politician, *familiaris* and (apparently) friend of Cicero, defended by the orator in 56 against a charge of *uis*. A solid identification of this figure with either the Caelius of Cat. 58 and 100 or the Rufus of Cat. 69 and 77 is attractive in the extreme, but remains impossible;[30] his name is included here on the basis of Cic. *Ep. Fam.* 8.1 and 8.3, each of 51 BCE, in the first of which Caelius mentions having sent Cicero a *uolumen*, and in the second of which he asks the orator for the dedication of a named dialogue as a testament to their shared *amicitia*.

- *S. Sulpicius Rufus* (106–43 BCE), orator, author of numerous legal works and a commentary on *Twelve Tables*, and a correspondent with Cicero (*Ep. Fam.* 4.5, 12). It is possible, if by no means certain, that he is to be identified with the Servius Sulpicius of Pliny *Ep.* 5.3; the appearance

---

[29] *Viuas... in litteris* (*Ep. Fam.* 9.26); the orator replies somewhat grumpily, *an quidquam me aliud egere censes aut possem uiuere, nisi in litteris uiuerem?* The significance of this admonition to "live in literature" is discussed in Part II.

[30] For representative arguments for and against this identification (among speculation that Caelius appears in other poems as well), cf. Arkins 1983; Forsyth 1976; and Noonan 1979.

of a Servius at Ovid *Trist.* 2.441–2 (*nec minus Hortensi nec sunt minus improba Serui / carmina*) may point to a positive identification with this patently "writing orator."

- *Q. Mucius Scaevola*, tribune of 54, poet (Pliny *Ep.* 5.3). Scaevola appears – by way of a statement of "Quintus Cicero" – at Cic. *de Leg.* 1.2, where he is made to comment favorably on Cicero's *Marius* (*de Leg.* 1.2). This Scaevola is not to be confused with the interlocutor of Cic. *de Orat.*, *de Rep.*, and *Lael.*, but his appearance at *de Leg.* may point to some acquaintance with the group.

- *P. Sestius* (b. early first century BCE?), orator and friend of Cicero who, in 56, defended Sestius against a charge of *uis*. It is almost indubitably this Sestius who appears at Cat. 44, when our poet complains that in the hope of attending a dinner at Sestius' he read one of the man's recent *orationes* – an attack on Antius – and grew violently ill as a result. This poem provides an important window into the world of literary conviviality in which individuals of varying age, aesthetic leaning, and (as we might imagine) social clique would meet, mingle, share, and discuss their literary productions.[31]

- *Suffenus*, poet, who appears at Cat. 14, 22. We know nothing of this Suffenus, who is linked at c. 14 with Caesius or the Caesii (unknown) and Aquinus or the Aquinii (if the former, possibly the poet of Cic. *TD* 5.63). As Thomson 1997: 22 notes, if the Aquinii of c. 14 is meant to refer to the Aquinus of *TD* 5.63, then it is possible that Suffenus is a real poet (rather than a character name for the "bad poet") whose tastes and abilities were at odds with those of Catullus and his closest companions. At c. 14, the sense is that this Suffenus – the only singular name given in the list of "bookshop poets" is one of the "wannabe" sorts Catullus would expel from his closest circle of textual comrades. The conciliatory tone at the end of c. 22 ("we're all a bit of a Suffenus"), however, may indicate Catullus' sensitivity to the vacillating borders of the Society; indeed, it is affectionate rather than invective in tone. Finally, the resonance between Suffenus and Alfenus Varus (see below) is tantalizing, and one might wonder whether "Suffenus" is a jocular, perhaps even affectionate, nickname used to refer to Catullus' friend Alfenus Varus when he engages in poetic activity.

- *L. Cornelius Sulla* (138–78 BCE), *dictator*, writer of *commentarii*, and poet (Gellius *NA* 1.12.16, 20.6.3; Plin. *HN* 22.12; Pliny *Ep.* 5.3). Sulla

---

[31] On the rejection of the idea that Catullus' desire to attend this dinner constitutes any form of parasitism or patronage, cf. Wiseman 1982: 41. I consider this poem more fully in Part II.

was the recipient of Lucullus' *commentarii* (see above), and he dedicated to Lucullus his own (Plut. *Luc.* 1). Sulla should likely be considered a senior member of this Society, and is perhaps more properly grouped with Catulus and Lucullus below; he was at any rate a man of literary interests and one who shows some evidence of having participated in a nascent textual culture of the late Republic.

- *Varus*, of Cremona, addressee of cc. 10 and 12, to be identified with either Quintilius Varus (a literarily minded individual and friend of Vergil and Horace [*Od.* 1.24], so Thomson 1997: 22) or Alfenus Varus the jurist and *cos. suff.* 39 (so Kroll *ad loc.*; cf. c. 10, noted above). Only c. 12 hints at participation in a sphere of textual production, but without a solid identification of which Varus we are dealing with, it is difficult to say more.
- *Veranius*, friend of Catullus, appears as the addressee of cc. 9 and (with Fabullus) 28, and is mentioned at cc. 12 (with his name once given in the diminutive) and 47 (again in the diminutive). As with Fabullus, discussed above, Veranius' inclusion in this group is purely circumstantial, and the name is a rare one for the period. He is certainly one of the poet's closest friends – whether he was also a writing friend is impossible to say.
- *Volusius*, apparent poet[32] and annalistic historian, whose poetry appears as an object of criticism at cc. 36 and 95 (this last in harsh contrast to the highly refined *Zmyrna* of Cinna). Catullus' charge against Volusius' poetry is one of logorrhea ("shitty sheets"); as we know nothing further of the individual's identity, we may surmise that he is either a member of the group, but one representative of a competing aesthetic, or – rather more tenuously – that he falls into the category of Suffenus, Egnatius (?), and Sulla *litterator*.

In our expanded group of "possible" members of the textual sphere, then, we have Aurelius, Furius Bibaculus, Caecilius, P. Valerius Cato, Q. Cornificius, Egnatius, Fabullus, Flavius, Furius, Gellius, M. Messalla, L. Papirius Paetus, C. Asinius Pollio, M. Caelius Rufus, S. Sulpicius Rufus, Q. Mucius Scaevola, P. Sestius, Suffenus, L. Cornelius Sulla, Varus, Veranius, and Volusius. If I were to include Lucretius in any way as a participant in this sphere – and as argued above, all evidence points to the contrary – it would only be here and, based both on his lexical predilections and the notable silence on his person in the authors with whom we are concerned, only on the outskirts. What we have for our expanded list are men who are known, or can be reasonably assumed, to have been of approximately

[32] For Volusius' identity as a poet as argued through the stylistics of c. 95, cf. Townend 1980.

equal and upper-class status (the case of Valerius Cato stands as an exception, and Furius and Aurelius are rather suspect), who show no evidence of having taken the literary or social role of *cliens*, and who seem to have had a certain degree of acquaintance, even if it is a contested or critical one, with the sphere traced at its beginnings from the evidence of Catullus and Cicero. This second group is an admittedly broad one; it raises rather more questions than it answers, and is almost fully dependent upon the agreement that the members of my first group constitute a "group" at all. But for as little as we know of the textual world of the late Republic, it is worthwhile to cast a wide net – and see what our catch brings.

Finally it will be useful to mention in brief two individuals who come on the scene rather too early to be included in our group, who show no evidence of having participated in textual exchange with any of our key figures, but who seem likely influential to later developments.[33]

The first is Q. Lutatius Catulus, respected "writing orator" and author of *commentarii* (*Brut.* 35.132), numerous epigrams (Apul. *Apol.* 9; Gellius *NA* 19.9.14; Cic. *DND* 1.79; cf. Pliny *Ep.* 5.3), and possibly an antiquarian "history";[34] he was one of the likely patrons of Archias, and is associated with Valerius Aedituus, Porcius Licinus, Volcacius Sedigitus, and Laevius (among others). Catulus is an interlocutor of *de Orator*, was the postmortem dedicatee and an almost certain interlocutor of the lost first book of the *Academica Priora* (Catulus died in 82 BCE; the dialogue dates from 45), and, with Lucullus and Cicero, an interlocutor of the second book of the *Academica Priora*, which was itself given in post-mortem dedication to Lucullus. His chronology places him in the very earliest years of late Republican textual practice, and he belongs to the group of men a generation earlier than Cicero. Nevertheless, Cicero's use of him in both *de Orator* and *Academica Priora*, as well as what we know of his work from later sources, may identify him as one of the earlier generation of writers whose practice Cicero identified with – or co-opted for – his own.

A second such figure is that of the immensely literarily interested L. Licinius Lucullus (cf. esp. Plut. *Luc.* 1.4–6). Lucullus was trained in Greek and Latin, a close friend of Hortensius and Sisenna, the author – on a dare of these two – of a *Marsic War* in Greek and Latin, the dedicatee of Sulla's

---

[33] If we were to expand this category on the basis of Cicero's *de Oratore* and *Brutus*, it would be a huge one, likely encompassing the bulk of patronal-class individuals – especially orators – of the end of the second century BCE. But as it is my argument that Cicero uses these texts in part to rewrite the august men of those years in his own image – and so to view his claims of their writing and circulation of texts with a grain of salt – it seems best to keep to primarily non-Ciceronian evidence for these years.

[34] On this see further Wiseman 1974a: 33, with additional bibliography on this possible "history."

commentarii (and, as noted above, dedicator, to Sulla, of his own), a patron of Archias, and responsible for acquiring, and then opening to the public, an extensive library. Cicero was favorably impressed by his writings, and makes mention of them in the context of writing the commentaries on his own consulship (*Ep. Att.* 1.19). Plutarch relates that Cicero and Pompey once angled for a dinner invitation at Lucullus' house (*Luc.* 42.1), and – as noted directly above – he was both an interlocutor and post-mortem dedicatee of the second book of the *Academica Priora*.

It is in short difficult to say to what degree either Catulus or Lucullus participated in the earliest stages of the textual group with which this study is concerned. However, in light of both their patent support of the literary arts and Cicero's evident desire to recast them as his dialogic partners, we may not be far off in locating the origins of our Society of Patrons in the literary interests and enthusiasm of these two men.

Bibliography

PRIMARY EDITIONS CONSULTED

Unless otherwise specified, all citations of Cicero come from the Oxford Classical Texts.

Baehrens, E. (ed.). 1885. *Catulli Veronesis liber*, vol 1. Leipzig: Teubner.
Benseler, G. E. (ed.). 1913. *Isocratis Orationes*. Leipzig: Teubner.
Blänsdorf, J. (ed.). 1995. *Fragmenta Poetarum Latinorum. Post W. Morel and K. Büchner*. Stuttgart: Teubner.
Diehl, E. (ed.). 1925. *Anthologia lyrica graeca*. Leipzig: Teubner.
Douglas, A. E. (ed.). 1966. *M. Tulli Ciceronis Brutus*. Oxford University Press.
Groningen, B. A. van (ed.). 1966. *Theognis: Le premier livre*. Amsterdam: Noord-Hollandsche.
Halm, K. F. (ed.). 1868. *M. Fabi Quintiliani institutionis oratoriae. Libri XII*. Leipzig: Teubner.
Heiberg, J. L. (ed.). 1910–1975. *Archimedis opera omnia, cum commentariis Eutocii*. Leipzig: Teubner.
Keil, H. (ed.). 1855–1880. *Grammatici Latini*. 7 vols. and suppl. Leipzig: Teubner.
Koestermann, E. (ed. *post* C. Halm and G. Andresen). 1936. *P. Cornelii Taciti libri qui supersunt*. Leipzig: Teubner.
Kroll, W. (ed. and comm.). 1989 (repr.). *C. Valerius Catullus*. Stuttgart: Teubner.
Leeman, A. D. (ed.). 1981–1996. *M. Tullius Cicero/De Oratore libri III*. Heidelberg: C. Winter.
Lindsey, W. M. (ed.). 1903. *T. Macci Plauti Comoediae*. Oxford University Press.
Malcovati, E. (ed.). 1970. *M. Tullius Cicero: Fasc. 4 Brutus*. Leipzig: Teubner.
Mayer, R. (ed.). 2001. *Tacitus. Dialogus de Oratoribus*. Cambridge University Press.
Mynors, R. A. B. (ed.). 1958. *Catulli Carmina*. Oxford University Press.
Peter, H. (ed.). 1914. *Historicorum Romanorum Reliquiae*, 2nd edn. Stuttgart: Teubner.
Pfeiffer, R. (ed.). 1949–1953. *Callimachus*. 2 vols. Oxford University Press.
Préhac, F. (ed.). 1961. *Sénèque: Des Bienfaits*. Paris: Société d'Edition "Les Belles Lettres."
Quinn, K. (ed.). 1970. *Catullus: The Poems*. London: MacMillan.

Reynolds, L. D. (ed.). 1965. *L. Annaei Senecae ad Lucilium Epistulae Morales.* Oxford University Press.

Shackleton Bailey, D. R. (ed.). 1965–1970. *Letters to Atticus.* 7 vols. Cambridge University Press.

Sutton, E. W. and Rackham, H. (eds. and transl.; rev. edn.). 1942. *Cicero: On the Orator, Books I–II.* Cambridge, Mass.: Harvard University Press.

Tyrrell, R. Y. and Purser, L. C. (eds.). 1894–1915. *The Correspondence of M. Tullius Cicero*, 2nd edn. Dublin: Hodges, Foster and Figgis.

West, M. L. 1978 (repr. 1996). *Hesiod: Works and Days.* Oxford University Press.

Wilkins, A. S. (ed.). 1963. *M. Tulli Ciceronis Rhetorica. de Oratore.* Oxford University Press.

Winterbottom, M. (ed.). 1970. *M. Fabi Quintiliani institutionis oratoriae. Libri Duodecim.* Oxford University Press.

Zetzel, J. E. G. (ed.). 1995. *Marcus Tullius Cicero. De re publica: Selections.* Cambridge University Press.

MODERN SOURCES

Adams, B. 1997. *E Pluribus Barnum. The Great Showman and the Making of U. S. Popular Culture.* Minneapolis, Minn.: University of Minnesota Press.

Adams, J. N. 1982. *The Latin Sexual Vocabulary.* Baltimore, Md.: Johns Hopkins University Press.

Andre, J. M. 1966. *L'Otium dans la vie morale et intellectuelle romaine, des origines a l'époque Augustéenne.* Paris: Presses Universitaires de France.

Andrews McMeel. 2005. *The Governator: 2005 Wall Calendar.* New Jersey. Andrews McMeel Publishing.

Apter, E. 1991. *Feminizing the Fetish: Psychoanalysis and Narrative Obsession in Turn-of-the-Century France.* Ithaca, NY: Cornell University Press.

———— 1993. "Introduction." In Apter and Pietz (eds.): 1–12.

Apter, E., and Pietz, W. (eds.). 1993. *Fetishism as Cultural Discourse.* Ithaca, NY: Cornell University Press.

Arkins, B. 1983. "Caelius and Rufus in Catullus." *Philologus* 127: 306–311.

Axtell, H. L. 1907. *The Deification of Abstract Ideas in Roman Literature and Inscriptions.* University of Chicago Press. (Reprinted New Rochelle, NY: Caratzas. 1987.)

Badian, E. (ed.). 1966. *Ancient Society and Institutions: Studies Presented to Victor Ehrenberg on his 75th Birthday.* Oxford: Blackwell.

———— 1982. Review of Saller (1982). *CP* 80: 348–349.

Baier, T. 1997. *Werk und Wirkung Varros im Spiegel seiner Zeitgenossen.* Hermes Einzelschriften 73. Stuttgart: Franz Steiner.

Balsdon, J. P. V. D. 1960. "Auctoritas, Dignitas, Otium." *CQ* 10: 45–50.

Barchiesi, A. 2001. *Speaking Volumes: Narrative and Intertext in Ovid and other Latin Poets.* London: Duckworth.

Barton, C. 1993. *The Sorrows of the Ancient Romans: The Gladiator and the Monster.* Princeton University Press.

Batstone, W. W. 1998. "Dry Pumice and the Programmatic Language of Catullus 1." *CP* 93.2: 125–135.

Beard, M., and Crawford, M. 1985. *Rome in the Late Republic*. Ithaca, NY: Duckworth.

Belfiore, E. 1994. "Xenia in Sophocles' Philoctetes." *CJ* 89: 113–129.

Bennett, S. 1997. *Theatre Audiences: A Theory of Production and Reception*, 2nd edn. New York: Routledge.

Benveniste, E. 1966. "Don et échange dans le vocabulaire indo-européen." In *Problèmes de linguistique générale*: vol. 1, 315–326. Paris: Gallimard.

Bernstein, W. H. 1985. "A Sense of Taste: Catullus 13." *CJ* 80.2: 127–130.

Bickel, E. 1953. "Salaputium: Mentula Salax." *RhM* 96: 94–95.

Bloomer, W. M. 1997. *Latinity and Literary Society at Rome*. Philadelphia, Pa.: University of Pennsylvania Press.

———— 2007. "Roman Declamation: The Elder Seneca and Quintilian." In Dominik and Hall (eds.): 297–306.

Bongi, V. 1943. "Note critiche sul carme XIII di Catullo." *Aevum* 17: 228–236.

Bowditch, P. L. 2001. *Horace and the Gift Economy of Patronage*. Berkeley, Calif.: University of California Press.

Bower, R. W. 1974. "Ineptiae and Ioci." *Latomus* 33.3: 523–528.

Boyancè, P. 1941. "Cum dignitate otium." *REA* 13: 172–191.

Brunt, P. A. 1965. "'Amicitia' in the late Republic." *PCPS* 191 n.s. 2: 1–20.

———— 1982. Review of Saller (1982). *Times Literary Supplement*, 19 Nov.: 1276.

Buchheit, V. 1975. "Catulls Literarkritik und Kallimachos." *Grazer Beiträge* 4: 21–50.

———— 1976a. "Catullus c. 50 als Programm und Bekenntnis." *RhM* 119: 162–180.

———— 1976b. "Sal et lepos versiculorum (Catull c. 16)." *Hermes* 104: 331–347.

Burger, R. 1980. *Plato's Phaedrus: A Defense of the Philosophical Art of Writing*. Birmingham, Ala.: University of Alabama Press.

Burgess, D. L. 1986. "Catullus c. 50: The Exchange of Poetry." *AJP* 107: 576–586.

Bury, R. de 1903. *The Love of Books. The Philobiblon of Richard de Bury*. Trans. E. C. Thomas. London: Alexander Moring, The de La More Press.

Bushala, E. W. 1981. "A Note on Catullus 106." *HSCP* 85: 131–132.

Butler, S. 2002. *The Hand of Cicero*. New York: Routledge.

Butor, M. 1968. *Inventory*. Trans. R. Howard. New York: Simon and Schuster.

Cairns, F. 1969. "Catullus 1." *Mnemosyne* 22: 153–158.

Camille, M. 1997. "The Book as Flesh and Fetish in Richard de Bury's *Philobiblon*." In D. Frese and K. O'Keeffe (eds.), *The Book and The Body*.: 34–77, University of Notre Dame Press.

Cavallo, G. 1975. *Libri, editori e pubblico nel mondo antico: Guida storica e critica*. Rome, Bari: Laterza.

Chandler, A. 1934. "The Nightingale in Greek and Latin Poetry." *CA* 30.2: 78–84.

Clack, J. 1976. "Otium tibi molestum est: Catullus 50 and 51." *CB* 5: 50–53.

Clarke, M. L. 1978. "Poets and Patrons at Rome." *GR* 25: 46–54.

———— 1996 (1953). *Rhetoric at Rome. A Historical Survey*, 3rd edn. New York. Routledge.

Clausen, W. 1970. "Catullus and Callimachus." *HSCP* 74: 84–95.

———— 1976. "Catulli Veronensis Liber." *CP* 71.1: 37–43.

Clay, D. 1975. "The Tragic and Comic Poet of the Symposium." *Arion* 2.2: 238–261.

Collins, J. H. 1952. "Cicero and Catullus." *CJ* 48.1: 11–17 and 36–41.

Connery, C. L. 1998. *The Empire of the Text: Writing and Authority in Early Imperial China*. Lanham, Md.: Rowman and Littlefield.

Connolly, J. P. T. 1997. "Vile Eloquence: Performance and Identity in Greco-Roman Rhetoric." Unpublished PhD thesis, University of Pennsylvania.

Connor, P. J. 1982. "Book Dispatch: Horace Epistles 1.20 and 1.13." *Ramus* 11: 145–152.

Conte, G. 1994. *Latin Literature: A History*. Trans. J. B. Solodow. Baltimore, Md.: Johns Hopkins University Press.

———— 1957. "The Unity of Catullus 68: A Further View." *CP* 52: 29–32.

Corbeill, A. 1996. *Controlling Laughter: Political Humor in the Late Roman Republic*. Princeton University Press.

Coulon, V. 1956. "Observations critiques." *RhM* 99: 245–254.

Courtney, E. 1985. "Three Poems of Catullus." *BICS* 32: 90–91.

Crowther, N. B. 1970. "ΟΙ ΝΕⲰΤΕΡΟΙ, *Poetae Novi* and *Cantatores Euphorionis.*" *CQ* 20.2: 322–327.

Daly, L. W. 1950. "Roman Study Abroad." *AJP* 71.1: 40–58.

———— 1952. "Callimachus and Catullus." *CP* 47: 97–99.

D'Arms, J. 1984. "Control, Companionship and *Clientela*: Some Social Functions of the Roman Communal Meal." *EMC/CV* 28: 327–348.

———— 1990. "The Roman *convivium* and the Ideal of Equality." In O. Murray (ed.), *Sympotica: A Symposium on the Symposium*: 308–320. Oxford. Clarendon Press.

———— 1999. "Performing Culture: Roman Spectacle and the Banquets of the Powerful." In B. Bergmann and C. Kondoleon (eds.), *The Art of Ancient Spectacle*: 301–319. New Haven, Conn.: Yale University Press.

Davisson, M. H. T. 1984. "Parents and Children in Ovid's Poems from Exile." *CW* 78: 111–114.

Deniaux, E. 1993. *Clientèles et pouvoir à l'epoque de Cicéron*. Rome: Ecole française de Rome.

Derrida, J. 1981. *Dissemination*. Trans. B. Johnson. University of Chicago Press.

———— 1994. *Given Time: I. Counterfeit Money*. Trans. P. Kamuf. University of Chicago Press.

Dettmer, H. 1986. "Meros Amores: A Note on Catullus 13.9." *QUCC* 24: 87–91.

Dimarogonas, A. D. 1995. "Pliny the Elder on the Making of Papyrus Paper." *CQ* 45: 588.

Dixon, S. 1993. "The Meaning of Gift and Debt in the Roman Elite." *EMC/CV* 37: 451–464.

Dominik, W. (ed.). 1997. *Roman Eloquence: Rhetoric in Society and Literature*. New York: Routledge.

———— 2007. "Tacitus and Pliny on Oratory." In Dominik and Hall (eds.): 323–338.

Dominik, W. and Hall, J. (eds.). 2007. *A Companion to Roman Rhetoric*. Malden, Mass.: Blackwell.

Douglas, A. E. 1960. "*Clausulae* in the *Rhetorica ad Herennium* as Evidence of its Date." *CQ* 10: 65–78.

——— 1995. "Form and Content in the Tusculan Disputations." In Powell, J. G. F. (ed.), *Cicero the Philosopher: Twelve Papers*: 197–218. New York and Oxford: Clarendon Press.

Dugan, J. 2005. *Making a New Man: Ciceronian Self-Fashioning in the Rhetorical Works*. Oxford University Press.

Dupont, F. 1997. "*Recitatio* and the Reorganization of the Space of Public Discourse." In T. N. Habinek and A. Schiesaro (eds.), *The Roman Cultural Revolution*: 44–59. Cambridge University Press.

——— 1999. *The Invention of Literature: From Greek Intoxication to the Latin Book*. Trans. J. Lloyd. Baltimore, Md.: Johns Hopkins University Press.

Edwards, C. 1993. *The Politics of Immorality in Ancient Rome*. Cambridge University Press.

——— 1997. "Unspeakable Professions: Public Performance and Prostitution in Ancient Rome." In Hallet and Skinner (eds.): 66–95.

Elder, J. P. 1966. "Catullus 1, his Poetic Creed, and Nepos." *HSCP* 71: 143–149.

Ellis, R. 1979. *A Commentary on Catullus*. New York and London: Garland.

Fantham, E. 1996. *Roman Literary Culture*. Baltimore, Md.: Johns Hopkins University Press.

——— 2004. *The Roman World of Cicero's* De Oratore. Oxford University Press.

Farrell, J. 2002. "Greek Lives and Roman Careers in the Classical *Vita* Tradition." In P. Cheney and F. A. de Armas (eds.), *European Literary Careers: The Author from Antiquity to the Renaissance*: 24–46. University of Toronto Press.

Feldherr, A. 1998. *Spectacle and Society in Livy's History*. Berkeley, Calif.: University of California Press.

Ferrari, G. R. F. 1987. *Listening to the Cicadas*. Cambridge University Press.

Finamore, J. F. 1984. "Catullus 50 and 51. Friendship, Love and *Otium*." *CW* 78: 11–19.

Finley, M. 1973 (repr. 1985). *The Ancient Economy*. Berkeley, Calif.: University of California Press.

Fitzgerald, W. 1995. *Catullan Provocations: Lyric Poetry and the Drama of Position*. Berkeley, Calif.: University of California Press.

Flores, E. 1976. "La dedica catulliana a Nepote e un epigramma di Cinna." *Vichiana* 5: 3–18.

Flower, H. 1996. *Ancestor Masks and Aristocratic Power in Roman Culture*. Oxford University Press.

Fordyce, C. J. 1961. *Catullus: A Commentary*. Oxford University Press.

Forsyth, P. 1976. "Tu cum Tappone: Catullus 104." *CW* 70: 21–24.

——— 1984. "The Lady and the Poem: Catullus 35–42." *CJ* 80.1: 24–26.

——— 1985. "Gifts and Giving: Catullus 12–14." *CW* 78.6: 571–574.

Fortenbaugh, W. 1989. "Cicero's Knowledge of the Rhetorical Treatises of Aristotle and Theophrastus." In W. Fortenbaugh and P. Steinmetz (eds.), *Cicero's Knowledge of the Peripatos*: 39–60. New Brunswick, NJ: Transaction.

Foster, H. 1993. "The Art of Fetishism: Notes on Dutch Still Life." In Apter and Pietz (eds.): 251–265.

———— 1990 (reissue). *The History of Sexuality: The Use of Pleasure*. Trans. R. Hurley. New York: Vintage.

Frank, T. 1919. "Cicero and the Poetae Novi." *AJP* 40.4: 396–415.

———— 1920. "Catullus and Horace on Suffenus and Alfenus." *CQ* 14.3/4: 160–162.

Fraser, P. M. 1972. *Ptolemaic Alexandria*. 3 vols. Oxford University Press.

Freud, S. 1953–1966. *The Standard Edition of the Complete Psychological Works of Sigmund Freud*. 24 vols. Trans. James Strachey. London: Hogarth Press.

Friedricksmeyer, E. 1973. "Catullus 49, Cicero, and Caesar." *CP* 68.4: 268–278.

———— 1985. "Catullus to Caecilius on Good Poetry." *AJP* 106: 213–221.

Frier, B. W. 1999. *Libri Annales Pontificum Maximorum: the Origins of the Annalistic Tradition*. Ann Arbor, Mich.: University of Michigan Press.

Geffcken, K. A. 1973. *Comedy in the* Pro Caelio. Mnemosyne Supplement 30. Leiden: Brill.

———— 1995. *Comedy in the Pro Caelio. With an Appendix on the* In Clodium et Curionem. Wauconda, Ill.: Bolchazy-Carducci.

Georges, F. 1976. *Deux Études sur Sartre*. Paris: Bourgois.

Gernet, L. 1981. "'Value' in Greek Myth." In M. Detienne (ed.), *Myth, Religion and Society*. Trans. R. L. Gordon. Cambridge University Press.

Gleason, M. 1995. *Making Men: Sophists and Self-Presentation in Ancient Rome*. Princeton University Press.

Godbout, J. T. and Caillé, A. 1998. *The World of the Gift*. Trans. D. Winkler. Montreal, QC and Kingston, ON: McGill-Queen's University Press.

Goerler, W. 1988. "From Athens to Tusculum: Gleaning the Background of Cicero's *De Oratore.*" *Rhetorica* 6: 215–235.

Gold, B. (ed.). 1982. *Literary and Artistic Patronage in Ancient Rome*. Austin, Tex.: University of Texas Press.

———— 1987. *Literary Patronage in Greece and Rome*. Chapel Hill, NC: University of North Carolina Press.

Goldberg, S. 2005. *Constructing Literature in the Roman Republic: Poetry and Its Reception*. Cambridge University Press.

Goldman, W. 1973. *The Princess Bride*. New York: Harcourt Brace Jovanovich.

Gowing, A. 2000. "Memory and Silence in Cicero's *Brutus.*" *Eranos* 98: 39–64.

Graf, F. 1992. "Gestures and Conventions: The Gestures of Roman Actors and Orators." In J. Bremmer and H. Roodenburg (eds.), *A Cultural History of Gesture*: 36–58. Ithaca, NY: Cornell University Press.

Green, C. M. C. 1997. "Free as a Bird: Varro *de Re Rustica* 3." *AJP* 118.3: 427–448.

Green, P. 1990. *Alexander to Actium: The Historical Evolution of the Hellenistic Age*. Berkeley, Calif.: University of California Press.

Greene, E. 1995. "The Catullan Ego: Fragmentation and the Erotic Self." *AJP* 116.1: 77–93.

Gregory, C. A. 1982. *Gifts and Commodities*. London: Academic Press.

Gruen, E. 1966. "Cicero and Licinius Calvus." *HSCP* 71: 215–233.

———— 1974. *The Last Generation of the Roman Republic*. Berkeley, Calif.: University of California Press.

———— 1992. *Culture and National Identity in Republican Rome*. Cornell Ithaca, NY: University Press.

———— 1996 (1990). *Studies in Greek Culture and Roman Policy*. Berkeley, Calif.: University of California Press.

Gunderson, E. 1996. "Catullus, Pliny, and Love-Letters." *TAPA* 127: 201–231.

———— 1994. "Ideology for an Empire in the Prefaces to Cicero's Dialogues." *Ramus* 23: 55–67.

———— 1998. *The Politics of Latin Literature*. Princeton University Press.

Haenni, R. 1905. *Die literarische Kritik in Ciceros* Brutus. Samen: Müller.

Hakamies, R. 1951. *Étude sur l'Origine et l'Évolution du Diminutif Latin et sa Survie Dans Les Langues Romanes*. Helskinki: Finnish Academy of Science and Letters.

Hall, J. 1996. "Social Evasion and Aristocratic Manners." *AJP* 117: 95–120.

Hallet, J. 1984. *Fathers and Daughters in Roman Society: Women and the Elite Family*. Princeton University Press.

———— 1988. "Catullus on Composition: Response." *CW* 81.5: 395–401.

———— and Skinner, M. B. (eds.). 1997. *Roman Sexualities*. Princeton University Press.

Hanssen, J. S. T. 1952. *Latin Diminutives: A Semantic Study*. Bergen: Grieg.

Hubbard, T. 1983. "The Catullan Libellus." *Philologus* 127: 218–237.

Hughes, J. J. 1997. "*Inter tribunal et scaenam*: Comedy and Rhetoric in Rome." In Dominik (ed.): 182–197.

Hunter, R. L. 1993. "Callimachean Echoes in Catullus 65." *ZPE* 96: 179–182.

Hutchinson, G. O. 2003. "The Catullan Corpus, Greek Epigram, and the Poetry of Objects." *CQ* 53.1: 206–221.

Hyde, L. 1983. *The Gift: Imagination and the Erotic Life of Property*. New York: Random House.

Immerwahr, H. R. 1964. "Book Rolls on Attic Vases." In C. Henderson (ed.), *Classical, Mediaeval and Renaissance Studies in Honor of B. L. Ullman*: vol. 1, 17–48. Rome: Edizioni di Storia e Letteratura.

———— 1973. "More Book Rolls on Attic Vases." *AK* 16: 143–147.

Irigaray, L. 1985. *Speculum of the Other Woman*. Ithaca, NY: Cornell University Press.

Janan, M. 1994. *"When the Lamp is Shattered": Desire and Narrative in Catullus*. Carbondale, Ill.: Southern Illinois University Press.

Janson, T. 1964. *Latin Prose Prefaces: Studies in Literary Conventions*. Stockholm: Almqvist and Wiksell.

Jay, M. 1993. *Downcast Eyes: The Denigration of Vision in Twentieth-Century French Thought*. Berkeley, Calif.: University of California Press.

Jensen, R. C. 1967. "Otium, Catulle, tibi molestum est." *CJ* 62.8: 363–365.

Johnson, T. and Dandeker, C. 1989. "Patronage: Relations and System." In Wallace-Hadrill (ed.): 219–242.

Kaiser, L. M. 1950. "Waves and Color in Catullus 65." *CB* 27: 2.

Kaplan, A. E. 1983. *Women and Film: Both Sides of the Camera*. New York: Routledge.

Kennedy, G. A. 1972. *The Art of Rhetoric in the Roman World, 300 B.C. – A.D. 300*. Princeton University Press.

Kenney, E. J. 1982. "Books and Readers in the Roman World." In E. J. Kenney and W. V. Clausen (eds.), *The Cambridge History of Classical Literature. Vol. II: Latin Literature*: 3–32. Cambridge University Press.

Kierdorf, W. 1980. *Laudatio Funebris: Interpretationen und Untersuchungen zur Entwicklung der römischen Leichenrede*. Meisenheim am Glahn: Anton Hain.

King, J. K. 1988. "Catullus' Callimachean carmina, cc. 65–116." *CW* 81.5: 383–394.

Kinsey, T. E. 1966. "Catullus 16." *Latomus* 24: 101–106.

Kirby, J. T. 1997. "Ciceronian Rhetoric: Theory and Practice." In Dominik (ed.): 13–31.

Knobloch, J. 1969. "Catullus 53.5 and Cicero." *RhM* 112: 23–9.

Kopytoff, I. 1986. "The Cultural Biography of Things: Commoditization as Process." In A. Appadurai (ed.), *The Social Life of Things: Commodities in Cultural Perspective*: 64–91. Cambridge University Press.

Krips, H. 1999. *Fetish: An Erotics of Culture*. Ithaca, NY: Cornell University Press.

Krostenko, B. A. 2001. *Cicero, Catullus and the Language of Display*. University of Chicago Press.

Kundera, M. 1997. *Slowness: A Novel*. Trans. L. Asher. New York: Harper Perennial.

Kurke, L. V. 1991. *The Traffic in Praise: Pindar and the Poetics of Social Economy*. Ithaca, NY: Cornell University Press.

Kuttner, A. 2005. "Cabinet Fit for a Queen: The Lithika as Posidippus' Gem Museum." In K. Gutzwiller (ed.), *The New Posidippus: A Hellenistic Poetry Book*: 141–163. Oxford University Press.

Kytzler, B. 1973. "Ciceros literarische Leistung in Brutus." In B. Kytzler (ed.), *Ciceros literarische Leistung*: 460–488. Darmstadt. Wissenschaftliche Buchgesellschaft.

La Penna, A. 2002. "Ritratti delle Lettere di Cicerone." In E. Narducci (ed.), *Interpretare Cicerone*: 1–23. Florence: F. le Monnier.

Lacan, J. 1977. *Écrits: A Selection*. Trans. A. Sheridan. New York. Norton.

Laughton, E. 1970. "Disertissime Romuli Nepotum." *CP* 65: 1–7.

Laurand, L. 1927–1928. *Études sur le style des discours de Cicéron*. Paris: Société d'édition "Les Belles Lettres."

Laursen, S. 1989. "The Apple of Catullus 65: A Love Pledge of Callimachus." *CM* 40: 161–169.

——— 1999. "Ciceronian '*Bi-Marcus*': Correspondence with M. Terentius Varro and L. Parpirius Paetus in 46 B.C.E." *TAPA* 129: 139–180.

Lee, G. 1990. *Catullus. The Complete Poems*. Oxford University Press.

Leeman, A. D. 1978. "Enstehung und Bestimmung von Ciceros De Oratore." *Mnemosyne* 31: 253–264.

Lévi-Strauss, C. 1969. *The Elementary Structures of Kinship*. Trans. J. H. Belle and J. R. von Sturmer. Boston, Mass.: Beacon Press.

Linderski, J. 1985. "The Dramatic Date of Varro, *De Re Rustica*, Book III and the Elections in 54." *Historia* 34.2: 248–254.

MacKay, L. A. 1933. "Catullus 53.5 '*di magni, salapantium disertum.*'" *CR* 47: 220.

MacKendrick, P. 1989. *The Philosophical Books of Cicero*. London: Duckworth.

Marcovich, M. 1982. "Catullus 13 and Philodemus 23." *QUCC* 11: 131–138.

Marx, K. 1981. *Capital, Vol. 1: A Critique of Political Economy*. Trans. B. Fowkes. New York: Random House.

Mauss, M. 1990 (1954). *The Gift: Forms and Functions of Exchange in Archaic Societies*. Trans. W. D. Halls. New York: Norton.

May, J. M. 1988. *Trials of Character: The Eloquence of Ciceronian Ethos*. Chapel Hill, NC: University of North Carolina Press.

Minyard, J. D. 1988. "The Source of the Catulli Veronensis Liber." *CW* 81.5: 343–354.

Morris, I. 1976. "Gift and Commodity in Archaic Greece." *Man* 21: 1–17.

Mulvey, L. 1989. *Visual and Other Pleasures*. Bloomington, Ind.: Indiana University Press.

Murgia, C. E. "Catullus 65 and Quintilian." Transcript of a lecture delivered at Harvard University; cited with permission of the author.

Murphy, T. 1998. "Cicero's First Readers: Epistolary Evidence for the Dissemination of his Works." *CQ* 48.2: 492–505.

Nappa, C. 1998. "Place Settings. *Convivium*, Contrast, and Persona in Catullus 12 and 13." *AJP* 119.3: 385–397.

———— 2001. *Aspects of Catullus' Social Fiction*. Frankfurt: Lang.

Narducci, E. 1997. *Cicerone e l'eloquenza Romana*. Rome: Laterza.

Nielsen, R. M. 1987. "Catullus and *Sal* (poem 10)." *AC* 56: 148–161.

Noonan, J. D. 1979. "*Mala Bestia* in Catullus 69.7–8." *CW* 73: 155–164.

Oliensis, E. 1997. "The Erotics of *Amicitia*: Readings in Tibullus, Propertius, and Horace." In Hallet and Skinner (eds.): 151–171.

———— 1998. *Horace and the Rhetoric of Authority*. Cambridge University Press.

Padilla, M. W. 2000. "Gifts of Humiliation." *AJP* 121 (2): 179–211.

Palmer, L. R. 1956. "The Concept of Social Obligation in Indo-European." In *Homages à Max Niedermann*. Collection Latomus 23: 258–269. Brussels.

Parry, J. and Bloch, M. (eds.). 1989. *Money and the Morality of Exchange*. Cambridge University Press.

Paxson, H. J. 1994. *The Poetics of Personification*. Cambridge University Press.

———— 1998. "Personification's Gender." *Rhetorica* 16 (2): 149–179.

Pearcy, L. T. 1994. "The Personification of the Text and Augustan Poetics in Epistles 1.20." *CW* 87: 457–464.

Pfeiffer, R. 1968. *History of Classical Scholarship from the Beginnings to the End of the Hellenistic Age*. Oxford University Press.

Phillips, J. J. 1986. "Atticus and the Publication of Cicero's Works." *CW* 79: 227–237.
Pietz, W. 1985. "The Problem of the Fetish, I." *Res* 9 (Spring): 12–13.
———— 1987. "The Problem of the Fetish, II." *Res* 13 (Spring): 23–45.
———— 1993. "Fetishism and Materialism: The Limits of Theory in Marx." In Apter and Pietz (eds.): 119–151.
Pinsky, R. 1996. *The Inferno of Dante: A New Verse Translation.* New York: Noonday Press.
Plasberg, O. 1892. *De M. Tullii Ciceronis Hortensio dialogo.* Leipzig: Fock.
Pontani, P. 2000. "The First Word of Callimachus' Aetia." *ZPE* 128: 57–59.
Purser, L. C. 1892. "Review: Plasberg on the *Hortensius* of Cicero." *CR* 6.10: 448–450.
Putnam, M. 1982. *Essays in Latin Lyric, Elegiac and Epic.* Princeton University Press.
Quilligan, M. 1991. *The Allegory of Female Authority: Christine de Pisan's "Cité des Dames."* Ithaca, NY: Cornell University Press.
Quinn, K. 1979. *Texts and Contexts: The Roman Writers and their Audience.* Routledge & Kegan Paul.
Raheja, G. C. 1988. *The Poison in the Gift: Ritual, Prestation, and the Dominant Caste in a North Indian Village.* University of Chicago Press.
Rathofer, C. 1986. *Ciceros "Brutus" als literarisches Paradigma eines Auctoritas-Verhältnisses.* Meisenheim: Hain.
Rawson, E. 1985. *Intellectual Life in the Late Roman Republic.* Baltimore, Md.: Johns Hopkins University Press.
Richardson, B. 1999. *Printing, Writers and Readers in Renaissance Italy.* Cambridge University Press.
Richardson, L., Jr. 1992. *A New Topographical Dictionary of Ancient Rome.* Baltimore, Md.: Johns Hopkins University Press.
Richlin, A. 1981. "The Meaning of *Irrumare* in Catullus and Martial." *CP* 76: 40–46.
———— 1992. *The Garden of Priapus: Sexuality and Aggression in Roman Humor.* New Haven, Conn.: Yale University Press.
———— 1997. "Gender and Rhetoric: Producing Manhood in the Schools." In Dominik (ed.): 90–110.
Ridley, R. T. 1983. "Falsi Triumphi, Plures Consulatus." *Latomus* 42: 372–382.
Roman, L. 2001. "The Representation of Literary Materiality in Martial's *Epigrams*." *JRS* 91: 113–145.
Roth, P. 1993. "The Theme of Corrupted *Xenia* in Aeschylus' *Oresteia*." *Mnemosyne* 46: 1–17.
Ruppert, J. 1911. *Quaestiones ad historiam dedicationis librorum pertinentes.* Leipzig: Teubner.
Sailor, D., and Stroup, S. C. 1999. "ΦΘΟΝΟΣ Δ' ΑΠΕΣΤω: The Translation of Transgression in Aiskhylos' *Agamemnon*." *ClAnt* 18.1: 153–182.
Saller, R. P. 1982. *Personal Patronage Under the Early Empire.* Cambridge University Press.

_____ 1989. "Patronage and Friendship in Early Imperial Rome: Drawing the Distinction." In Wallace-Hadrill (ed.): 49–62.

Sandulescu, C. 1970. "Cicero und Homer." *StudClas* 12: 53–68.

Sandy, G. N. 1978. "Indebtedness, '*scurrilitas*,' and Composition in Catullus (44, 1, 68)." *Phoenix* 32.1: 68–80.

Sarkisan, J. 1983. *Catullus 68. An Interpretation*. Leiden: Brill.

Sartre, J. P. 1956. *Being and Nothingness. An Essay on Phenomenological Ontology*. Trans. H. E. Barnes. New York: Washington Square Press.

Saunders, C. 1944. "The Nature of Rome's Early Appraisal of Greek Culture." *CP* 39.4: 209–217.

Schenker, D. J. 2006. "The Strangeness of the Phaedrus." *AJP* 127: 67–87.

Scherf, J. 1966. *Untersuchungen zur antiken Veröffentlichung der Catullgedichte*. Spudasmata 61 Hildesheim: Olms.

Schrift, A. D. (ed.). 1997. *The Logic of the Gift. Toward an Ethic of Generosity*. New York: Routledge.

Schwabe, L. 1862. *Quaestiones Catullianae*. Giessen: Ricker.

Sciarrino, E. 2004. "Putting Cato the Censor's *Origines* in its Place." *ClAnt* 23.2: 323–357.

Scott, W. C. 1969. "Catullus and Calvus (Cat. 50)." *CP* 64.3: 169–173.

Seaford, R. 1994. *Reciprocity and Ritual: Homer and Tragedy in the Developing City-State*. Oxford University Press.

Seager, R. 1974. "Venustus, lepidus, bellus, salsus: Notes on the Language of Catullus." *Latomus* 33: 891–894.

Sedgwick, W. B. 1947. "Catullus X: A Rambling Commentary." *GR* 16: 108–114.

Segal, C. 1970. "Catullan *Otiosi*: the Lover and the Poet." *GR* 17: 25–31.

Sherwin-White, A. N. 1985. *The Letters of Pliny: A Historical and Social Commentary*. Oxford University Press.

Singleton, D. 1972. "A Note on Catullus' First Poem." *CP* 67.3: 192–196.

Skinner, M. (ed.). 2007. *A Companion to Catullus*. Malden, Mass.: Blackwell.

Spitzer, P. 1993. "Les Xénia, morceaux sacrés d'hospitalité." *REG* 106: 599–606.

Stafford, E. 2000. *Worshipping Virtues: Personification and the Divine in Ancient Greece*. London: Duckworth.

Starr, R. J. 1987. "The Circulation of Literary Texts in the Roman World." *CQ* 37: 213–223.

Steel, C. E. W. 2001. *Cicero, Rhetoric, and Empire*. Oxford University Press.

Steiner, D. 1994. *The Tyrant's Writ: Myths and Images of Writing in Ancient Greece*. Princeton University Press.

Stewart, A. F. 1997. *Art, Desire, and the Body in Ancient Greece*. New York: Cambridge University Press.

Stewart, S. 1993. *On Longing: Narratives of the Miniature, the Gigantic, the Souvenir, the Collection*. Durham, NC: Duke University Press.

Strathern, M. 1988. *The Gender of the Gift: Problems with Women and Problems with Society in Melanesia* (Studies in Melanesian Anthropology 6). Berkeley, Calif.: University of California Press.

Strodach, G. K. 1933. "Latin Dimunitives in –ello/a- and –illo/a-." Dissertation, University of Pennsylvania.

Stroup, S. C. 2003. "*Adulta Virgo*: The Personification of Textual Eloquence in Cicero's *Brutus*." *MD* 50: 115–140.

——— 2006. "Invaluable Collections: The Illusion of Poetic Presence in Martial's *Xenia* and *Apophoreta*." In R. R. Nauta, H.-J. Van Dam, and J. J. L. Smolenaars (eds.), *Flavian Poetry*: 299–313. Leiden. Brill.

——— 2007. "Greek Rhetoric Meets Rome: Expansion, Resistance, and Acculturation." In Dominik and Hall (eds.): 23–37.

Sullivan, J. 1991. *Martial: The Unexpected Classic*. Cambridge University Press.

Sumner, G. V. 1973. *The Orators in Cicero's Brutus: Prosopography and Chronology*. University of Toronto Press.

Svenbro, J. 1993. *Phrasikleia: An Anthropology of Reading in Ancient Greece*. Trans. J. Lloyd. Ithaca, NY: Cornell University Press.

Tatum, W. J. 1988. "Catullus' Criticism of Cicero in Poem 49." *TAPA* 188: 179–184.

——— 1997. "Friendship, Politics, and Literature in Catullus: Poems 1, 65 and 66, 116." *CQ* 47 (2): 482–500.

Thomas, L. 1993. "Friendship and Other Loves." In N. K. Badhwar (ed.), *Friendship: A Philosophical Reader*: 48–72. Ithaca, NY: Cornell University Press.

Thomson, D. F. S. 1967. "Catullus and Cicero: Poetry and the Criticism of Poetry." *CW* 60: 225–230.

——— (ed.). 1997. *Catullus*. University of Toronto Press.

Toner, J. P. 1995. *Leisure in Ancient Rome*. Oxford University Press.

Townend, G. B. 1980. "A Further Point in Catullus' Attack on Volusius." *GR* 27: 134–136.

Turner, E. G. 1968. *Greek Papyri. An Introduction*. Oxford University Press.

Usener, H. 1901. "Italische Volksjustiz." *RhM* 56: 1–28.

Van Sickle, J. 1968. "About Form and Feeling in Catullus 65." *TAPA* 99: 487–508.

Vernant, J.-P. 1990. *Myth and Society in Ancient Greece*. New York: Zone.

Ville, G. 1981. *La gladiature en Occident des origines a la mort de Domitien*. Rome: Ecole française de Rome.

Volkmann, R. E. 1885. *Die Rhetorik der Griechen und Römer*. Leipzig: Teubner.

Vollmer, E. 1892. *Laudationum funebrium Romanorum historia et reliquiarum editio*. Jahrbücher fur Klassiche Philologie Suppl. 18: 445–528.

Walde, A., and Hofmann, J. B. 1965. *Lateinisches Etymologisches Wörterbuch. Vierte Auflage*. Heidelberg. C. Winter.

Wallace-Hadrill, A. (ed.). 1989. *Patronage in Ancient Society*. New York: Routledge.

Waltz, R. 1909. *Vie de Sénèque*. Paris: Perrin.

Weiss, M. 1996. "An Oscanism in Catullus 53." *CP* 91.4: 353–359.

White, P. 1974. "The Presentation and Dedication of the *Silvae* and the *Epigrams*." *JRS* 64: 40–64.

——— 1978. "*Amicitia* and the Profession of Poetry in Early Imperial Rome." *JRS* 68: 74–92.

——— 1982. "Positions for Poets in Early Imperial Rome." In Gold (ed.): 50–66.

———— 1993. *Promised Verse. Poets in the Society of Augustan Rome.* New Haven, Conn.: Harvard University Press.

———— 1982. "Phases in Political Patronage of Literature in Rome." In Gold (ed.): 3–27.

———— (ed.). 2003. *Seneca. De Otio, de Breuitate Vitae.* Cambridge University Press.

Winkel, L. C. 1979. "Some Remarks on the Date of the *Rhetorica ad Herennium.*" *Mnemosyne* 32: 327–332.

Wirszubski, C. 1954. "Cicero's *Cum Dignitate Otium*: A Reconsideration." *JRS* 44: 1–13.

Wiseman, T. P. 1974a. *Cinna the Poet and other Roman Essays.* Leicester University Press.

———— 1974b. "Catullus 68.157." *CR* 24: 6–7.

———— 1980. "Looking for Camerius: The Topography of Catullus 55." *PBSR* 48: 6–16.

———— 1982. "*Pete nobiles amicos*: Poets and Patrons in Late Republican Rome." In Gold (ed.): 28–49.

Wohl, V. 1998. *Intimate Commerce: Exchange, Gender and Subjectivity in Greek Tragedy.* Austin, Tex.: University of Texas Press.

Wood, N. 1988. *Cicero's Social and Political Thought.* Berkeley, Calif.: University of California Press.

Woodman, A. J. 1966. "Some Implications of *otium* in Catullus 51.13–16." *Latomus* 24: 217–226.

Wray, D. 2001. *Catullus and the Poetics of Manhood.* Cambridge University Press.

Wray, M. 1998. "Fetishizing the Fetish." *Bad Subjects* 41 (online publication) ("Fetish").

Wyke, M. 1987. "Written Women: Propertius' *Scripta Puella.*" *JRS* 77: 47–61.

Zagagi, N. 1982. "A Note on *munus, munus fungi* in Early Latin." *Glotta* 60: 281.

———— 1987. "Amatory Gifts and Payments: A Note on *Munus, donum and data* in Plautus." *Glotta* 65: 129–132.

Zanker, P. 1993. "The Hellenistic Grave Stelai from Smyrna: Identity and Self-Image in the Polis." In A. W. Bulloch, E. S. Gruen, A. A. Long, and A. Stewart (eds.), *Images and Ideologies*. 212–230. Berkeley. Calif.: University of California Press.

———— 1995. *The Mask of Socrates. The Image of the Intellectual in Antiquity.* Trans. A. Shapiro. Berkeley, Calif.: University of California Press.

Zetzel, J. E. G. 1982. "The Poetics of Patronage in the Late First Century B. C." In Gold (ed.): 87–102.

———— 2003. "Plato with Pillows: Cicero on the Uses of Greek Culture." In D. Braund and C. Gill (eds.), *Myth, History and Culture in Republican Rome: Studies in Honour of T. P. Wiseman*: 119–138. Exeter: University of Exeter Press.

Zicàri, M. 1965. "Sul primo carme di Catullo." *Maia* 17: 232–240.

Index locorum

This index strives to be illustrative rather than exhaustive. Incidental citations of passages or phrases in Cicero (especially *Brutus* and *de Oratore*) and Catullus are generally not included in what follows. Citations of works that appear in the footnotes – lists of individual passages or entire works that support the argument at hand but are not central to it (thus their placement in the footnotes) – tend not to be included. I have made some exceptions to this, however, especially for citations from Greek works, and when the use of a citation as a *comparandum* may aid the argument as a whole. I hope to have restricted what follows to those citations, and the discussions surrounding them, that will be most useful to the reader.

Aristophanes
  Batrakhoi 1059, 246 n. 76
  Nephelai 137, 246 n. 76

Auctor
  Rhetorica ad Herennium 4.53.66, 246

Aulus Gellius
  Noctes Atticae
  1.5.3, 120 n. 8

Catullus (C. Valerius Catullus)
  Carmina
  1, 219–221
  1.1–3, 33
  1.1–2, 88
  10.1–4, 43
  12, 73
  14, 78–79
  16, 224
  33, 137
  42.1–6, 235
  44.7–12, 158
  49, 226
  50, 229–230
  51.13–16, 55
  65, 83
  68b.149–152, 88

Cicero (M. Tullius Cicero)
  Brutus
  1.1, 192, 272
  5.19, 31, 239
  5.20, 241

6.22, 251
6.25, 252
11.42, 28
13.51, 256
20.264, 133
30.113, 89
49.183, 161
50.189, 161
51.192, 127, 130
53.198–54.199, 162
82.283, 259
96.328, 239, 262
96.333, 260, 263
97.332, 163
de Divinatione
2.6–7, 90
2.30.63, 60
de Finibus
2.3.7, 10
2.21, 249
3.10, 59
3.14, 59
de Lege Agraria
2.4.9, 49
de Legibus
2.19, 246
2.28, 246
de Officiis
1.48, 96
1.92, 59
1.150, 118
2.4, 58
3.1, 91
3.33, 96

Index rerum et nominum

Names, concepts, and terms mentioned in passing, and names of literary characters, are generally omitted. Brief citations of oft-cited texts (*Brutus, de Oratore*) and incidental citations of texts in general, are not included; terms that may easily be gleaned from the Table of Contents (*otium*; *munus*; *uendibilis*, etc.) tend not to be included. References in footnotes are included only if they seem to add to the argument as a whole.